Benjamin Harrison ⋅ *Hoosier President*

✩　　✩　　✩

Also by the Author

Benjamin Harrison: Hoosier Warrior, Through the
Civil War Years, 1833-1865
Benjamin Harrison: Hoosier Statesman, From the
Civil War to the White House, 1865-1888

Benjamin Harrison

Hoosier President

By

HARRY J. SIEVERS

Published by American Political Biography Press

Newtown, CT

Reprinted with the permission of the
Arthur Jordan Foundation

Published by
AMERICAN POLITICAL BIOGRAPHY PRESS

Library of Congress Catalog Card Number 96-78889
ISBN Number 0-945707-18-5

39 Boggs Hill
Newtown, Connecticut
06470-1971
Tel: (203) 270-9777 ✧ Fax: (203) 270-0091
E-Mail: APBPress@EarthLink.Net

WWW.APBPRESS.COM

This is the second printing of the first edition.

All publications of
AMERICAN POLITICAL BIOGRAPHY PRESS
Are dedicated to my wife
Ellen and our two children
Katherine and William II

This particular book is
Dedicated to:

James Bond Stockdale 09/09/65
Ron Storz 04/28/65
Dennis L. Thompson 02/07/68

And all the others.

Acknowledgments

LORD ACTON, who found history an inspiration for the soul, epitomizes my thoughts as this Harrison trilogy is completed. Two decades of research and writing have resulted in an Actonian-like spiritual uplift. Gratefully I now thank hundreds who, in one way or another, assisted me. Their patient efforts in seeing the *Hoosier President* and the author through to publication are deeply gratifying.

Two previous prefaces have articulated my gratitude to family, friends and colleagues between 1949 and 1959. To re-list their names here is unnecessary: each knows his contribution, and each has my renewed appreciation for support unfailing. In the last eight years an even greater indebtedness has been contracted. Difficult as it is to liquidate so vast a human debt, one must try and beg indulgence for oversights and space limitations.

At the Library of Congress, courtesies were renewed and enlarged by John McDonough and Roger Preston in the Division of Manuscripts; by Fred Shelley, who directed a talented team in microfilming and indexing the Harrison Papers; by L. H. B. Obear, chief of the Loan Division. Also the Photographs and Prints Division and the American Law Section contributed significantly to this volume. Georgetown University's inter-library loan expert, Miss Margaret Ticknor, has rendered favors characteristic of the entire staff. White House curator James Ketchum and his wife, Barbara, have helped generously. So has the staff at the National Geographic, where special thanks go to Abigail Brett. Also in Washington the Pan American Union, the State Department and the National Archives offered guidance and easy access to new materials. With sorrow is noted the death of State's chief historian, Dr. E. Taylor Parks. Before illness won out, he entrusted me to my life-long archives consultant and friend, Judy Carroll.

In neighboring Maryland, the Johns Hopkins University, Loyola College (especially the late and distinguished History chairman,

Dr. Harry W. Kirwin), and Professor Dick Walsh (Georgetown University), editor of the *Maryland Magazine of History*, all extended a willing hand. A hundred miles north, Philadelphia proved itself a City of Brotherly Love. The archives of the Pennsylvania Historical Society and of St. Charles Seminary (Overbrook) filled many a gap. My special gratitude, however, goes to the Sisters of the Blessed Sacrament, St. Elizabeth's Convent, Cornwells Heights, Pa. Here Foundress Katharine Drexel's papers disclosed a new aspect of the Harrison era. First, Mother General Anselm, and then Mother David, along with archivist Sr. M. Francisca, Sr. Ignacita, and Sr. Consuela Marie, the talented biographer of Katharine Drexel, provided me with a home, an office and the sundry tools of research. Perhaps only the late Mother M. Philip Neri knows my partially unfulfilled desire to make better known the American story of a banker's heroic daughter who gave self and fortune to educating the American Indian and the Negro.

Investigation of new evidence relating to the boundary dispute between Venezuela and Guyana opened diplomatic, legal, and historical doors in Washington, London, Paris, Rome, Berlin, Mexico City, and several other urban centers. Harrison's legal work for Venezuela was particularly appreciated by Senor Dr. Marcos Falcon Briceno, Venezuelan Foreign Minister under President Romulo Betancourt. Consultations with Dr. Falcon in Washington soon led me to government archives in Caracas. Here two distinguished Jesuit historians, Fathers Hermann Gonzalez Orapesa and Pablo Ojer, entered my life. Joint research in their country, in Mexico, in England and Europe, and in the United States has been unforgettable. My debt to them, and to Dr. Adolfo Taylhardat, remains large.

In Washington, diplomatic courtesies extended by Venezuelan Ambassador Tejera-Paris; Dr. Carlos Pérez de la Cova, Minister Counselor for Economic Affairs; Dr. Enrique Tarchetti, First Secretary; Juan Lopez de Cebellos, Second Secretary, and by hidden workers like Yolande Anzech, Isabel Andino and Stella Blanco have been unlimited. In Caracas, Senor Bernardo Bermúdez, Dr. Raul Nass, Senor Jose Angel Ruiz-Mendez, and Dr. Walter Brandt, who is now Venezuelan Ambassador to Georgetown, Guyana, deserve special thanks. The present Venezuelan Foreign Minister, Senor Dr. Ignacio Iribarren Borges, has shown himself a friend, a lawyer, a historian, and, of course, a diplomat.

Benefactors in Chicago are too numerous for individual listing. Still, I must thank the Chicago Historical Society, the home of the Melville W. Fuller papers, and Willard L. King, the genial lawyer-biographer of Chief Justice Fuller. Mr. King shed important light on the boundary dispute between Venezuela and British Guiana. Helpful, too, was George B. Young, co-author of a current work on American diplomacy. In the library of the Chicago *Sun-Times* presides my devoted friend Joe Simmons, whose family and profession I have seen grow. Behind the scenes in Illinois worked and prayed sterling souls like Pat and Bob Trainor, the Senior Tom Keoghs, and the late Marie Trainor.

High above Cayuga's waters is perched the John M. Olin Research Library of Cornell University. Here archivist Edith M. Fox, now emeritus, and archival director Herb Finch effectively guided me through the Andrew D. White and George Lincoln Burr manuscripts. Twin sojourns at Ithaca were enhanced by association with Msgr. Don Cleary and Fr. Dick Tormey, of the Newman Oratory, and by Jesuit colleagues Dick Doyle, John Hoodack, and Clem Schneiders, graduate students at the time. In nearby Syracuse, the facilities of Le Moyne College were offered and accepted. Fr. William Reilly, S.J., President; Fr. Andrew Brady, S.J., Guidance Counselor, and Fr. Bob O'Connell, S.J., know my deep appreciation. Solid support also emanated from Peter and Rosemary Carr of Camillus, N. Y.

At many turns lawyers have helped the cause of research. From a chance meeting with William R. Joyce, Jr., Washington head of the New York law firm of Curtis, Mallet-Prevost, Colt & Mosle, grew an association and a friendship of several years. Suffice it to say that Joyce, a fellow alumnus of Loyola University, Chicago, took an interest in international lawyer Ben Harrison and in his biographer. This resulted in a "second base of operations" at the Federal Bar Building, Washington, and a third in the ancient Wall Street offices of Mallet-Prevost's firm. Here Manuel R. Angulo, nonagenarian lawyer and judge, Otto Schoenrich, and others illuminated the story of the Harrison and Mallet-Prevost partnership at Paris during the long, hot summer of 1899. Judge Schoenrich has published part of the story in the *American Journal of International Law* (July 1948), but more will follow the publication of this volume. Special thanks go to Mary Malovin, who helped me with the correspondence of Mallet-Prevost, and to

Jesse Knight, who graciously provided material possessed by the second Mrs. Mallet-Prevost.

In Mexico City, Alex Hoagland, the Mallet-Prevost firm representative, arranged an interview for me with Adela A. Allen, Esq., whose husband, the late Perry Allen, served the American Boundary Commission (1896–1897) and the Arbitral Tribunal at Paris (1899). No one could have been more hospitable or more cooperative than Mrs. Allen and her family. Also in the same area, the Guilermo Cussi, the Daniel O'Brien, and the Paul Content families befriended a gringo researcher at every turn. So did Ben Cooper, head of the Firestone operation in Mexico City.

Closely connected with the Mallet-Prevost and Perry Allen papers were files in Washington, D.C., editorial headquarters of the *American Journal of International Law*. Here Eleanor Finch, daughter of the late Dr. George Finch, confirmed the roles played by Schoenrich, Mallet-Prevost, Allen, and a fourth lawyer-editor, the late William Cullen Dennis. The latter's son, David W. Dennis, who practices law in Richmond, Indiana, opened to me his home and his father's papers.

New England, always kind to Harrison, also served the author well. Yale University Library archives yielded pertinent material on David J. Brewer, whom Harrison appointed to the Supreme Court. In Boston, both the Athenaeum and the Massachusetts Historical Society staffs made work a pleasure. Special thanks go to John Cushing, Mrs. Fischer, and Professor Richard Welch. The latter, an authority on the Force Bill of 1890, also advised me on using the George F. Hoar papers. On a personal level the Jimmy Kelly family of Waltham gave me several assists.

Along the Ohio River, at Evansville, Indiana, and at Louisville, Kentucky, countless friends helped me research and write the Harrison story. Particularly, I thank Roy and Mary Ryan, who often combined personal loyalty with family generosity in aiding me to locate the papers of William Lindsay Scruggs, author, forgotten diplomat and powerful propagandist.

The search for the Scruggs material began in Louisville, where Ed Killelea manages the local office of Merrill Lynch, Pierce, Fenner and Smith. Final dividends came in Nashville, Tennessee, where Harry Denison and Tom Mackenzie put me in touch with affable attorney Walter M. Robinson, Jr., and his cooperative wife, Margaret Ann Robinson. Their sense of history and their kindness gave me the opportunity of examining the Scruggs letters and diary. Thus the role of Harrison's minister to Caracas became increasingly clear. Miss McGrath, secretary to Mr. Robinson, Jr., knows my appreciation for her extraordinary kindness. Also the Robinsons put me in touch with Mrs. C. J. Horne, the Roswell, Georgia, descendant of William L. Scruggs. Missing letters were made available by Mrs. Horne, her sister, Mrs. Sam P. McKenzie of Atlanta, and their understanding mother, Mrs. Margaret Scruggs McMillan. Their hospitality and friendship have made it possible to recreate a lost chapter in American diplomatic history. So did the kind efforts of Dr. Dave Barton and his wife, Lolly, in Boise, Idaho.

The above acknowledgments and those following partially reflect the story behind the Harrison story. To stay within bounds, this tale must conclude with a brief expression of debt to friends in the four key cities of Indianapolis, Plattsburgh (N. Y.), Washington (D. C.), and the greater New York area. These areas saw the biographical trilogy experience its literary beginnings, middle, and end.

Indianapolis has increased the number of helping hands and hearts since 1960. My primary debt is to the Trustees of the Arthur Jordan Foundation whose patient support continued under the chairmanship of Emsley W. Johnson, Jr. Retirements and new appointments have changed nothing. Obviously efforts to complete Benjamin Harrison's life would have been stymied without the Foundation's financial support. No one knows this better than myself and Jerry Carrier, Executive Secretary and Auditor. He proved himself a friend at court, especially when the research in newly discovered archives delayed publication. To single out any trustee for special commendation would be unfair. Yet Cliff Hart, the late Dick James, and their friend and associate, Jim Richardson, have conspired personally to keep me on free-moving wheels. Other friends have offered Father bed, board and encouragement. This same circle of friends have helped in erecting a new home for my Jesuit family, the present faculty of Brebeuf Preparatory School. Among my close associates and supporters there are the Rector, Fr. Bill Schmitt, and Development Director, Fr. Jack Williams. I congratulate them and the Sons of St. Ignatius who have launched a Jesuit educational first in central Indiana. Likewise, I am indebted to Bill Finneran of Bobbs-Merrill Co., Inc. His Irish wit and stamina have created an atmosphere of responsible publishing in that venerable company.

The McGowans, the first I met in Indianapolis, continue to multiply in family and in personal kindness. I thank them and the Jim McNutts, who are raising their own gridiron squad, for favors unlimited. I note sadly the passing of J. B. Lanagan, a true Christian gentleman.

In the North Country, Bellarmine College (Plattsburgh) afforded me a teacher's podium between 1956 and 1964. Faculty, students and friends in town have my deep thanks. Fr. Tom Fleming and the late Fr. Andrew L. Bouwhuis never wavered in their support. Bro. Jerry Gordon and our late librarian, Bro. Denis Murry, made my lot an easier one.

Off campus, David and Mary Glenn, Jack and Gayle Fitzpatrick, the Arthur de Grandpres, Sheila Fitzpatrick, and a whole host of relatives helped the cause. In all operations, literary, pastoral, and professional, I am grateful for prayerful support of a fine Dominican nun, Sr. Mary Paul.

Washington, D. C., has been a good home. Helpers came in droves to assist a cleric run a research office. Some friends prefer anonymity perhaps for security reasons, but I gladly note my appreciation for the friendship provided by the following families in the greater D. C. area: Mrs. Helen Tansill, Mr. and Mrs. Charles Missar, Mr. and Mrs. David Klausmeyer, Jr., Mr. and Mrs. Thomas Keogh, Cdr. and Mrs. Louis Sarosdy, Mr. and Mrs. Paul Minnich, Mr. and Mrs. George Towner, Mr. and Mrs. William R. Joyce, Jr., Mr. and Mrs. Milec Kybal, Dr. and Mrs. Earl Vivino, Mr. and Mrs. Jeremiah P. O'Donovan, Dr. and Mrs. Tim O'Donovan, Dr. Maxine Schurter, Mr. and Mrs. Joseph Lucas, Jr., Mr. and Mrs. Eugene Burke, Mrs. John Lively and family, Capt. and Mrs. R. B. Mulholland, Mr. and Mrs. Walter Sheridan, Mr. and Mrs. Robert A. Shaffer, Dr. and Mrs. Edmond Fitzgerald, Carmen Sarmiento and former Ambassador Emilio Sarmiento, Adm. and Mrs. Thebaud, Mr. and Mrs. Ed Mitchell, Mr. and Mrs. Jerry Hanifin, Mr. and Mrs. Robert H. McNeill, the Joseph Gerretys and Mrs. Hazel Mann.

Other Washingtonians conspired to make life and work ever so rewarding. There were Mr. and Mrs. Gerald Oudens, whose children, Elizabeth and Matthew, offered a hand in typing at the "office"; Mr. and Mrs. Eugene Cacciamani and their daughter, Amy;

Mr. and Mrs. Kevin Maroney, whose Tim, Pat, Eileen, and Kathy leaped over educational barriers while Harrison III resisted confinement between hard covers. Their contributions have been direct and indirect, and I want to express heartfelt gratitude.

At Gonzaga, in downtown Washington, I lived nearly three years with a stimulating group of fellow Jesuits who staff our high school and parish. Through Fr. Rector, the Rev. William F. Graham, S.J., I say "thank you" and pray that God may reward each and every one. In the Tenley Circle area looms "Immaculata"—a junior college and a high school conducted by the Sisters of Providence whose roots are in Hoosier soil at St. Mary-of-the-Woods, near Terre Haute, Indiana. A decade of close association with administrators, faculty and students makes a complete listing unfeasible. Through Sr. Theresa Aloyse, Sr. Mary Clare, Sr. Robert, and current superior, Sr. Marian Thomas, I want to express my sincere appreciation for their hospitality and kindness. Immaculata Chapel, a D. C. haven for the late Cardinal Ritter of St. Louis, is that and more for this peripatetic biographer.

I left the Potomac on January 1, 1967, for reassignment in the Empire State, where a twofold operation came into view. One embraced Loyola College and Seminary, the College of Letters and Philosophy of Fordham University. It is located at Shrub Oak, N. Y., where an understanding rector, Fr. John Dineen, and a provident vice-president, Fr. Leo Daley, head up a faculty and a community which claim my allegiance as a professor of history. My "history majors" are understanding and a generous faculty lends ready assistance. Our genial dean, Fr. Lorenzo K. Reed, has arranged a compatible teaching schedule, and the library, under Frs. Cunnion and Flood, offer needed help at every turn. Other unsung heroes, including our Jesuit Brothers, deserve special mention, as does the Fr. Provincial, the Very Rev. Robert A. Mitchell.

The second "operations point" is the *American House,* a mid-Manhattan editorial office and residence, where some ten Jesuits produce the National Catholic weekly, *America,* a journal of opinion. My assignment as an assistant editor last February has opened several more windows on the world of ideas. A friend of long standing, Fr. James A. Sheridan, S.J., directs community affairs, and a former mentor, Fr. Thurston N. Davis, S.J., has served as Editor-in-Chief for the last 12 years. Both have encouraged my efforts with Harrison, as have my colleagues on the editorial staff. To all I say thank you.

Many old friends and several new acquaintances have happily crowded my final years with Harrison. Freeman Cleaves, Civil War expert and talented biographer, has helped me with points of organization and style. His skill, coupled with the friendship of Mrs. Gwen Cleaves, has truly indebted me to him. The Procarios of Valhalla, N. Y., and the Satriales of the Bronx have contributed editorial suggestions and have become my devoted friends and a strong support for my mother. Mark Nevils, the man who makes Boeing better known, has taken a personal interest in this book. So have Larry Grow and Sharland Trotter, who have saved me from errors and ambiguities. From across the country old Air-Force friends have rallied to my assistance. In addition to Dr. Dave and Lolly Barton, who combed the Idaho State Archives at Boise, I thank Dr. and Mrs. Linn Tompkins, who covered Columbia, S. C., for me; Dr. and Mrs. Russ Ferrigno sent help from Windsor, Conn., while Dr. Harry and Edna Willey of Point Pleasant, N. J., have been most generous and interested.

Finally, authors owe family an apology for neglect over months at a time. This volume's dedication suggests, I hope, a son's gratitude to a queen-like mother. Her prayers have contributed most to the completion of the task. The Healy, Cheasty, McCarthy, Murphy, and Roesch families know their contribution to a kinsman. And within the family circle by association ranges my indefatigably devoted secretary, Mrs. Bernard Wohlfert of Washington, D. C. She fathomed tired dictabelts, calendared countless collections, typed and retyped to perfection endless versions of sundry chapters, and during crisis sessions managed to keep clients happy and informed. This recognition hardly cancels a debt; only God can do this.

For expert help in securing a photograph for the back of the jacket I thank three modern-day Matthew Bradys: Jack Cheasty, Dave Knox and Jeff Shields.

Harry J. Sievers, S.J.
America House
New York, N. Y.

Contents

List of Illustrations

(between pages 174 and 175)

xvii

Benjamin Harrison

Hoosier President

CHAPTER I

His Own Boss

A GOOD CARTOONIST, one who gets quickly to the heart of a matter, can often capture a people's mood more readily than can the hard-bitten reporter. This proved to be the case on January 12, 1889, when the humor magazine *Judge* featured Bernard Gillum's weekly cartoon neatly captioned: "HIS OWN BOSS."[1] It pictured President-elect Benjamin Harrison securely astride and driving an elephant, the G.O.P. symbol. Directly behind Harrison in the howdah were depicted certain leading Republicans: James G. Blaine, Warner Miller, Thomas Collier (Boss) Platt, Senator John Sherman, Senator Matthew (Boss) Quay, and Senator William B. Allison. The words beneath the portrait reflected the thought uppermost in the minds of politicians, office-seekers and voters.[2]

Harrison, now in his fifty-sixth year, had one of the last full beards of the Civil War era. Son of a congressman, grandson of a President, and great-grandson of a signer of the Declaration of Independence, the man about to become the twenty-third President of the United States was of a family whose name had been known to Americans from the early days of Colonial Virginia. His carefully trimmed gray beard, full and square-cut, contrasted with a pink-white complexion and two gentle, often twinkling, sometimes piercing, blue eyes. The man destined to serve as the nation's Centennial President stood barely five foot six. That he was also slightly rotund appeared to detract from his stature. Yet the onetime brigadier general was both graceful and energetic. He easily wore dignity, and his intellectual abilities and honesty of purpose

[1] *Judge*, XV, 217. This magazine ranked with *Puck* and *Life* as a great comic weekly. Published each Friday, *Judge* had a circulation of more than 40,000.

[2] Cartoons in this era were usually bold, slashing pictures, full of action and merciless in satire. See Frank Luther Mott, *American Journalism*, pp. 512–13.

were acknowledged by Grover Cleveland, the retiring President.

Integrity formed the backbone of Harrison's character. As William Allen White, editorial writer of the Kansas City *Star*,[3] put it, one had to admire his "instinct to do the polite, honest, dignified thing in every contingency."[4] Editor White could easily generalize on what many already knew. The Harrison who was to enter the White House was respected as a man who stood high in legal circles although as a national political leader he was largely untried. His active intellect firmly backed by moral courage, he was regarded as a bulwark of political decency. He labored as both an ethical lawyer and a praying churchman in his works, and he intended to pilot national affairs under a strict interpretation of the Constitution.

Government, in Harrison's view, was the servant of the people. And because he felt that it was the right of the people to make their own laws, he based his political philosophy on the premise that: "to govern best is to govern least." Determined to exercise only the most basic functions of his office, Harrison would cling to this creed. Editor White also believed that "in writing the history of the United States it may be that future historians will go back to the . . . administration of Harrison to find an example of a constitutional president."[5]

Reaching decisions in a methodical, legalistic way had long characterized Benjamin Harrison as a leader of the Indiana bar and as a United States senator from that state. To Whitelaw Reid, vigorous editor of the influential New York *Tribune,* he "was of a deliberate habit of mind and not only took his own time but kept his own counsel."[6] Harrison's colleagues saw him as one of those lawyers who often take weeks to make up their minds in the face of conflicting evidence. This explains why Harrison, immediately after his triumph over Cleveland in the presidential contest of 1888, entered on a long period of silent and watchful waiting which

---

3 In 1895 White bought the Emporia (Kansas) *Gazette* for $5,000 and won for it a national rating within a year (Mott, *op. cit.*, pp. 470–71; 570–71) .

4 William Allen White, *Masks in a Pageant,* p. 66. He alleged that Harrison "seems always to have felt it more important to be a gentleman than to be an orator with a smart answer in any contest." Actually Harrison's skill in extemporaneous speaking often enabled him to be smart and a gentleman at the same time. See Eugene Gano Hay, "Benjamin Harrison: An Appreciation," a 16-page typed manuscript in the E. G. Hay MSS. Hay knew Harrison intimately from 1876 until 1901.

5 White, *op. cit.,* p. 89.

6 Royal Cortissoz, *The Life of Whitelaw Reid,* II, 121.

often exasperated both friends and opponents. At the outset, he cherished two convictions. One centered on a profound sense of the difficulties he faced and the other on his belief that he himself could best guide the ship of state.

Yet the General's correspondence and his talks with friends and advisers such as Indiana's Attorney General Louis T. Michener,[7] helped to shape his plans for the new administration. He would have many opportunities to listen to visiting politicians and he read countless letters, some suggesting suitable names for his Cabinet.[8]

Michener, the man whom Harrison most wanted as a member of his official family, reluctantly refused, feeling bound to discharge the duties of his state office until the expiration of his term. In 1881, when invited to enter Garfield's Cabinet, Senator-elect Harrison had used the same reasoning.

However disappointing to Harrison, Michener's decision did not prevent the two men from discussing freely the complexities of appointing a strong Cabinet. The President-elect told Michener that he wanted able, conscientious, loyal-minded men of irreproachable character, who would be thoroughly qualified to perform their duties; he wanted men who were Republicans in political faith, although it was not imperative that they should have held office or have been active in party campaigns in the nation.[9]

Harrison quite agreed with another old friend, Ohio Senator John Sherman, who felt that the appointees must represent Republican policy and ideas rather than mere factions or cliques. Eager office-seekers could derive little hope from Harrison's avowal that he would choose Cabinet officials who would administer the patron-

---

7 Michener had served as Harrison's Warwick in the campaign of 1888. He first met the General casually in 1876, 1879 and 1880, but during the winter of 1883 while Harrison was in the U.S. Senate, the latter showed Michener marked attention. They often talked at length and spent weekends at Harrison's Indianapolis home. At the 1884 state convention, Michener almost single-handedly routed the forces of Walter Q. Gresham, thus cementing his friendship with Harrison. See "The Formation of the Cabinet," undated typed memorandum in Michener MSS.

8 Newspapermen and reporters led the parade to Harrison's door. W. J. Arkell, proprietor of *Judge*, headed one delegation from New York and made certain that his cartoonist, Bernard Gillum, interviewed the President-elect. The volume of incoming mail, now part of the Harrison MSS., contained innumerable names of candidates for the cabinet. (Hereafter the Harrison MSS. in the Library of Congress will be cited as (L.C.).)

9 "Formation of the Cabinet," Michener MSS., details the Harrison-Michener conversations on the subject and pinpoints the General's reluctant acquiescence to Michener's wishes.

age not in their own selfish interests but for the good of the country. Apparently this policy put many senators, congressmen and local bosses on the defensive from the beginning. Two things must be understood, Harrison told Stephen B. Elkins, who once had backed Blaine: "First, that a Cabinet selection is, in such a strong sense a personal matter, that the selection of one person is in no sense a disparagement of another; and second, that Cabinet officers are not to be state bosses."[10]

For Harrison to adhere to this policy would require no little courage. In that era, Republican senators and state bosses represented powerful business and financial interests rather more than they did the collective citizenry. Expedient-minded beings who endorsed the spoils system were in reality lobbyists for the New York Central, the Union Pacific, or the Southern Pacific. Similarly, insurance, coal, iron, and steel interests claimed senators and political bosses from both Eastern and Middle Atlantic states. From personal experience Harrison also knew that cotton and silver had their coteries in the upper house. Nor could it be denied that these groups, representing as they did vast capitalistic enterprises, had contributed liberally to Harrison's campaign fund.[11]

In deciding early that he alone would "drive the elephant," Harrison insisted with Elkins that he had to consider

not only men, but their adaptation to the particular place which I may be able to assign to a state. I must also have regard, a very high regard, to party harmony, not only in the state, but in the whole country–for these appointments are general. I would think it bad taste, as well as very bad politics, to allow any cabinet officer to use his position to weaken or destroy the proper influence of any other Republican leader. Indeed, it is quite probable that his influence in local matters would be less rather than more.[12]

With these principles fixed in his mind, Harrison set out to build a strong Cabinet.

10 Harrison to Stephen B. Elkins, January 18, 1889, Elkins MSS. Elkins for many years had been a "practical politician of national fame and power," and next to Michener perhaps did most to elect Harrison. In 1889, however, Elkins did not inspire in Harrison the confidence that in 1891 resulted in his becoming Secretary of War.

11 W. A. White, op. cit., pp. 79–80, contends that "the largest sum of money that has ever been raised to elect a candidate was raised to elect Harrison President." For an evaluation of this statement, see Harry J. Sievers, Benjamin Harrison: Hoosier Statesman, pp. 413–29 (chapter titled "Boodle and Victory").

12 Harrison to Stephen B. Elkins, January 18, 1889, Elkins MSS. Indianapolis Journal, March 5, 1889.

Harrison regarded selecting the personnel of the official family as the first really important act of any administration.[13] Colonel E. W. Halford, who resigned as editor of the Indianapolis *Journal* to become Harrison's private secretary,[14] recalled how many came to advise the President-elect. On one occasion a group of Ohioans dropped in, and Congressman Benjamin Butterworth, acting as spokesman, described in vivid detail the type of a man thought most desirable in a Cabinet post. After hearing him out, Harrison pointedly remarked: "Major Butterworth, we are in entire agreement in this matter. Kindly give me the name of the gentleman you have been describing."[15]

Despite newspaper gossip appearing to guarantee pre-election promises made in Harrison's name, the Cabinet was entirely open. Thus the task of selection would be all the more difficult, the chances of committing some blunder all the greater. Harrison knew that if he should choose friendly and experienced advisers from Congress, he might seriously weaken party representation there. The clamor for sectional recognition would gain force, since the Pacific Coast, New England and the South would hardly be outdone by the Midwest or by the larger states on the Atlantic seaboard. If only he might confine his selections to Alaska, Harrison wrote James G. Blaine, he could easily arrange an excellent slate and at the same time preserve party harmony.[16]

It was not long, of course, before a host of Blaine's friends, with the Maine man's masterly connivance,[17] filled the mails with urgent pleas for his appointment to the portfolio of State. Though Harrison had already determined to do so, he kept the decision to himself since any premature move might lead to quick inferences— that a deal had been made at the Chicago convention, or that

13 Benjamin Harrison, *This Country of Ours*, p. 105. For an insight into Harrison's view on the office of President and on the machinery of the national government, see pp. 68–180. This volume, comprised mainly of essays written by Harrison, first appeared in 1897.

14 Before Halford's decision to become Harrison's private secretary, the General had secured the temporary services of Eugene Gano Hay and De Alva S. Alexander. See E. G. Hay, *art. cit.*, p. 6.

15 E. W. Halford, "General Harrison's Attitude Toward the Presidency," *Century Magazine*, June 1912, p. 306.

16 Harrison to Blaine, February 1, 1889, as cited in A. T. Volwiler (ed.), *The Correspondence Between Harrison and Blaine*, p. 51.

17 Oscar Doane Lambert, *Stephen Benton Elkins*, pp. 126–30, and David Saville Muzzey, *James G. Blaine*, pp. 388, 390, show conclusively that Blaine wanted to be Secretary of State and that he requested Davis, Elkins and others to intercede for him.

Blaine and not Harrison was handpicking the names. He therefore was able to keep matters firmly in hand.[18] He still believed
Blaine to be capable of great public service provided he would
serve the administration first and himself second, possibly a large
order in any political arena.[19]

To some few unbiased minds, Blaine seemed the logical choice
for State.[20] Sharing with Harrison the title of leading Republican
he had come, in 1884, within 1,200 votes of the presidency. Four
years later his support had proved decisive in Harrison's nomination and election.[21] Many Republicans intimately knew and liked
the graceful, urbane Blaine who had served as Speaker of the
House, senator, and Secretary of State during President Garfield's
brief reign. On the other hand there were many vigorous foes
whose hostility stemmed from the old political scandals and feuds
that had plagued the administrations of Hayes, Garfield, and
Arthur.[22]

Political pressure on Harrison was bound to grow. Vigorous
pleas on Blaine's behalf were rivaled by impassioned protests
against him. His critics had a point in urging that as Secretary of
State he would rule the administration or wreck it. One ominous
threat came in the mail from a G.O.P. leader in Missouri. "Attempt to put James G. Blaine in your Cabinet," Harrison was

18 By so doing, Harrison later admitted, "I could keep my own counsel and act
upon my own judgment." In "Harrison's Memoranda on His Relations with Blaine,"
a document preserved in Harrison MSS. It was prepared on May 22, 1893 at Indianapolis—less than three months after Harrison had left the White House. Volwiler,
op. cit., pp. 294–303, made it public in 1940.

19 W. A. White, op. cit., p. 93, points out how easily Blaine could cease to be an
ally and become a liability to the administration. He noted: "In a convivial day,
Blaine kept open house and a delectable table. The home of the Secretary of State
rivaled in political importance the White House itself, and for good-fellowship
Blaine's establishment far outshone the Presbyterian menage on the Avenue."

20 Before the inauguration Whitelaw Reid observed: "It has been evident from
the outset that General Harrison started his cabinet-making with two points settled."
One was Blaine for State, the other was that the Treasury should go West. See Cortissoz,
op. cit., p. 121.

21 As Matthew Josephson, in The Politicos, p. 438, observes: "For Blaine's extremely
popular stumping in 1888—he was then a legendary figure, a Prince Hal of politicos
to a generation which had known him from its infancy—had clearly helped to win
the day."

22 Volwiler, op. cit., p. 9, alleges that Blaine's appointment "would alienate thousands of voters—on the one side, idealistic, independent Mugwumps; and on the
other, uncompromising, aggressive 'stalwarts,' followers of General Grant." Some still
distrusted Blaine because of his Roman Catholic connections, while others recalled
the "Rum, Romanism and Rebellion" incident of the 1884 campaign.

warned, "you will meet the death of a Lincoln or a Garfield.[23] Other letter writers opined that Blaine's appointment would prove a serious handicap at the very least.[24]

Lack of universal backing irked Blaine's friends and wounded the vanity of the Plumed Knight himself. Especially in Indiana, Judge Walter Q. Gresham learned, were the Blaine men "very bitter—so bitter that they can hardly contain themselves." Harrison, they contended, had completely ignored the party's elder statesman. Indeed, Gresham's correspondent predicted an explosion "unless Harrison does something decent pretty soon."[25] Thus the game of Blaine intrigue *vs.* Harrisonian caution continued until, on January 17, 1889, five days after the publication of the *Judge* cartoon, Harrison broke his silence. In a brief formal note, Blaine was offered the portfolio of State. Significant was an enclosed "private and confidential" letter which the General had laboriously rewritten.[26] At the outset Harrison outlined policy:

We have already a pretty *full* understanding of each other's views as to the general policy which should characterize our foreign relations. I am especially interested in the improvement of our relations with the Central and South American States. We must win their confidence by deserving it. It will not come upon demand. Only men of experience, of high character and broad view, should be sent even to the least important of these States. In all this I am sure you will be a most willing *coadjutor,* for your early suggestions and earnest advocacy have directed public opinion to that subject.

Switching from Latin America to Europe, Harrison explained to Blaine the national need for settling peacefully and justly the

23 James Finley to Harrison, January 2, 1889, (L.C.), Vol. 55. The warning scarcely seems that of a crank, as the writer was chairman of the Republican Club of Kansas City.

24 Henry C. Johnson to John Sherman, John Sherman MSS., as cited in Volwiler, *op. cit.*, p. 9. Johnson felt that there was some truth to the report published at home and abroad that Harrison ran as a "mere proxy of Mr. Blaine" where the General would be a marionette "with Mr. Blaine manipulating the wires."

25 Walter Wellman to Walter Q. Gresham, January 12, 1889, Gresham MSS. Harrison's ignoring of Blaine during the formative period of the administration did not sit well with many of Blaine's close friends such as Elkins, Hale, Halstead, Reid and Kerens. Their letters of guarded disappointment are in (L.C.), Vols. 47–57, *passim.*

26 Harrison respected Blaine's ability but harbored feelings of distrust. In (L.C.) remains a penciled draft of his "personal" covering letter to Blaine. It clearly shows the torture of many revisions and deletions. This draft, as the late Professor Volwiler observes, reveals the "absence of trusting cordiality between the two leaders to a greater extent than does the final letter." See Volwiler, *op. cit.*, p. 45, n. 2.

outstanding differences with major European powers. He know-
ingly added that "your familiarity with the origin and ... history
of our diplomacy, would give you great advantage in dealing with
them." Hardly entirely cordial, Harrison admonished Blaine as
to the need for preserving harmony in the party:

... the continuance of Republican control for a series of presidential
terms is, I think, essential to the right settlement of some very grave
questions. I shall be very solicitous to avoid anything that would promote dissensions, and very desirous that the civil service shall be
placed and conducted on that high plane which will recommend our
party to the confidence of all the people. This purpose is absolutely
disassociated with any selfish thought or ambition. I will be quite as
ready to make proper concessions as to ask others to do so. Each member of my official family will have my *full* confidence and I shall expect
his in return.[27]

Blaine accepted at once, assuring his complete accord with Harrison's principles and policies. He further promised at all times
to be in close communication in his role as "certifying officer" for
the Chief Executive. He added what Harrison most wanted to
hear: "Foreign Affairs are in their inception and management ex-
clusively Executive and nothing decisive can be done in this important field except with the President's personal knowledge and
official approval."[28]

Although Harrison had determined to keep his Cabinet a secret
until the entire slate could be announced and sent to the Senate
for confirmation, a report of Blaine's acceptance appeared in New
York and Washington newspapers on January 26, 1889.[29] Before
long an avalanche of criticism rolled over Harrison. The Chicago
Tribune's sentiments were typical: "First and Foremost, James G.
Blaine will be Premier of the Harrison Administration, and the
mugwumps can put that in their pipe and smoke it."[30] The same

---

27 Volwiler, *op. cit.*, pp. 45–48. In the original draft Harrison had written: "You
have never allowed any provocation to lessen your zeal & effort as a Republican and I
am sure that your wide acquaintance with our public men will enable you to give me
valuable suggestions and very efficient aid in preserving that happy unity which in
the recent election brought us success." In the actual copy sent to Blaine, Harrison
deleted the above sentence.

28 Blaine to Harrison, January 21, 1889, (L.C.), Vol. 61.

29 Indianapolis *Journal*, January 27, 1889 reprinted these New York and Washington
dispatches under the caption: "The first authentic cabinet news leaked." (Hereafter
this paper and the Indianapolis *Daily Sentinel* will be cited as the *Journal* and
Sentinel, respectively.)

30 January 30, 1889.

Republican leader in Missouri who had earlier predicted Harrison's assassination if Blaine were appointed, was fuming: "You are a gone goose. You and your party is [sic] dead to the world."[31]

Quite naturally the Democratic organs, anxious to fan the fires of factionalism among Republicans, followed the lead of the New York *World* which had bluntly declared that "Gen. Harrison's administration is predestined to failure. It will go down in history as a parallel of that of Rutherford B. Hayes."[32] Other Republican leaders regarded Blaine's appointment with undisguised regret. New Jersey's William J. Sewell, the brigadier general[33] whose Senate term paralleled Harrison's, informed his colleague and hunting partner that "the settled assurance that Blaine is to be Secretary of State has made a great number of men very lukewarm as to the success of the Administration."

Sewell, moreover, emphasized a point of which Harrison was already aware: "It is going to be difficult to frame a Cabinet acceptable to the country with Blaine as the cornerstone."[34] Harrison, however, would not retreat. Instead he drew some consolation from the assurance that a number of sagacious Republicans regarded him as a strong man in the Cabinet. Periodically, as might have been expected, the Indianapolis *Journal* contended that the cabinet would be essentially Harrison's, and at every meeting "the head of the table will be where he sits."[35]

The man whom Harrison most wanted for the Treasury portfolio was Senator William Boyd Allison, the Iowan master of finance whom President Garfield had tried to lure into his official family. On January 17, 1889, the same day that Blaine had been invited into the Cabinet, Allison also received an official tender and a covering letter in which Harrison strongly urged his acceptance of the Treasury office.[36] When no definitive answer was forth-

31 James Finley to Harrison, February 12(?), 1889, as cited by Volwiler, *op. cit.*, p. 13. Copy also in (L.C.).

32 The *World* contended that "there is a cloud on the Republican horizon. Two months ago it was a mere speck, but it has grown very rapidly since and now has threatening proportions" (*ibid.*).

33 Irish-born Sewell had immigrated to Chicago and finally settled in Camden, N.J. He played a heroic part in the Battle of Chancellorsville and was breveted brigadier general. In 1896 he received a Congressional Medal of Honor. For his friendship with Harrison in the Senate (1881–1887), see Sievers, *op. cit.*, pp. 195, 208.

34 Sewell to Harrison, February 5, 1889, (L.C.), Vol. 65.

35 *Journal*, January 5, 1889. During January and February this idea gained prominence.

36 Harrison to Allison, January 17, 1889, (L.C.), Vol. 59.

coming, the President-elect, then in Indianapolis, summoned Allison from Washington for a conference on January 27th and 28th. During the 27 hours Allison remained as Harrison's house guest the two men spent a great deal of time in private conference. Once again Allison was offered the post; acceptance was urged on the grounds of public and party considerations. The Senator remained undecided, although Harrison in his own mind felt certain that Allison would agree, once he had returned to Washington. Allison's biographer noted that acceptance was generally expected.[37]

Back in the Senate chamber once again, the cautious and conservative "Hawkeye" listened to the chatter of "can Allison stay out?" and, inevitably, to much contradictory advice from his colleagues. Wisconsin's Senator John C. Spooner joined Senator Preston B. Plumb of Kansas in advising him to accept.[38] On the other hand, friends from New York and Iowa thought he should decline. For two days Allison wrestled with his problem, and, as he assured Harrison, "I have tried to bring my mind in accord with yours."[39] Finally, on January 31, 1889, in a "My dear General" letter, Allison wrote that he felt it was his imperative duty to decline the Treasury post.[40]

Harrison, who had already read some newspaper gossip on the subject, found Allison's decision very disappointing and deemed further negotiations useless.[41] The turn of events only served to increase his perplexity arising from political pressure from the East, especially from New York, where Boss Platt and former Senator Warner Miller both ardently desired the Treasury post. The

37 Leland L. Sage, William Boyd Allison, p. 237, writes: "Everyone believed that he had been offered a Cabinet post, and of course everyone expected him to accept it."

38 John Coit Spooner to Harrison, January 30, 1889, (L.C.), Vol. 63. See also Dorothy Ganfield Fowler, John Coit Spooner: Defender of Presidents, pp. 116–19, for the close relationship between Harrison and Spooner during the formative period of the administration.

39 Allison to Harrison, January 31, 1889, (L.C.), Vol. 63. This letter of declination was discovered after Professor Sage had published his admirable biography of Allison. See Sage, op. cit., p. 370, n. 30.

40 In analyzing Allison's refusal, Sage, op. cit., p. 239, lists the following reasons: "The comparative security of his Senate seat as against the uncertainty of the length of tenure in the Cabinet; the great expense involved in Cabinet social obligations; the vast amount of petty desk work. But the real reason was the possibility that his successor might be the hated William Larrabee, the man whose [senatorial] ideas on railroad regulation were now anathema to Allison's best friends, General Dodge and Charles E. Perkins."

41 Harrison to Allison, February 4, 1889, (L.C.), Vol. 64. See also Sage, op. cit., p. 238. Harrison could have, and probably did, learn the same news from the Indianapolis Journal; e.g., see Harrison to Blaine, February 1, 1889, (L.C.), Vol. 64.

two candidates, each a leader of rival factions within the party, had strong and influential supporters. Moreover, Platt had vigorously advanced the claim, totally unfounded,[42] that he had a letter in Harrison's own handwriting promising him the appointment to the post.

Although he recognized his political debt to the New Yorkers who had swung the electoral vote to his column in 1888, Harrison felt it wise to select someone from another state for the Treasury post. A New Yorker would be chosen for a less important cabinet post. In this decision Harrison stood alone, encountering the repeated opposition of his own political lieutenant, Louis T. Michener, who felt that there should be at least one able political manager in the Cabinet. Even prior to Allison's refusal, Michener had urged earnestly and often the appointment of Thomas C. Platt, whom he regarded as having "undoubted integrity, great abilities as a business man, a loyal nature, and remarkable skill as a party manager." Harrison remained adverse to Michener's suggestion. He had decided to grasp the reins himself, and the official family circle was not wide enough to include a state boss. This Michener regarded as political naïveté. He said candidly that "the fact is that in the winter of 1889 Harrison was afraid, though he did not say so in words, to put a powerful practical politician in the Cabinet, lest his presence there would cause criticism of his administration. . . ."[43]

For the Treasury, Harrison refused to look to any Eastern state, despite heavy pressure from trading and industrial interests.[44]

42 *The Autobiography of Thomas Collier Platt,* ed. Louis J. Lang, pp. 206–8. For the rebuttal of this unfounded charge see Halford, "General Harrison's Attitude Toward the Presidency," *loc. cit.;* also Sievers, *op. cit.,* p. 348, n. 73, and p. 395.

43 Michener, "Formation of the Cabinet," Michener MSS. From the viewpoint of practical politics, Michener had a strong case, arguing that both factions, if passed over, would take offense and "in time unite against the administration and do the party and the President infinite harm." Not nearly as sensitive to the possible charge of "bossism" and "corruption" as was Harrison, Michener maintained that if Harrison had "appointed Mr. Platt, the head of the faction that embraced 9/10's of the party in the state, the other faction, as a matter of self-preservation, would acquiesce presently, and support the administration loyally. . . ." In 1889 Harrison refused to see it Michener's way. By 1891, however, he appointed Stephen B. Elkins as Secretary of War. Michener simply recalled: "Harrison had grown wiser" and had brought a powerful boss and manager into the official family.

44 Wharton Barker, a steel industrialist, had supported Harrison for the presidency as early as 1884. In 1889, in return for campaign contributions collected and in gratitude for "delivering the Irish vote," Barker fully expected the Treasury portfolio. See *Journal,* February 1, 1889, and Barker to Harrison, February 8, 1889, (L.C.), Vol. 66.

Instead he turned his thoughts to the West, where an abundant crop of Cabinet candidates had grown tall. Ohio alone boasted three impressive candidates: Congressman William McKinley, former Governor Charles Foster, and Senator John Sherman. During the Hayes' administration Sherman had filled the Treasury post with distinction. Although the Senator had disclaimed any desire for executive office under the new administration, he playfully advised Harrison: "You should feel like a gallant young gentleman entering upon life with a world of girls about him, free to choose—to propose, but not to dispose."[45]

Harrison showed himself quite willing to propose, but his interest centered on Minnesota rather than on Ohio. Here lived Ohio-born William Windom, a lawyer who had represented Minnesota as a Republican through five terms in Congress and another decade as United States senator. In 1881 he resigned to accept the Treasury portfolio under Garfield.[46] When Harrison learned that Allison would not join his official family, he sought information far and wide on Windom's availability and competence.

Early reports seemed promising. Minnesota's Senator-elect, William Drew Washburn, assured Harrison that Windom's appointment would convey confidence to the country.[47] Senator Henry Blair of New Hampshire supported Windom for an entirely different reason. He told Harrison that such a move would please the temperance sentiment in the party, gleefully adding that "as you know, he helped to organize and is identified with the Anti-Saloon movement . . . and perhaps one or two cold water fellows will do well sandwiched in with us wine dippers."[48]

Opposition to Windom soon developed on two fronts. In Washington, Hoosier Congressman George W. Steele reported that a majority on the Hill regarded Windom as an inept politician.[49] And National Committeeman J. S. Clarkson told L. T. Michener the same tale, alleging that Windom not only refused to work during the 1888 campaign but had even taken a pleasure trip to

45 John Sherman, *Recollections of Forty Years in the House, Senate and Cabinet*, p. 795.

46 *Biographical Directory of the American Congress, 1774–1949*, p. 2032. Also, in addition to the usual newspaper sketches, *Appleton's Annual Cyclopedia and Register of Important Events of the Year 1889* (n.s., Vol. XIV), p. 802, summarizes Windom's life.

47 Washburn to Harrison, February 3, 1889, (L.C.), Vol. 64.

48 Henry Blair to Harrison, February 4, 1889 (*ibid.*).

49 George W. Steele to Harrison, February 8, 1889 (*ibid.*).

avoid speaking.[50] Senator Preston B. Plumb opposed Windom on personal grounds, while Minnesota Congressman John Lind sourly remarked: "If President Harrison wants to get a Wall Street broker, why doesn't he take a New Yorker?"[51]

On this score Stephen B. Elkins advised Harrison that the Minnesotan had "lent his name too freely to one or two business ventures . . . not fairly established," though he admitted that current financial circles in Wall Street now regarded him as "safe, sound and conservative."[52] Since this aroused the President-elect's suspicions, he determined to investigate the matter both personally and by proxy.

In addition to Senator-elect Washburn, who was already committed to Windom's cause, Harrison had two other Minnesota friends who knew Windom well. These men, Eugene Gano Hay and General A. B. Nettleton, owner and publisher respectively of the Minneapolis *Tribune*, were invited to Indianapolis. Hay himself later recalled:

The President-elect received us cordially and apparently welcomed all we said in Mr. Windom's favor. He, however, told us that he had heard from some source that Windom had certain connections with Wall Street that if true could render him unavailable.[53]

Closely questioned by Harrison, the two friends could not settle his lingering doubts. Consequently, they took the next train for New York, and within 24 hours were in conference with Windom at the Fifth Avenue Hotel. He was able to satisfy his guests, who promptly informed Harrison that Windom indeed had no dubious Wall Street connections. A week later Windom himself, by invitation of the President-elect, visited Indianapolis. It was then, as Hay stated, that he was offered the position of Treasury Secretary.[54]

The choice of John Wanamaker as Postmaster General, a post usually awarded to the "Cabinet Politician," fooled nearly every experienced Republican leader except Boss Quay, the chairman

50 J. S. Clarkson to L. T. Michener, February 16, 1889, (L.C.), Vol. 66.

51 Lind's comment to Congressman Steele, in Steele to Harrison, February 8, 1889, (L.C.), Vol. 64.

52 Elkins to Harrison, February 4, 1889, Elkins MSS.

53 Hay, *op. cit.*, p. 10.

54 *Ibid.*, p. 11. This squares in all details with the account in the *Journal*, February 17, 1889. Harrison did not consult Michener on the Windom appointment. See "Formation of the Cabinet," Michener MSS., p. 3.

of the National Committee. Indeed, until the very morning of the inauguration even Matt Quay found himself on tenterhooks.[55] When newspapers gossiped about a possible Wanamaker appointment, party leaders flooded Indianapolis with protests—with only Quay abstaining.

The report also drew fire from reformers within both parties. The mere thought of a political tyro as chief dispenser of patronage struck dread into the hearts of local Republican leaders who had starved during the Cleveland administration. Philadelphians knew the Wanamaker store but few across the nation knew the energetic, fifty-two-year-old merchant prince. Even Harrison himself had not yet met the man who had managed the financial aspects of the campaign.[56]

As one of a number of other Cabinet considerations, Wanamaker was first proposed by Quay, who had visited Indianapolis in mid-December.[57] Between Christmas and mid-January the President-elect actively sought an estimate of Wanamaker's character and competence. He requested a detailed report from Charles Emory Smith, editor of the Philadelphia Press and Wanamaker's wealthy neighbor. Harrison quickly learned that the substantially united sentiment of Pennsylvania supported the Philadelphia merchant who "represents . . . new blood . . . fresh spirit . . . progressive ideas." Smith advised Harrison that Wanamaker should have a share in his administration because:

. . . he embodies the qualities and attributes that would make him a pillar of strength to you, and I do not think I over-estimate it in regarding him as the most important new factor that has come to our politics.[58]

Harrison, an expert listener, found he had to balance Smith's appraisal against a less favorable and temperate judgment leveled

55 Frank William Leach to Professor A. T. Volwiler, July 20, 1938, a letter incorporated by Volwiler into (L.C.).

56 Matthew Josephson, op. cit., p. 440, alleges Wanamaker donated $50,000 to the Republican war chest. Most Democrats regarded this figure as too low. Though a Republican since the party's first presidential canvass in 1856, Wanamaker had been a political unknown until he served successfully as the National Advisory Chairman of the Finance Committee during the 1888 campaign. See Sievers, op. cit., pp. 378–79, 426–27.

57 According to H. A. Gibbons, John Wanamaker, I, 260, Quay told Harrison that Wanamaker had been "the tower of saving strength."

58 Charles Emory Smith to Harrison, January 3, 1889, (L.C.), Vol. 55.

against Wanamaker by an old Pennsylvania soldier who warned: "You do not need the Philadelphia tailor—a Jew inwardly—a sharper and rich. . . . He is not and cannot become a statesman."[59] Another City of Brotherly Love resident styled Wanamaker a "colossal hypocrite and humbug."[60]

Understandably bothered, Harrison determined to summon Wanamaker to Indiana, especially when he learned that the Philadelphia merchant had booked passage for Europe.[61] On January 17th the President-elect invited him to come west for a conference. A prompt reply indicated how much Wanamaker coveted recognition;[62] four days later he arrived at the Hoosier Capital where he lunched and conferred with Harrison for some four hours. As usual, reporters could come by no positive information, though Wanamaker's biographer pointedly observed:

Harrison and Wanamaker took to one another immediately. It was a sudden discovery of affinity. Each was unlike what the other had expected. Harrison was not as stiff and unbending as Wanamaker had thought he would find him. Wanamaker was far from being the ambitious business man ready to accept office as a *quid pro quo*.[63]

There is no doubt that Harrison decided then and there to offer the Philadelphia merchant a place in his official family. Wanamaker not only promised to accept the Cabinet dignity but he also agreed in advance to the appointment of James S. Clarkson as Assistant Postmaster General.[64]

Shortly after the Indianapolis meeting, the assaults of politicians and the sharp criticism of newspapers continued unabated until March 3, 1889, eve of the Inauguration. The President-elect, already in Washington, summoned Chairman Quay to his quarters

59 F. P. Davidson to Harrison, December 31, 1888, (L.C.), Vol. 54.

60 John C. Wilkinson to Harrison, January 19, 1889, (L.C.), Vol. 60.

61 John R. Paxton to Harrison, January 10, 1889, (L.C.), Vol. 57. Paxton informed Harrison that Wanamaker was scheduled to leave for Europe on January 17. Harrison then advised Paxton to have Wanamaker delay his trip until he could invite the Philadelphian to Indianapolis. With characteristic caution the President-elect warned that such an invitation should not be construed as a Cabinet "conclusion."

62 Gibbons, *op. cit.*, I, 265. By courtesy of the heirs and Walter Berry, vice-president of the Wanamaker store in Philadelphia, this author has had the privilege of examining Wanamaker's papers and the research notes compiled by Mr. Gibbons and his staff.

63 *Ibid.*, I, 266.

64 F. W. Leach to A. T. Volwiler, July 20, 1938, *loc. cit.* Clarkson had seemed to be the leading contender for the post of Postmaster General. He had served Harrison well as vice-chairman—under Quay—of the National Committee. See Sage, *op. cit.*, pp. 234–37.

in the Arlington Hotel. The sequel, with Quay's secretary Frank W. Leach waiting downstairs, reveals the torment suffered by Harrison in arriving at decisions. Leach later recalled that

After an hour with the President-elect, Quay came to the street-floor where I was awaiting him, and told me to get ready to leave for Philadelphia by the next train, see Wanamaker and bring him to Washington at once. Quay, who seemed greatly distressed and worried, told me General Harrison had informed him that some prominent men recently had declared to him that certain important corporate interests (I do not recall what they were: something like oil interests, perhaps, such as caused so much trouble under Harding) had been promised by Mr. Wanamaker, while collecting campaign funds, certain favors, at the hands of the Harrison administration. Harrison told Quay this matter must be cleared up or he would not name Wanamaker.[65]

Leach caught the midnight train for Philadelphia and at 3:00 A.M. met Wanamaker who proved the charge utterly devoid of truth. Leach and Quay conveyed the testimony to Harrison shortly before the Inauguration.[66]

During January and February, when many distinguished men stopped by to see General Harrison, only a few came by invitation. Whenever invited guests arrived, such as Allison, Windom and Wanamaker, the visit stirred cabinet gossip to the boiling point. After each interview, however, the press failed to secure comment from either the visitor or from Harrison. Only after the Inauguration would the country read the whole story. The truth is, however, that once the names of Blaine, Windom, and Wanamaker became fixed in Harrison's mind, he had comparatively little trouble in selecting the five remaining members of his official family.[67] As Louis T. Michener recalled: "It was not at all difficult to satisfy Harrison that former Governor Proctor of Vermont should be made Secretary of War, or that John W. Noble of Missouri should be Secretary of the Interior."[68]

Redfield Proctor, rated as "an original Harrison man" at the nominating convention,[69] had a good war record, with a wound to

---

65 Leach to Volwiler, *loc. cit.*

66 *Ibid.* Leach, who complained that he had experienced a "strenuous 24 hours," recalled that he had cleared the charges against Wanamaker only a "half-hour" before the Inauguration.

67 With the raising of the Department of Agriculture to Cabinet status on February 9, 1889, Harrison had eight high offices to fill.

68 "Formation of the Cabinet," Michener MSS., p. 5.

69 *Journal*, February 19, 1889.

prove it; furthermore, he owned one of the largest marble enterprises in the country. A native Vermonter, Proctor had been graduated from Dartmouth just over the New Hampshire line, had studied law in Albany and practiced in Boston until he went to war with the 15th Vermont Infantry. After filling several elective offices, he became Governor of Vermont in 1878.[70]

On February 18, 1889, Harrison invited Proctor, then returning from California, to stop at Indianapolis. Private Secretary Halford alerted the *Journal* readers lest they forget that the party leader in the Green Mountain State had seconded the General's nomination and had acted as chairman of the only delegation that cast its vote solidly from first to last for Harrison. Although Proctor spent only a short time with the President-elect, Harrison very likely offered him the portfolio of War on that occasion.[71]

As Secretary of the Interior, Harrison selected John Willock Noble, a St. Louis lawyer who enjoyed a "high reputation of probity, learning and industry." His background resembled Harrison's; Ohio-born, both had matriculated at Miami University. Noble, however, finished at Yale where he was graduated in 1851. He first practiced law in St. Louis, then in Keokuk, Iowa. At the outbreak of the war, he became adjutant of the 3rd Iowa Cavalry and compiled an impressive combat record to gain a brigadier's star. During the railroad strike of 1877, General Noble, like Harrison in Indianapolis, had organized his fellow citizens to maintain order and law enforcement. His prosecution of the Whiskey Ring in St. Louis won him such admirers as Supreme Court Justice Samuel F. Miller and former Attorney General Benjamin Bristow. Before Harrison departed for Washington, Noble had accepted the office of Secretary of the Interior.[72]

Harrison's selection of his own law partner, William Henry Harrison Miller, as Attorney General, surprised all but Hoosiers themselves. Early in February, according to Michener, Harrison had determined to appoint one genuine friend from his own state, one whose fidelity and qualifications he could not doubt. William Evarts of New York had been urged upon him, but Harrison still turned to Miller, who had never been active in politics. After Harrison told Michener that he feared he would deeply offend

70 *Appleton's Annual Cyclopedia . . . (1889)*, pp. 802–3.

71 *Journal*, February 19, March 6, 1889.

72 *Appleton's Annual Cyclopedia . . . (1889)*, p. 804; *Journal*, February 19, 21, March 6, 1889. The fact that Mrs. Noble was house-hunting in Washington on February 20th is good circumstantial evidence of an offer made and accepted.

some Indiana leaders by such an appointment, Michener began interviewing leading Republicans in each congressional district, telling them what Harrison really wanted. County newspaper editors cooperated and as Michener put it: "In less than ten days the sky was free from clouds and Miller was selected."[73]

Until the very last minute, the hardest political nuts for Harrison to crack proved to be Wisconsin and New York. At the national convention both delegations had dropped their favorite sons to support Harrison. No two states found themselves in a better position to demand recognition in the new Cabinet, and at the same time no other states found themselves so badly divided by political factions within the party.

Among Wisconsin's several cabinet candidates, John Coit Spooner had been prominently mentioned for Attorney General. Even before Harrison decided on his own law partner for this post, Spooner had withdrawn his name from consideration, thereby freeing himself for a dual role: confidential adviser to Harrison and mediator between Wisconsin's two leading aspirants for cabinet posts—three-time Governor Jeremiah McLain Rusk and State Chairman Henry Clay Payne. Fired with political ambition, Rusk tried to outmaneuver Payne in seeking the War, the Navy, or the Agriculture Department. Weeks of anxious waiting followed, with Senator Spooner at times pushing Harrison to invite Rusk into the official family circle.[74]

Rusk, like Harrison and Windom, had geography on his side. Born in Ohio, he was reared on a farm, achieved distinction by his rare fighting qualities in the army, afterward served three terms in Congress, then became an extremely popular governor of Wisconsin. Uncle Jerry, as his friends called him, found himself in the valley of Harrison's indecision until the day before the Inauguration. Spooner, already intimate with Harrison, called on the President-elect once again, and at the eleventh hour the Senator successfully landed Governor Rusk in the Cabinet as the first Secretary of Agriculture in the nation's history.[75]

73 "Formation of the Cabinet," Michener MSS., p. 5.

74 Fowler, op. cit., pp. 116–17. Harrison had invited Spooner three times to Indianapolis. He came twice, the second visit being over Christmas Day.

75 Halford's Diary, (L.C.), entry for March 3, 1889, reads in part: "This afternoon after conference with Spooner appointment of Rusk to Agricultural Department was determined upon. Halstead and myself suggested Clarkson." See also Fowler, op. cit., p. 118.

The selection of a New Yorker for the Cabinet vexed Harrison from the day of his election until two days before his Inauguration. The Empire State had given Harrison a plurality of more than 13,000, but G.O.P. gubernatorial candidate Warner Miller lost his race to the incumbent Democratic Governor, David B. Hill, by more than 19,000 votes. General Harrison had promptly wired: "I am greatly grieved at your defeat. If the intrepid leader fell outside the breastworks, the column, inspired by his courage, went on to victory."[76]

When the press printed Harrison's picturesque message of sympathy, Warner Miller's supporters became more confident. Furthermore, his friends argued strongly that his defeat made him a logical candidate for the new Cabinet. Boss Platt, already sorely disappointed at being scratched from the list of Cabinet eligibles, vowed that neither Miller nor Miller's choice should go into the Cabinet. By the time Harrison had arrived in Washington, the factional feud had grown bitter. Compromise seemed impossible, although representatives of both Platt and Miller debated the matter with the President-elect.[77]

Harrison still walked alone. He felt he could side with neither faction though he must somehow reward New York. Finally, and against the advice of Michener, Clarkson, and Elkins, Harrison conferred with Senator Frank Hiscock and subsequently settled on Benjamin Franklin Tracy, a Brooklyn attorney who had been mentioned as a possibility for Attorney-General.[78] As had been his custom, Harrison would make no decision until he could arrange to talk with the candidate. Private Secretary Halford's diary, March 1, 1889, relates the sequel: "General Tracy reached here and had an interview with the General at night. Offered Navy and accepted it."[79]

Tracy, indeed, could present the kind of credentials Harrison wanted. This future Secretary of the Navy had already had an attractive career in the military and at the bar. Decorated for gal-

76 D. S. Alexander, *Four Famous New Yorkers*, pp. 130, 132.

77 T. C. Platt, *op. cit.*, pp. 205-8; *Journal*, January, February, March 1, 2, 3, 1889.

78 D. S. Alexander, *op. cit.*, p. 133, reports on Hiscock's agreeable relations with Harrison. *Journal*, March 4, 1889, carried a "special" entitled "Solving New York's Problem." It speculated as to who first suggested General Tracy's name to President Harrison. It reported that "credit should be given to Franklin Woodruff, and to his nephew, Timothy L. Woodruff . . . also to Senator Hiscock and J. Sloat Fassett."

79 (L.C.), Vol. 69. *Journal*, March 4, 1889 reported that Blaine regarded Tracy with high favor.

lantry at Spottsylvania during the Wilderness Campaign, Tracy
quickly rose from colonel to brigadier general. He later served
with credit as New York assemblyman, as a district attorney of the
State and of the United States, and as a judge of the Court of
Appeals.[80] Such a man Harrison found easy to accept—no matter
what seasoned political lieutenants might feel. The day following
the Harrison-Tracy meeting, a New York City attorney wrote to
Washington:

Alexander the Great *cut* the "Gordian Knot,"—you have done better—
you have untied it . . . the choice of General Tracy as one of your
advisers . . . will be received with a deeper and more general satisfaction throughout the State than any other you could have made. He is a
broad man—national not personal in his politics—he leads no faction—
he is simply and thoroughly Republican.[81]

Although Harrison could draw some slight consolation from
scanning letters dealing with the Tracy appointment,[82] he had
scarcely settled the party feud within the Empire State. Platt's only
solace came with the knowledge that he had kept Warner Miller
out of the Cabinet, while Miller and his supporters grew resentful
and depressed. With Tracy in the cabinet, Hiscock in the Senate,
and Levi P. Morton as Vice-President, neither the Platt nor the
Miller faction felt encouraged.[83] Harrison's own leadership was
paramount even though Tom Platt and Warner Miller decided to
take their separate political paths.

All in all, in naming his own Cabinet, Harrison had given the
party managers little or no say.[84] As Elkins unhappily noted, "Republicans complain that of the eight men in the Cabinet only one
of them was in the Convention. Not one of the whole Cabinet did
anything for you to bring about your nomination and . . . this is

80 *Journal*, March 6, 1889; D. S. Alexander, *op. cit.*, p. 133.

81 John A. Grow to Harrison, March 2, 1889, (L.C.), Vol. 69.

82 James M. Scovel wired Harrison from Philadelphia that "General Tracy is an
inspiration"; and Major General Isaac Catlin sent an encomium on Tracy's "gallan-
try . . . ability and integrity." See Scovel and Catlin to Harrison, March 2, 1889 (*ibid.*).

83 D. S. Alexander, *op. cit.*, p. 134.

84 T. C. Platt, *op. cit.*, pp. 205–8; L. T. Michener, "Formation of a Cabinet,"
loc. cit.; E. W. Halford, "General Harrison's Attitude Toward the Presidency," *loc. cit.*
All this evidence contradicts Josephson, *op. cit.*, p. 438, who quotes Harrison as saying:
"When I came into power I found that the party managers had taken it all to
themselves."

an abandonment of friends. . . . A chill . . . is already felt. . . ."[85] Elkins, of course, had failed to receive full consideration from Harrison who made some amends by naming him Secretary of War in 1891.

In the final analysis, Harrison had leaned with conviction toward age and experience in choosing his Cabinet—only Attorney General Miller and Postmaster General Wanamaker were younger than he.[86] In the other departments Windom's 61 years gave him seniority, and Blaine at 59 came next. Secretary of War Proctor, Secretary of Navy Tracy, and Secretary of Agriculture Rusk all admitted to 58 years, and Interior Secretary Noble would be 58 on October 26th. Though Blaine, Windom, and Wanamaker had not seen service during the Civil War, Tracy, Noble, and Rusk had all been breveted brigadier generals. Redfield Proctor had risen from quartermaster to colonel, and William Henry Harrison Miller's friends called him Captain on the strength of his service as a Hundred Day volunteer. Finally, after shuffling the deck for his "Legal Deal," Harrison had come up with six lawyers and two businessmen. Each member of the cabinet was a churchgoer, although Wanamaker and his Sunday school received the most newspaper attention.[87] The President's friends, including of course, ex-President Rutherford B. Hayes, acclaimed the final slate as excellent.[88]

85 S. B. Elkins to Harrison, March 8, 1889, (L.C.), Vol. 70. He warned Harrison that "already predictions are made that in the next election you will lose the House by fifty majority, also New York, Indiana and Ohio." Elkins tempered the report with his personal judgment: "Of course, I do not share all these apprehensions, but in my judgment there is ground for fear."

86 Harrison, at age 55, had seven years on Miller and four years over Wanamaker. For the story of the Harrison-Miller friendship and law partnership, see Sievers, op. cit., pp. 65–66.

87 On Wanamaker and "The New Kind of Sunday School," see Gibbons, op. cit., I, 181–94. Like Harrison, Wanamaker was a Presbyterian elder who, as Gibbons alleges, "could be relied upon to help the President in keeping politics as clean as possible in Washington." Ibid., p. 263. The Journal, January, February, and March, 1889, passim, reprinted many national press reports on Wanamaker's religious activities.

88 Hayes to Harrison, March 5, 1889, (L.C.), Vol. 69; W. W. Holden to Harrison, March 6, 1889, ibid. Perhaps more satisfying to Harrison was the Inauguration Day wire he received from John C. New, William Wallace, J. A. Wildman, L. C. Walker, Lew Wallace and T. P. Haughey from Indianapolis: "As old friends and neighbors we congratulate you and the nation . . . and we cordially endorse your selection of Cabinet" (ibid.).

CHAPTER II

Prelude to High Office

HARRISON'S POLITICAL INDEPENDENCE both baffled and estranged some G.O.P. workers whose Cabinet suggestions were not honored.[1] Yet to fulfill party pledges it was necessary to maintain harmony in Washington where the Republicans held control and also in the nation at large in which political loyalties were more evenly divided. Harrison believed the responsibility to be his and, should failure ensue, then that also. The task at hand was to accommodate party pressures, within the limits of his own conscience and ideals.

Harrison had affirmed in his campaign speeches his belief in a protective tariff and had promised some relief from the competition of foreign-made cheap goods. He had addressed himself to immigrant workers as well as to the farmers and industrialists across the nation. Standing before some 1,000 persons who had come from Terre Haute to his front porch, Harrison had stressed what he believed to be the American way:

The smoke of your factories goes up night and day. The farms about your city have become gardens, and the cordial and harmonious relations between the railroad shop and the factory and the farms that lie about have a conspicuous illustration with you. You have found that that policy which built up these shops, which maintains them, gives employment to the largest number of men, is the best thing not only for the railroads that do the transportation, but for the workingmen who find steady employment at good wages, and for the farmers who supply their needs.[2]

1 Harrison bristled that he had "made no war on anyone and do not intend to; but I think I know the proper limit of patience and self-respect" (Harrison to Elkins, February 18, 1889, Elkins MSS.). Yet the latter lamented: "So far as I can make out, not one of your friends who stood by you firmly and conspicuously before and during the Convention is to find a place in your Cabinet..." (Elkins to Harrison, February 19, 1889, (L.C.), Vol. 68).

2 Explaining that doubled imports from England would aid that country but not the workingmen of America, Harrison called for a "wise selfishness" at home. See *Speeches of Benjamin Harrison*, Charles Hedges (compiler), pp. 73–76.

Once dominantly agricultural, the nation was beginning to feel industry's challenge—something that would divide an old from a modern America.[3] Harrison was aware of the change. His own words had stamped him as something more than a passive champion of that evolution in technology which is summed up in the term Social Darwinism.[4] He had inherited political and economic principles from the Europe of the seventeenth and eighteenth centuries; yet he felt that America, physically and socially, was still in the making. As had his predecessors in the White House, including Grover Cleveland (later called a conservative Republican by Woodrow Wilson),[5] Harrison saw, in the words of Henry Steele Commager, "an America . . . self-confident, self-contained, self-reliant, and conscious of its unique character and of a unique destiny."[6] As Chief Executive, moreover, he would identify himself with "men of humanitarian impulse" and "probe for the cause of extensive poverty in the midst of material progress."[7] Some expected from him a stronger leadership along social and political lines than had been experienced under Cleveland.[8]

Harrison, in brief, had shown himself aware that a protective tariff might entail higher consumer prices, that currency problems might be solved only by inflation and freer coinage of silver, that

3 Henry Steele Commager, The American Mind, pp. 41–54, describes this transition as "The Watershed of the Nineties." See also Harold U. Faulkner, Politics, Reform and Expansion: 1890–1900, pp. 1–22.

4 Harrison, never subscribing to unqualified laissez faire economy, had enjoyed some strong labor support during the 1888 campaign.

5 Morton Borden (ed.), America's Ten Greatest Presidents, p. 169.

6 Op. cit., p. 41. See also William J. Sewell to Harrison, January 1, 1889, (L.C.), Vol. 58. He advised that "there is a general settling down amongst the business community and in railroad managements, we are going to have very prosperous times."

7 Samuel P. Hays, The Response to Industrialism: 1885–1914, p. 41. Within a decade Harrison would conclude that "each citizen has a personal interest . . . in the tax return of his neighbor. We are members of a great partnership, and it is the right of each to know what any other member is contributing to the partnership and what he is taking from it. It is not a private affair; it is a public concern of the first importance." See Benjamin Harrison, Views of An Ex-President, ed. Mary Lord Harrison, pp. 355–56.

8 A. B. Nettleton to E. W. Halford, January 21, 1889, (L.C.), Vol. 61, pointed to the statesmanship needed by new Republican leaders. The victorious party must be held together not by "finesse, patronage and sharp political management, but by satisfying the mass of people who rendered the verdict of November 1st." Also Benjamin H. Bristow to Judge George Denny, January 21, 1889, Bristow Letterbooks, noted: "I have full faith in Ben Harrison politically and personally and therefore supported him with much pleasure."

veterans might require service pensions, that a stronger navy and a new merchant marine would be almost mandatory, that federal regulation would be needed for trust and monopolies, and that the Negro must be guaranteed the voting franchise.

In uptown Indianapolis on New Year's Day, General and Mrs. Harrison threw open their warm red-brick house to receive the traditional callers. Between 2:00 and 8:00 P.M., nearly 2,000 persons came to greet them.[9] Workingmen with their wives and daughters mingled with fashionably dressed society. Properly attired in their long Prince Albert coats, the General and his son Russell headed the receiving line that welcomed the crowd.

Harrison seemed to reserve his warmest greetings for three close friends—General Lew Wallace, his campaign biographer; ex-Governor Albert G. Porter, his former law partner; and onetime U.S. Senator Joseph E. McDonald, a Democrat who had crossed party lines in the recent campaign. New Hampshire Senator Henry W. Blair, a man whom Harrison viewed somewhat warily, came to urge that Congress be called into extra session. Desiring prompt passage of his much-debated Educational Bill, Blair had scheduled several lectures on the subject in Indiana and elsewhere in the Midwest.

A wearied Harrison listened patiently, and following the last handshake, he hurried off to a celebration prepared by the George H. Thomas Post of the G.A.R. Despite the late hour and the fatigue he felt, Harrison enlivened the festivities with some forceful words. A free ballot and an honest count throughout the land, Harrison insisted, should be "a matter above and beyond any question of partisanship. . . . A free vote, honestly given and fairly counted, is the safeguard of our institutions."[10]

Though the meeting was not a public affair, yet Harrison had seized the occasion to broadcast his aversion to the suppression of free suffrage. He would like to hear, he concluded, "a bugle-call throughout the land demanding a pure ballot."[11] He soon learned

9 *Journal,* January 2, 1889.

10 *Journal,* January 2, 9, 1889, as cited from Philadelphia *Press.*

11 As a senator, Harrison had stated: "We may place the U.S. Marshals at the polls, if we ever recover the Presidency again. . . ." See Sievers, *Benjamin Harrison: Hoosier Statesman,* pp. 274–75.

that his views had aroused Eastern Mugwumps, who began to consider him aggressive and radical and not, as they had hoped, "conciliatory . . . toward the South."[12] Harrison had fired the opening
salvo in what would prove to be the new administration's bitterest
battle. He called for the strict enforcement of the Constitution and
its guarantees of civil rights for Negroes in the South.[13]

After arranging for White House delivery of two splendid Studebaker carriages priced at $1,600 and $1,300, the General, on January 14th, learned that the Presidential electors of Indiana had
cast their ballots as expected for Harrison and Levi P. Morton.
The one contest of the day centered on the selection of an elector
to act as special messenger to the U.S. Senate. By lot the privilege
fell to William H. Penfield, a lawyer from New Albany. The fifteen
electors then marched from the State House to Harrison's home,
where they needed no introduction.[14] Some twenty states north of
the Mason-Dixon Line were casting 233 electoral votes for Harrison and Morton; sixteen of the South, joined by Connecticut
and New Jersey, counted 168 votes for Cleveland and Allen G.
Thurman.

The day, however, really belonged to General Alvin P. Hovey,
who was leaving Congress to become Indiana's new Governor.
Harrison listened intently to Hovey's inaugural address at the State
Capitol. While the President-elect fully endorsed an oratorical
plea to safeguard the ballot, to curb trusts and monopolies, and to
give Indiana good roads, he heard nothing concerning the much-
discussed issues of service pensions and land bounties for veterans.[15] Within an hour, Harrison could explain the Governor's
silence. Returning home he found there the chiefs of the National
Service Pension Association, a powerful pension lobby which

12 *Journal*, January 9, 1889. Also R. S. Taylor to Harrison, February 10, 1889, (L.C.),
Vol. 66, pleaded for a mild, conciliatory approach to the southern problem, predicting
that "among the conspicuous events of your administration will be some decisive steps
towards the settlement of the Negro question."

13 The Republican platform of 1888 promised effective legislation to secure the
integrity and purity of elections, and charged that the suppression of the ballot was
"a criminal nullification of the Constitution and the laws of the United States." See
Vincent P. De Santis, *Republicans Face the Southern Question*, p. 198.

14 *Journal*, January 15, 1889.

15 Hovey, who believed his shouts for service pensions had elected him to Congress, has aptly been described as the General John Logan of Indiana. See Mary R.
Dearing, *Veterans in Politics*, p. 367.

claimed Governor Hovey as its head.[16] Apparently it was for Harrison to discuss service pensions in his own inaugural speech.[17]

A President-elect must see everyone, and everyone came: business people, office-seekers, war veterans and labor men. Among the most persistent callers were a group of Negro leaders from the South headed by Bishop W. J. Gaines of the African Methodist Episcopal Church in Georgia, who was accompanied by Bishop B. T. Turner of Philadelphia, and by the Rev. Dr. James A. Handy of Washington, D.C.[18] General Harrison, it was reported, gave an attentive hearing to their impassioned plea that "the colored man be recognized to the fullest extent merited by his advancement and his numerical strength,"[19] but again no promise was given.

A white delegation from Decatur, Alabama, also called, but all they could get was Harrison's acknowledgment that he was

. . . glad to know that the people of the South were now everywhere awakening to the importance of protecting the promising industries of that section, especially their growing manufacturing interests.[20]

Harrison also briefly touched on the need for the South to attain some independence in industry, and thus the delegates left Indianapolis much encouraged by his attitude and remarks.

Inasmuch as Harrison either had little to say or would say very little, the public was unable to focus its views. It was believed, for example, that Reconstruction policies would be revived to protect voters against intimidation. Others thought that Harrison would ignore the Negroes and would work with native white leaders. Some theorized that Harrison would woo high-tariff Democrats in the South. And still another idea prevailed that the new President

16 *Journal*, January 15, 1889. C. A. Powers, Secretary of the Association, had twice written to Harrison during the 1888 campaign (June 27, July 6, 1888), requesting an outright pledge to work for service pensions. Secretary Halford successfully forestalled a positive commitment. See *Sentinel*, March 11, 1890, and Dearing, *op. cit.*, pp. 367, 378, 397–98.

17 Harrison's long, sympathetic discussion of veterans and pensions in his Letter of Acceptance had emboldened the soldiers. See Hedges, *op. cit.*, p. 113.

18 *Journal*, January 24, 1889. Harrison had requested the views of friends on the southern question, and he had seriously considered some southern soldiers for Secretary of War. See Harrison to former President Rutherford B. Hayes, January 22, 1889, (L.C.), Vol. 61 (a photostat from Hayes Memorial Library, Fremont, Ohio).

19 *Journal*, January 24, 1889.

20 *Journal*, January 27, 1889.

would cripple boss rule in the South by a wary distribution of the patronage.[21]

As the Harrisons prepared to leave for Washington, the Pennsylvania Railroad refitted a ten-year-old presidential car known only as No. 120. It had been used by the company president, G. B. Roberts, who offered it for the new President's inaugural run.[22] A second car, the Maywood, would carry relatives and friends, and the press would ride in the Iolanthe. Monday, February 25, 1889, dawned mild and cloudless. The family rose early to breakfast, Harrison read from the Bible and conducted the usual morning prayers. It is hardly possible even to guess at the General's inner thoughts, but his secretary, Elijah Halford, found him "badly broken up. . . . and full of tears when the time came to take his leave."[23]

But for all Indianapolis it was a great day. Hundreds swarmed about North Delaware Street to form a lively procession as Harrison rode off at 2:30 P.M. with Governor Hovey and former Congressman William H. English. Banners waved and guns were fired, and in front of the New Denison Hotel, members of the Indiana legislature, standing abreast, saluted, wheeled, and joined the march. From windows and balconies downtown, women waved their handkerchiefs to Mrs. Harrison who was in the second coach, her arms full of roses. With a G.A.R. band falling into line ahead of the General's carriage, now solidly flanked by a citizens' honor guard, it took nearly an hour for the procession to cover the fifteen short blocks to the station.

The way was finally cleared for Harrison to reach the train's rear platform. After studying the crowd for a moment, he drew a thin manuscript from his coat pocket. His talk was brief:

. . . I love this city. It has been my own cherished home. Twice before I have left it to discharge public duties and returned to it with glad-

21 Articles from the Greensboro (N.C.) North State, the New York Graphic, and the Philadelphia North American, reprinted in the Journal, January 28, February 3, 4, 1889, speculated widely on the new administration's attitude toward the South. Privately Harrison had concluded first to study the political, social, and economic problems of the area, and then to adopt a policy as "national as a law" that would know neither South, North, East, nor West. See De Santis, op. cit., pp. 195–96; and Henry Cabot Lodge to Harrison, April 4, 1889, (L.C.), Vol. 73.

22 G. B. Roberts to Harrison, January 9, 1889, (L.C.), Vol. 57. After it was refurnished, the press styled the car a "veritable Oriental palace." See Journal, February 24, 25, 26, 1889.

23 "Private Diary of E. W. Halford," February 25, 1889, an excerpt in (L.C.), Ac 49500 ADD. 7.

ness, as I hope to do again. It is a city on whose streets the pompous displays of wealth are not seen. It is full of pleasant homes, and in these homes there is an unsual store of contentment.

The memory of your favor and kindness will abide with me and my strong desire to hold your respect and confidence will strengthen me in the discharge of my new and responsible duties. Let me say farewell to all my Indiana friends. For the public honors that have come to me I am their grateful debtor. They have made the debt so large that I can never discharge it.

There is a great sense of loneliness in the discharge of high public duties. The moment of decision is one of isolation. . . .[24]

Waves of cheers came from the crowd.

The train made its way slowly through villages and cities where crowds, brass bands, and even booming cannon halted progress. Harrison found it necessary to speak from the rear platform at the border town of Richmond, and at Piqua, Ohio, where Governor Joseph B. Foraker, who had climbed aboard, stood at his side.[25] At Columbus the crowd was estimated at 20,000, or about one-fifth of the city's population; at 10:00 P.M. at Newark, Ohio, as the bells of some 50 locomotives in the Baltimore & Ohio yards clanged wildly, every factory whistle blew. The din served to awaken the President-elect, who had gone to bed early, but there was no further personal appearance that night.

Harrisburg, Pennsylvania, was reached after breakfast, and, forgoing a visit to the capitol building despite the urging of a welcoming committee, Harrison was able to inform the crowd at the station that his mother's birthplace was not many miles away, in one of Pennsylvania's beautiful valleys.[26]

Since no political gains could be made in Washington, D.C., which Congress ruled and where no citizen could vote, the presidential party was taken quietly from the train at the Ninth Street freight depot. Presumably this was the efficient way, but crowds awaited in vain the arrival at the Sixth Street passenger station. The public uproar which resulted prompted Harrison, who had

24 Hedges, op. cit., p. 191; Journal, February 26, 1889.

25 Not missing a chance to make political capital, Governor Foraker also showed Harrison off before some 2,000 citizens who had gathered at the Urbana, Ohio, depot. See Journal, February 26, 1889.

26 On August 12, 1831, Elizabeth Irwin of Mercersburg, Pa., married John Scott Harrison, son of General William Henry Harrison (Sievers, Benjamin Harrison: Hoosier Warrior, p. 18).

been taken by surprise, to make known his regrets. His almost secret entry into the Capital had been arranged without his request
or authority, it was strongly implied.[27] Rooms were taken in the
Johnson House annex of the massive-windowed Arlington Hotel
on Vermont Avenue. A large display of orchids in the Louis XIV
parlor interested Mrs. Harrison, who had received dozens of other
floral tributes. Secretary Halford busied himself with stacks of mail
as the Harrisons rested.

[27] *Journal*, February 28 and March 1, 1889.

CHAPTER III

Launching the
Centennial Administration

BY MARCH 1st, Harrison had completed writing his Inaugural speech and so was able to receive several congressmen and their wives at his hotel. He himself made one important call. The five minutes that he spent at the White House on the morning of March 2 was reciprocated by President Cleveland's return visit of ten minutes that afternoon.[1]

On that same day a relentless rain pelted the city, turning the streets into mud holes and drenching the red, white, and blue bunting already strung along Pennsylvania Avenue buildings. Rarely a prisoner of the weather, Harrison also called on Senators John Sherman and George F. Edmunds that day. He already had read a draft of his speech to two Cabinet choices, Blaine and Windom,[2] and now he won the approval of his two old Senate friends. Harrison returned to his hotel and scratched in a few revisions of his own. Near midnight Secretary Halford was retyping the address for the last time, worried only by a forecast of continued bad weather for the Inauguration.[3]

[1] Cleveland had invited Harrison to call at the White House, and took pains to assure his successor that he was ready to do everything possible to make the transition "easy and agreeable" (Cleveland to Harrison, February 15, 1889, (L.C.), Vol. 67). Harrison's immediate reply was a cordial acceptance (Harrison to Cleveland, February 18, 1889, (L.C.), Vol. 68). Although Cleveland had not called on outgoing President Arthur in 1885, and Andrew Jackson had refused to visit the retiring John Quincy Adams in 1829, no rancor existed between Harrison and Cleveland, who would return to fight another day four years thence.

[2] Halford's Diary, (L.C.), March 2, 1889. Both men were reported as greatly pleased with the Inaugural draft. Blaine offered one verbal amendment, and Harrison adopted it.

[3] *Ibid.*

A steady downpour on Sunday, March 3, which kept the Harrisons from church services, continued throughout the night. At dawn the heavy clouds contrasted with the bright banners that signaled the early arrival of civil and military marching clubs with their various brass bands. Soon the strains of martial music filtered through alleyways, private homes, and hotel lobbies—murdering sleep. As one Washingtonian sensed it: "Before the dawn the din began."[4]

Shortly after 10:00 A.M., and with a few hundred spectators braving the rain, the Presidential party left the Arlington Hotel in a closed carriage drawn by four beautiful grays. Mrs. Harrison joined others of her family at the Willard Hotel, the General continuing on to the White House, where some 200 survivors of the Seventieth Indiana presented arms and saluted their old commander. Once inside, Harrison exchanged greetings with Grover Cleveland and the two men entered an open carriage for the ride to the Capitol. Cleveland held fast to an umbrella which afforded some overhead shelter for both, and warmth was provided by a heavy bearskin blanket. Harrison began waving to dampened sightseers crowding against police lines along Pennsylvania Avenue as a crescendo of cheers rose from under tightly clustered umbrellas.

With military contingents experiencing some difficulty in clearing the way for the carriage, progress was slow. A multitude of onlookers was already solidly massed east of the Capitol, where a platform had been erected at the foot of the steps. In the Senate, the closing proceedings were being witnessed by the members of the House, the Supreme Court Justices, foreign diplomats, and other guests. Levi P. Morton, dignified yet spruce, was sworn in as Vice-President and the Senate was declared adjourned, but it immediately reconvened in the extra session that Cleveland had ordered at Harrison's request. The ceremonies were running late and threatening the tradition of swearing in the new President at high noon, as Morton began to administer the oath to newly elected Senators. With a long pole, the clock was pushed back a good quarter hour by Captain Bassett, otherwise known as "Old Father Time."[5] Minutes later the assemblage arose as Cleveland and Harrison entered arm in arm, followed by Senators George Hoar, Shelby Cullom, and Francis Cockrell, the top men of the Inaugural Committee.

4 *Journal*, March 5, 1889.
5 Edna Colman, *White House Gossip*, p. 199.

Mrs. Harrison's party, having occupied seats in the Senate gallery, departed in advance of the procession of dignitaries. With her father, Dr. John Witherspoon Scott, now 89, and children, Russell and Mary, Mrs. Harrison was escorted by General George B. Williams to the uncovered inaugural stand, where a black sea of upraised umbrellas confronted them.[6] As the crowd first glimpsed Harrison—just after one o'clock—a welcoming roar rose, continuing until all had been seated.

His head uncovered and bowed, Harrison placed his right hand on an open Bible held by the Court clerk, while Chief Justice Melville Fuller stood by. Quietly he repeated the oath by which he was inaugurated the twenty-third President of the United States. Donning once again his high silk hat, and standing erect in the Prince Albert coat tailored for him in Indianapolis,[7] the new President drew his speech from his pocket.

Harrison could allude to the blessings that followed on territorial expansion—an increase in population and in corporate wealth. There were now nearly 60,000,000 United States citizens better fed, clothed, and housed than ever before. He credited neither political party, but attributed American growth to the benign influences of education and of religion, and appealed for further progress. He called for greater effort to form a more perfect Union based on a broadened industry by which the cotton states and the mining territories might begin to match strides with New England and the thriving Atlantic Seaboard. Noting that the "mill fires were lighted at the funeral pyre of slavery," Harrison urged that free men of the smelting furnace and the mill might make of material things a better servant, and he renewed his campaign promise of a protective tariff.

A strong antisectional note was maintained as Harrison urged, in effect, no "Southern policy" (as had been asked by some Republican leaders). "Laws are general, and their administration should be uniform and equal" without special regard for sections; the Negro had been granted the right to vote, in both North and

6 *Journal*, March 5, 1889.

7 The tailor was Frederick William Pich, a German immigrant, employed by the Indianapolis firm of A. J. Treat and Son (information supplied to the author by Anna A. Pich of Indianapolis. See also *Indianapolis Evening News*, February 26, 1962). The black broadcloth material, the gift of John F. Plummer III of New York, was made by the Springville Company, Rockwell, Connecticut. See John F. Plummer to Harrison, February 5, 1889, (L.C.), Vol. 65.

South. After pointing an accusing finger at trusts and monopolies,[8] the President pledged social justice for all men.

The new Administration's foreign policy would be vigilant of national honor and insistent on the commercial and personal rights of American citizens everywhere. The essence of the Monroe Doctrine was recalled. "We have a clear right," said Harrison, "to expect that no European government will seek to establish colonial dependencies upon the territory of . . . independent American States." Since the flag would follow every U.S. citizen "in all countries and in many islands," he urged the building of a modern navy and an efficient merchant marine. More convenient coaling stations, better dock and harbor privileges would be required. Noninterference in the affairs of foreign governments and arbitration of international quarrels would be America's contribution toward world peace, but Harrison was putting national strength first.

Early statehood for the territories, a free ballot, and a plan to pension war veterans and their families were advocated. Then as now, a promise of government assistance evoked the loudest and most enthusiastic demonstration of the day. On the other hand, Harrison pledged himself to enforce the civil service law fully and without evasion. Spoilsmen could well agree that honorable party service would by no means disqualify a man from public office; but when Harrison added that "in no case will it be allowed to serve as a shield for official negligence, incompetence or delinquency," silence followed, broken only by a meaningful "Ah."[9]

A plea for more universal education and a deeper patriotism ended the Inaugural, which Editor Murat Halstead considered a "document of extraordinary literary as well as political merit."[10] As a chilled crowd applauded warmly, the President turned aside to embrace his wife and daughter Mary.

8 While staying at the Arlington Hotel, Harrison had accepted the gift of an enormous Siberian bloodhound as a watchdog. A reporter remarked that the animal symbolized the protective tariff. Harrison agreed, and added that the hound "looks very much like an over-fed monopolist" (*Journal*, February 27, 1889).

9 *Ibid.*, March 5, 1889.

10 Murat Halstead to Harrison, March 7, 1889, (L.C.), Vol. 69: "We have so recently talked about literary matters, the construction of addresses . . . that I feel bound to say that your Inaugural address is certainly a document of extraordinary literary as well as political merit. This is, I believe, the universal opinion; and a great number are at pains to say so in the most extravagant terms, who are not accustomed to enthusiasm."

By early afternoon the downpour had lapsed into a fine, driving mist, but still the parade from the Capitol to the White House moved quite slowly. A crowd estimated at between 40,000 and 50,000 were chanting Harrison's name and adding the cry for "Four, four, four years more." It was a name and a chant familiar to many old-timers who could recall when President William Henry Harrison, on a white horse, led a procession of 4,000 citizens to the White House. They remembered, too, that rain had also swept the city on that March day in 1841. There was a natural feeling that the new President "had inherited some of the unadulterated blood . . . of his grandfather."[11]

After the traditional White House luncheon, Harrison and Morton entered the reviewing stand to witness a splendid parade. Close by sat General John C. Frémont, whom Harrison had supported as the first Republican nominee in 1856. Here too was General William Tecumseh Sherman, wearing a G.A.R. badge on his Prince Albert lapel. During the next four hours, fast-marching units of infantry, artillery, cavalry, Navy men, Marines and the National Guard held the attention. As the military segment of the parade ended, numerous G.A.R. posts passed in review.

Business, civic, and political clubs with multicolored uniforms carried life-sized pictures of President Harrison as a "Big Chip Off the Old Block." Next passed the smartly attired Cowboy Club of Denver, led by Buffalo Bill astride the silver-gray stallion that had been presented by the Sultan of Turkey to General Grant, followed by a blue-coated mass of Minnesotans with flaming torches. A contingent of red-shirted firemen carrying red, white and blue umbrellas resembled a prairie fire. Several groups were forced by darkness to disband before reaching the reviewing stand, but the final contingent to greet the President, just at dusk, were the Harrison and Morton Negro Marching Clubs from Virginia.

At least one newspaper described the parade as the grandest civil and military pageant yet seen in Washington.

The Inaugural Ball would be held in the ordinarily cheerless Pension Office Hall on Judiciary Square, but in three months' time an army of decorators had transformed the barnlike interior into a luxurious salon adorned with fresh flowers and rare plants. A crowd of 12,000, many arriving early, spilled across the acre of tile floor reserved for dancing. Marine Band Leader John Philip

[11] Clem Studebaker to Benjamin Harrison, March 25, 1892, (L.C.), Vol. 138.

Sousa had composed the "Presidential Polonaise" for the occasion, and two bands played continuously.

President and Mrs. Harrison arrived at 10:30 P.M., an hour when festivities were well under way. The First Lady's costume had been a matter of gossipy uncertainty for months and she did not disappoint her admirers. Her apricot and pale gray satin gown was fronted with cut velvet of the same shade, with plaiting of pale gray on either side. Hers was a natural beauty and radiance, enhanced by the simplicity of her dress.

Throughout the evening, President and Mrs. Harrison appeared on one balcony or another as required by protocol, and at a signal from Band Leader Sousa, they descended the balcony to lead the grand promenade. Back in the White House, the worn President and his wife retired almost immediately.[12]

Despite the wet weather, all, or nearly all, had gone well. Though the newspapers would make much of the fact that Frances Folsom Cleveland, wife of the ex-President, had attended neither the Inaugural ceremonies, the White House luncheon, nor the Inaugural Ball, Carrie Harrison declined to regard the omission as a personal affront. The First Lady slept soundly, and after breakfast the next morning sent the young Mrs. Cleveland a bouquet of red roses—presumably in graciousness, perhaps in consolation. A letter of gratitude was of course received at the White House,[13] but Mrs. Cleveland's words to a colored servant would be recalled by historians: "Take good care of all the furniture and ornaments in the house for I want to find everything just as it was when we come back again . . . four years from today."[14]

In a moment of neighborly feeling, President and Mrs. Harrison had committed an indiscretion. They had suggested to their Hoosier neighbors and friends that when they were in town they should call, assuring one and all that the White House latchstring would always be out. Thus long before noon on the day following Inauguration, many Hoosiers began their calls. Each was greeted by the President with a handclasp, and then shown through the

12 *Journal,* March 5, 1889.

13 Frances F. Cleveland to Mrs. Harrison, March 5, 1889, (L.C.), Vol. 69.

14 Although several newspapers reported that Mrs. Cleveland, a popular First Lady, had wished to attend all the Inaugural functions, Allan Nevins, *Grover Cleveland,* p. 448, states that she "departed defiantly." John and Alice Durant, *Pictorial History of American Presidents,* p. 194, repeat this story.

White House by Harrison's son-in-law, Bob McKee. "Ben's Boys" of the Seventieth Indiana Regiment surrounded the President as a volunteer guard in the East Room where the reception line seemed never to end. When, in mid-afternoon, the crush of callers became too great, the White House doors were bolted until order could be restored. During an undisturbed family dinner, Harrison was heard to remark that he had "probably shaken the hands of 8,000 persons since daylight,"[15] but open house prevailed for two days longer, while regular executive business remained at a standstill.

During a quiet evening, Harrison reorganized the White House clerical and domestic staffs. With the oath administered by Colonel William Henry Crook, the disbursing agent of the White House, Elijah W. Halford was sworn in as the President's private secretary.[16] Other appointments included Captain E. S. Dinsmore, who would take charge of the lower floor of the White House, and stenographers Frank Tibbott and Alice Sanger, whose loyalty Harrison had known in Indianapolis.[17] All but one of the domestic servants retained their posts.

Although courtesy calls at the White House soon dwindled, the demands of office-seekers and their patrons daily reached new highs. Henry C. Bowen, publisher of the New York *Independent*, begged a good consulship for his son.[18] Chicago attorney Alexander Sullivan, eloquent spokesman of an Irish Republican group, felt that "brainy, honest, and genuine" Patrick Egan certainly deserved a minister's post south of the border. Not only had Egan, a recent Irish *emigré*, supported Harrison, but he had also defended Charles Stewart Parnell in his crusade for Irish liberty.[19] The President's old law partner, William P. Fishback, spoke on behalf of Democrat George W. Julian, who desired to be retained as Surveyor General of New Mexico. For the important post of Minister to England, Stephen B. Elkins urged the immediate appointment

---

15 *Journal*, March 6, 7, 1889.

16 Halford, who had never held public office, was a man of strong character and positive convictions. It was rightfully thought that his individuality would make him valuable to Harrison as a confidential assistant.

17 Alice Sanger had been employed as a stenographer by the law firm of Harrison, Hines and Miller. After the election she vacationed in Europe and returned to Indianapolis in time to accompany Harrison to Washington for the Inauguration.

18 Henry C. Bowen to Harrison, March 5, 1889, (L.C.), Vol. 69.

19 Alexander Sullivan to Matt O'Doherty, March 6, 1889, *ibid*.

of Whitelaw Reid on the score that he was the unanimous choice of the Republican press.[20]

In troublesome New York, personal friend John F. Plummer threatened to resign the presidency of the powerful Business Men's Republican Association, unless Boss Platt's foe, Joel B. Erhardt, was named Collector of the Port of· New York. Prominent senators came with or sent in their lists, and even Vice-President Morton apologized for making two rather bold personal requests— one that his brother-in-law, W. F. Grinnell, be transferred from Bradford in northern England to London as Consul General. Bellamy Storer, with whose father Harrison had read law in Cincinnati, sought appointment as Minister to the Netherlands.[21] Many wires and letters urged that Colonel Fred Grant be named Minister to China;[22] while Harrison's real or pretended kinsmen asked assistance in a struggle to keep the wolf from the door. And so the flood rose.

By mid-March, Washington had been inundated by office-seekers and office "brokers." One eyewitness to the confusion swirling about the Government Departments and Washington hotels was the veteran Benjamin H. Bristow, the capable reformer who served as Grant's Secretary of the Treasury.[23] It surpassed anything he had ever seen in the Capital. As he wrote to Judge Walter Q. Gresham, "every old dead-beat whom we used to know in the army and about Washington after the war has turned up as an office-seeker. Senators and M.C.'s crowd the rooms of the Cabinet offices, plying the disreputable vocation of office-brokers. . . ." Bristow maintained that everyone turned out of office by Cleveland had now returned to ask for his old job back. Thousands more, who had never held any office, blithely sought appointment on the ground that they had never been so employed. Moreover,

20 S. B. Elkins to Harrison, March 8, 1889, (L.C.), Vol. 70. On March 12, 1889 Elkins came to Washington and closeted himself with the President in Reid's behalf. See S. B. Elkins to Whitelaw Reid, March 13, 1889, Reid MSS.

21 L. P. Morton to Harrison, March 11, 1889, (L.C.), Vol. 70. In the case of Bellamy Storer's desires, the approach to Harrison was made by Ohio Governor J. B. Foraker. See J. B. Foraker to Harrison, March 16, 1889, (L.C.), Vol. 71.

22 Grenville Mellen Dodge spearheaded the plea that Fred Grant be appointed to China. See G. M. Dodge to W. B. Allison, N. E. Dawson, J. S. Clarkson, and James G. Blaine, March 16, 1889, Dodge Records, Vol. 12.

23 By exposing the "Whiskey Rings," Bristow brought the Grant Administration into serious trouble. In 1876, being already endeared to the reformers and highly regarded by business, Bristow tried to succeed Grant in the presidency. See Malcolm Moos, The Republicans, pp. 142–45.

men removed by Cleveland on charges of corruption sought rein-statement as a matter of self-vindication. At the office of Attorney General Miller, former Solicitor General Bristow saw what he considered to be a good part of the entire population of the state of Indiana. The Kentuckian told Gresham:

I was beset on all sides by dead beats & incapables for recommenda-tions. I got away as soon as possible—disgusted by the disgraceful scram-ble. It doesn't lie in our mouths to talk any more about the "hungry and thirsty democracy."[24]

If Bristow left Washington a confirmed believer in the necessity for radical civil service reform,[25] he did not feel any more strongly than the President, who had to remain at his post and somehow bring order out of political chaos.

At his first Cabinet meeting, on the afternoon of March 7th, Harrison outlined his policy on major appointments and patron-age distribution, remarking that he would rely heavily on the judgment of those present as to the fitness and character of each name he would send to the Senate for confirmation. By promising to refer all office-seekers to the respective Departments, Harrison would avoid the cross-fire that would result if one faction could approach the President directly, while others channeled their endorsements through the proper Cabinet members. This pro-cedure, he explained, would allow him more time to deal with the larger aspects of executive policy. He made it clear, however, that he would reserve to himself the final decision as to the char-acter and fitness of every appointee.[26] In effect, Harrison made it known that he would have no kitchen Cabinet; furthermore, he had served notice that the spoils system, already entrenched in the political machines of several states, including Pennsylvania and New York, would be no part of his Administration. This was another slap at machine politics, otherwise known as "senatorial courtesy." As the word got around, many a startled leader, whose

24 Bristow to Gresham, March 22, 1889, Gresham MSS., Vol. 37, a revelatory eight-page letter.

25 Bristow had no fears of an aristocracy of officeholders under permanent civil service. Rather, the distribution of offices on the spoils theory excited his apprehen-sions for the future. He confessed to Gresham that he favored "a body of trained men *condemned* to hold office for life to attend to the actual business of govern-ment, while the Prest. & Cabinet play at politics" (*ibid*.).

26 Halford's Diary, (L.C.), March 7, 1889; also, *Journal*, March 8, 1889.

treasure-looting prerogatives were being challenged, decided to test the President's sincerity.[27]

National Committee Chairman Matt Quay made the first move. As United States Senator from Pennsylvania, he called on his good friend the President to present a long list of names of Pennsylvania Republicans whom he and the senior senator, J. Donald Cameron, had selected for marshals, district attorneys, collectors, and postmasters in the various cities. Harrison, who recognized Quay's immense political service during the campaign, politely requested information concerning each man on the list. The practical Quay tried to explain that this was unnecessary, since he and Cameron had agreed to guarantee their choices. But Harrison replied that he thought the appointive power was entitled to know the fitness and character of every man whose name it sent to the Senate. Quay again tried to assure his host that there need be no anxiety as to the Senate's confirmation of the proposed appointees, as he would see to that himself. The President stiffened, for he knew that beyond the Senate

. . . lay the great public, to which he as President felt himself responsible, and that no matter whom senators might recommend or what the Senate might do in the way of confirmation, if an appointee turned out badly, the President, not the senators or the Senate, would be held responsible.[28]

In terminating the interview, Harrison requested that letters of endorsement be filed. Again claiming senatorial courtesy, Quay declined. This marked a parting of the ways. No doubt Harrison was determined at the outset to ram the lesson home. He would initiate his own inquiries, he said, hoping that the result would corroborate the other's judgment. Thus began an estrangement that would end in open hostility.

Other senators and congressmen tried their luck in the White House. Illinois Senator Charles B. Farwell wanted a spoils system based on Republican votes cast in a presidential election. The number and the kind of appointments deserved by a given state could thus be accurately determined, and senators and congressmen could act accordingly. Harrison's rejection of the scheme

27 E. W. Halford, "General Harrison's Attitude Toward the Presidency," *Century Magazine*, June 1912, pp. 307–8.

28 *Ibid.*, p. 308. The authenticity of Halford's article is supported by W. H. H. Miller who supplied pertinent data (W. H. H. Miller to E. W. Halford, March 22, 28, 1912, in Miller Letterbooks).

apparently provoked a bitter attack from Senator Farwell, who also would go his own political way.[29]

There is no doubt that Harrison's idea of a legal deal had dashed the hopes of spoilsmen. A whispering campaign begun in the Capitol corridors soon reached the ears of Walter Wellman, who headed the Chicago *Tribune's* Washington bureau. Wellman suavely shared the gossip with Harrison's political foe, Judge Walter Q. Gresham:

You may be interested in knowing that we have one of the smallest Presidents the U.S. has ever known. He is narrow, unresponsive and, oh, so cold! The town is full of grumblers. Nobody appears to like H., though, of course, many tolerate him for what he can give out; there is no administration element in town ... Senate very cold toward H. ...

There are bitter complaints ... Senators call and say their say to him, and he stands silent. . . . As one Senator says: "It's like talking to a hitching post."[30]

It was as if Harrison was a forerunner of Silent Cal.

Despite feverish pressure for office, Harrison managed to give priority to major nominations without neglecting postmasters, marshals, and port collectors. With the Dakotas, Montana, and Washington territories clamoring for statehood, he appointed to office those who were citizens of the territories they were to serve. Apparently this marked a departure from Cleveland's policy, which, said Whitelaw Reid's New York *Tribune,* "had made the Territories a dumping ground for disreputable adherents whom it was important to placate or convenient to reward."[31] Harrison believed it desirable to place control with those who understood the people and the needs of the future states, and who would have a stake in their prosperity when admitted to the Union.[32]

29 Miller to Halford, March 22, 1912, Miller Letterbooks, recalls: "What you say about Farwell I can readily believe, for he manifested the same temper to me with reference to the appointment of a district attorney in Chicago; he thought no questions should be asked after he had made a recommendation."

30 Walter Wellman to Walter Q. Gresham, March 20, 1889, Gresham MSS., Vol. 37. Wellman seems to have had as his informants the two Illinois Senators, Farwell and Cullom. The newspaperman reported that in the Senate, Harrison could count no more than three or four friends. He concluded: ". . . it is early to form an opinion, but H. seems now to be a single termer. . . ."

31 New York *Tribune,* March 14, 1889.

32 Indianapolis *Journal,* March 14, 1889; New York *Tribune,* March 13, 14, 1889. In the matter of territorial nominations, both papers stated that Harrison had proved his intention to stand by the national platform of the party, which declared that "pending the preparation of statehood, all offices therefore should be selected from the bona fide residents and citizens of the Territory wherein they are to serve."

In filling the diplomatic posts, which attracted nearly as much attention as the Cabinet, Harrison showed himself decisive and independent. When Edward J. Phelps resigned his London mission, Harrison, much to the surprise of everyone, including Secretary Blaine, named Robert Todd Lincoln, the lawyer son of the martyred President. Lincoln, however, had been War Secretary under both Garfield and Arthur,[33] and Theodore Roosevelt, a leader in the fight for civil service reforms, hastened to say that the choice was admirable.[34] It was Blaine's view, of course, that patronage should be used to satisfy political debts, and he hardly needed Elkins' pointed reminder to Whitelaw Reid that not only had Bob Lincoln supported Gresham against Harrison, but that he had also gone abroad soon after the nomination, taking no part whatever in the campaign.[35]

Little or no surprise, however, greeted the subsequent announcement that Whitelaw Reid would be the American Minister to Paris, replacing Robert M. McLane. Rated as "second to none" as the influential editor of the New York *Tribune*, Reid had graduated from Ohio's Miami University four years after Harrison. His was a staunch Republican family, and before he had reached voting age, he campaigned for Frémont. A fluency in French, coupled with known literary and diplomatic skills, made him a prime candidate for either the Court of St. James's or Minister at the Elysée in Paris. But since the *Tribune* supported Irish Home Rule and had publicly endorsed Gladstone over Lord Salisbury, now the Prime Minister, consideration of the editor for the London post was brief. It was Harrison's further thought that the *Tribune* could remain more independent of British influence with Reid happily placed in Paris.[36]

A German-American hostility had been inherited from Cleveland, largely because Prince Otto von Bismarck had insisted on

33 Leonard D. White, *The Republican Era*, p. 139, judges that Bob Lincoln "became Secretary of War without enthusiasm and left little impress upon the Department." The friendly N.Y. *Tribune*, March 28, 1889, characterized Lincoln's cabinet service as having been outstanding.

34 Theodore Roosevelt to Henry Cabot Lodge, March 27, 1889 as cited in Elting E. Morison (ed.), *The Letters of Theodore Roosevelt*, I, 155. Three weeks later he wrote: "I think our new minister, Bob Lincoln, is a very good fellow" (Theodore Roosevelt to Sir Cecil Arthur Spring-Rice, April 14, 1889, *ibid.*, p. 157).

35 Stephen B. Elkins to Whitelaw Reid, March 28, 1889, Reid MSS. Both Elkins and Blaine tried hard to get the English mission for Reid.

36 Royal Cortissoz, *The Life of Whitelaw Reid*, II, 123–25; see also *Journal*, March 20, 1889, an editorial entitled "The First Class Missions."

making Samoa a German protectorate. Diplomatic parleys in-
volving England, Germany, and the United States had proved
fruitless in 1887, and until the Berlin Conference on Samoan
affairs would open on April 29, 1889, there lingered the threat of
war. Theodore Roosevelt was intrigued by a situation that evoked
interpreting phrases from his active pen:

Just at present our statesmen seem inclined to abandon the tail of the
lion, and instead are plucking vigorously at the caudal feathers of that
delightful war-fowl, the German eagle—a cousin of our own bald-
headed bird of prey. Frankly, I don't know that I should be sorry to
see a bit of a spar with Germany . . . while we would have to take
some awful blows at first, I think in the end we would worry the Kaiser
a little.[37]

Harrison hoped to send a strong three-man team to the Berlin
Conference. Even before filling the British and French missions,
he had named three Samoan Commissioners. He crossed party
lines to appoint Democrat George H. Bates, a Delaware lawyer
whose protest against German imperialism was on file in the State
Department.[38] John A. Kasson and William Walter Phelps, also
named, were both Republicans with diplomatic experience who
shared the views of Bates. Phelps, a member of the House Foreign
Affairs Committee in three Congresses, was regarded by Harrison
as particularly able, and soon after the Conference he would be
named Minister to Germany.[39]

Even the lesser diplomatic appointments reflected Harrison's
concern for fitness. Californian John F. Swift, named Minister to
Japan, had negotiated an 1880 treaty with China. For the Spanish
mission he chose wealthy Thomas W. Palmer, a onetime senator
who had traveled widely in Europe and had lived in Cádiz. The
New York *Sun* approvingly noted that Palmer "learned their
language . . . speaks it fluently and knows Spanish history by
heart."[40] When Harrison named Frederick Dent Grant, the son
of the General, to the Court of Vienna it brought a letter of deep
gratitude from the war hero's widow, Julia Dent Grant.[41] Named

37 Theodore Roosevelt to Sir Cecil Arthur Spring-Rice, April 14, 1889, *loc. cit.*

38 *Frank Leslie's Illustrated Weekly,* March 23, 1889; see also *Foreign Relations of
the U.S.,* 1889, pp. 237–78.

39 *Congressional Record* (51st Cong., 1st sess.), Vol. 21, Part I, pp. 108, 222.

40 New York *Sun,* March 12, 1889.

41 Julia D. Grant to Harrison, April 8, 1889, (L.C.), Vol. 74, writes that her son
will be "loyal and true" and a credit to the Administration.

as Minister to Italy was Albert Gallatin Porter, who had nominated Harrison for the presidency. Porter was the second of Harrison's former law partners to gain public recognition. (Miller,
of course, was now Attorney General. William Wallace, a third
partner, remained in Indianapolis, but as that city's new postmaster.)

As had several other Presidents, Harrison found newspaper
editors and publishers among the most numerous, insistent, and
sometimes the best-qualified applicants for the foreign service.
After screening out the political hacks, he fixed on four from the
press for diplomatic posts. Besides Whitelaw Reid, he nominated
Charles Allen Thorndike Rice, the 38-year-old editor of the
North American Review, for Russia;[42] and John Hicks, editor of
the *Oshkosh* (Wisconsin) *Northwestern*, for Peru.[43] John A.
Enander, author of the first history of the United States published
in the Swedish language, and the Chicago editor of the popular
Swedish-American *Hemlandet*, was named Minister to Den-
mark.[44]

Not only these, but the appointment of other editors to lesser
posts, including postmasterships, began to irritate reformers who
asserted that as a senator, Harrison had criticized "the subsidized
press." Bitterly opposed to Harrison before his election, the *Nation* now reminded the President that Grandfather William on
Inauguration Day had issued a warning against all attempts to
subsidize the press through the use of executive patronage.[45]
Theodore Roosevelt, however, did not openly join the attack. He
did admit privately that the man in the White House had made
many individually good appointments, but added: "I am utterly
against editors being given political positions."[46] The independent
New York *Evening Post* somewhat perversely derided editors as
diplomats: "As an office seeker, or an office expectant, the editor

---

42 This brilliant personality, who gave the *North American Review* a position of
influence and intellectual leadership, died before he could assume office.

43 Hicks was born in Auburn, New York in 1847 and died in San Antonio, Texas
in 1917. His fame as diplomat and editor was associated with his residence in
Wisconsin.

44 Born in Sweden in 1842, and educated there, Enander came to the U.S. in
1869. He was an outstanding lecturer and educator in the Chicago area. See New
York *Tribune*, March 13, 1889.

45 Cited in James E. Pollard, *The Presidents and the Press*, p. 543.

46 Roosevelt to Henry Cabot Lodge, March 27, 1889, cited in *Letters of Theodore
Roosevelt*, I, 155.

is much out of place . . . it is both humiliating and unseemly."[47]

This form of attack, however, found favor with neither the nation's press in general nor with the Administration, particularly after the Senate rejected Harrison's nomination of Murat Halstead, editor of the Cincinnati Commercial Gazette, as Minister to Germany. With indefatigable labor and a genius for enterprise, Halstead had made the Commercial Gazette one of the greatest papers west of the Alleghenies.[48] Regarding this friend and supporter as a man of singular fitness, personal honor, and political honesty, Harrison had wanted a "stubborn and implacable fighter"[49] to worry Bismarck a bit. The Senate had other ideas. Since many senior legislators well remembered Halstead's harsh excoriation of corruption within their ranks, this was a time for revenge. After a heated debate in executive session, much of which was leaked to the newspapers, the nomination was thrown back at Harrison, who thus sustained his first defeat at the hands of his own party.

Certain newspapers that had rebuked the President for nominating editors for high office now turned on the Senate. The principle at stake appeared to be freedom of the press. Congressman Charles A. Boutelle, a Bangor, Maine editor, wired Harrison: "In rejecting Murat Halstead's nomination for the reason stated the Senate has struck one of the most desperate blows ever aimed at the liberty of the press."[50] The brilliantly eloquent Henry Watterson, whose Louisville Courier-Journal editorials were widely circulated in other Democratic newspapers, sounded a similar note: "The rejection of Mr. Halstead carries with it primarily a warning from the Senate to the press of the country to look to its utterances when dealing with that body or any of its members."[51]

Senator Spooner, who had defended Halstead in the closed-door Senate session, raised the important point that "if newspaper men were to be held responsible for the opinions expressed in the heat of a campaign, or in the course of great public excitement, few . . . could ever hope to pass into the realm of office-

---

47 New York Evening Post, March 18, 1889.

48 Frank Luther Mott, American Journalism, pp. 459–60.

49 Louisville Courier-Journal, March 30, 1889, a clipping in (L.C.), Vol. 73.

50 C. A. Boutelle to Harrison, March 30, 1889, (L.C.), Vol. 72. He added: "I hope you will resist it with all your power."

51 Courier-Journal, ut supra.

holding."[52] And so the controversy raged. Although Watterson warned that "whenever a Senator is publicly criticized he will bide his time to get revenge by stabbing his critic in the back and in the dark," the Senate declined to reconsider.

While Halstead's rejection was personally disappointing, Harrison set aside a suggestion that the editor be appointed after the Senate adjourned. For one thing, he preferred to hold to the rule that Executive appointments be made by and with the advice and consent of the Senate, which was responsible for judging a nominee's competency, fitness and character;[53] and for another, Halstead's fitness for the Berlin post at this particular time had been validly questioned. Serious diplomatic differences between the United States and Germany existed already, and Senator Henry M. Teller, a Republican, had argued that Halstead's influence and excitable temperament might disrupt proceedings at the forthcoming Berlin Conference on Samoa.[54] Senator George F. Edmunds, the wily Vermonter, whose counsel Harrison valued, told the President to forget the matter, and he did so.[55] The whole episode served to demonstrate Harrison's innate conservatism and his regard for the letter of the law set forth in the Constitution.

After the new Administration had functioned only two weeks, the New York *Herald*, which had opposed Harrison's election, admitted that "the man on the box knows how to drive." Recalling that there were many in the President's own party

who dolorously prophesied that he would be the tool of Mr. Blaine, the obedient servant of the imperious senatorial set, the prey of the great herd of office-seekers, and the victim of faction leaders . . .

the New York Democratic paper concluded that

so far he is none of these things. Mr. Harrison remains President, and we may as well tell him that in this he has greatly pleased the mass of his own party, and the people in general.[56]

Such praise from the enemy camp was quickly taken up by the Republican press, which widely reproduced the editorial. As could

52 New York *Tribune*, March 30, 1889.
53 Benjamin Harrison, *This Country of Ours*, p. 109.
54 *Journal*, April 3, 1889.
55 George F. Edmunds to Harrison, April 2, 1889, (L.C.), Vol. 73. Edmunds, who had been in the South recuperating from a bronchial infection, had not taken part in Halstead's rejection. He counseled the President not to make an interim appointment of Halstead as Minister to Berlin.
56 New York *Herald* as cited in the *Journal*, March 18, 1889.

be expected, the Indianapolis *Journal* endorsed these views. Hoosiers, it added, had often witnessed the fearlessness, mingled with courtesy and justice, of Benjamin Harrison.[57]

The wailing of disappointed office-seekers aside, Harrison's honesty of purpose as translated into action had proved him a true independent. He was warmly supported by *Leslie's Weekly,* which viewed him as wise and fair.[58] A Boston *Traveller* correspondent used picturesque language in epitomizing his stand: "The President is firm, not headstrong . . . no mulishness in his composition"; yet he could also "say No so loud and sharp that it will make your teeth rattle."[59]

Harrison's own feelings in these few crowded weeks were no secret to his intimate friends. He was pleased by apparent success in giving the lie to the Democratic sneers that he was "Caretaker of the White House," and "not a safe man to be President,"[60] yet he found the pressure at times almost unbearable. Kinsmen, in particular, failed to understand the actual situation of a man who could do some things but not all. From Keokuk, Iowa, Cousin Lucy Howell wrote: "Surely there is no . . . impropriety in your giving a few of the 82,000 offices . . . to your needy but honest and capable relatives. The charge of nepotism made by his enemies did not kill General Grant . . . and he gave 29 offices to his own. . . ."[61]

Harrison placed the letter in a private drawer and replied after a few days. He hoped Cousin Lucy would realize "how I am beset by family friends all over the country, and that I am here exercising public duties and cannot give full play to my personal wishes. General Grant had a claim upon the forebearance and affection of his countrymen that I do not have. The distressing part of my

[57] The sentiments of an editorial entitled "Two Weeks of President Harrison," *Journal*, March 18, 1889.

[58] *Frank Leslie's Illustrated Weekly*, April 13, 1889, carried an editorial entitled "One Month of Harrison." It made the point that Harrison had shown his wisdom in putting the right man in the right place, under circumstances which might well have discouraged one of less independence of character. The piece concluded by noting that "even among Democrats there is a disposition to treat the Administration fairly. And it is very generally understood that it is the Administration of General Harrison himself."

[59] *Journal*, April 22, 1889, copied this undated Washington dispatch to the Boston *Traveller*.

[60] This was the position of the *Nation*, July 19, 1888, as cited by Pollard, *op. cit.*, p. 539.

[61] Lucy Howell to Harrison, April 7, 1889, (L.C.), Vol. 74.

life here grows out of the fact that I am necessarily scattering so many disappointments."[62]

Within weeks of his Inauguration, Harrison had come to experience the truth expressed in his farewell to Indianapolis: "The moment of decision is one of isolation."

[62] Harrison to Lucy Howell, April 13, 1889, *ibid.*

CHAPTER IV

In the White House

D URING THESE FIRST weeks of his Administration, Harrison was able to make himself popular with some Washingtonians. On nearly every pleasant afternoon he would be seen taking a long walk of three or four miles, either along Connecticut and Massachusetts avenues, or on 16th Street as far as the District line—two of the most pleasant promenades in the city. Accompanied by a member of his family or by Private Secretary Halford, or sometimes by a visitor, Harrison set a brisk pace that often tired the others.

Harrison dressed simply, wearing a "plain black overcoat, buttoned tightly around his rotund form, a pair of brown kid gloves, a tall hat, and a shining black silk tie."[1] If recognized, he would stop and chat briefly. More often he discussed the work or happenings of the day with Halford, always a good listener. Once the Secretary posed a significant question: "I asked the President if he had ever seriously thought about being President. He said the thought had been with him many times when suggested by others, but he had never been possessed by it or had his life shaped by it."[2]

Harrison sometimes varied his routine by driving a dark green landau into Maryland or Virginia. He took special pride in the four family horses, all Kentucky thoroughbreds, named Abdullah, Billy, Lexington, and John. As Albert Hawkins, the veteran Negro coachman, would have it, these were the finest horses in the presidential stables since he had been at the White House.[3] Sometimes driving a buggy without coachman or footman, Harrison managed the reins skilfully. This habit of daily exercise and recreation,

1 Frank G. Carpenter, *Carp's Washington*, p. 296.
2 Halford's Diary, (L.C.), April 21, 1889.
3 *Journal*, March 18, 22, 1889, and Carpenter, *op. cit.*, p. 304.

which often included billiards on rainy days,[4] led one Washington correspondent to write that "President Harrison . . . is showing himself more democratic than any of his predecessors of the past decade."[5] Harrison at the same time was finding Washington people as friendly as his Indianapolis neighbors.

The President found difficulty in settling his family into a fairly comfortable routine in the White House. Whereas Cleveland had existed as a bachelor during the first half of his term, the Executive Mansion was quite filled now with Harrison's daughter's family and his wife's relatives. One paper observed: "President Harrison is the only living ruler who can gather at his table four generations in the direct line from Great-grandfather Scott,"[6] including the General's three baby grandchildren—and the five bedrooms of the White House were thus found inadequate. Ninety-year-old Dr. John W. Scott, Mrs. Harrison's father, had resigned his clerkship in the Pension Office to live with his daughter.[7] Mary McKee, the President's daughter, who had inherited much of her father's executive ability, had come to help her mother with the social schedule; and she moved in with Benjamin (Baby) McKee, not yet two, and with tiny Mary Lodge McKee, who would celebrate her first birthday on the 4th of July. Fortunately, Harrison's son Russell would divide his time between Montana and New York; but his wife Mary and child Marthena would live in the White House. Also helping Mrs. Harrison to some extent was her older sister, Mrs. Russell Lord (Lizzie) whose health was not robust. When, late that November, Mrs. Lord died, her daughter, Mary Dimmick, a charming young widow of 30, joined the family circle to aid her Aunt Carrie.[8] Thus all three of the younger women bore the name of Mary. To avoid confusion, Mrs. McKee was called Mamie, Mrs. Russell Harrison May, and Mrs. Dimmick Mame. No wonder that the First Lady found the Executive Mansion too small and the life there sometimes confusing.

[4] Halford's Diary, (L.C.), March 19, 1889; Bess Furman, *White House Profiles*, p. 249.

[5] Carpenter, *op. cit.*, p. 304. Also the New York *Tribune*, March 14, 1889, noted that the Harrisonian informality enabled the new Administration to surpass the earlier Jeffersonian simplicity (article entitled "Jefferson is Outdone"). Similar conclusions were reached by the New York *Times*, February 15, 1891.

[6] *Statesman* (Yonkers, N.Y.), March 28, 1889.

[7] Dr. Scott died at the White House, November 29, 1893, in his ninety-third year.

[8] Elizabeth Lord was taken seriously ill during the summer of 1889, while her two married daughters, Mrs. Dimmick and Mrs. Parker, were in Europe.

Mrs. Benjamin Harrison was not the first President's wife with a large family to complain of the discomfort of living in the White House while it was used also for official business.[9] She was the first, however, to offer ideas for improving the situation. In her campaign for personal privacy and more ample living quarters, Carrie Harrison did not limit herself to any one plan; with her assistance, three were devised by architect Fred D. Owen. One called for a separate residence to be erected on 16th Street; another for minor additions to the White House as it stood. The third, using the White House as a starting point, envisioned several new structures to be built around a hollow square.[10]

Mrs. Harrison's immediate task, however, was a general cleaning up of the old mansion. For one thing, faulty plumbing had caused a green mold to form on the walls; and on foggy or heavy days escaping sewer gas polluted the air. Made ill towards the end of March, Carrie left the problem to her husband while she went south for a short time to rest. The entire house was to be scrubbed, cleaned, and repaired.[11]

She returned to the task initiated by President Chester A. Arthur, who had cleared out 24 wagonloads of goods left by former tenants. Several rooms on the floor next to the roof were found filled with old books and public documents plus cobwebs and dust. More wagonloads were taken away, and this was only a beginning.[12] No dusty corner escaped Mrs. Harrison's eye in that spring cleaning of 1889.[13] Ants, cockroaches, and rats had to be exterminated once the old, rotting floorboards—five layers in some places—were removed from the basement and ground floors. From start to finish it took weeks for the laying of clean new floors.

White House cuisine was also something of a problem for the plain-living Hoosiers. The steward, Hugo Zieman, had enticed a French lady-cook from the British legation, whose menus, replete

---

[9] Amy La Follette Jensen, *The White House*, p. 138, gives a pictorial explanation of crowded conditions.

[10] Furman, *op. cit.*, p. 250 ff., notes that this plan "contemplated the development of the entire White House grounds as a hollow square, enclosing a 'Private Court' with an 'Allegorical Fountain' in its center. The Pennsylvania Avenue side of this square would consist of 'Present (1792) Mansion' with round pavilions at either end joined to it by connecting corridors. The side across from the Treasury would be 'The Historical Art Wing'; that across from the State, War and Navy Building the 'Official Wing.'"

[11] *Journal*, April 7, 1889.

[12] *Journal*, May 12, 1889.

[13] Frank G. Carpenter, *op. cit.*, p. 302.

with rich pastry and sauces, Harrison disliked. One newspaper commented: "The new cook's dishes laid him out"; and so Madame Pelouard, who thus lives in history, was finally discharged. She threatened to sue,[14] but that came to nothing. Mrs. Harrison promptly engaged a colored cook from Kentucky, Dolly Johnson, whose plain fare pleased the President, and whose state dinners, moreover, showed real artistry. With a Virginia girl named (and called) Mary, to help her, she did such all-around good work that everything went smoothly in the White House kitchen, although Zieman of course resigned to go elsewhere. Philip McKim, onetime steward of the Metropolitan Club and later in the employ of John Hay, the diplomat, filled the vacancy quite expertly. McKim was Scotch-Irish and personally popular.[15]

Aside from cooking, the distaff side of the White House apparently gave Harrison little concern. With her sturdy midwestern upbringing and practical experience, Carrie Harrison felt no embarrassment in dealing with Washington society. She actually appeared capable of running the domestic machinery—"a four generation home—with part of her day and still to find time for fine needlework, literature, china painting and orchid culture."[16] She had taught china painting in Indianapolis, and now in the White House she brought in another expert to help with a new class. A professor of French was then engaged to instruct the wives and daughters of several Cabinet families, along with other society people. In all there were about twenty-five students, most of whom attended both classes. And by donating much of her handiwork to church bazaars and other charities, Mrs. Harrison easily won new friends.

She designed the Harrison family china set, and it was said that her brush decorated hundreds of porcelain dishes for Washington ladies wanting them for heirlooms. "Many a baby whose parents have named him for the President has received a milk set painted by Mrs. Harrison with cunning Kate Greenaway children," remarked Washington correspondent Frank G. Carpenter. Indeed, the First Lady left few White House utensils unadorned, deco-

14 New York *Sun*, October 22, 1889, also reported that the New York *World*, which was circulating all sorts of stories about the President's table, was urging the suit against Harrison.

15 New York *Sun*, October 22, 30, 1889.

16 Furman, *op. cit.*, p. 249.

rating even the "candlesticks, cheese covers, crackerboxes, flower-
pot saucers . . . milk pitchers and chocolate jugs."[17] Also Carrie was
fond of history and its associations with such common things as
the contents of an old china closet that had to be replaced.[18] Thus
she began the White House collection of the china of past Presidents.

With equal enthusiasm Mrs. Harrison met her formal social
duties. The reception of the diplomatic corps, held in the Red
Parlor on March 14th, was a distinct success, and the press reported
that the Harrison ladies were charming. Standing beside the First
Lady was her daughter, Mamie McKee, whose vivacious spirit
would dominate future functions there. She was, like her mother,
both clever and tactful. Secretary Halford noted that the reception
honoring the Japanese Prince and Princess came off handsomely,
and the pleased John Hay called it "one of the prettiest parties . . .
seen in the White House." Although sometimes weary, the President conducted himself well at these functions. The easy informality that prevailed on the occasion of the Supreme Court's first
formal call contrasted favorably with a rather stiff affair held four
years earlier when Cleveland ruled alone.[19]

The Harrison household was run on methodical lines. An 8:30
breakfast, followed by prayers led by either the President or Dr.
Scott, enabled Harrison to get an early start on the day's business,
which was interrupted only by a light lunch at 1:30. Following his
brisk walk or drive late in the afternoon, the President rejoined the
family for dinner at 6:30.[20]

At mealtime little Benjamin McKee's high chair was pulled
close to his grandfather, whose affection for his little namesake
became the talk of the country. Citizens heard that Nellie Grant's
old room had been turned into a nursery for the Harrison grandchildren, including the infant Mary Lodge McKee, christened

17 Frank G. Carpenter, op. cit., p. 301. Though Mrs. Harrison frequently painted
flowers, leaves, shepherdesses, and milkmaids, her favorite design was a four-leafed
clover.

18 Ibid., p. 252. Carrie Harrison's interest in history stemmed from her Indianapolis days. She had already preserved many souvenirs of the 1840 and 1888 campaigns (Journal, February 25, 1889).

19 Journal, March 18, 1889. As a senator, Harrison had come to know all of the
Justices and had maintained close relations with several of them.

20 A. J. Halford, "Mrs. Harrison in the White House," Ladies' Home Journal,
Vol. VII, No. 4 (March 1890).

there by Dr. Scott with water from the River Jordan, and cousin Marthena, "the beauty of the group—sweet and winning, a gentle, quiet little thing."[21] But Baby McKee got so much attention from the press and from office-seekers that Secretary Halford finally had to ask that the reporters tone down their stories, "lest people . . . should come to believe the tales about this child's having more influence than the members of the Cabinet."[22] In this respect, Baby McKee was even linked with Vice-President Morton, who owned the palatial Shoreham Hotel with its magnificent bar, and Postmaster General Wanamaker, who reportedly still taught the largest Sunday-school class in America. Party regulars would have none of it, save perhaps Morton's whiskey:

> The baby runs the White House,
> Levi runs the bar;
> Wanny runs the Sunday school,
> And, damn it, here we are.[23]

Toys of every manufacture and design came to the White House —a French mechanical dog, then a live pony and a cart, complete with harness and lap robe, which Baby McKee rode daily. Popular pictures showed him in either a tasseled silk tennis cap or a natty yachting cap as a participant in both sports on a miniature scale. Numerous childlike antics appeared in the press, and one day even the President lost his patience, the Cleveland *Leader* reported:

When the Harrisons first moved into the White House, this child had not yet learned how to walk well. He still often crawled about like a crab. Many a visitor in the President's study felt a warm little arm around his leg in the midst of his interview. One day during a conference when Benny's presence was not noticed, a roll of important papers disappeared. A frantic search was made by the President's secretary, who could not hold back a cry when he pulled the window draperies aside and found Baby McKee stirring the contents of a huge spittoon with the precious roll. Grandpa for once lost his patience with his darling child, and sent him off with his nurse, while the secretary was set to clean the brown stains off the documents.[24]

21 Frances Cavanagh, *They Lived in the White House*, p. 104.

22 Carpenter, *op. cit.*, p. 298.

23 *Report of the Benjamin Harrison Memorial Commission*, p. 155.

24 As quoted in Carpenter, *op. cit.*, p. 299. Chief among Baby McKee's antics were playing the roles of a wounded soldier and a speech-making President.

All three grandchildren had the run of the mansion and of the broad White House lawn where sightseers would try to catch a glimpse of the trio romping with a pet collie, or riding behind the pony or a billy goat dubbed "His Whiskers." It cannot be doubted that they gave the serious President many hours of happiness.

Contrary to a report that the President would choose no particular church on the Sabbath, Harrison reserved a pew in the new Presbyterian Church of the Covenant, on the southeast corner of Connecticut Avenue and N Street, a fashionable neighborhood. No work was done on Sunday and mail was left unopened. As Marthena Harrison recalled: "Afternoon walks were the only diversion permitted younger members of the household," the evenings being spent quietly at home.[25] The young people in the household nevertheless brought back dancing as a regular part of the formal receptions—"for the first time since its banning by Mrs. Polk."[26]

Lurking beneath the air of genteel gaiety were two formidable problems that Harrison had inherited from Cleveland and the Fiftieth Congress. The first involved the alleged violation of American rights in the Bering Sea, where Canadian seal hunters slaughtered herds of these valuable animals. By 1886 the fur seal question had become an acute diplomatic problem. American and European women were demanding more sealskin coats and muffs, enhancing the value of the skins many times over. This in turn fostered the killing of the female as well as the male, both on land and in the water. So wanton was the slaughter that the seal population, estimated a few years earlier at over four million, was threatened with extermination.[27]

---

[25] Unidentified newspaper clipping (Washington *Star*?), in possession of Marthena Harrison Williams; A. J. Halford, "Mrs. Harrison in the White House," *loc. cit.*

[26] Furman, *op. cit.*, 250. The return of dancing evoked a strong protest from Reuben C. Richards to Mrs. Benjamin Harrison, March 26, 1889, Marthena Harrison Williams MSS. Richards maintained that "dancing cannot be done in the name of Christ."

[27] Thomas A. Bailey in *A Diplomatic History of the American People*, p. 446, observed that the nub of the problem came to this: "Swimming females cannot be distinguished from males, and the death of a female ordinarily meant the loss of a nursing pup on the land, and an unborn pup in the seal. Since about half of the animals shot in the water were not recovered, every skin obtained in the open sea represented the death of approximately four seals." As the number of poaching schooners increased, the seal herds decreased. As higher prices were paid for skins still obtainable, the fear of extermination of the species was not an empty one. Hence the *contra bonos mores* position of the Harrison Administration.

United States revenue cutters began to seize Canadian schooners —even beyond the three-mile limit. The Canadian government, through the British Minister in Washington, protested with some justice that such seizures violated freedom of the seas. The United States took the position that the wholesale destruction of seals actually corrupted public morals. While neither Secretary of State Blaine nor Harrison questioned that the seas were free beyond the three-mile limit, they argued that "the law of the sea is not lawlessness." Even during diplomatic exchanges, American seizure of foreign ships in Bering Sea waters continued.

The entire affair would take a long time to settle. Two days before Harrison's Inaugural, the Congress had taken action which authorized the President to proclaim American rights and jurisdiction within the Bering Sea. On March 21st, Harrison officially warned all persons "against entering the Bering Sea for unlawful hunting of fur-bearing animals,"[28] and the revenue cutters were set to work. While no one at home doubted the President's willingness to act in the national interest,[29] the diplomatic quarrel was not to be resolved during the Harrison regime.

The opening of the Oklahoma Territory to white settlers was another complicated issue. As a senator, Harrison had championed statehood for those territories already organized, but had blocked the indiscriminate seizure of public lands by railroads and monopolistic interests.[30] In every instance he had insisted on orderly procedure. Oklahoma, however, presented several problems which he now felt obliged to lay before the Cabinet.

Long before Congress had ever appropriated the several million dollars necessary to acquire from the Indians clear title to the Oklahoma country, this heartland had seethed with discontent and lawless adventure. Federal troops had frequently evicted prospectors and other trespassers; in early 1889 the Oklahoma borders witnessed the presence of "boomers" or raiders eager to enter and

28 Indianapolis *Journal*, March 22, 23, 1889, and New York *Tribune*, March 23, 1889.

29 *Report of the Benjamin Harrison Memorial Commission*, p. 190, notes this violent dispute with Great Britain and concludes that while "The United States adopted an untenable position, from which she was at last obliged to retire . . . (she) obtained a primary objective, namely the protection of the fur seals. . . ." The final issue was settled by arbitration at Paris on August 15, 1893. The Harrison Administration had struck a blow for the freedom of the seals, while a mixed international tribunal declared for an open sea. For concise summary, see Richard B. Morris, (ed.), *Encyclopedia of American History* (1953 edition), pp. 284-85.

30 See Harry J. Sievers, *Benjamin Harrison: Hoosier Statesman*, pp. 241-42; 281-83.

to stake claims, legally if possible, illegally if not. Responding to petitions by lumbering, mining, and real-estate interests, Congress authorized the President to proclaim the land open to settlement. The hastily drawn Oklahoma Bill called for the establishment of a single U.S. Court for the Indian Territory; that it failed to prescribe adequate legal machinery sorely perplexed Harrison. On March 27th, he designated noon of April 22nd as the hour for the opening of the Territory.[31]

Attorney General Miller recounted that the Administration felt a "good deal of anxiety" lest the 5,000 or more "Sooners," or would-be settlers, already tented at points of entry, should rush in lawlessly and shed blood "at a time and place where there was no civil government whatever, and no one with a semblence of official authority to establish such a government."[32] Previously the army had kept out intruders, but after opening day for the Sooners who could say what jurisdiction it would enjoy over hordes of anxious settlers?[33] As the Attorney General recalled it, the President and the Cabinet finally agreed that

. . . our people had always been equal to every emergency of that kind, and have often established and maintained order where there was no law, and made and administered government de facto in the absence of government de jure. It was safe to assume that it would be done in Oklahoma.[34]

Future homesteaders, most of them well armed, answered the noonday bugle blast with a wild rush over the border. Upward of 50,000 entered the Territory, made their claims, laid out town sites, and established temporary municipal governments. One writer described it as a "spectacle unparalleled even in the annals of

31 *Congressional Record*, (50th Cong., 2nd sess.), Vol. 20, Part III, p. 2671, shows President Cleveland signing the bill (H.R. 1874) to establish a U.S. Court in the Indian Territory. Cleveland gave his approval on March 2, 1889. For the March 27 proclamation, see *Journal*, March 28, 1889; and E. Benjamin Andrews, *The History of the Last Quarter Century of the United States: 1870–1895*, II, 198–200.

32 W. H. H. Miller to C. M. Sarchet, July 15, 1909, Miller Letterbooks. Miller, in answering Sarchet's inquiry of July 6, 1909, confessed that "after a lapse of twenty years my recollection of the Cabinet discussions touching the opening of Oklahoma are not very distinct."

33 Harrison to George F. Edmunds, April 17, 1889, a photostatic copy in author's possession by courtesy of the Historical Society of Pennsylvania. Attorney General Miller's recollection was that "the President might, if necessary, use the army to keep the peace—for of law and authority there was none."

34 Miller to Sarchet, July 15, 1909, *loc. cit.*

Western civilization—the birth of a new country in a single day."[35] Before noon Guthrie had been a mere town site. By nightfall on April 22nd, it was a city of nearly 10,000. Within six months the Territory had 29 schools, 38 churches, and 22 newspapers.

The inevitable skulduggery aside, Harrison and Miller, when asked for their interpretation of it all, praised the dominant soldier element among the settlers. The war veteran, they believed, harbored respect for order "learned in many hard campaigns," having become convinced that "regulated liberty is the only liberty worth having."[36] An act to provide a temporary government for the Territory and to enlarge U.S. Court jurisdiction within its borders would be signed on May 2, 1890, following prolonged debate.

[35] *Appleton's Annual Cyclopedia* . . . *1889,* p. 675.
[36] Miller to Sarchet, *loc. cit.*

CHAPTER V

In the Footsteps of Washington

WITH THE PASSAGE of one hundred years since 1789, Harrison found himself the central figure in the Centennial of the birth of a nation. From April 29th to May 1st, New New York City was to commemorate the first Inauguration of George Washington at the head of plain old Wall Street. The festivities would give him some respite from avid office-seekers, while thousands of citizens would have a chance to see and greet the twenty-third President. Despite correspondent Henry L. Stoddard's view that Harrison had "an extreme distaste for . . . 'playing to the galleries,' "[1] the opportunity for a good press was hardly overlooked by friends of the Administration.

Descendant of a signer of the Declaration of Independence, Benjamin Harrison, the fifth of that name in Virginia, the new President had a strong sense of history to which he gave voice on various occasions, such as the 1876 Centennial of the signing of the Declaration of Independence in Philadelphia. Evidently impressed, a local paper had hailed him as a Demosthenes.[2] Again, as a U.S. Senator, Harrison had been called upon to speak at the centennial of Cornwallis's surrender at Yorktown. Since the ceremonies planned by the civic leaders of New York would be of much greater importance, Harrison would take due care to dignify the patriotic event scheduled in the nation's first capital.

Bipartisan support had been available for the Centennial planning. President Cleveland's final message had requested action by

1 Henry L. Stoddard, *As I Knew Them*, p. 164. Working at this time as secretary for Stephen B. Elkins, Stoddard came to know Harrison. In 1927 he ranked Cleveland, Theodore Roosevelt, and Wilson as the three outstanding Presidents between Lincoln and Coolidge but wrote that "I feel as though I were doing an injustice to Benjamin Harrison not to crowd him into the three, for, intellectually, he outranked them. He was the ablest of them all" (*ibid.*, p. 36).

2 Philadelphia *Times*, October 26, 1876.

the Congress, which fixed April 30, 1889 as a national holiday. (Harrison's own Inaugural address further suggested that the Supreme Court might properly celebrate its own centennial.)[3] Clergymen across the land noted that religion and patriotism had been united in us as a people from the very beginning; and the President decided that it should be a day of national thanksgiving: "[let] the people of the entire country repair to their respective places of Divine Worship, to implore the favor of God that the blessings of liberty, prosperity and peace may abide with us."[4]

Harrison was forced by the exigencies of public business to turn aside a flood of requests for personal appearances along the route from Washington to New York taken by George Washington; April found him meeting three times a week with the Cabinet. When lumbago kept Blaine home and abed much of the time, Harrison assumed personal direction of the State Department. To American diplomats en route to Berlin, he issued instructions for a strong stand to protect U.S. interests in Samoa.[5]

Just prior to leaving for New York City, at an informal dinner held at the White House, Harrison accepted a gold Centennial medal to wear in his lapel. The decoration was inscribed with the profile bust of Washington, encircled by thirteen stars and the Roman fasces, symbol of strength in unity. On the reverse side, sculptor Augustus Saint-Gaudens had framed the coat of arms of New York City with a border of 38 stars representing as many states now in the Union.[6] Caroline Harrison was completely surprised to receive from her husband an eighteen-carat gold brooch which was ingeniously devised to match the medal.[7]

3 Charles Hedges (comp.), *Speeches of Benjamin Harrison,* p. 165.

4 Harrison noted that on the day of Washington's Inauguration all New York churches had prayed "for God's blessing on the Government and its first President." See C. W. Bowen (ed.), *The History of the Centennial Celebration of the Inauguration of George Washington as First President of the United States,* p. 162 (cited hereafter as *Centennial History*).

5 Albert T. Volwiler (ed.), *Correspondence between Harrison and Blaine,* pp. 59–61. Halford's Diary, (L.C.), entries for April 9, 23, 25, 1889, confirms Harrison's determination that the American Commissioners face up to Bismarck.

6 *Centennial History,* pp. 138–39. Saint-Gaudens directed the work but modeling the medal was done by Philip Martiny. Hence both names appear on the medal. An inexpensive bronze replica of the Centennial medal was struck and placed on public sale.

7 At Harrison's request the Queen's jeweler in England had designed a bold enameled shield, set with rubies and bearing the coat of arms of the Washington family (Robert S. Roberts, of Leamington, England, to Harrison, April 5, 1889, Marthena Harrison Williams MSS.).

An hour or so before midnight on April 28th, the Harrisons and the Levi P. Mortons, accompanied by the Cabinet (less Blaine) and the Supreme Court Justices and their families, boarded sleeping cars bound for Elizabeth, New Jersey, where early the next morning Governor Robert S. Green and the first of the day's several twenty-one-gun salutes greeted the Centennial President. After breakfast with the Governor, Harrison and his party entered carriages to ride to Elizabethport, passing beneath several wooden arches decked with flowers. Groups of young women dressed in white welcomed the visitor and showered him with roses.[8] At Elizabethport, a twelve-oared white barge, flying the President's blue flag, carried Harrison and Morton to the U.S.S. *Despatch* anchored in the deeper waters off Port Richmond. The roar of cannon and the unrelenting blast of steam whistles from factories and harbor craft nearly deafened the ears of the party. The ship headed for upper New York Harbor, closely followed by three puffing steamboats filled with dignitaries.[9]

Admiral David Dixon Porter and General William Tecumseh Sherman escorted Harrison to the upper deck to witness a naval display. Using binoculars, Harrison inspected ten ships of war, including four new steel cruisers: the flagship *Chicago,* flying the colors of the Navy Secretary, and the *Atlanta, Boston,* and *Yorktown.* In line, too, was the U.S.S. *Brooklyn* back from its Asiatic station, flying a homeward-bound pennant 500 feet long. Several revenue cutters, in place since early morning, also awaited the approach of the slow but stately *Despatch.*

As the President passed, each ship dipped colors and fired salutes. Equally impressive was the sprawling array of merchant ships which towered over numerous harbor tugs and fashionable yachts.[10] Flag-smothered mastheads turned the harbor into a rainbow, and despite the choppy waters Harrison remained at his reviewing post for more than two hours. The scene indeed contrasted sharply with Washington's crossing by barge in 1789. The

8 *Appleton's Annual Cyclopedia . . . 1889,* p. 604. A similar honor had been accorded Washington who, like Harrison. stopped the parade and thanked the girls.

9 Named the *Sirus, Erastus Wiman,* and the *Monmouth,* the vessels are pictured in *Centennial History,* pp. 188 ff.

10 *Ibid.,* 202, lists two divisions of merchant ships with five squadrons each, "comprising in all one ocean steamship, forty-four steamboats, one hundred and seventy-one steam tug-boats, fourteen steam propellers, six steam yachts, eight steam ferryboats, seventeen steam lighters, and six barges." In addition to the ships in line, it was reported that a large number of steamboats, steam yachts, and tugboats followed the *Despatch.*

U.S. then had no navy, and the only shots fired came from the Spanish corvette *Galveston* and from one lonely merchantman. The progress achieved since that early day did not escape Harrison. Though he had told Blaine in Washington that he had no speech even in outline for delivery at the Centennial,[11] he was beginning to gather material.

Just off Wall Street, Harrison stepped into a barge manned by twelve retired sea captains who rowed him to shore—a service their predecessors had performed for George Washington. Here Governor David B. Hill and Mayor Hugh J. Grant, aided by New York's senior citizen Hamilton Fish, extended an official welcome. Military and patriotic groups joined ranks and headed for the Equitable Building on Broadway, where more than 2,000 people awaited Harrison's arrival at the Lawyer's Club. Nearly everyone sought the President's hand, including some thirty governors who were first in the reception line. Among the clergy present was Henry Codman Potter, Episcopal Bishop of New York and a man whom Harrison would have reason to remember before the festivities closed.[12]

The late afternoon procession from the Equitable Building to City Hall Park left Harrison with the memory that "all the store signs and all the show windows were covered with the flag," with "not a suggestion of commerce on the whole route."[13] Just as the merchants of lower Wall Street had erected a massive arch covered with red, white, and blue silk at the corners of Front and Wall Streets, so was the old Post Office festooned with the national colors. Further on, yards of bright-hued bunting draped the *Herald, Times, Tribune, World,* and *Sun* buildings, where they formed a thriving newspaper hub. When the procession neared City Hall, police had difficulty in restraining the swarming crowd.[14]

[11] Volwiler, *op cit.,* p. 61. Harrison, who always felt mental anguish before any address, had complained to Blaine that he found executive tasks too distracting to concentrate on his Centennial speeches.

[12] Elting E. Morrison (ed.) *Letters of Theodore Roosevelt,* I, 165, n. 5. Potter was scheduled to deliver the sermon on April 30 at St. Paul's Chapel in the presence of the President and two former Presidents.

[13] Benjamin Harrison to Mrs. Jesse Benton Fremont, May 17, 1898, (L.C.), Vol. 172 (Tibbott transcript).

[14] *Centennial History,* pp. 225–26.

Outside the Governor's Room at City Hall stood files of little girls—two from each grade school in the city—and an honor guard of their older sisters. Armed with lilies of the valley and roses, they compelled "the gray-haired, serene-faced Chief Magistrate" to run "the pleasant gauntlet of a floral fusillade." The President greeted each child with a smile, and attentively listened to their memorized words of welcome.[15] Flanked by Mayor Grant and Governor Hill, he shook hands with another 5,000 well-wishers and curiosity-seekers who managed to gain entrance before the doors were finally locked at 5:00 P.M.

Following a fine dinner given by Stuyvesant Fish, the Harrisons hurried to the Metropolitan Opera House to witness a gala Centennial Ball. Unlike his illustrious predecessor, Harrison did not lead the quadrille made famous by George Washington. With 10,000 others he applauded a re-enactment of the dance, accepted some refreshments, and then left for Vice-President Morton's Fifth Avenue home. It was now well after midnight, and if the first day in New York was any indication of what might come, the Centennial President needed nothing more than he needed a good night's rest.

First, however, he reviewed with his wife the April 30th program, which was billed as the most important of the three-day fête. Prior to staring at some eleven miles of soldiery over a six-hour period, Harrison would have to attend religious services, some literary exercises, and an informal luncheon. Following the very long military review, the day would close with a festive banquet and much speech-making at the Opera House. Although the day also called for two talks by the President who "never made a poor speech,"[16] unpreparedness did not keep him from deep slumber.

Artillery salutes at sunrise awakened the President and many New Yorkers long before a scheduled 9:00 A.M. service at St. Paul's Chapel. Standing at Broadway and Vesey Streets, old St. Paul's loomed more as a landmark than a church, and on this day it appeared somewhat overdecorated for a house of prayer. Everywhere pyramids of flowers, flanked by palms and other plants, caught the

15 *Ibid.*, pp. 239, 247. College senior Annie Abrahams spoke for the youthful gathering and presented the President with an illuminated copy of her address, beautifully bound in black Russian leather.

16 Stoddard, *op. cit.*, p. 181.

eye, and huge American flags hung from the ceiling. Entering quietly by a side door, Harrison was escorted to the George Washington pew; nearby were seated ex-Presidents Hayes and Cleveland, along with the members of the Supreme Court and of the Cabinet. As the clock in the steeple struck nine, the choir intoned the opening hymn, and so began a program of scripture readings interspersed by choral selections.

Bishop Potter mounted the venerable pulpit and Harrison settled back to await a polished eulogy. The expectation was that the first President and his Centennial successor would come in for a goodly share of routine compliments, but no. With something of the fire of an ancient prophet, Potter lauded Washington's simplicity and integrity but only in contrast to the self-seeking manifested by latter-day government officials. A professed Republican the minister heaped maledictions on the body politic for having exchanged "Washingtonian dignity for Jeffersonian simplicity" that led so easily to "Jacksonian vulgarity," materialism, and "practical politics"; and as he went on and on, it became rather plain that his words were directed against men now in power. The growth of wealth, the prevalence of luxury, and the amassing of large material forces were cited as the "standing menace to the freedom and integrity of the individual." Potter further charged that it was "impossible to reproduce today either the temper or the conduct of our fathers" as long as national leaders mistook bigness for greatness and confounded gain with godliness.[17]

The startled congregation showed signs of uneasiness as the renowned Bishop continued to speak his mind. Lucidly and with careful diction Potter lashed out at the spoils system as practiced by the reigning G.O.P. or whoever:

The conception of the national government as a huge machine existing mainly for the purpose of rewarding partisan service—this is a conception so alien to the character and conduct of Washington and his associates that it seems grotesque even to speak of it. It would be interesting to imagine the first President of the United States confronted with someone who ventured to approach him upon the basis of what are now commonly known as "practical politics."[18]

17 Harry Thurston Peck, *Twenty Years of the Republic: 1885–1905*, p. 196. See also H. C. Potter, "National Bigness or Greatness—Which?", *North American Review*, CLXVIII, No. 509 (April, 1899), 436.

18 For the full text of Potter's sermon see the *Centennial History*, pp. 277–81, or the *Journal*, May 1, 1889.

The sermon would be interpreted by Democrats, Mugwumps, and independent reform groups as a criticism of Harrison's tolerance of certain Republican bosses intent on the spoils of political victory.[19] Two days later newspaper reporters asked Potter for some explanation. Potter wryly observed that he hated "taffy and platitudes," and during the Centennial, "I wasn't needed for that. . . . There were plenty who were sure to pay sounding compliments to Mr. Harrison." The scramble for office, he explained, had disgusted him. Had President Harrison yet given a single hour to statesmanship?[20]

Through it all, even after he had read the Potter interview, Harrison had little to say. Every U.S. President, since Andrew Jackson and his men let down the bars completely, had had his difficulties with fat and lean spoilsmen, and whether Potter understood the situation or not, Harrison had been contending valorously with them for several months thus far. Somehow he would go down in history as that cold little man in the White House who gave most political bosses no undue amount of his time. Too, his remarks at the very next ceremony held at the Federal Sub-Treasury building indicated that he was in accord with the preacher, when he said there: "Self-seeking has no public observance or anniversary."[21]

Long before the church service had ended, thousands had swarmed to Wall and Nassau streets, the site of Washington's first Inauguration. Patriotic decorations in the grand manner hid most of the Doric design of the Sub-Treasury building that had replaced the original Federal Hall. Gilded eagles with a wing-spread of 25 feet hid the main frontal columns, and the structure itself was completely covered by national and state flags. Even the long flight of broad steps leading from the street was hidden by a wooden platform and seats to accommodate 1,200 people. Stretching the entire length of the roof was a double row of signal flags proclaiming: "First in War, First in Peace, and First in the Hearts of his Countrymen."[22]

19 Peck, *op. cit.*, p. 197. Such an interpretation was taken in editorials in the New York *Herald, Sun*, and *Evening Post*, May 1, 1889.

20 *Journal*, May 4, 1889. This pro-Harrison organ dismissed the sermon as the work of "Pessimist Potter."

21 *Report of the Benjamin Harrison Memorial Commission*, p. 158; *Speeches of Benjamin Harrison*, pp. 210–11.

22 *Centennial History*, p. 286.

Soon after ten o'clock, the President's carriage and a cavalcade of dignitaries arrived and Gilmore's famous band struck up "Hail to the Chief" as they ascended the platform. Seated in Washington's chair, Harrison thoughtfully fingered the first President's Inaugural Bible. Chairman Elbridge T. Gerry, who opened the exercises, referred to "that sacred volume [as] silently attesting the basis on which our nation was constructed and the dependence of our people upon Almighty God."[23] An invocation and a reading of "The Vow of Washington," written for the occasion by 80-year-old John Greenleaf Whittier, preceded the orator of the day, the celebrated Chauncey Mitchell Depew.

Depew's distinctive bald head and canny expression had graced banquet tables for a generation, and only Mark Twain rivaled him as an after-dinner speaker.[24] On this day he would disappoint no descendants of the Founding Fathers. Having eulogized several members of that august group, including Harrison the signer, the orator let it be known that the spirit of Washington now filled the Executive office.[25]

When it was Harrison's turn to address the audience, dozens of cameras were focused upon him from the surrounding housetops.[26] When the cheering crowd of some 10,000 permitted him to speak, he referred to Washington in a few brief sentences as one who "teaches us today this great lesson: That those who would associate their names with events that shall outlive a century can only do so by high consecration to duty. Self-seeking has no public observance or anniversary."[27] A benediction by Michael A. Corrigan, Roman Catholic Archbishop of New York, closed the morning program.

A six-hour-long parade up Fifth Avenue was something of an elaborate re-enactment of the Harrison Inauguration, although obviously it was proving more comfortable than the rain-soaked pageantry in Washington. It was to be distinctly military. With General Sherman again at his side, Harrison sat in a pavilion

23 Ibid., pp. 290–91. The speaker was the grandson of Elbridge Gerry, the member of Congress in 1789 who had performed a similar service at Washington's Inauguration.

24 Stoddard, op. cit., pp. 267–72, pays tribute to Depew's career and life "full of friendships, full of honors, full of health and full of years."

25 Centennial History, p. 306.

26 Journal, May 1, 1889. Every notable phase of the three-day celebration was well photographed. The better pictures were reproduced in the Centennial History.

27 Report of the Benjamin Harrison Memorial Commission, p. 158.

erected in Madison Square to review some 50,000 troops marching past. Regular Army and Navy forces, including battalions from West Point and Annapolis, National Guard units, and numerous G.A.R. contingents participated.[28] The loudest ovation greeted 12,000 New York Guardsmen with a splendidly mounted cavalry troop. Second in numbers were 7,000 Pennsylvanians in full battle gear marching behind Governor James A. Beaver, a legless General, securely strapped to his saddle. Major General John M. Schofield, serving as Chief Marshal, reported to War Secretary Redfield Proctor that the troops, militia and Regulars, "could be concentrated at any point and made an effective army in an exceedingly short time."[29] Harrison said publicly that "perhaps never in the history of our nation have we been so well equipped for war upon the land as now." The Administration, however, was obviously peaceably disposed, with no military actions ever under discussion.[30]

Open-air concerts and a festive display of fireworks entertained the crowds that evening as the Harrisons and 800 guests sat at the Opera House banquet.[31] The thirteen wines listed on the menu represented the number of toasts to be proposed; through the two-hour marathon of words that followed, Mayor Grant, the toastmaster, skillfully handled the reins. The last to speak as he responded to the toast "The United States of America," Harrison had his turn well after midnight, paying a tribute to the American flag.[32] New York's great thoroughfares, said he, "dedicated to trade, have closed their doors and have covered the insignia of commerce with the Stars and Stripes."[33] The President continued:

These banners with which you have covered your walls, these patriotic inscriptions, must come down, and the ways of commerce and of trade be resumed again here; but may I not ask you to carry these

28 *Centennial History*, pp. 346–49. Captain Daniel M. Taylor, Ordnance Department, U.S.A., noted in his official report to the Adjutant General in Washington: ". . . it is gratifying to one who knows the weakness of our Regular Army to see in the National Guard the reserve army."

29 *Ibid.*, p. 347.

30 Harrison observed: "We have never seen the time when our people were more smitten with the love of peace" (*ibid.*, p. 382).

31 *Appleton's Annual Cyclopedia . . . 1889*, p. 606.

32 For an extended treatment of this theme consult Harry J. Sievers, *President Benjamin Harrison and Our Country's Flag*, a five-page brochure reprinted from the *National Magazine of History* (November, 1952).

33 *Centennial History*, p. 382. An editorial writer for the New York *Independent* commented that Broadway "had been closed to business, because something higher than business was in our hearts" (Sievers, *op. cit.*, p. 3).

banners that now hang on your walls into your homes, into the public schools of your city, and into all your great institutions where children are gathered, and to drape them there, that the eyes of the young and of the old may look upon that flag as one of the familiar adornments of every American home.[34]

Thus began Harrison's personal crusade to develop greater love for the flag by having it raised over every schoolhouse and ordering it flown above the White House and the Executive Departments in Washington.[35]

The ceremonies ended as Harrison received a committee from the Jesuit college of St. Francis Xavier, which presented a poetic tribute to Washington written in 27 languages.[36] The scholars were duly thanked for their efforts, and the President returned for the night to Vice-President Morton's house.

Artillery salutes from harbor forts and naval vessels announced the dawn of the final Centennial day. A weary Harrison had no choice but to rise early and resume his post of honor at the Fifth Avenue grandstand. Civic and industrial leaders had promised a parade that would surpass the military review both in pageantry and in numbers. At ten A.M., as the floats began to move past, the President appeared attentive and pleased.

Following the units of local collegians were French, German, Irish, Italian, Scottish, and Swiss immigrant groups in native costumes. Volunteer firemen demonstrating every variety of equipment drew loud cheers. Almost explosive was the greeting accorded 2,000 of the Ancient Order of Hibernians, and 2,500 Tammany Braves. Various trade associations—bakers, butchers, plasterers, and piano-makers—marched past. Historic tableaux depicting John Smith, Henry Hudson, and William Penn drew applause; scenes from the life of Washington commanded much interest. There were wonderful allegorical floats honoring Arion,

34 *Centennial History*, p. 382.

35 Benjamin Harrison to John J. McCook, June 22, 1894, (L.C.), Vol. 160. Harrison assured his correspondent that "You are quite right in assuming that I feel the fullest sympathy with this movement to display the National Flag over all our public and educational institutions. I gave orders that the Flag should be displayed over the Executive departments and over the White House while I was in Washington; and during the Washington Centennial Exercises in 1889 in New York, I suggested that the Flag, which during the parade hung over the business houses of the city, should be sent to the school houses. A love of the Flag and an understanding of what it stands for should be sedulously promoted in all our educational institutions."

36 *Centennial History*, p. 382.

Bacchus, Prince Carnival, and Christmas, as well as floats bearing scenes derived from the great German composers.

It was three o'clock in the afternoon when four huge trucks rolled by the President's stand, each depicting an aspect of the nation's industrial progress. At this juncture, a timely interruption in the parade allowed Harrison to retire gracefully. Taking leave of his wife and family, who were to remain in New York for another week, he hurried to Jersey City and boarded his train. Newspapermen remarked that he seemed not tired but "thoroughly refreshed" as he waved a farewell from the rear platform.[37] Through it all, even the Bishop Potter episode, Harrison had remained serene.

Still house-bound with lumbago, Secretary Blaine sent Harrison a note on his first morning back in the White House. "My dear Mr. President," he began,

Very glad you are back safe & sound! I congratulate you on both your speeches in New York. They were exceedingly apt, sententious and dignified in both instances. I would not think it worthwhile to pay this compliment to one who always speaks admirably, but for the fact that you felt your two months of wearisome official labor had disabled you from doing your best. You proved that you had judged yourself erroneously.[38]

If the President was pleased by Blaine's courtesy, he was also well satisfied by the Secretary's report that "on Samoan affairs we have thus far gained every point." The Berlin Conference was three days old, and a diplomatic victory over the young Kaiser Wilhelm at the outset of the new Administration would result in enormous prestige.[39]

37 New York *Tribune*, May 2, 1889.

38 James G. Blaine to Benjamin Harrison, May 2, 1889, as cited in Volwiler, *op cit.*, p. 61. Forced to forgo the Centennial festivities himself, Blaine was represented there by his son Walker, who accompanied the Presidential party to and from New York.

39 See George H. Ryden, *The Foreign Policy of the United States in Relation to Samoa*, pp. 422–522.

CHAPTER VI

The Task of Civil Service Reform

HARRISON'S ADMINISTRATION witnessed the usual struggles for power. The Legislative and Executive branches were in conflict, as were the professional politicians and the reformers over the merit system and customary patronage. Realizing that the two problems were closely related, Harrison determined that the Executive branch should take the offensive. By selecting a Cabinet congenial to him and by exercising a degree of independence in filling major posts at home and abroad, the new President had made a vigorous start. But as the weeks wore on he discovered that the power of appointment had become the most exacting, unrelenting and distracting of his duties. By the fall of 1889 he would confess: "Every day that I am here and every appointment I dispose of only adds to the load of distress that I carry, resulting from the fact that so many friends are disappointed."[1]

If the political history of the Harrison Administration is a struggle between the conscience and ideals of an earnest, high-minded Executive and the power and pressure of the party machine, it also reflects the morals of an era devoid of an efficient national civil service.

Not only was Harrison intent on getting congressmen out of his house so that he could go to bed, but, whether piqued or not by Bishop Potter's remarks at old St. Paul's in New York, he determined to intensify the struggle with the spoilsmen.[2] Assistance of sorts was available. In the 1880's, civil service reform had stirred

---

1 Harrison to William Henry Smith, October 19, 1889, (L.C.), Vol. 89 (Tibbott transcript). This contradicts the popularly held but uncritical interpretation of Harold U. Faulkner, *Politics, Reform and Expansion: 1890–1900*, p. 96, who declares that Harrison found congenial the task "of finding jobs for loyal Republicans."

2 Harry J. Sievers, *Benjamin Harrison: Hoosier Statesman*, p. 384, records candidate Harrison's promise "to do his best so that at the end of his term some progress should have been made in civil service reform."

73

human passions. Its proponents—the cheerful and confident Lucius Swift of Indianapolis; the hard-hitting and ofttimes disdainful New York editor, E. L. Godkin; and spidery Carl Schurz, who urged that the President be a St. George against the spoils dragon —spoke and wrote on the subject so constantly as to become repetitious.

In Harrison's day, some of the fiercest struggles of American politics would be waged over reform. No set official policy would work, nor could it, as long as any loyal party man had a hand in the hiring and firing. By appointing John Wanamaker, a political outsider and a man of probity, to head the Post Office Department, the Administration waged war on "the plunderbund of politics which fattened on post offices,"[3] and what was practically a clean sweep was carried out. First Assistant Postmaster General James S. Clarkson began "decapitating a fourth-class postmaster every five minutes"[4]—all to make room for some 30,000 Republican successors.

Despite an uproar raised by reformers, Harrison did nothing to stay Clarkson's axe.[5] So overwhelming and persistent were the demands of eager office-seekers meanwhile, that even congressmen darted away to hide, and some even changed their residences to escape importunities. As a well-known White House occupant, Harrison was unable to adopt the latter stratagem.[6]

Harrison's record in Indiana had won the approval of Theodore Roosevelt, a supporter of civil service reform, who expected the President to show himself a reformer. With the shifting of postmasters in New York City, however, young Roosevelt appeared disillusioned. Harrison's choice was Cornelius Van Cott, a regular Republican who had worked his way up through the usual municipal offices. His replacement of Postmaster Henry G. Pearson was cited by Roosevelt as "an awful black eye to the party here; a criminal blunder."[7] Roosevelt, who regarded Van Cott as a Platt

3 William A. White, *Masks in a Pageant*, p. 81.

4 William Dudley Foulke, *Lucius B. Swift*, p. 41.

5 Clarkson openly admitted his role as chief dispenser of patronage. On May 25, 1889 he assured General Grenville M. Dodge: "I am most anxious to get through with my task here and leave. I am simply on detail from the National Committee, to see that some of the men who fought with us splendidly last year are rewarded" (Dodge Records, Vol. 12, p. 167).

6 The President's daughter complained that "we, none of us, have had any time to take care of ourselves. . . ." Mary Harrison McKee to Eugenia Peltz, April 28, 1889, Messinger MSS.

7 Theodore Roosevelt to Henry Cabot Lodge, March 30, 1889, as cited in Elting E. Morison (ed.), *Letters of Theodore Roosevelt*, I, 156 (hereafter cited as *Letters*).

henchman, complained bitterly that Harrison had strengthened the Platt machine in New York City, and predicted that it was "still quite in the cards that Cleavland [sic] may come in again in '92."[8] But when Harrison elevated Ernest Howard Crosby, New York lawyer, progressive politician, and philanthropist, to a judgeship, Roosevelt grew slightly less critical. "I do hope," said he, "the President will appoint good Civil Service Commissioners."[9]

Harrison had ideas of his own, and apparently Roosevelt fitted into them. The New Yorker had been disappointed in not gaining the post of Assistant Secretary of State, yet Harrison early in his Administration had spoken of him favorably in recognizing his talents.[10] Roosevelt was certainly known as a bitter foe of the spoils system, whatever his talents. So it was that on May 3, 1889 he was asked to come to the White House.[11]

Harrison offered him the post of Civil Service Commissioner and, on May 7th, impressed by the challenge implicit in the offer, Roosevelt accepted. The post had real meaning for the zealous young reformer who later would acknowledge that Harrison "gave me my first opportunity to do big things."[12] To Roosevelt, what was coming would be big—it would, in fact, be no less than the Presidency.

Harrison had a second Commission vacancy to fill, and this choice had to fall to someone agreeable to Roosevelt. He selected Colonel Hugh S. Thompson, educator, orator, and twice Governor of South Carolina, a post he resigned in 1886 to become Assistant Secretary of the Treasury under Cleveland. It appeared fairly plain that Harrison had appointed a strong Commission.[13] Thus in mid-May, 1889, a new era for civil service reform dawned in Washington.

8 *Ibid.*, Theodore Roosevelt to Cecil Arthur Spring-Rice, April 14, 1889.

9 Theodore Roosevelt to Henry Cabot Lodge, April 1889, printed in H. C. Lodge (ed.), *Selections from the Correspondence of Theodore Roosevelt and Henry Cabot Lodge, 1884–1918*, I, 77.

10 Memorandum by L. T. Michener, "Theodore Roosevelt's Appointment to the Civil Service Commission," April 1889, in Michener MSS., Box 2.

11 E. W. Halford to Theodore Roosevelt, May 3, 1889, Cowles MSS. Copy to author by the courtesy of the late Professor Howard K. Beale who in 1956 published *Theodore Roosevelt and the Rise of America to World Power*.

12 Memorandum of L. T. Michener, *loc. cit.*

13 To Theodore Roosevelt, Colonel Thompson, even though a Democrat, was "a trump," while holdover Commissioner Charles Lyman was considered "honest, hard-working, and very familiar with the law" (Theodore Roosevelt to Henry Cabot Lodge, September 27, 1889, *Letters*, I, 192).

Even before Roosevelt and Thompson took office, reform advocate E. L. Godkin displayed some thoughts on the subject in the *Nation:* "The President gave on Tuesday the first tangible indication of a desire to redeem the pledge of his letter of acceptance, in the matter of civil service reform." Without meaning to overlook Thompson, whom he regarded as neither a "dummy" nor a "weakling," Editor Godkin spotlighted Roosevelt as "erratic and impulsive, but . . . energetic, enthusiastic, and honest, and may be relied on to see that the law is faithfully executed."

Godkin went on: "The Commission as now constituted is the best we have had, and makes one feel as if the Potter sermon were really beginning to tell."[14] All this proved timely, even serving to undercut George William Curtis, whose annual message to the Civil Service Reform Association had strongly censured the President for violating the spirit of civil service reform. Countering Curtis, the Indianapolis *Journal*, without mentioning the new appointments, found it

. . . remarkable that, while the Mugwumps are criticizing the President for violating the spirit of civil service reform, many office-seekers and Congressmen are criticizing him for observing its spirit too closely. One set of critics finds fault with him for making too many removals from office, and another set for not making enough nor making them fast enough. Between the two the President cannot do better than to keep right along as he has been, discharging his duty in his own way and time, and improving the Civil Service by every appointment he makes.[15]

Despite the fact that office-seekers as well as reformers roundly abused the President, most citizens, free from special interests, believed he was serving the public well.

Theodore Roosevelt began his duties as Civil Service Commissioner with the assurance that the law would be honestly executed. "No attempt to get around the law in any way will be permitted; and the Democrats and the Republicans alike will have fair play," he wrote Lucius Swift, the reform leader in Indianapolis.[16] It soon became evident that the Commission would not rest satisfied with verbal slaps at the spoilsmen. The three officials went to New York

14 *The Nation*, XLVIII (May 9, 1889), 375.

15 *Journal*, May 9, 1889.

16 Theodore Roosevelt to Lucius B. Swift, May 16, 21, 1889, *Letters*, I, 162.

for an on-the-spot investigation. After hearing testimony bearing on fraud in the conduct of Custom House civil service examinations, the Commission recommended and secured the removal of three employees. Not only Roosevelt, but Harrison also seemed pleased by this early success. Assured of official support, the Commissioner outlined a tour to include Indianapolis, Chicago, and Milwaukee. "The West knows much less about civil service reform than the East, and there will be a row,"[17] observed Theodore Roosevelt, briskly rubbing his hands over the prospect.

As President Cleveland had done in 1888, Harrison reviewed a Decoration Day parade in New York. The following day, May 31, 1889, was a quiet one in Washington, but in rain-swept western Pennsylvania, swirling waters from a broken reservoir near Johnstown took several thousand lives and ten million dollars worth of property. Reports reaching Harrison the next morning told of a mountain of water fifty feet high and thirty feet wide at first, but widening to half a mile, bearing houses, factories, bridges, and corpses upon its angry crest until it all but swept Johnstown from this earth. Even locomotives weighing twenty tons were tossed about "as if the law of gravity had been repealed."[18]

Harrison promptly wired Pennsylvania Governor J. A. Beaver: "My heart is burdened for your smitten people." Every kind of Federal assistance was offered. The guiding spirit at a Washington public meeting, a tired and worried President seemed to forget "official distinctions and everything else except his desire to have the city give generously."[19] Willard's Hotel was made a provisions depot, $10,000 was subscribed in a short time, and a supply train soon left the city.

While the nation was recovering from the shock of the disaster, the influential Philadelphia *North American* carried an editorial occasioned, as the editor said, by the spate of political criticism directed against a President who had taken a stand on the patronage. Since the article found a prominent place in the Harrison

17 Theodore Roosevelt to Henry Cabot Lodge, June 24, 1889 (*ibid.*, p. 166). The three customs employees were charged with "laxity, negligence and fraud," and one was prosecuted for criminal violation of the law.

18 E. Benjamin Andrews, *The History of the Last Quarter Century in the United States: 1870–1895*, II, 204–5.

19 A Washingtonian's letter in the *Philadelphia Record*, as cited in the *Journal*, June 11, 1889.

scrapbook, one may assume that it had been carefully read by the President. It ran:

It is already known and admitted that President Harrison is President. The murmurs of the small politicians who are said to "run" things testify to the headship of the President. The small bosses are impatient of the deliberation of the President. They declare that they are tired of waiting.[20]

The suggestion was offered that the spoilsmen "nap for a few months so that they might awake like giants refreshed. . . . the President will not always please the men who assume to 'run' things."[21]

Scarcely a day passed without some public debate on spoils versus merit system,[22] and many private letters reached the White House. A correspondent who disapproved of the new order of things was George A. Mott of New York, a prominent attorney and regular Republican. "To be frank with you," Mott wrote Harrison,

. . . Your administration . . . , so far as the distribution of local patronage is concerned, has been a failure, here and elsewhere, in my judgment and in the judgment of many of my neighbors and friends who warmly supported you; and it is no secret that the feeling of hostility is already very outspoken and widespread.[23]

Of course, the spoilsmen—especially in Indiana—were full of angry objections to any hint of a change in the rules. Hoosier Republicans made no effort to hide their disdain for anybody and anything connected with civil service reform. In the state capital a group organized as the Indianapolis Republican Club came to be better known as the Kickers' Club. "The principal object," it was said, "seems to be to complain."[24]

Party workers in Indiana were found to be particularly disgruntled, and now an elated and zealous Roosevelt was heading West. In Indianapolis, he investigated complaints against City Postmaster William Wallace, whom Roosevelt thought a "well meaning weak old fellow."[25] Wallace, however, was none other than a former law partner of Harrison, who had just appointed

20 As cited in the *Journal*, June 1, 1889.
21 *Ibid.*
22 For example, *Journal*, June 1, 4, 14, 15, 18, 19, 22 24, 28, 1889; New York *Tribune*, June 4, 12, 30, 1889.
23 George A. Mott to Harrison, June 10, 1889, (L.C.), Vol. 79.
24 Louis T. Michener to E. W. Halford, May 11, 1889, (L.C.), Vol. 76.
25 Theodore Roosevelt to Henry Cabot Lodge, June 24, 1889, *Letters*, I, 235.

him postmaster at $3,000 a year. Wallace, now 64, was the brother of General Lew Wallace, author of *Ben Hur* and Harrison's campaign biographer. He obviously needed his job, having assumed the debts of a prodigal son. Although always considered a man of integrity, he was now charged with the illegal removal of three employees. Wallace offered his defense in a letter to Secretary Halford, assuring him of his good intentions:

Let me assure the President that I intend to observe the Civil Service Law. I have observed it. The records in my office show it. If at the beginning technical omissions have been made they have been unintentional. I confess to no technical knowledge of the laws.[26]

Harrison, however, could hardly intervene. Two illegal removals and one appointment were disclosed by the Commission, and Roosevelt saw to it that certain individuals responsible were summarily dismissed. Nevertheless, no real fault could be found with Wallace, an efficient and honest executive,[27] who was permitted to remain in office until his death two years later.

It did appear, however, that while a new broom may be expected to sweep clean, Roosevelt had proved a little too thoroughgoing. State Attorney General Michener, although careful to style himself as "earnestly in favor of civil service reform,"[28] was one who waxed indignant over the New Yorker's apparent arrogance. The White House therefore was advised:

Theodore Roosevelt . . . was positively insulting to the Republicans he met and extremely agreeable to every interest hostile to the Republican party. . . . Four-fifths of the Indiana Republicans despise it [Civil Service reform]. When they go out in the back yard in the morning and spit, they like to think they are spitting on Foulke, Swift, Roosevelt, and George Will Curtis.[29]

Despite the fact that Roosevelt's intentions were highly moral, his manner came to be prejudicial to the cause.

His next stop was in Milwaukee, where Postmaster George H. Paul, a Cleveland appointee, had his own system of competitive examination. When Roosevelt discovered that test papers had been re-marked so that Paul could obtain the men he wanted in office,

26 William Wallace to E. W. Halford, June 21, 1889, (L.C.), Vol. 80. He insisted: "My assistants have all, from the first, been instructed to be most careful not to give offense by failure to comply in the letter and spirit of the law." Irving McKee, "Ben Hur" Wallace, p. 233.
27 Foulke, op. cit., p. 38. Two years later Roosevelt referred to Wallace's administration as a "model" (Letters, I, 235, n. 2).
28 Louis T. Michener to E. W. Halford, June 29, 1889, (L.C.), Vol. 81.
29 Michener to Halford, August 19, 1889, (L.C.), Vol. 84.

he was so infuriated that his pen fairly flew. The man was "about as thorough paced a scoundrel as I ever saw—an oily-gammon, church-going specimen";[30] and he begged Harrison to remove him from office at once. But Postmaster Paul had his defenders and Roosevelt his critics among persons in high places, whatever their politics.

In Harrison's Cabinet there was John Wanamaker, whom Roosevelt characterized as "outrageously disagreeable as he could possibly be"; among civil service reformers there was Dorman Eaton, one of Paul's college friends who considered Roosevelt "too impetuous"; and there was Frank Hatton, editor of the Washington *Post*, a former Postmaster General and an articulate foe of civil service reform.[31]

Until he could obtain all the facts in the Paul case, therefore, Harrison would delay action even though Roosevelt was growing tense. Toward the end of June the reformer advised Congressman Henry Cabot Lodge as to the hard row he was then hoeing:

I have made this Commission a living force, and in consequence the outcry among the Spoilsmen has become furious; it has evidently frightened both the President and Halford a little. They have shown symptoms of telling me that the law should be rigidly enforced where the people will stand it, and handled gingerly elsewhere.[32]

The law, however, was to be enforced "up to the handle *everywhere*, fearlessly and honestly." Roosevelt wined and dined Secretary Halford in pressing for Presidential action in removing Paul, and he continued to exhort his friend Lodge that reform and Administration good were one and the same:

Dwell on the fact that is to Harrison's credit, all that we are doing to enforce the law. I am part of the administration; if I do good work, it redounds to the credit of the administration. This needs to be insisted on, both for the sake of the Mugwumps and for the sake of Harrison himself.[33]

30 Theodore Roosevelt to Henry Cabot Lodge, June 24, 1889, *Letters*, I, 235; also Theodore Roosevelt to E. W. Halford, July 24, 1889, (L.C.), Vol. 83.

31 George William Curtis to Colonel Silas W. Burt, July 29, 1889, Burt MSS. Tension over the issue became so great that the House Committee on Reform in the Civil Service was finally instructed to conduct a Congressional investigation. The Committee's report, issued in June 1890, vindicated the conduct of Roosevelt and Thompson.

32 June 29, 1889, *Letters*, I, 167.

33 Ibid., p. 168, July 1, 1889. Roosevelt was convinced that he had already strengthened the Harrison Administration "by showing, in striking contrast to the facts under Cleveland, that there was no humbug in the law now."

But countering Lodge in the House were men like veteran Republican Congressman Thomas M. Browne of Indiana, who labeled the civil service system "a cumbersome piece of political patchwork" and advocated its abolition, as well as the repeal of the Pendleton Act, which provided for competitive examinations.[34] While this and similar attacks were embarrassing Harrison, Roosevelt became even more resolute.

In an effort to restore party unity in Indiana, Harrison's old campaign manager, L. T. Michener, accepted the post of State Party Chairman in mid-July.[35] Assistant Postmaster General Clarkson of Iowa, who had a hand in many appointments, informed Michener that he was the man for the place, and emphasized the importance of his new duty:

Let me say to you that it is absolutely necessary for your friend, the President, that you continue your state to be Republican. I know your affection for him and your pride in him. There is no man anywhere who can render him the service and make him so secure as you can.[36]

At the outset of his Administration Harrison came under heavy pressure from Negroes to do something for them by way of patronage—especially in the South. He proposed to appoint some Negro postmasters in large southern cities and to go beyond his predecessors in rewarding the colored man with other federal jobs. He needed support and got it from First Assistant Postmaster General Clarkson.

Clarkson, a former editor of the Des Moines *Register* and an ally of Senator William B. Allison, was close enough to Harrison to be influential in overturning an unwritten law of the Treasury that no Negroes be appointed to office in that department. As Assistant Postmaster General, Clarkson had already put some thousand Negroes in rural post offices and had appointed hundreds

---

34 *Journal*, June 27, 1889.

35 Michener left a memorandum on his becoming State Chairman in July 1889, replacing J. N. Huston who had resigned to take the post of Treasurer of the United States. He declared: "I took the office only because I felt in that place I could be of service to him [Harrison] and his Administration" (Michener MSS., Box 2, July 1889).

36 James S. Clarkson to Louis T. Michener, August 26, 1889, Michener MSS. Three weeks earlier Senator Matthew [Boss] Quay had written to express his personal pleasure at Michener's decision and to advise the new chairman to cooperate more closely with Clarkson and Dudley. He closed with the promise that "we will strengthen your hands to the utmost of our ability." M. S. Quay to L. T. Michener, July 30, 1889, Michener MSS., Box 1.

more as letter carriers and railway mail clerks.[37] Thus, he readily adopted the cause of Norris Wright Cuney, a G.O.P. Negro leader from Texas and candidate for Collector of the Port of Galveston. Harrison meanwhile had been induced to go along with the Treasury Department, which drew the color line against Cuney, but Clarkson and his friend happened to call at the White House at just the right time.

With Treasury Secretary Windom there at his elbow, Harrison had just signed the appointment of another candidate for the post. whose name had been written in on a document ready at hand. "That's not the right name," Clarkson stoutly protested. "In conferences . . . you decided to appoint Mr. Cuney." Harrison began pacing the floor. "I remember now but the Department . . . has caused me to change my mind." He put it up to Clarkson: "Would you give the most important position in Texas . . . to a Negro?" Sensing victory, Clarkson answered firmly: "Yes." Harrison deleted the original name and wrote in Cuney's. "I am glad you called my attention to the matter in time," he told Clarkson.[38]

Likewise that summer, Harrison named the 72-year-old Negro leader Frederick Douglass[39] as U.S. Resident Minister and Consul General to Haiti. It was traditional Republican policy to reward a few Negro leaders, as in fact President Rutherford B. Hayes had done. Harrison, although no torch-bearer like Clarkson, at least would not abandon the Negro.[40]

[37] James S. Clarkson to Henry Lincoln Johnson, June 22, 1912, Clarkson MSS. (Library of Congress), Box 4. Johnson was a Georgia Negro and a delegate to the Republican convention of 1912. The numbers given in the text are Clarkson's own.

[38] The basic source for the Cuney episode is Vincent P. De Santis, *Republicans Face the Southern Question*, pp. 223–24, and n. 116. This in turn is based on Maud Cuney Hare, *Norris Wright Cuney, A Tribune of the Black People*, pp. 120–22; Huntsville (Alabama) *Gazette;* April 13, 1889; New Orleans *Weekly Pelican*, April 13, 1889. Northern Negro Republicans petitioned strongly for equal recognition at the hands of the Harrison Administration, for example, J. M. Townsend to E. W. Halford, July 31, 1889, (L.C.), Vol. 83.

[39] To Douglass was attributed the oft-repeated warning: "The Republican party is the ship; all else is the sea." See Henry Lee Moon, *Balance of Power: The Negro Vote*, p. 68. Also Stanley P. Hirshson, *Farewell to the Bloody Shirt*, p. 122.

[40] De Santis, *op. cit.*, p. 223, observes: "Harrison continued to carry out the traditional Republican policy of rewarding a few Negro leaders. . . . Names like Bruce, Smalls, Douglass, Lynch . . . which had appeared in Hayes' appointment list reappeared on Harrison's."

CHAPTER VII

A Vacation With Politics

INVITATIONS here and there—to the unoccupied cottage of Mrs. Ulysses S. Grant at Long Branch, New Jersey, to John Wanamaker's place at Cape May, and to the Newport mansion of George P. Wetmore, onetime Rhode Island governor—failed to sway Harrison from a decision to take his family to Deer Park in western Maryland for the summer. This was an agreeable mountain retreat developed by the West Virginia millionaire Henry G. Davis with the help of his son-in-law and business partner, Stephen B. Elkins. Industrial and political leaders of both parties knew the place, and Harrison knew it particularly well, since it was at a party conclave there that he had inherited the mantle of G.O.P. political leadership from James G. Blaine.[1] The Harrisons did enjoy the surf and the sea breezes at the Wanamaker cottage at Cape May one June weekend,[2] but ex-Senator Davis's offer of a sizable cottage was felt to be the best as well as the least expensive.

Harrison accepted in absentia honorary degrees of doctor of laws conferred by Princeton University and by Miami University in Ohio. "The wearing of decorations, either as an attachment to my name or person, is not to my taste, but this is one that will not require use to keep it from decay," he notified President E. R. Graven of Princeton.[3] A Fourth of July celebration organized by Henry G. Bowen, editor of the influential *Independent,* called him to Woodstock, Connecticut, in company with Interior Secretary Noble,

1 Oscar D. Lambert, *Stephen Benton Elkins,* pp. 103–4; Allan Nevins, *Grover Cleveland,* p. 305; Harry J. Sievers, *Benjamin Harrison: Hoosier Statesman,* pp. 200, 309, 317; *Journal,* July 25, 1889.

2 *Journal,* June 23, 1889. The Presidential family enjoyed a standing invitation from Postmaster General Wanamaker to use his Cape May cottage.

3 Harrison to Rev. E. R. Graven, D.D., June 28, 1889, (L.C.), Vol. 80. Princeton honored the President on June 19, 1889, and Miami conferred its degree one week later.

Navy Secretary Tracy, and Supreme Court Justice Samuel F. Miller. It was pointed out that President Garfield had visited the place on July 4, 1881, and that a good number of important party men would be Bowen's guests. Indeed, Senators Joseph Hawley and Orville Platt, and Governor Morgan G. Bulkeley of Connecticut climbed aboard the train along the way, as well as the four congressmen from that State. Congressman Thomas B. Reed of Maine, candidate for Speaker of the House, was prominent among the welcoming party, and Harrison was seen in earnest conversation with him that evening.

Harrison planted a liberty tree during the formal 4th of July program the next day. The Presidential tour then took him into Rhode Island, where a state election would be held that fall, and the return trip was made from Newport aboard the U.S.S. *Despatch* via Long Island Sound.[4] An inspection of the Brooklyn Navy Yard occupied Harrison and Tracy for part of the next day. Some big warships were being built—the largest then in the world—as the nucleus of a modern U.S. Navy. The Cleveland Administration had not progressed beyond the building of cruisers, none above 5,000 tons.

At Deer Park, the twelve-room villa looked, according to the Indianapolis *Journal,* "like a Swiss chalet, with . . . a pointed red roof and deep verandas . . . sitting midway on an upland . . . and behind a high hill bearing a dense growth of oaks." Mrs. Harrison organized the downstairs for the immediate family, and designated the garret—four rooms—as servants' quarters. The necessary household furnishings and a two-seated surrey had been shipped from Indianapolis. Harrison's study, "the presidential office," as Carrie Harrison called it, faced east and commanded a sweeping view of the Allegheny Range. Mrs. Harrison sought Halford's help in preparing rod and reel equipment for use, since reports had it that the Youghiogheny River was harboring three-pound trout.[5] Once her chores were completed, the First Lady devoted herself to palette and brush until her husband could escape Washington, which he found very oppressive in early July, when the weather was at its worst.

4 New York *Sun,* July 2, 3, 6, 7, 1889; *Journal,* July 4, 1889. Beyond the fact that Blaine and future House Speaker Reed had urged him to stop in Rhode Island, the President, who held membership in the Society of Cincinnati, was to be honored by that state's chapter (Nathan Greene to Benjamin Harrison, July 5, 1889, (L.C.), Vol. 81).

5 *Journal,* July 6, 17, 18, 21, 22, 23, 27, 28, 31, 1889, featured detailed stories on all activities at Deer Park.

By mid-month Harrison joined the family for a few days, returned to Washington for a Cabinet meeting, and then decided that any further conferences should be held at Deer Park. After only a few days, the President assured Secretary Blaine, then at Bar Harbor, Maine: "I am much more comfortable here than in Washington and am getting a good deal of rest. . . . The morning hours I have been giving to work upon some matters that required leisure for continuous thought."[6]

The only immediate member of the family absent from Deer Park was Russell Harrison. Then on a European tour where he was flying high, dining with queens and princes, he relied upon his mother to keep him informed.[7] If Russell had access to American newspapers, he would have learned that each day for hours Baby McKee exercised his rather rotund grandfather. In the absence of a Presbyterian church, Harrison attended Sunday services in a tiny Gothic chapel where he listened to Methodist, Episcopalian, and Presbyterian ministers. Beyond the regular outdoor diversions of walking, carriage riding, hunting, and fishing, the President frequented the bowling alley connected with the nearby hotel, losing to Attorney General Miller at billiards, and to Private Secretary Halford at tenpins. Even the discovery of a "four leaved clover" brought him no luck.[8] On July 30th, he sat at a dinner given by ex-Senator Davis. Among the invited guests were James Cardinal Gibbons, Treasury Secretary Windom, and Stephen B. Elkins. This was the first time that the President and the Cardinal had met, and it marked the beginning of cordial relations which lasted through the years.[9]

Harrison had promised Secretary of State Blaine that he would visit him in August after stopping at the White House en route. As

---

6 Harrison to Blaine, July 9, 1889, cited in A. T. Volwiler (ed.), *Correspondence Between Harrison and Blaine*, pp. 66–67; also Harrison to Blaine, July 26, 1889, Blaine MSS., Vol. 3.

7 Caroline S. Harrison to Russell Harrison, July 27, 1889, R. B. Harrison MSS. By courtesy of the Vigo County Historical Society the author had access to these papers in Terre Haute. Since that time they have been transferred to the archives of Indiana University at Bloomington.

8 *Journal*, July 17, 1889.

9 Harry J. Sievers, "The Catholic Indian School Issue and the Presidential Election of 1892," *Catholic Historical Review*, XXXVIII, No. 2 (July 1952), 144–45, 146, 150. For a description of the relationship between President Harrison and Cardinal Gibbons see John Tracy Ellis, *The Life of James Cardinal Gibbons, Archbishop of Baltimore*, I, 373–74; II, 390–93.

the President stepped from the train at the B.&O. depot, flanked by Halford and Windom, he appeared healthy and sunburned.[10] He had to meet Civil Service Commissioner Roosevelt, who had been seething over the retention of Postmaster Paul at Milwaukee after the Commission's critical report had been filed. Roosevelt's reaction sizzled through the mails to Henry Cabot Lodge:

I do wish the President would give me a little active, if only verbal encouragement; it is a dead weight to stagger under, without a particle of sympathy from any of our leaders here, except old Proctor. I am a little weary over the case of the Milwaukee postmaster; he has a strong pull, and the President has slumbered on his case over a week; if he is not dismissed, as we recommend, it will be a black eye for the Commission, and practically an announcement that hereafter no man need fear dismissal for violating the law; for if Paul has not violated it, then it can by no possibility be violated.[11]

In the same post Roosevelt wrote Secretary Halford at Deer Park. Labeling Postmaster Paul a "liar," he begged for an invitation to visit Deer Park, but was advised that the President would see him at the White House on August 1st.[12] Roosevelt was grateful for that much, although unconvinced that Harrison would ever carry a big stick. He replied to his friend Lodge:

Today I caught a glimpse of the President, and repeated to him the parable of the backwoodsman and the bear. You remember that the prayer of the backwoodsman was "Oh Lord, help me kill that bar; and if you don't help me, Oh Lord, don't help the bar." Hitherto I have been perfectly contented if the President would preserve an impartial neutrality between me and the bear, but now, as regards Postmaster Paul of Milwaukee, the President *must* help somebody, and I hope it won't be the bear. I guess he'll stand by us all right; but the old fellow always wants to half-do a thing.[13]

Actually, Harrison had heard him out without indicating his final decision. Within a couple of days Roosevelt headed for the Rockies and his summer vacation, while Harrison began his rail and sea journey to Maine. What the anxious Commissioner did not know was that the President would accept Paul's resignation,

10 *Journal*, August 2, 1889.
11 July 28, 1889, as cited in *Letters*, I, 175. According to Roosevelt the Commission's report on the Paul case was filed on July 18, 1889.
12 Roosevelt to Halford, July 28, 1889, (L.C.), Vol. 83. Halford's immediate answer gratified Roosevelt (Roosevelt to Halford, July 30, 1889, (L.C.), Vol. 83).
13 August 1, 1889, *Letters*, I, 182. It should be noted that Lodge, who was to be Blaine's house guest during Harrison's sojourn in Maine, was expected to press the issue both with the President and with Private Secretary Halford.

notifying him that if he had not resigned, he would soon have been removed.[14]

Political necessity, coupled with a concern for party unity, apparently made the President determined to tour the state of Maine. Despite the discomfort of summer train travel, he would go where he seemed to be wanted. Political pulse-taking was one of Secretary Blaine's several accomplishments, and Harrison had been glad to learn that

I have been profoundly gratified with the general, I may say the universal, tone of approbation which your administration has thus far secured from the great mass of people who have no interest except in just and wise and pure government. I am sure you need not allow yourself to be bothered by the complaints of disappointed self-seekers whether in or out of Congress. You will find the air here very beneficial to you in every respect.[15]

On Blaine's urging him to give as much time to Maine as he could, Harrison decided on a ten day visit, from August 6th to 16th, with some of that time to be spent in New Hampshire. Travel arrangements for the presidential party were handled by Blaine's eldest son, Walker, Solicitor for the State Department. With War Secretary Redfield Proctor, Treasury Secretary William Windom, and E. W. Halford, Harrison entrained for Jersey City and there boarded the Fall River liner *Pilgrim*.[16] After a smooth overnight voyage, he was wined and dined in Boston as the guest of the Commonwealth. Everywhere he received an enthusiastic welcome, and Faneuil Hall was unable to accommodate an overflow crowd of several thousand well-wishers. Other than a few words of thanks here and there, the President made no speeches. As he departed via the Boston and Maine Railroad he was advised that he was riding behind a new 45-ton locomotive christened "Tippecanoe." At Lawrence and Haverhill, at Exeter, New Hampshire, and Berwick,

---

14 The Harrison solution did not please Roosevelt who called it "a half-and-half, boneless policy . . . neither ennobling nor inspiring" (Roosevelt to Lodge, August 8, 1889, *Letters*, I, 185–86).

15 Blaine to Harrison, July 22, 1889, (L.C.), Vol. 83.

16 Harrison's trip "way down East" was featured daily by the *Journal*, and the New York *Sun*, August 7, 8, 9, 10, 1889. Illness of the First Lady's father, Dr. J. W. Scott, coupled with a natural dislike for crowds and extensive travel, caused Mrs. Harrison to cancel plans to accompany the President (Caroline S. Harrison to Mrs. James G. Blaine, July 22, 1889, Blaine MSS., Vol. 3; and Caroline S. Harrison to Russell Harrison, July 27, 1889, Russell Harrison MSS.).

Maine, cheering throngs forced the speeding train to halt, and, at the state line, governors, senators and congressmen relieved each other as official escorts. During the run from Berwick to Portland, Congressman Tom Reed again engaged the President in armchair conversation.[17] At Augusta, the state capital and home town of Blaine, Harrison went to the rear platform and shook many hands, a scene repeated at Waterville and Bangor. As the circuitous 301-mile rail journey came to an end, host James G. Blaine escorted the President aboard the Bar Harbor ferry.

Next morning there began an enjoyable Maine vacation at Stanwood. Buckboard rides, lawn parties, and formal dinners added variety to the everyday picnic fare. Congressman Henry Cabot Lodge escorted the President to various points of interest, and even along that remote shore, Harrison was sought out by former Illinois Congressman John R. Thomas, Senator Eugene Hale of Maine, the Russian Minister, Baron Rosen, and many others, some bearing gifts. Harrison, meanwhile, made several appointments, granted two stays of execution, and talked politics with Lodge. On August 10th, Navy Secretary Tracy arrived aboard the *Despatch* and joined the political circle at Stanwood.

Returning, Harrison inspected the Sewall shipyards at Bath, a suitable place for his public assertion that he would endeavor to promote the rebuilding of the American merchant marine.[18] Harrison quite meant what he said as the nation had lost much of its ocean-carrying trade, which, at various times in its history, had been one of its most prosperous industries. Crossing into New Hampshire, the President visited the busy mill city of Manchester and placid Concord, the state capital.

"These visits," Harrison wrote Secretary Blaine upon his return

17 At each unscheduled stop Harrison was introduced by Reed, and the President shook hands with many of the congressman's constituents. Reed, of course, had hoped to entertain the Harrison party at Portland for a few days but the President had early refused this invitation (Thomas B. Reed to Harrison, July 21, 1889, (L.C.), Vol. 83).

18 New York *Sun*, August 20, 1889. The *Sun* editor interpreted Harrison's remarks as a major policy statement. A week later the Indianapolis *Journal*, in a lengthy editorial entitled "The United States and Foreign Trade," supported the President's intention of expanding the merchant marine. The editor reprinted Harrison's campaign promise in part and added: "But we do not mean to be content with our own market. We should seek to promote closer and more friendly commercial relations with the Central and South American states. . . . We are not to be frightened by the use of the ugly word 'subsidy.' We should pay to American steamship lines a liberal compensation for carrying our mails, instead of turning them over to British tramp steamships."

to Washington, "were accompanied by the most hospitable atten-tions."[19] He obviously enjoyed himself throughout, was always in a good mood, and "really jolly a part of the time," Blaine notified Elkins, who was advised, too, that the President had spoken of him with kindly regard. Blaine added:

I did not lose the opportunity to respond pointedly and expressed once my great regret that you were not included in the Cabinet. His single reply was that residence alone stood in the way—*alone* was quite dis-tinctly expressed. I did not deem it wise to press any views on that phase of the case because it is so soon to be changed and because I thought by not appearing to be urgent, I would have a larger reserve of power at the critical moment of *opportunity.*

Blaine candidly admitted that the President "is a man with whom nothing is gained by argument or urgency at the wrong time. I have learned that lesson well. He is a very true and a very sincere man. He gains in my regard I may say daily—I am satisfied that you will in the end have full reason to know him as your unswerv-ing friend."[20]

On that same day Henry Cabot Lodge had pen in hand. In a candid frame of mind, the young congressman who had spent so much time with Harrison expressed himself to Theodore Roose-velt as "gratified beyond any expectation" by what the President had said concerning the civil service reform movement.

He is thoroughly in favor of the reform. He believes that the offices should be taken out of politics. He thinks that the reform suffered dur-ing Cleveland's rule and his only hope is that we will be able to re-establish and rehabilitate the law, to prove that it is *not* worked so as to let in only candidates of the ruling party and to extend it so far as he can. . . . He also said that he should urge the matter upon Con-gress and ask for increased appropriations. He spoke of you in the highest terms (this is exact) said you were doing excellent work, and that you had shown yourself practical and fully alive to commending the system to the approval of the country.

Lodge continued his confidential note with observations that may not have been pleasing. The President's only criticism, said he, was this: "I wish he [Roosevelt] would not have so many

---

19 Harrison to James G. Blaine, August 16, 1889, as cited in Volwiler, *op. cit.,* p. 74. The *Journal,* August 16, 1889, reprinted Harrison's speeches to the New Hampshire legislature, to a large assembly of the citizens, and to a local G.A.R. group.

20 James G. Blaine to Stephen B. Elkins, August 15, 1889, Elkins MSS.

interviews. Actions speak better and are sufficient." With further
food for reflection Lodge continued:

I have given you the substance just as it was precisely. He has the
idea that the reform has been discredited and needs to be carefully
commended to the country by wise execution to show that it is reasonable and honest and not hypocritical and fanatical. His dread is
lest such opposition should be raised as would defeat the reform which
he rightly thinks would be a great misfortune to him and the party. . . .
You are fighting the evil of patronage hand to hand and know all
about it but I am sure the President means to stand by you and you
must not be impatient if he does not move as fast as you would like.
The cry of the Spoilsmen is ever in his ears and seems more important
than it is but he feels that he is helpless to do anything unless he keeps
his party together and therefore moves cautiously. I think all is going
well. Even our Civil Service *Record* begins to give Harrison credit.[21]

This letter showed Roosevelt that he was appreciated, and it may
have lent him some stability of mind. At least he would have no
further quarrel with the President.

As for newspaper gossip of an estrangement between the President and the Secretary of State, nothing was farther from the
truth.[22] In mutually cordial letters of warm appreciation, both
written on August 16th, Harrison was concerned lest he had not
thanked the Blaines sufficiently; while the Secretary styled the
President's journey to New England a "triumphal progress." After
commenting on the popular feeling for Harrison in New England,
Blaine concluded:

Your visit—which I hope may have yielded you some personal pleasure
and given you a slight recreation—has, I am very sure, strengthened the

---

21 Lodge to Roosevelt, August 15, 1889, Lodge MSS. Lodge, who had found the week
at Bar Harbor "very interesting and amusing," fully explained to his more impetuous friend the resignation of Milwaukee Postmaster Paul. He confided that Harrison's action "was entirely sufficient as it expressly endorsed your action and committed the President to its support." Lodge, moreover, chided Roosevelt for prema-
turely concluding that Harrison had followed a half-and-half and boneless policy.
The long letter concluded with the judgment that Secretary Halford was "a gentleman and a good fellow . . . thoroughly honest. He is also entirely serious on the
matter of civil service although he may not be as radical as you and I." For a typed
carbon of this long and important letter, the author is indebted to Professor Edward
A. White of California, who had access to the Lodge MSS. and the Roosevelt
Files (1909–1919).

22 In mid-July, Blaine's resignation as Secretary of State was rumored by the New
York *Herald* and the New York *Sun*. Both papers reported that Blaine's health was
poor but no poorer than the relations between himself and the President. Vehement
denials by other Cabinet members were widely published in the Republican press,
and on July 16, Harrison dismissed the false rumor as "the attempt to create a
sensation." He avowed openly that "there was not the slightest foundation for the
report" (*Journal*, July 17, 1889).

administration by giving to the "plain people" a free opportunity to manifest their profound confidence and esteem for you personally and officially.

Let me thank you for the honor of your visit to my home which gave great gratification in many directions.[23]

Thus, in mid-August, 1889, President Harrison and his official family were at the apex of good understanding and harmony.

23 James G. Blaine to Harrison, August 16, 1889, (L.C.), Vol. 84. A copy of the Harrison to Blaine letter of the same date may be found in Volwiler, *op. cit.*, p. 74. The note was unusually personal and warm.

CHAPTER VIII

The David Terry Case

A s CHIEF EXECUTIVE of a broad country, Harrison would find himself concerned at times with events in the turbulent West. Small wars arose out of collisions between Indians and land-hungry settlers, one ending in the Battle of Wounded Knee in South Dakota, December 29, 1890, an affair Harrison briefly referred to as "very bloody."[1]

More far-reaching and quite as fatal to the chief protagonist at least was the shooting of a former Chief Justice of the California Supreme Court by a U.S. deputy marshal in line of duty. Assigned to guard U.S. Supreme Court Justice Stephen J. Field, then on circuit duty as (until 1891) was the custom, Deputy David Neagle shot and killed David S. Terry at a California railroad station on August 14, 1889.[2]

Neagle's revolver ended the stormy career of a man with blood Attorney General Miller to write the final chapter in the case. David Terry was a venturesome personage of his time, a fighter in the Texas war under Sam Houston, a slayer of a California vigilante in a street melee, and, again, of an anti-slavery U.S. Senator, David S. Broderick, an affair that ended his career on the bench.[3]

1 Harrison to Mrs. H. S. Howell, January 19, 1891, (L.C.), Vol. 118, (Tibbott transcript). "I have followed very closely, and kept a pretty strong hand on the Indian matter. It is a great gratification to know that it has been closed so speedily."

2 *Journal*, August 15, 16, 1889; Carl B. Swisher, *Stephen J. Field: Craftsman of the Law*, p. 321.

3 Terry became Chief Justice of the California Supreme Court in October 1857, after serving as an Associate Justice from 1855 (Professor John S. Goff, University of Southern California, to the author, March 30, 1956. Also see Goff article, "A Letter from Mrs. David S. Terry to the President's Wife," in *Historical Society of Southern California Quarterly*, Vol. XXXIX, No. 3 [September 1957], 211–16). A. E. Wagstaff's *Life of David S. Terry* was authorized by Judge Terry's son. A better documented biography is A. Russell Buchanan's *David S. Terry, Dueling Judge.*

Some years later he would wear the Confederate gray, and he took the center of the stage after the war by becoming attached to a woman of uncertain past who was involved in a resounding legal quarrel over money. The judge who delivered the opinion in the ultimate disposition of the case was Stephen J. Field, who had served with Terry on the California bench prior to his appointment to the U.S. Supreme Court.

The legal quarrel in essence was between Sarah Althea Hill, the onetime mistress and presumptive widow of U.S. Senator William Sharon of Nevada, and the Senator's son and heir. After a series of court battles in which Terry, as an associate counsel for the fair defendant took part, marrying the lady meanwhile, Justice Field read the opinion of himself and two associate judges upholding the charge that the Sharon-Hill marriage papers had been forged.[4] When the defendant Sarah Terry interrupted with: "You have been paid for this decision," she was ordered removed. In the uproar that followed, David Terry stepped between his wife and the marshal, putting his hand inside his coat, and two court attendants forcibly escorted him from the room. One of them, David Neagle, wrested a knife from his grasp, and a pistol was taken from Mrs. Terry's satchel. Husband and wife were sentenced for contempt of court, Terry to six months, Sarah to 30 days in the Alameda County jail.[5]

Seldom had a county jail housed so distinguished a prisoner as a former Chief Justice of the California Supreme Court. The sheriff and his wife did everything possible to make the Terrys comfortable, even surrendering their own beds to the distraught couple. While serving his sentence, Terry was heard to declare that when he got out he'd horsewhip his antagonist, Field. "The earth is not big enough to hide him from me," Terry told his wife, assuring her that no jury "would convict anyone for killing that old villain."[6] Wife Sarah appeared to be of like mind.

As tempers cooled, Terry asked the U.S. Supreme Court for leave to file a petition for a writ of habeas corpus. On September 17, 1888, Justice John M. Harlan, appearing for the Court (Field, of course, excused himself from the case) denied Terry's plea. An

---

4 Oscar T. Shuck, *History of the Bench and Bar in California*, pp. 173–88, has a factual account of the Sharon Will cases.

5 Swisher, *op. cit.*, p. 336, puts Mrs. Terry's jail sentence at three months.

6 *Ibid.*, p. 337.

appeal to President Cleveland for a pardon likewise proved unsuccessful. When a friendly Alameda County sheriff sought to parole Terry for good behavior, Justice Field, it was said, urged that Terry be confined for the full period of six months.

Under the strain of enforced idleness, Terry waxed indiscreet. In lengthy letters sent to the *Political Record,* a nonpartisan weekly in San Francisco, Justice Field was set down as a cowardly gambler who accepted bribes, and other ugly charges were bruited. Both in and, later, out of jail the Terrys continued to utter threats of what they would do to Justice Field when he returned to California on circuit duty. Somewhat alarmed, Field's friends in Congress tried to dissuade him from making the trip west in the summer of 1889.[7] Field, who insisted on going, put on a brave front:

I cannot and will not allow threats of personal violence to deter me from the regular performance of my judicial duties at the times and places fixed by law. As a judge of the highest court in the country, I should be ashamed to look any man in the face if I allowed a ruffian, by threats against my person, to keep me from holding the regular courts in my circuit.[8]

President Harrison and Attorney General Miller soon found themselves discussing the situation because of "convincing" evidence of threatened violence against Field. Miller was advised to warn the U.S. marshal for the northern district of California "to exercise unusual caution . . . for the protection of his honor, Justice Field, or whoever. . . ."; and it was Harrison's mind too that "no effort on the part of the government shall be spared to make them feel entirely safe and free from anxiety in the discharge of their duties."[9]

On the Coast, it was decided that deputies appointed to protect the federal judges should be strangers to the Terrys; Harrison and Miller agreed. U.S. Marshal John G. Franks then engaged David Neagle, who was short, strong, and quick on the draw, for $5 a day. But, as we have seen, the previous September Neagle was one who had helped escort Terry from the courtroom and to disarm him.

7 Sister Maria Margaret Quinn, C.S.J., "William Henry Harrison Miller," (unpublished Ph.D. dissertation, Catholic University of America, 1965). pp. 126-28.

8 G. C. Gorham, *Attempted Assassination of Justice Field,* pp. 74-75, as cited by Swisher, *op. cit.,* p. 343.

9 A copy of Miller's letter of instruction, dated April 17, 1889, may be found in the *Journal,* September 6, 1889. Also in the National Archives, Miller to John Franks, April 27, 1889, Department of Justice, Incoming Correspondence File 8165-88.

Although it is doubtful that Neagle *was* remembered,[10] newspapers pictured it as a collision course. Terry was reported as saying: "The Supreme Court has reversed its own decision in the Sharon case and made my wife out a strumpet. What can a person do in the face of the Sharon millions? It is infamous." Justice Field was portrayed as self-confident almost to the point of being offensive and "sometimes hot-tempered and vindictive."[11]

Deputy David Neagle met Justice and Mrs. Field and party at Reno, and safely escorted them to San Francisco. Field refused to carry a gun, explaining:

I will not carry arms, for when it is known that judges of our courts are compelled to arm themselves against assaults in consequence of their judicial action it will be time to dissolve the courts, consider the government a failure, and let society lapse into barbarism.[12]

On August 13th the party boarded a sleeper bound for Los Angeles where Field was to hold court. Alert to danger at Fresno, where the Terrys resided, Deputy Neagle had the porter awaken him before the train reached the station. When he saw both the Terrys climb aboard he told Field, who took the news rather calmly. Further on at Lathrop, a breakfast stop, Field decided to eat in the station restaurant rather than in the dining car. The Terrys entered later, and on catching a glimpse of Field, Mrs. Terry hurriedly left.

The brooding Terry, coming up from behind, struck the Justice twice about the head. Neagle leaped to his feet crying, "Stop that, I am an United States officer!" and believing Terry might be reaching for his knife, the deputy quickly fired twice.[13] The man slumped to the floor as his wife, who came running, threw herself upon his limp body, crying that "they" had killed her only friend. Justice Field was hurried back to his Pullman compartment and a guard was placed at the door.

10 Swisher, *op. cit.*, p. 345, who cites the correspondence *In re Neagle*, 135 U.S. 1.

11 Wagstaff, *op. cit.*, pp. 314–15, as cited by Swisher, *op. cit.*, p. 346; Willard L. King, *Melville Weston Fuller*, pp. 127–28.

12 Gorham, *op. cit.*, p. 86.

13 In a statement made in San Francisco Federal Court three weeks later (September 6, 1889), Neagle testified: "I believe Terry would have cut me to pieces, and perhaps Judge Field, if I had not acted promptly. He looked like a maddened giant. I knew he had always carried a knife and I believe that he had one on him then. I knew him to be a giant in strength, and proposed to take no chances with him. For that reason I held my pistol in both hands so that he would not take it away from me" (*Journal*, September 7, 1889).

Reports of the affair at Lathrop, which made black headlines all over the country, reached President Harrison on his way to Washington from Bar Harbor. Solicitor General Chapman inquired of Attorney General Miller, then on vacation in Indianapolis, as to how the government might handle the defense of Deputy Neagle, then in jail at Stockton.[14]

On Saturday, August 17th, Harrison and Miller conferred at Deer Park. Miller thereafter instructed U.S. District Attorney Carey of California to defend the unhappy prisoner. There began an eight month battle between federal and state courts for jurisdiction. Ultimately the U.S. Supreme Court would decide.

The tactics of Mrs. Terry put the government on the defensive for the moment; soon she would bring Mrs. Harrison in. Although she wanted both Field and Neagle lynched, the fair Sarah had to be content with a formal complaint charging them with murder.[15] Field then obtained a writ of habeas corpus to protect Neagle, who was spirited from Stockton to San Francisco. Arrested and detained on Mrs. Terry's testimony, Field was released on his own recognizance, with a bond fixed at $5,000. Mrs. Terry then took her appeal to Mrs. Benjamin Harrison.

"My Dear Madam." In a barely legible scrawl, the First Lady could sense another's distress. "I believe," Sarah began,

you are a woman with all the attributes that go to make up a sober good woman with a woman's heart—and being so I ask you to take up my great trouble to the extent of seeing that this persecution of me is stopped—have your husband remove the District Attorney and Marshal Franks and fill their places with Republican gentlemen—these men now in office got their positions through Judge Field and do anything he may desire—they have murdered my husband in cold blood.

After explaining how Field had been a courtroom enemy, Sarah Terry continued,

I at the time the 3 of last September was three months towards being a mother—and when I heard that Judge so slander me—I thinking of my little unborn—became excited and Judge Field ordered me dragged from the court room . . . in dragging me from the room I was injured [so] that I lost my child—and Judge Field ordered that I should not have the privilege of a hospital. . . .

14 Chapman to Miller, August 16, 1889, Ex. and Cong. Letterbook V, 225 N.A.

15 Swisher, op. cit., pp. 349–50. Mrs. Terry insisted that Field had hired Neagle to shoot Terry. "If my husband had killed Justice Field the crowd would have lynched him . . . and now . . . you will not help me punish the murderers of my husband."

It was a rather protracted outburst yet the petitioner had few friends so perhaps she could make one. . . .

Marshal Franks says Attorney General Miller ordered that he have the secret service men follow us and hound us around—and now that my husband is murdered—they today not being satisfied with what they have done—dragged me from a sick bed into court. . . . If Miller thought it necessary to have Marshals protect Field—why did he not have the fact published and dress the Marshal in officers clothes—instead of dressing him like a dude.

Declaring that she and her husband had been "persecuted something terrible," Sarah Terry begged Mrs. Harrison to ask the President to act. "He can order this persecution stopped and allow me to have peace with my dead. I put this matter in your hands—and as a woman to a woman I ask you to come to my aid—and stop this awful persecution."[16]

A U.S. Circuit Court decision that Neagle, in acting as a federal officer (and as engaged by a U.S. marshal), was not liable under state law resulted in his discharge. The state of California appealed on the ground that there was no federal law which could be applied. Neagle, therefore, was subject to trial in the state court.[17]

Prior to the arguments before the U.S. Supreme Court, Harrison brought the Terry-Field-Neagle case to the attention of Congress. He anticipated the legal quibble with a recommendation that

. . . more definite provision be made by law, not only for the protection of federal officers, but for a full trial of such cases in the United States Courts. In recommending such legislation I do not at all impeach either the general adequacy of the provision made by the State laws for the protection of all citizens or the general good disposition of those charged with execution of such laws to give protection to the officers of the United States. The duty of protecting its officers, as such, and of punishing them who assault them on account of their official acts, should not be devolved expressly or by acquiescence upon the local authorities.[18]

16 Marthena Harrison Williams, granddaughter of President Harrison, loaned the writer Mrs. Terry's undated letter to Mrs. Harrison. John S. Goff, *art cit.*, p. 216, n. 2, suggests that it was written between August 14 and September 3, 1889.

17 Annual Report of the Attorney General, 1889, XIV, as cited by Sr. Maria Margaret Quinn, pp. 130–31. See also U.S. Rev. Statutes, 753. As early as August 16, the *Journal* argued: "This is one of those cases in which the government . . . is justified in exercising a power not granted in the Constitution [which] . . . nowhere provides for the protection of Justices of the Supreme Court, either in the performance of their duty, or from bodily danger on account of such performance. . . . There is a higher law than constitutions, and even courts will recognize the higher law when necessary."

18 *Public Papers and Addresses of Benjamin Harrison*, p. 47. Harrison's first annual message, December 3, 1889, is on pp. 36–65.

Harrison sought to strengthen the Justice Department by appointing Judge William Howard Taft of the Ohio Superior Court as Solicitor General. An able jurist in his own right, Taft backed Attorney General Miller's brief for the original release of Neagle on habeas corpus.[19] Two eminent New York lawyers, Joseph H. Choate and James A. Carter, also submitted a brief in behalf of Neagle. No one could doubt that the President and the Justice Department were exerting every effort to protect Neagle.[20]

Arguing before the Supreme Court and in the presence of an audience "composed . . . chiefly of lawyers of national reputation," Attorney General Miller maintained that the power of self-preservation, so utterly essential to the existence of government, made it mandatory for the Executive branch to protect the Judicial. President Harrison's views on the necessity of safeguarding the judiciary were well known. If judges were to be protected at all, Miller argued, the Executive must employ the services of federal marshals. Further, since the national government and the obligations it imposed were supreme, any supposed right or claim of state contravening such an obligation must yield. No state court could question Neagle for official conduct as a federal officer. Miller's arguments won high praise,[21] and as one historian wrote: "No case within the past ten years has attracted more attention."[22]

A White House dinner for the Supreme Court Justices and their wives was given on April 8, 1890, while decision in the case was still pending, and it could be asked whether on that occasion any views were influenced.[23] In any event, six days later, Justice Samuel Miller read a majority opinion which strikingly resembled Attorney General Miller's argument. While admitting that Deputy Marshal Neagle's assignment was not traceable to any definite statutory

19 William Howard Taft to Alphonso Taft, February 26, 1890, Taft Papers (family correspondence).

20 Gherhardi Davis to J. C. Bancroft Davis, January 20, 1890, in J. C. B. Davis MSS. The Chicago *Inter-Ocean*, as cited in the Indianapolis *Journal*, August 16, 1889, held the opinion that "no irate lawyer shall be able to intimidate the court."

21 Horace Speed to Harrison, January 25, 1893, (L.C.), Vol. 155. Speed was present in the Supreme Court when the Neagle case was argued. See also *In re Neagle*, 135 U.S. 1, 16 (1889); Sr. Maria Margaret Quinn, pp. 132–37.

22 Hampton Carson, *Supreme Court of the United States*, II, 550; also Grosvenor Lowry to J. C. B. Davis, March 27, 1890, in J. C. B. Davis MSS.

23 Three regular State dinners were given during the winter. First the Cabinet, then the diplomatic corps, and then the Supreme Court Justices were entertained (Benjamin Harrison, "The Social Life of the President," *Ladies' Home Journal*, XIV, No. 5 [April 1897], 3–4.

provision, the majority decision held that the order to protect Justice Field from anticipated violence—an order given with the consent of President Harrison—was merely an expression of the Chief Executive's duty to "take care that the laws be faithfully executed." It sustained the President as the principal conservator of "the peace of the United States."[24] Neagle therefore was set free without trial.

Chief Justice Melville Fuller, a Maine man, had joined with Justice Lucius Quintus Cincinnatus Lamar, a states rights Southerner, in dissenting from the majority opinion, Justice Field abstaining. Both justices had been appointed to the Court by President Cleveland, a Democrat, and both leaned toward a strict construction of the Constitution. It was left to them, therefore, to defend a state's juridical rights against presumed federal encroachment. The absence of a federal law authorizing a trial for murder was cited.[25]

Public opinion, which was almost unanimous in its approval of Neagle's action, supported the six justices of the majority opinion. An able critic has judged that the Neagle decision was the broadest interpretation, up to that time, of the implied powers of the national government under the Constitution,[26] and that Harrison had acted strongly to "preserve the peace of the United States."

Although Justice Field had taken no part in the decision, his associates were aware of his deep concern over the outcome. He had given Deputy Neagle a gold watch inscribed: "Stephen J. Field to David Neagle, as a token of appreciation of his courage and fidelity to duty under circumstances of great peril at Lathrop, California, on the fourteenth day of August, 1889."[27] An elegant social event was the celebration dinner given by Attorney General and Mrs. Miller for the President and Mrs. Harrison to which most of the Cabinet members and their wives were invited. Whatever may or may not have been said, possibly some thought was given the pitiable Sarah Terry. There could have been no one to speak for the woman caught in the grinding mills of the law. Even

---

24 *In re Neagle*, 133 U.S. 1, 59 (1890). Accounts may also be found in the New York *Times*, April 15, 1890; and in Charles Fairman, *Mr. Justice Miller*, p. 307.

25 Cleveland wrote Fuller, April 16, 1890: "I am very submissive to your court but I dont believe in that doctrine either" (Wallace Papers as cited by King, *op. cit.*, pp. 141, 360).

26 Charles Warren, *Supreme Court in United States History*, II, 697.

27 King, *op. cit.*, p. 141.

when she asked that room for her grave be left by that of her husband a cold voice was heard: "There is a general sentiment that she should not permit that valuable ground to remain unoccupied."[28] Whatever its future occupancy, Sarah Terry, in March 1892, was found insane and committed to the State Asylum at Stockton. For 45 years she lived on with her mental illness, at first acute mania which became chronic. Death finally came on February 14, 1937, and she was buried next to her husband in the Stockton cemetery.

[28] *Journal*, April 16, 1890. The harshest verdict was handed down by the *Journal*, an Administration organ: "Althea Hill Sharon Terry will have a chance to sit down on the back doorstep of her infamous career and wish she had never been born. She has been the devil's chambermaid ever since she was a big girl and has given the old fellow a great many points in her life. She will probably continue in the same capacity as long as she lives and receive at least the compensation she deserves" *(ibid.,* August 19).

CHAPTER IX

Presidential Strategy and the First Pan-American Conference

W HEN HARRISON drove up to the White House on Friday afternoon, August 16th, after an absence of nearly two weeks,[1] he could count more perhaps on the future welfare of the nation as a whole than on perfect harmony within his official family. He had not assumed the presidency without his own opinions on foreign policy;[2] for, unlike Arthur and Cleveland, he had determined to do more about Latin America. By mid-August, everyone close to him knew that he would seek close economic ties with the emancipated republics to the south. Fully prepared to jettison isolation as an instrument of national policy, he had entrusted the State portfolio to Blaine, a long-time advocate of hemispheric solidarity.[3] After consulting Navy Secretary Tracy and Attorney General Miller,[4] Harrison was ready to take the first step in nearly a decade toward improving western hemispheric cooperation and understanding.

Thus a new policy for the Americas was carefully formulated during the summer of 1889, though it was camouflaged by an outward emphasis on vacation jaunts, ceremonial speeches, social tri-

---

[1] *Journal*, August 17, 1889.

[2] Ernest R. May, *Imperial Democracy*, p. 17, overlooks the Blaine-Harrison agreement on Latin-American affairs between January and August, 1889.

[3] Russell Henry Bastert, "James G. Blaine and the Origins of the First International Conference of American States" (unpublished Ph. D. thesis, Yale Univ., 1952), pp. ii-v; Alice Felt Tyler, *Foreign Policy of James G. Blaine*, pp. 166–74.

[4] Walter Russell Herrick, Jr., "General Tracy's Navy" (unpublished Ph. D. thesis, Univ. of Virginia, 1962), pp. iii–iv. See also Herrick's, *The American Naval Revolution*, pp. 10–11.

umphs, and party bickerings.[5] The new inter-American system envisioned would be based on improved trade, diplomacy, and mutual defense.

In recent years, plans for an international American congress had been introduced in Washington three times in Arthur's Administration and twice in Cleveland's, but all were killed in committee. Finally, in May 1888, a bill which became law without Cleveland's signature asked the President "to invite the several governments of the Republics of Mexico, Central and South America, Haiti and Santo Domingo, and the Empire of Brazil" to meet in Washington in 1889.[6] On instructions from Cleveland, Secretary of State Bayard invited eighteen countries to an inter-American conference which could properly consider and discuss all "measures that shall tend to preserve the peace and promote the prosperity of the several American States."[7]

Although some leaders feared that the conference could result only in the political and commercial ascendancy of the United States in this hemisphere, only Santo Domingo refused outright, while revolution-ridden Haiti delayed acceptance of the invitation.[8] October 2, 1889 was chosen as the opening day for the Congress.

While arrangements were in progress south of the border, the presidential campaign of 1888 had shifted into high gear. The Democrats had failed to mention South America in their platform, but a Republican plank pledged trade expansion "with our Pacific territory, with South America, and with the islands and further coasts of the Pacific ocean."[9] By his letter of acceptance, nominee Harrison not only promised a foreign policy characterized "by friendship and respect . . . dignity and firmness," but he also spe-

---

[5] Only an occasional article on the International American Conference interrupted the steady flow of editorials and news stories on the President's day-by-day activity. See Benjamin Harrison Papers (Presidential Papers Microfilm), Series 16, Scrapbooks 1–9.

[6] Tyler, op. cit., pp. 174–75; Appleton's Annual Cyclopedia . . . 1889, p. 440.

[7] James W. Gantenbein (ed.), The Evolution of Our Latin-American Policy, pp. 49–52, summarizes eight points of Bayard's invitation, which was dated July 13, 1888.

[8] Ibid., p. 358. The Mexican Minister said that "it was apprehended by some . . . that the object of the United States in convening the conference was to obtain decided political and commercial advantages. . . ." (Matías Romero, "The Pan American Conference," North American Review, CLI, No. 406:3 [September 1890], 356).

[9] Appleton's Annual Cyclopedia . . . 1888, p. 776–77, contains the full text of the platform.

cifically pledged the cultivation and extension of "diplomatic and commercial relations with the Central and South American States."[10] This bit of campaign oratory raised a question in the minds of citizens of South America and overseas as well. If elected, would Harrison lead a commercial crusade to break British and European monopoly of trade with South America?

Six weeks before his Inauguration, Harrison told Blaine that the new Administration meant to win Latin confidence "by deserving it."[11] Blaine, who, "more than any other statesman, personified the momentous change of his nation's attitude toward Latin America,"[12] quite agreed that growing industrial production made expansion into foreign markets a necessity. Both entertained high hopes for the 1889 conference. There was talk of a customs union, inter-American rail and steamship lines, trademark and copyright laws, and arbitration treaties.[13]

In his inaugural address Harrison had asked for an enlarged merchant marine that would guarantee a greatly increased flow of national goods to foreign markets. Only by the establishment of American shipping lines, along with reliable and rapid means of communication, could expanded trade with South America be realized. While bent on acquiring strategic bases in the Caribbean, Harrison sought to allay Latin fears of U.S. designs. Coercion, he said, would not be used in obtaining coaling stations or other trading privileges.[14] This policy certainly had Blaine's support.[15]

10 Letter of Acceptance, September 11, 1888, *Public Papers and Addresses of Benjamin Harrison*, p. 7.

11 Harrison to Blaine, January 17, 1889, as cited in Volwiler (ed.), *Correspondence Between Harrison and Blaine*, p. 44.

12 Walter La Feber, *The New Empire: An Interpretation of American Expansion 1860–1898*, p. 106. This volume, winner of the 1962 Beveridge Award of the American Historical Association, is an excellent interpretation of America's emergence as a world power during the Harrison era.

13 Tyler, *op. cit.*, p. 176. Harrison and Blaine adopted the eight-point program outlined in Bayard's invitation. The conference would be "consultative and recommendatory only."

14 *Public Papers and Addresses of Benjamin Harrison*, pp. 31, 33.

15 Blaine regarded it as "one of its highest duties" that the United States enlarge the area of its foreign trade. He supported the Republican belief that "under the beneficent policy of protection we have developed a volume of manufactures, which in many departments, overruns the demands of the home market." In 1890 he concluded: "Our great demand is expansion. I mean expansion of trade with countries where we can find profitable exchanges." For complete text of Blaine's Waterville speech, see the New York *Tribune*, August 30, 1890.

Harrison and Blaine considered the task of choosing ten U.S. commissioners to attend the Pan-American congress to be a matter of prime importance. Political adherents, convinced that the President had determined to shape a new inter-American policy,[16] flooded Washington with letters or came in person to voice a conviction that the first business of the Pan-American Conference was to be business.[17] Bankers, shippers, and industrialists led the way in suggesting men whose experience in business, coupled with some diplomatic skill, would guarantee "the cooperation of the nations of the American continent in the establishment of an American continental policy."[18]

Harrison's problem, of course, was to select delegates from various areas who had high standing in business. Presumably, most would be gifted with some diplomatic insight. He well realized the necessity of appointing men with reputations for personal integrity, so that self-interest would be subordinated.

Although many felt that personal friendship and party politics would influence Harrison's choice, which to some extent was true, he let it be known that only a bipartisan group could succeed in making the conference run smoothly,[19] and by July had the acceptances of eight commissioners. Andrew Carnegie, who boasted that "American steel production had passed Great Britain's and stood first in the world," headed the list, which also included two New England Republicans, Cornelius Newton Bliss and Thomas Jefferson Coolidge.[20] Though Bliss had moved to New York City, where he was active in politics, he still remained one of the largest textile mill owners in New England. Coolidge, the Boston financier and merchant, was a king in the cotton-spinning industry and a future director of numerous banks and railroads.[21] Harrison reached out to the West Coast for Morris M. Estee, whose law firm had helped

---

[16] Harrison's associate, Murat Halstead, had assured Blaine's friends of this determination prior to the Inauguration. (See Murat Halstead to Walter William Phelps, February 4, 1889, Reid MSS.). To insure the success of this new foreign policy Halstead had urged Reid's appointment as Navy Secretary and had counseled sending William Evarts as Ambassador to Great Britain.

[17] Bastert, op. cit., p. 431.

[18] Halstead to Phelps, February 4, 1889, Reid MSS.

[19] Particularly significant are the John F. Plummer letters to Harrison, (L.C.), of April 11, 1889 (Vol. 74) and May 16, 1889 (Vol. 76).

[20] Concise Dictionary of American Biography, pp. 144–45 (cited hereafter as the CDAB); Bastert, op. cit., pp. 428–30.

[21] CDAB, on Bliss and Coolidge, pp. 83, 188.

to put a Republican back in the White House.[22] To provide some political balance he named John F. Hanson, a Georgia industrialist and a protective tariff Democrat, and William Henry Trescot, a South Carolina lawyer and onetime Assistant Secretary of State, who had Blaine's confidence, as well as actual knowledge of Latin American affairs born of diplomatic work with Mexico, Chile, Bolivia and Peru.[23] Appointments from the Midwest included former U.S. Senator John B. Henderson, who had left Missouri to practice law in Washington, and Clement Studebaker, an Indiana friend who had become the world's largest carriage and wagon manufacturer.[24]

Two others on the list, John R. G. Pitkin of Louisiana and William Pinckney Whyte of Maryland, resigned their commissions to assume other duties. Whyte became the Attorney General of Maryland, while Harrison made Pitkin U.S. Minister to the Argentine Republic.[25]

Harrison and Blaine agreed on William Eleroy Curtis, journalist, traveler, and publicist, as special agent in charge of preparations for the Pan-American Conference.[26] Though not yet forty, Curtis had served on President Arthur's South American Commission, visiting all Latin America, and had published *The Capitals of South America*, a reference book for interested members of the House and Senate. Curtis, who was on good terms with many legation officials in Washington, found himself in a key position to "promote his conviction that in trade with Latin America lay untapped reservoirs of wealth for the United States."[27]

Early in the summer, Curtis opened the Pan-American Conference headquarters at New York's Fifth Avenue Hotel. He corresponded with various boards of trade and chambers of commerce across the nation, collecting much information; furthermore, he

---

22 Harry J. Sievers, *Benjamin Harrison: Hoosier Statesman*, p. 363, details Estee's role as Chairman of the Notification Committee, which came to Indianapolis on July 4, 1888.

23 Bastert, *op. cit.*, p. 429; *National Cyclopedia of American Biography*, XIII, 576–77; *CDAB*, p. 1079.

24 *CDAB*, p. 1028. The original Studebaker company was established at South Bend in 1852.

25 Blaine concurred that he thought it very wise to send Pitkin to the Argentine Republic. (Blaine to Harrison, July 25, 1889, (L.C.), Vol. 83.)

26 *Journal*, July 28, 1889.

27 Bastert, *op. cit.*, pp. 433–35.

laid plans for the South American delegates to visit agricultural and industrial cities before settling down to the work of the Congress. This plan enjoyed Harrison's active support,[28] and Warner P. Sutton, formerly Consul General in Mexico, was sent to help Curtis in New York.

As the summer wore on, statistics and opinions dealing with economic affairs facing the Conference were channeled to the American delegates. For those who wished to read, reports were available on such matters as steamship subsidies, tonnage, import and export tables on Latin America, customs regulations, coinage and precious metals, copyright and patent laws, weights and measures, reciprocity treaties, port charges, extradition, and ship sanitation and quarantine. And the President himself cordially encouraged bankers, merchants, and manufacturers convened at Delmonico's to discuss how they might best promote friendlier relations within the Hemisphere.[29]

Replacements for Pitkin and Whyte had yet to be named when Blaine reminded his chief that "as the Democrats only got three out [of] ten in the original appointments it might be well to give them both these—making the Comm[in] 6 to 4."[30] Among more than a dozen candidates reported as ready to accept, if not scramble for the two vacant posts, Blaine strongly favored David Dudley Field, an able New York lawyer interested in codifying the law of nations, although tinged with the brush of Boss Tweed. Also favored was a onetime New York reform mayor, William R. Grace. But W. R. Grace and Company had commercial and banking offices in most large South American cities, and Grace himself was too largely involved in Chilean and Peruvian affairs to serve as a commissioner.[31] Harrison scuttled both suggestions. The President knew well the inner history of the Grant Administration, which was deeply tainted by self-interest.

Information supplied by Curtis led Harrison to regard more favorably another New Yorker, 50-year-old Charles Ranlett Flint,

[28] Organizations such as the Union League Club and Business Men's Republican Association of New York, whose membership embraced the most prominent shipping interests, enjoyed more influence with Harrison than did the professional politicians. See W. E. Curtis to Halford, August 1, 17, 1889, (L.C.), Vol. 84.

[29] Series 2 of Harrison Papers on Microfilm reveals much national interest in Harrison's attitude toward the Conference.

[30] Blaine to Harrison, July 25, 1889, as cited in Volwiler, *op. cit.*, p. 69.

[31] Grace was known in some quarters as the "pirate of Peru" (Blaine to Harrison, August 25, 1889, *ibid.*, pp. 79–80).

whose shipping business acumen was as strong as his tie with the Democratic Party. Like his father before him, who owned the largest number of sailing vessels engaged in South American commerce, Flint became a leading figure in the Spanish American Commercial Union.[32] Also he had a good political record. As an enterprising Democrat who belonged to the Tilden-Dana protective-tariff wing of the party, Flint had solid Republican backing. When he readily accepted the commission post, business leaders rejoiced, and John F. Plummer advised the President: "I want your administration to have the credit of taking the strong initiative that shall result in what I feel sure is to occur in the future, that of a firm, well-established trade communication between North and South America."[33]

For the tenth delegate Harrison proposed either Henry Gassaway Davis, former U.S. Senator from West Virginia, or Edward A. Burke, a protectionist Democrat from Louisiana who had achieved success and fortune as newspaper owner and as a speculator in real estate.[34] Merchant, lumberman, and railroad-builder Davis, father-in-law of Stephen B. Elkins, obviously had the inside track. Sometime between Harrison's fifty-sixth birthday on August 20th and the gala dinner party given the President at Deer Park by Davis, on August 31st, the appointment was offered.[35] By early September, Davis signified his acceptance and noted the fact, without further comment, in his journal.[36]

Shortly after noonday at the White House on October 2, 1889, the opening social event of the International Congress saw delegates escorted in by a cheerful and happy Blaine, who leaned on

[32] Curtis informed Halford that Flint served on the Board of Directors of the Spanish American Commercial Union, was well connected with several banks, and traded mostly with Brazil and the Argentine Republic by "shipping general merchandise to those countries and bringing back wool and hides."

[33] Plummer to Harrison, August 1, 1889, (L.C.), Vol. 84.

[34] Harrison had some personal acquaintance with Burke as well as with Davis. Both men were Democrats, spoke Spanish, knew well Central and South American affairs, favored protection, believed in subsidizing ships, and had taken great interest in the success of the International American Congress (Harrison to Blaine, August 16, 1889, in Volwiler, *op. cit.*, p. 75).

[35] The Harrison papers reveal that the President appointed Davis and Flint on August 29, 1889, and the press gave the move wide coverage on August 30, the eve of the dinner party tendered the President by H. G. Davis. Guests included Wall Street financiers, merchants, industrialists, and politicians.

[36] Charles N. Pepper, *The Life and Times of Henry Gassaway Davis (1823–1916),* pp. 106–7.

the arm of Minister Matías Romero of Mexico. In the vestibule, a scarlet-uniformed Marine Band gave them a musical salute as they promenaded in pairs with Walker Blaine and Charles Flint of New York ending the procession. After a brief stop in the East Room to examine the presidential portraits, the delegates were greeted by each member of the Cabinet, and at two o'clock President and Mrs. Harrison came downstairs. Wearing a tightly buttoned Prince Albert coat with a Grand Army badge on the lapel, Harrison appeared to be in a mood somewhat thoughtful, if not a little apprehensive.[37]

The national airs of all the countries represented were played as appetites grew keen. During luncheon in the elaborately decorated dining room, informal conversation prevailed until the President indicated that Blaine should now open the first business session, and then excused himself. In an address reported as generally excellent, the Secretary fostered an amicable atmosphere at the outset by saying:

No conference of nations has ever assembled to consider the welfare of territorial possessions so vast and to contemplate the possibilities of a future so great and so inspiring. . . .

We believe that hearty cooperation, based on hearty confidence, will save all American States from the burdens and evils which have long and cruelly afflicted the older nations of the world.

We believe that a spirit of justice, of common equal interest between the American States, will leave no room for an artificial balance of power like unto that which has led to wars abroad and drenched Europe in blood. . . .

We believe that standing armies, beyond those which are needful for public order and the safety of internal administration, should be unknown on both American continents.

We believe that friendship and not force, the spirit of just law and not the violence of the mob, should be the recognized rule of administration between American nations and in American nations.[38]

But since the post of chairman or president of the Congress usually went to the host country, competition immediately arose between John B. Henderson, chairman of the U.S. delegation, and William Henry Trescot of South Carolina, whose long diplomatic

[37] Clipping of October 2, 1889, (L.C.), (Benjamin Harrison Scrapbook Series, Vol. 9). Blaine and Miller wore cutaways, while Rusk and Noble joined the President in wearing the G.A.R. emblem.

[38] James G. Blaine to the First International American Conference, in Gantenbein, op. cit., pp. 54–56.

experience made him the better equipped. Hence a spirit of contention in the American delegation threatened to disrupt the work of the Congress. Harrison, who was notified, passed on word that Blaine be elected—and so he was.[39]

The start of a tour through northern and midwestern industrial areas was the first order of business next day. Escorted by William E. Curtis and military officers familiar with the Spanish and Portuguese tongues, the delegates left Washington by train for West Point. A six weeks' trip of some 6,000 miles was planned, to reveal "our manufactures and our massive and mighty agricultural products, also our military resources in case of war, and to impress them on general principles that the United States is . . . richly worth trading with."[40]

The inspection of New England manufacturing centers took less than a week. Thriving industry impressed the visitors, and they found even more to admire in the many schools in cities and towns. After leaving the East Coast for the country beyond the Alleghenies, the delegates made a Sabbath pause at Niagara Falls. The rapid pace had rather wearied the travelers, who were heard to remark that "it is always better to have a clear and definite idea of a few things than confused notions concerning a great many."[41]

After inspecting the stockyards and grain elevators at Buffalo, the delegates were entertained at Erie, Cleveland, and Detroit, spending many hours at the University of Michigan. Reporters who traveled westward with the delegates noted that the visitors were seeing the real America. As the New York *Herald* observed:

The further West the members of the international conference go the better idea of the country they are obtaining. They were beginning now to see the type of men who have made the country what it is—the busy, pushing, brainy, restless men of resources, who build up cities in a year, so to speak, where before was a wild country. And therefore Uncle Sam's guests are the more deeply impressed with the character of the nation.[42]

---

[39] Romero, *op. cit.*, p. 365, reported that the suggestion regarding Blaine came from Harrison. The Argentine delegation urged technical objections to having a chairman or a president come from outside the ranks of the delegates, and hence absented themselves from the meeting which chose Blaine.

[40] The Worcester *Times*, October 9, 1889, from A. Curtis Wilgus, "James G. Blaine and the Pan-American Movement," *Hispanic American Historical Review*, V (1922), 662–708.

[41] Worcester *Times*, October 9, 1889.

[42] As cited in Boston *Traveller*, October 8, 1889.

At South Bend, Indiana, home of delegate Clem Studebaker, several manufacturers displayed their wares in a large auditorium, a practical idea which eliminated much travel from one plant to another. The itinerary provided for visits to the University of Notre Dame and St. Mary's College nearby, followed by dinner at the Studebaker home. There the South Bend *Tribune* interviewed the delegates, whose festive mood showed them in favor of a Pan-American alliance.[43]

Chicago proved to be the highlight. Besides touring the famous stockyards and the meat-packing plants, the delegates visited the Pullman Company and spent some time in Marshall Field's Department Store. As the tour moved through Wisconsin and Minnesota, with stops at Milwaukee, St. Paul, and Minneapolis, a new *entente cordiale* was developing among the delegates. At a St. Paul banquet, Venezuelan delegate Señor Peraza thanked the people of the United States for their so marked cordiality, for the delegates had "found that the hearts of the American people grow warmer as we travel westward." His remarks reflected western informality, particularly the observation: "In New England we were entertained as honored guests . . . in Wisconsin and Minnesota you receive us as brothers."[44] American newspapers, which speculated on the impressions received by their southern neighbors, could quote the Minneapolis *Tribune* which reported late in October:

First of all, the South American delegates have been impressed with the equal distribution of wealth in the United States as compared with what they have at home. . . . They are impressed with the stability of the buildings here, and think they point to the solidity and stability of the country generally. The public school system was of great interest to them. . . . The fire departments in the large cities have been seen with great interest. . . .[45]

After visiting Sioux City and Omaha, the delegates turned eastward. In Missouri they stopped at Kansas City and St. Louis, and in Illinois were entertained at the capital city of Springfield. Harrison's home city of Indianapolis accorded them a warm welcome on November 1st, and Cincinnati greeted them on election day, impressing them by the orderly procedure at the polls.[46] At Pitts-

43 October 17, 1889.
44 St. Paul *Daily News*, October 24, 1889.
45 October 25, 26, 1889.
46 New York *Tribune*, November 6, 1889.

burgh, Commissioner Andrew Carnegie escorted them through his huge steel mills. As a finale to six weeks on the road, Philadelphia provided a brilliant reception for the delegates and their families at the Union League Club. In the same environs Postmaster General John Wanamaker did double duty as a department store head and as a host close to the Harrison Administration.[47]

Harrison kept a close eye on the progress of the touring delegates. Despite some press opposition at home, and cries of alarm from abroad,[48] the President regarded the movement as a sign of a brighter era for the Western Hemisphere. When a Kansas City industrialist called at the White House en route to Mexico City, where he planned to talk with Mexico's president prior to extending his business there, Harrison assured him of most friendly feelings toward the republics to the south. Mindful of the hostility and fears of nations, he grasped the opportunity to say that

The United States of America were happily situated in one respect in which they differed from the great nations of Europe, namely, in that they had, and could have, no colonizing policies. . . . if there ever had been in the past a tendency on the part of the Americans to look with jealousy or unfriendly envy upon the possessions of their neighbors to the South that tendency had long ago passed away.[49]

Nor did the President disguise the fact that "the temper exhibited by the American people toward the present Conference had greatly gratified him and seemed to him to assure a most cordial feeling on the part of our country toward the deliberations of the Conference." Although the business sessions of the Pan-American meeting were still a week away, he forecast "a greater intimacy with our neighbors at [sic] the South," and left no doubt in the

---

47 Harrison regretfully had to decline an invitation to attend the Union League Club's dinner held on November 11. See William C. Houston to Harrison, November 2, 1889, Harrison Papers on Microfilm, Series 2.

48 Wilgus, art. cit., pp. 701–8, details the opinions of both antagonistic and sympathetic newspapers. The foreign press, on the whole, was hostile to the idea of the Congress. Typical was the Diritto of Rome (September 30, 1889) which saw two dangers arising from the All-American Congress, "namely, the hegemony of the Anglo-Saxon over the Latin race, and a coalition of all the states of America against the products of Europe." The New York Nation of April 24, 1890 would assert that "the real object was to enable a few steamship owners to get their hands into the U.S. Treasury."

49 Edward M. Shepard to Halford, November 8, 1889, Harrison Papers on Microfilm, Series 2. Shepard wrote out his recollections of Harrison's interview in order to share it with President Porfirio Díaz of Mexico.

minds of his hearers that he "looked for great things from the Conference."[50]

On November 18th, after a brief respite to recover from more than six weeks of travel, the Conference convened and organized for business in the usual way. Various bills, when introduced, were referred to one of seventeen committees. Upon being reported back, the bills were then debated and voted on, each nation being empowered to cast one vote.[51] All in all 70 meetings were held, and Blaine managed to attend 44 of them. When tempers flared in the absence of the Secretary of State, a summons would often bring him to the floor of the Conference where he acted to adjust all differences quickly.[52] Aside from a ten-day recess for the Christmas and New Year's holidays, the delegates were occupied almost daily until adjournment on April 19, 1890.

In his parting words, Secretary Blaine expressed himself cautiously to the delegates. "The extent and value of all that has been worthily achieved by your Conference cannot be measured today," he said. "We stand too near it. Time will define and heighten the estimate of your work; experience will confirm our present faith; final results will be your vindication and your triumph."[53] Harrison's farewell, though guarded, was optimistic. "We rejoice," the President said, "that you have found in the organization of our country something which commends itself to your own. We shall be glad to receive new lessons in return."[54]

The next two and a half years of the Harrison Administration would justify to a large degree the doctrine that had called for a larger trade with our Southern neighbors. Apparently public opinion was ready to support a policy of American trade expansion. The hostile New York *Nation* may have clamored that results were small, but the influential New York *Herald* and New York

50 *Ibid.*

51 Committees set up to facilitate the work of the Conference comprised: Executive, Customs Union, Communication of the Atlantic, Communication of the Pacific, Communication of the Gulf of Mexico and Caribbean Sea, Railroad Communications, Customs Regulations, Port Dues, Sanitary Regulations, Patents and Trade-Marks, Weights and Measures, Extradition, Monetary Convention, Banking, International Law, General Welfare, and Rules (Wilgus, *art. cit.*, pp. 696–97).

52 Gail Hamilton, *Biography of James G. Blaine*, p. 680; also *Sen. Exec. Doc.* No. 231, pp. 112–14; 142–43. Edward Stanwood in *James Gillespie Blaine*, p. 316, comments on the conciliatory attitude of the delegates despite contrasts in temperament, language, and custom.

53 Blaine's remarks are cited in Gantenbein, *op. cit.*, pp. 57–58.

54 *Public Papers and Addresses of Benjamin Harrison*, p. 278.

Tribune joined in the view that the Americas could and should be better united. The *Herald* urged the high goal of a continental policy, observing: "From this day the Monroe Doctrine passes by process of diplomatic evolution into a stage of higher development. There is an American continental policy to be worked out and consummated."[55] The *Tribune* viewed results as "most important, albeit indirect" and "likely . . . to promote the highest ends of civilization." Harrison, who usually read the *Tribune*'s friendly pages, could say amen to that and to sonorous phrases faintly reminiscent of Lincoln's "unfinished work" and "the great task remaining before us" delivered in a nationalist setting. "The Congress has ended," declared the *Tribune,*

but the work of American unification has barely begun. The ground has been leveled, the way has been opened for securing united action on the part of the eighteen commonwealths which will promote the enlightened self-interest of each and the common welfare of all; and it now remains for the United States to take the initiative and to complete a great work of high civilization.[56]

55 April 31, 1890.

56 As cited in Wilgus, *art. cit.,* pp. 700–701. The paper came daily to the White House. After Harrison read it, staff members usually clipped articles which were placed in the Harrison Scrapbooks.

CHAPTER X

A Crisis Over Pensions

Harrison's cautious approach to his office would be tested by the powers backing pensions for Civil War veterans. It was readily expected that the Executive would willingly tap the Treasury in behalf of those who had saved the Union. Harrison's successful campaign for the Senate had earned him the title of "the Soldiers' Senator."[1] Twice a Republican Senate had passed liberal pension legislation introduced by Harrison, which then lost in the Democratic House. In the campaign against Cleveland, Harrison had cited the wartime toil and suffering of Union veterans, and the plight of their survivors. Further, his declaration that a nation should not use "an apothecary's scale to weigh the rewards of the men who saved the country" had hardly hurt his image with the G.A.R. Just after the great Encampment of 1888, the G.A.R. Committee on Pensions visited the President-elect, who gave cordial assurance of his warm interest and of his desire that "generous pensions to the defenders of the Union should be granted."[2]

The General thus served prompt notice that needy veterans should get relief. The more liberal pension advocates were also pleased that the President's official family included four generals:— Windom in the Treasury, Rusk in Agriculture, Tracy in Navy, and Noble as Secretary of the Interior, guiding pension policy. Speculation ran high about who would serve as Commissioner of Pensions under General John Noble. Harrison's mail reflected strong support for Corporal James R. Tanner, the G.A.R. com-

[1] Donald L. McMurry, "The Bureau of Pensions During the Administration of President Harrison," *Mississippi Valley Historical Review*, XIII, No. 3 (1926), 344.

[2] Harry J. Sievers, *Benjamin Harrison: Hoosier Statesman*, pp. 209–10, 284–85, 299, 377–78; and *Journal*, August 29, 1889, "Inside History of Pension Legislation."

mander from New York who had lost both legs in the Second Battle of Bull Run.[3]

Not only was the mail heavy from New York, but Senator John Sherman of Ohio joined his brother General William T. Sherman, Harrison's onetime commander, on Tanner's behalf. Harrison himself could hardly forget the campaign efforts of Tanner, who had gone about "representing Cleveland as an inhuman monster and Benjamin Harrison as an angel of mercy carrying a purse hanging mouth downward." Tanner was also on record as claiming that more money would be paid out for pensions if Harrison won.[4] And Tanner had told General Sherman: "If I achieve the office, I shall run it on the idea that it is the duty of all of us to assist a worthy old claimant to prove his case rather than to hunt for technical reasons under the law to knock him out."[5] On March 23, 1889, Harrison sent Tanner's nomination to the Senate, which promptly confirmed him as the new Commissioner.[6]

The dynamic and vocal advocate assumed his duties with enthusiasm, noting that "there was a mighty tide of humanity surging into the Pension Office [and] claiming my personal attention."[7] To friend and foe he explained that "for twenty years I have been only able to plead, but now I am thankful that at these finger tips there rests some power."[8] Pension critics dismissed this as the muttering of a "loudmouthed Grand Army stump speaker"[9] who had run a successful pension agency while clerking in the New York Custom House. However, Tanner the partisan went his own way. Claiming that he had Harrison's directive to be "liberal with the boys," he intended "just as soon as possible . . . to call in every one of the certificates of pension . . . and reissue them on the basis of truth . . . though I may wring from the hearts of some the prayer, 'God help the surplus.' "[10]

The actual program was for pensioning as many as possible and

3 McMurry, art. cit., p. 345.

4 Donald L. McMurry, "Political Significance of the Pension Question, 1885–1897," Mississippi Valley Historical Review, IX, No. 1 (1922), 30.

5 Tanner to Sherman, January 5, 1889, W. T. Sherman MSS., as cited by Mary R. Dearing in Veterans in Politics, p. 393.

6 Congressional Record (Special Session Senate, March 4, 1889 ff.), Vol. 21, Part I, pp. 40, 42.

7 New York Sun, October 21, 1889 (special interview by Tanner).

8 McMurry, "Bureau of Pensions . . . ," pp. 343–64.

9 Ibid., p. 345.

10 Ibid., pp. 346–47; Dearing, op. cit., p. 393; Nation, XLVIII (1889), 438–40.

increasing the existing rates. When charged that his handouts were lavish and illegal,[11] Tanner declared he would "drive a six-mule team through the Treasury."[12] But by mid-June powerful Democrats appeared at the White House to demand the Corporal's removal. Already alerted by Tanner,[13] Harrison referred the matter to Secretary Noble, whose feelings toward the veteran soldiers were indeed as liberal. But after a probe was ordered, evidence of the new Commissioner's disobedience and jobbery began to jar the existing harmony within the official family.

Noble had prudently forbidden any 48-hour decisions unless destitution or death threatened a claimant—a directive Tanner chose to ignore. Called on the carpet, the Commissioner openly and boldly argued that Noble was powerless to interfere with or even review decisions of the Bureau of Pensions on the grounds that too much pension may have been granted. The Secretary's power of review, Tanner held, extended only to cases in which a claim had not been approved.[14] Tanner then wrote Noble a letter (released to the press some three months later) in which he dauntlessly attacked the Secretary's authority. Noble's strongly worded reply to Tanner was also sent to the White House.

Tanner seemed quite hopeless. Not only did he try to block Noble's investigation, but he began to argue publicly that he was guilty only of granting more liberal pensions than his predecessor. After about three weeks of such badgering, Noble cited Tanner, in the Annual Report of the Secretary of the Interior, for disrespect and insubordination to the last degree.[15]

Newspapers began to comment editorially on the affair. The Boston *Post* asked whether Tanner thought he had the whole U.S. Treasury at his disposal. "If Tanner does not go soon," clamored the New York *World*, "the surplus will—and the Republican Party after it." Pension attorneys and lobbyists came in for strong Democratic criticism. A warning was sounded against the danger of converting federal rule into a "government by the Grand Army of the Republic for the Grand Army of the Republic," which in turn

---

11 Tanner's distribution of public funds was made with little or no regard for the strict letter of the law, customary Pension Bureau procedure, or rules promulgated by Secretary Noble. See McMurry, "Bureau of Pensions . . . ," pp. 347–49.

12 Dearing, *op. cit.*, p. 393.

13 Tanner to Harrison, June 19, 1889, (L.C.), Vol. 79. Tanner requested the President to call for any and all papers in cases where irregularity was alleged.

14 *Annual Report of the Secretary of the Interior (1889)*, pp. clii–cliv.

15 Leonard D. White, *The Republican Era*, pp. 178–79.

would result in a "Grand Army for Revenue only."[16] A few scandalized Republicans joined in; certain newspapers which had defended Tanner began to change their tune. Solid support came only from Indiana and elsewhere in the Midwest.[17]

Harrison's correspondence that summer indicates that the Tanner problem was much more than a tempest in a teapot. Rumors of Tanner's forced resignation disturbed G.O.P. leaders. Ohio Governor Joseph B. Foraker, then in the heat of a re-election campaign, wired Harrison to "stand by Commissioner Tanner." He further advised that "Republican sentiment here is all with him and his removal would injure us greatly."[18] From Indiana, where Louis T. Michener, Harrison's astute political manager, had just been elected chairman of the G.O.P. state committee, came a strong plea that the President avoid any break with Tanner until after the fall elections.

Although Michener was quite capable of quieting troubled waters by himself, he sought to influence Harrison to come to Indianapolis by way of Cincinnati and show himself to the public. An appropriate event presented itself—on August 22nd the cornerstone of the great Soldiers' and Sailors' Monument (a memorial suggested in 1884 by Senator Harrison) was to be laid in Indianapolis. Moreover, on August 23rd the Seventieth Indiana Regiment would hold its annual reunion. The political importance of a visit at this time was lost on no one.

It was on his fifty-sixth birthday, August 20, 1889, that Harrison boarded a Baltimore and Ohio sleeper at Deer Park to go home. In the party were Agriculture Secretary Rusk and Attorney General Miller, along with some minor officials, mostly soldiers in federal jobs. Significant was the presence of General Dan Ransdell, U.S. Marshal of the District of Columbia and a supporter of Commissioner Tanner. Ransdell, who had fought under Harrison at Resaca, where he lost an arm, was one Hoosier who called him "Ben" before, during, and after the Presidency.[19]

As the Presidential party reached Cincinnati, cannons boomed and crowds cheered. The first person to grasp Harrison's hand in

16 McMurry, "Bureau of Pensions . . . ," p. 348.

17 L. T. Michener to E. W. Halford, September 10, 1889, (L.C.), Vol. 86.

18 J. B. Foraker to Harrison, August 3, 1889, (L.C.), Vol. 84.

19 Of Ransdell, Harrison wrote: "He was Marshal of the District of Columbia while I was President, and conducted his office with great efficiency—greatly to the satisfaction of the judges. . . . He is very popular and has the esteem of everybody" (Harrison to William Jay Turner, May 20, 1898, (L.C.), Vol. 172).

full view of thousands of voters was candidate Joseph Foraker, followed by Cincinnati's Mayor Mosby. After a public reception in the Burnet House, where a magnificent chandelier had highlighted many of the famous,[20] Harrison visited a new chamber of commerce building, and recalled his earlier days as a country boy in rustic surroundings. While enjoying the hospitality of the Queen City and shaking hands with hundreds of veterans, the President made it clear that he came "not only as an officer of the Nation, but as a brigadier. I appreciate the fact that I see before me not only representatives in business, but loyal supporters of our great Union."[21]

The short run to Indianapolis evoked nostalgic memories. Cheering throngs crowded the stations and lined the tracks at Hamilton and at Oxford, Ohio, a land where he had won a college degree, a Phi Delta Theta scroll, and a loyal wife. Twice the President violated his self-imposed "no speaking" injunction, but he regretted only the fact that he was unable to grasp the hand of Dr. Robert Hamilton Bishop, his onetime professor, who was somewhere in the crowd at the Oxford station.[22] At the Indiana state line Hoosier Governor Hovey and Indianapolis Mayor Denny took over from Governor Foraker and Mayor Mosby. In thanking the welcoming party, Harrison displayed a sensitiveness to the esteem of his neighbors. "If, when my public career is ended," the President said, "I can return to you, the happy possessor of your respect and good will, I shall not leave public office with regret."[23]

The usual brass bands at Indianapolis, along with fireworks, flags, and marching veterans, greeted Harrison, who was "looking heavier and better than when he left" six months before. Wearing a dark gray suit and a silk hat resting firmly on his head, this favorite son of Indianapolis was escorted to the New Denison Hotel. Two hours and several brief speeches later, Harrison retired.

The laying of the cornerstone of the Soldiers' and Sailors' Monument had become a national event. More than 40,000 were attracted to that center of Indianapolis now called Monument Circle

---

20 Eminent personages received there included Jenny Lind, Abraham Lincoln, General Grant and General Sherman, Prince Albert, and the Hungarian patriot Kossuth.

21 *Journal*, August 22, 1889.

22 Harrison to R. H. Bishop, August 26, 1889, a photostat in (L.C.), Vol. 85.

23 *Journal*, August 22, 1889. That Harrison prized the respect of his countrymen undoubtedly caused him no little anxiety in dealing with the Tanner affair.

to witness the ceremonies and the parade. Some 8,000 veterans escorted the presidential party to the spot from which there would rise a slender spire of Indiana limestone to honor all Hoosiers who had died for freedom and national unity.

Scanning the crowd during long-winded preliminary speeches, Harrison was able to recognize old friends and comrades. He then spoke without manuscript of "a monument about which the sons of veterans, the mothers of our dead, the widows that are yet with us, might gather, and pointing . . . say, 'There is his Monument.' "[24]

Heartened by waves of cheering as he thanked the living and dead for their contributions in blood, skilled labor, and essential funds, Harrison reminded his hearers that this was one nation, one of free men:

This is a monument by Indiana to Indiana soldiers. But I beg you to remember that they were only soldiers of Indiana until the enlistment oath was taken; that from that hour until they came back to the generous state that had sent them forth they were soldiers of the Union. So that it seemed to me not inappropriate that I should bring to you today the sympathy and the cheer of the loyal people of all the States.

The monument, the President concluded, commemorated not only the death of slavery but the birth of a new and united desire "to hold up the dignity and honor of our free institutions, and to see that no harm shall come to our country, whether from internal dissensions or from the aggressions of a foreign foe."[25]

Harrison's voice, a reporter noted, had risen higher and higher "until it rang out clear as a bugle." At the end, a tribute of silence was broken by loud and prolonged applause. "The speech had touched their hearts." Said the Terre Haute *Express:* "It was well that President Harrison came back to his home state. The hearty welcome and endorsement he received will give him courage to go on his good course." The Columbus *Republican* decided that "more and more it will appear to the people that the Presidential chair has never been filled by an abler or more patriotic man than Benjamin Harrison."[26]

24 *Journal*, August 22, 23, 1889. Berlin-born Bruno Schmitz, who had designed the Victor Emmanuel Monument at Rome, was the designer and supervising architect.

25 *Speeches of Benjamin Harrison*, Charles Hedges (comp.), pp. 214–15.

26 *Journal*, August 26, 1889, carried a long column of comment on how the state press viewed the cornerstone ceremonies and the President's address.

Nor was the political impact of the visit overlooked by the press of the state: "Indiana will stand by General Harrison."[27] For a moment, at least, the agitation over pensions and Tanner was quieted. The next day Harrison attended the reunion of his old regiment before heading back to the summer White House at Deer Park, but his thoughts inevitably turned to the 22nd Annual G.A.R. National Encampment to be held in Milwaukee.

Both Harrison and General Noble hoped that the controversial Tanner, if he were to appear at all, might be a *silent* participant at Milwaukee.[28] Despite an urgent appeal to stay away, Tanner went to Milwaukee where he received a hero's welcome. The Grand Army debated resolutions endorsing their favorite—who, at that very moment, was under investigation by the Secretary of the Interior. A spirited debate resulted in a resolution that at once cleared Tanner and left the door open for an inquiry into his acts:

We thank President Harrison for his appointment of our comrade James Tanner . . . and . . . notwithstanding the assault made on him we declare our complete confidence in his integrity and our approval of his endeavors to do all that he can under the laws for the veterans of the war and in connection with him we ask a full investigation of his administration of the affairs of the Pension Bureau.[29]

Until Secretary Noble reported to Harrison, political friends would bend every effort to bring Tanner into line, but to no avail, since he still flaunted pension rules. No statement from Harrison appeared, even after he received Noble's report and handed it to Tanner at a White House meeting on September 11th. Also present were Attorney General Miller, Navy Secretary Tracy (who had made a special trip from New York) and Postmaster General Wanamaker of Philadelphia. Inevitably, rumors cropped up. One story had the embarrassed President supporting Noble while offering Tanner a New York post as federal marshal. Personal Secretary Halford quickly denied the report, as did Navy Secretary Tracy. Meanwhile, from Indianapolis, G.O.P. Chairman Michener

27 The Frankfort *Evening News* summarized the opinion of Harrison: "Facts are, he is an honest, capable man, and above all a patriot in the true sense of the term. Such a man is always close to the hearts of the masses" *(ibid.).*

28 Dearing, *op. cit.,* p. 395, alleges that Harrison feared that Tanner might commit the Administration to service pensions. Others feared that an aroused Encampment might pass anti-Administration resolutions.

29 *Journal,* August 30, 1889.

wrote Halford that he understood "Mr. Tanner will resign . . . will be compelled to resign." The man who knew Harrison best told Halford: "I do not believe that Mr. Noble will be able alone to bring about this result, and therefore I judge that the President has reached the conclusion that he must have Mr. Tanner's resignation at once."[30] Dated September 10th, the letter may have reached Harrison shortly before he sent U.S. Marshal Dan Ransdell to Tanner's Georgetown home on a midnight mission on the 11th.[31] A friend of both the President and the Commissioner, Ransdell argued that Tanner would be doing Harrison an injustice if he failed to resign of his own accord. Apparently Tanner agreed. The following afternoon he left the Pension Bureau, not to return again as Commissioner. To the White House came a letter of resignation, effective at the President's pleasure.[32] Harrison replied that it would become effective upon appointment of a successor and told Tanner: "Your honesty has not at any time been called into question."[33]

As soon as the exchange of letters had been fed to an eager press, the President again retreated to Deer Park. Tanner's removal troubled him, despite the views of Navy Secretary Tracy, who wrote from his New York law office to say that "so far as I can gather public sentiment, you made no mistake about Tanner. I don't think it will amount to even a ripple."[34] The usually astute Cabinet member could not have been more mistaken.

From Indiana and Ohio came a flood of protest and criticism,

[30] Michener to Halford, September 10, 1889, (L.C.), Vol. 86.

[31] *Journal*, September 13, 1889.

[32] Dated September 12, 1889 and published the following day, Tanner's letter admitted that the differences with Noble had caused Harrison considerable embarrassment *(ibid.)*.

[33] Harrison also sent Tanner a private letter saying: "It has been suggested to me that it will be agreeable to you to have a leave of absence until your successor is appointed . . . [which] will probably not be done immediately" (Harrison to Tanner, September 12, 1889, (L.C.), Vol. 86.

[34] Benjamin F. Tracy to Harrison, September 13, 1889, (L.C.), Vol. 86. Tracy said that personally he was more satisfied than ever with the solution arrived at. Other expressions of hearty approval may be listed as follows: William Cogswell to Halford, September 13, 1889, (L.C.), Vol. 86, in which he requested that Halford tell the President that "Tanner was losing votes for us every day, and provoking a reaction of sentiment against the best interest of our deserving ex-soldiers." Henry Cabot Lodge to Harrison, September 17, 1889, (L.C.), Vol. 87: "Your action has been as wise and judicious as it has been courageous and right." Nathaniel McKay to Harrison, September 12, 1889, (L.C.), Vol. 86. McKay, who styled himself as spokesman for the good Republicans of New York City and Brooklyn, wrote: "This will add fresh laurels to your national fame for rare sagacity and even-handed justice."

with a few exceptions.[35] Indianapolis let fly with both barrels. General Lew Wallace advised Harrison that he was now "receiving more adverse criticism over this affair than any since his inauguration . . . all from soldiers."[36] Governor Hovey and Attorney General Michener, lamenting Tanner's loss, urged that he be placed in another post. Chairman Michener reported "a great deal of soreness and discontent . . . among the soldiers; the resignation has made the soldiers more clamorous than ever. . . ."[37] And as Grand Army Chief George S. Merrill stated: "The veterans [are] very generally in revolt . . . deeming the removal of Tanner a blow at the liberal construction of pension laws and against liberal pension legislation."[38] This report by a man who had been eight years chairman of the G.A.R. Pension Committee and who had befriended the Administration, proved quite unsettling to the President. Where might a suitable replacement for Tanner be found?

It would prove to be a long and hard search. The post was refused by two G.A.R. luminaries, Major William Warner of Kansas City, Missouri,[39] and Major George Merrill of Massachusetts.[40] As time passed, nearly every friendly senator and politician touted a favorite for the job, an obvious plum. More than a month later, on October 16th, Harrison confided to one aspirant, Major George W. Steele of Marion, Indiana, that "I have been looking, both as to locality and as to some special qualities, in the new Commis-

35 Harrison Papers on Microfilm, Series 2, Reels 67, 68, reveal that some conservative Republicans approved the Tanner removal; from Fort Wayne came the assurance: "You have lost nothing in the estimation of old soldiers here by your prompt retirement of Corporal Tanner." A Danville (Indiana) correspondent praised Harrison for saying to Tanner, "You did wrong."

36 Lew Wallace to Halford, September 14, 1889, (L.C.), Vol. 86. Wallace had advised Tanner to resign, saying that "your enemies want you to antagonize the President. Don't."

37 L. T. Michener to Harrison, September 17, 1889, and Michener to Halford, September 23, 24, 25, 1889, (L.C.), Vol. 87.

38 Merrill to Harrison, September 30, 1889, (L.C.), Vol. 88. Merrill had been at the Milwaukee Encampment and had supported the compromise resolution which thanked Harrison for appointing Tanner but which also opened the door for the investigation. He defended Harrison's removal of Tanner.

39 William Warner to Harrison, September 16, 1889, (L.C.), Vol. 86. Warner wrote that business interests kept him from accepting the commissionership and thus aiding "as best I could in carrying out your wise and liberal policy towards the old soldiers and sailors." Warner was serving his second term as Republican congressman from Missouri (1885–87; 1889–91).

40 Merrill had the backing of Henry Cabot Lodge and Senator G. F. Hoar. Both Warner and Merrill had defended the President. James F. Tanner to Harrison, September 20, 23, 1889, (L.C.), Vol. 87, worked against Merrill and for General Lucius Fairchild.

sioner of Pensions, realizing that the question of this appointment is quite a different one from what it was. . . ."[41] An Illinois veteran, however, General Green B. Raum, was already being considered, and on October 19th was appointed. Raum, who had served under Grant and who had reinforced Harrison's brigade at Resaca, enjoyed some repute as a lawyer; during two terms as Commissioner of Internal Revenue, he had put that branch of the Treasury Department in good working order.[42]

Back home in Indiana, according to Michener, the President's move had restored confidence among veterans. "Such soldiers as I have seen today from Governor Hovey on down," Michener wrote, "commend in the highest terms, the appointment of the new Commissioner. I hope he will know how to keep his tongue between his teeth, and I believe he will." Raum's selection, Michener concluded a few days later, had greatly relieved a strained situation in Indiana. Evidently the President's manager himself was breathing more easily, since he added that "until that appointment was made, the situation in soldier circles was the most alarming I ever knew. Now everybody is praising the selection and looking forward with a great deal of hope to what you will say in your message on the pension question."[43]

At this point, Harrison felt that he could unburden himself as he did in a letter to Lieutenant Governor Ira J. Chase of his home state. "Can it be possible," the President asked

that there is any soldier who fought for the maintenance of the law who can expect of the Executive and the administrative department of the Government anything but the application of the law? Could any greater harm be done to the cause of progressive relief to our soldiers than to have the country suppose that any administrative officer could modify the law at his pleasure?

The law, liberally construed—for the canons of construction require such laws to be liberally construed—is the only safe standard for any of us; and I am sure that the soldiers will not ask for anything else. When we leave that we are in the realm of favoritism.

41 (L.C.), Vol. 89. Harrison added that "if personal considerations were to control, there is no one of those named who could be or would be preferred to you."

42 Indianapolis *Journal* and New York *Sun*, October 20, 1889. Senator John Hipple Mitchell of Oregon first suggested Raum at the end of September. Both Tanner and Noble favored the appointment, and Harrison used the occasion to warn them to bury their former differences. Only the Secretary complied (see New York *Sun*, October 21, 1889, wherein Tanner "told all" to a Democratic reporter).

43 L. T. Michener to Harrison, October 19, 23, 1889, (L.C.), Vol. 89.

When I come to speak to Congress I shall be at liberty to say something as to a modification of the law; but until then there is nothing
left for me, or those under me, except the kindly and equal application of the law, favorably interpreted.[44]

Before he sent his first annual message to Congress, Harrison
clarified once and for all the Administration's desire for a new
pension policy. He had inherited manifest inequalities in the existing law that needed to be remedied. Wounds or disease having an
origin in the war entitled veterans (duly mustered into the United
States service) to a pension under the Arrearages Act of 1879.[45]
"Two of the three necessary facts, viz., muster and disability, are
usually susceptible of easy proof," reasoned the soldier-President,
"but the third, origin in service, is often difficult, and [in] many
deserving cases impossible to establish." Harrison's senatorial experience, as well as his association with Pension Commissioner
W. W. Dudley, had made him keenly aware of loopholes in the
law and of frauds actual and potential. Lawyer and ex-soldier, the
Hoosier President would tell Congress:

That very many of those who endured the hardships of our most bloody
and arduous campaigns, are disabled from disease that has a real but
not traceable origin in the service I do not doubt. Besides these there is
another class composed of men, many of whom served an enlistment of
three full years, and of re-enlisted veterans who added a fourth year of
service, who escaped the casualties of battle and the assaults of disease,
who were always ready for any detail, who were in every battle line of
their command, and were mustered out in sound health, and have,
since the close of the war, while fighting with the same indomitable
and independent spirit the contests of civil life, been overcome by
disease or casualty.[46]

Thus the stage was set for a pension plank in the President's recommendations to Congress. Despite strong G.A.R. pressure for a
simple and outright service pension, Harrison asked for legislation
granting "a pension to such honorably discharged soldiers and

44 Harrison to Chase, October 21, 1889, (L.C.), Vol. 89. This explanation came in response to Chase's letter and days after President Charles W. Eliot of Harvard had
delivered his Boston denunciation of the pension system as "a crime against all
honest soldiers"; see McMurry, "Bureau of Pensions . . . ," p. 363.

45 Leonard D. White, op. cit., p. 209, claims that "the result of this legislation was
to validate undreamed of arrears culminating over more than a decade." It opened
the door to many fraudulent claims. See Richard B. Morris, (ed.), Encyclopedia of
American History, p. 259.

46 Public Papers and Addresses of Benjamin Harrison, p. 56.

sailors of the Civil War . . . [who] are now dependent upon their own labor for a maintenance, and by disease or casualty are incapacitated from earning it." Aware that "the pension-roll already involves a very large annual expenditure," the President judged that it was completely consistent with national honor to show even greater generosity to those who served "so gallantly and unselfishly."[47]

A seeming weakness in the appointment of Corporal Tanner, the G.A.R. furor over his forced resignation, the temporary lack of harmony within the Cabinet, and the threat to Republicans at the polls—all seemed to fade into nothingness by June of 1890. Congress passed and Harrison signed a Dependent and Disability Pension Bill into law. Not only did Harrison and the Republican majority in Congress discharge a debt to the "old soldier," but it was G.O.P. legislation that shaped the principle of the service pension to provide for minors, dependent parents, and widows.[48] It may be noted that between 1891 and 1895 the number of pensioners rose from 676,000 to 970,000. By the time Harrison left office, the yearly appropriations for pensions had increased from $81 million to $135 million. Not an unmixed blessing, this law by 1907 had cost the Government over a billion dollars.[49] The President and the G.O.P. legislature had outdone Corporal Tanner although with regard for due process. Ultimately, the Fifty-first Congress was referred to as "the Billion-Dollar Congress," which evoked from House Speaker Thomas B. Reed the comment: "Yes, but this is a billion-dollar country."[50]

47 *Ibid.* Harrison pointed out that many of the men who would be included in this form of relief were already dependent upon public aid. He felt that it was inconsistent with national honor "that they shall continue to subsist upon the local relief given indiscriminately to paupers."

48 White, *op. cit.*, pp. 209–10, concludes that "with the passage of years it became essentially a *service* pension plan." The G.A.R. hailed it as "the most liberal pension measure ever passed by any legislative body in the world." Cited by William H. Glasson, *Federal Military Pensions in the United States*, p. 233.

49 Dearing, *op. cit.*, p. 400. This estimate seems solidly based on the studies made by McMurry and Glasson.

50 Harry Thurston Peck, *Twenty Years of the Republic, 1885–1905*, p. 224. Harrison, in his first annual message, told Congress he would not be deterred by the prospect of large annual expenditures.

CHAPTER XI

Facing the Nation

REPORTS FROM BUSINESS during the summer and fall of 1889 showed a record volume of trade, with mills and factories running full time and fields yielding their bounty. Indeed, from Iowa came word of "an unprecedented crop of everything."[1] Hoping to master pension and tariff problems, civil service reform, and the silver issue, Harrison believed it essential to convene a special session of Congress. After soliciting some views, both pro and con, he was persuaded to think otherwise by Cabinet members who met at the White House on September 7, 1889. Secretary of State Blaine, who was absent, reminded him by letter of certain risks involved—any injury to the small Republican majority on the day assigned, possibly during the course of travel, for which the President might be blamed. Blaine then referred to other extra sessions, that of 1797, which marked the beginning of John Adams's political downfall in his view, and to the unfortunate James Madison, who called two extra sessions "against the better judgment of the War Party" and Henry Clay. Martin Van Buren had started out with an extra session, then stumbled on to defeat. John Tyler's defection dated "in the popular mind from the extra session of 1841, which was called by your grandfather."[2]

Party men could see that Harrison was making good progress publicly, both at the Old Log College (Presbyterian) near Philadelphia where he was hailed as "a Christian President,"[3] and at

1 William B. Allison to Harrison, September 8, 1889, (L.C.), Vol. 86.

2 Blaine agreed with Harrison's contention that the business of the country might possibly need a special session, but maintained that it was not necessary unless a quorum of the House were guaranteed, so that they could organize safely and go promptly to work. The Maine man felt safe in saying "We can safely abide the result on an appeal to the business men of the country" (September 4, 1889, (L.C.), Vol. 86).

3 *Journal*, September 6, 8, 10, 16, 1889; New York *Sun*, September 8, 1889.

the seventy-fifth anniversary celebration of the Fort McHenry bombardment, where he reviewed a parade for several hours, standing the whole time.[4] In early October he watched the colorful Knights Templar, then in Washington for their triennial conclave, stream past a stand placed on the White House grounds. He attempted to greet them all the next day at a reception, but of the 20,000 or more who came, possibly no more than one-third were able to see the President.[5] In November, he lauded Catholic educational leaders at ceremonies marking the opening of Catholic University in Washington.[6]

These diversions were a welcome relief from the burdens assumed in the White House, where Harrison had to deal with domestic worry as well as hard work, and, at times, sheer loneliness. At Deer Park his stay had been brightened by Baby McKee, "a jolly boy—not a bit spoiled, and he and I had some famous times." With the McKees absent from the White House that fall, Harrison confessed that he missed the children so much "that it is a meager comfort only to hear from them."[7] Whenever Mrs. Harrison made shopping trips to Philadelphia or visited her ailing sister in New York, the President was full of complaints. After a bleak day devoted to work on his first annual message to Congress, he confided to Mame Dimmick: "Your Aunt Carrie did not return yesterday as I expected and I am for another Sunday the sole occupant of this big house—about which I wander without any sense of its being a home."[8] The house on Delaware Street, Indianapolis, was known to Harrison as home.

Preparations for the Fifty-first Congress brought a change in business hours at the White House. Congressmen could continue to call each day except Monday, but only between 11:00 A.M. and 12:30 P.M., while the hours of public receptions in the East Room, already restricted to Mondays, Wednesdays, and Saturdays, were curtailed. Harrison would have had little protection otherwise because of the illness of Secretary Halford who, on October 4, 1889,

4 Harry J. Sievers, *President Benjamin Harrison and Our Country's Flag*, a pamphlet reprinted from the *National Magazine of History* (November 1952).

5 *Journal*, October 10, 1889.

6 *Journal*, November 13, 14, 1889. The President and the Cabinet attended both the dedicatory ceremonies and a banquet. Secretary Blaine also spoke briefly.

7 Harrison to Mary Scott Dimmick, September 28, 1889, Walker MSS. The McKees were then in Indianapolis.

8 Harrison to Mary Scott Dimmick, November 10, 1889, Walker MSS.

collapsed at his desk. Halford underwent a painful operation two
days later, giving rise to care and anxiety on this account.[9] Harrison still managed to keep quite well, although admitting to edgy
and nervous feelings in the absence of his closest aide. When Halford was able to resume his normal duties, the President seemed to
relax somewhat and renewed the custom of an afternoon stroll or
carriage ride. Halford, however, did hear him remark, as the two
were returning from a brisk walk: "There is my jail," pointing at
the White House.[10] On only two occasions during October did the
President avail himself of recreation or entertainment. Late that
month he attended the races at the District's Ivy City track, and on
the 29th, for the first time since his Inauguration,[11] he took Mrs.
Harrison to Albaugh's Opera House to witness a performance of
the celebrated Rhea in *Josephine, Empress of the French*.[12]

Work on the message to Congress was interrupted by the occasional admission of new states into the Union, first North and
South Dakota, then Montana and Washington, all of them together containing little more than a half million people. Quite
aware of sectional jealousies as leaders of the North and South
Dakotans surrounded his desk at the White House, Harrison bade
Secretary Halford spread some newspapers before him, push the
two proclamations face down beneath them, and then shuffle the
pile. When it was impossible to tell which was which, Secretary of
State Blaine pulled one proclamation toward the edge of the President's desk, exposing only the space for Harrison's signature.
The procedure was repeated, then Halford reshuffled the docu-
ments before exposing them. Following the usual handshaking, the
North and South Dakotans left the White House quite satisfied.
Identical wires went out to the two state governors, who were advised that both proclamations were signed at 3:40 P.M., "the first

9 *Ibid.* The New York *Sun*, October 9, 1889, reported that "Private Secretary Halford
is lying at the White House where on Sunday a surgical operation was performed
on him by Dr. Sowers. It was successful, and the Doctor says that with a few weeks'
rest Mr. Halford will have entirely recovered."

10 E. W. Halford, "General Harrison's Attitude Toward the Presidency," *Century
Magazine* (June 1912), 305–10.

11 As reported in the Washington *Sunday Star*, November 11, 1956. The track was located at Florida Avenue and Fenwick Street, N.E.

12 *Journal*, October 31, 1889; New York *Sun*, October 30, 1889. Secretary and Mrs.
Rusk, and Attorney General and Mrs. Miller completed the Presidential party, which
occupied two stage boxes. W. H. H. Miller to Sam Miller, October 31, 1889, Miller
Letterbooks, reported it as good entertainment.

instance . . . of twin states—North and South Dakota—entering the Union at the same moment."[13]

Montana and Washington shed territorial status in rapid succession, becoming the forty-first and forty-second states. Land of explorers, fur traders, gold miners, Indians, cowboys, and stock growers, Montana held much interest for Harrison, whose son Russell was secretary of the Montana Stockgrowers Association, as well as owner of the Helena *Daily Journal*. When Washington next received statehood, it was noted that Montana gold was in the pens used to sign the document. For the Republican party, political gold had been mined with a gain of eight senators and five representatives from the four states.[14]

It was evident that the nation awaited Harrison's first message to Congress. Indiana G.O.P. Chairman Michener was writing Halford that he hoped the message would "put our people to thinking more about public policies and less about offices . . . but it will take a strong and ringing document to do it."[15] After a regular Cabinet meeting on Friday morning, November 22nd, Harrison closeted himself with Treasury Secretary Windom to discuss some troublesome financial aspects of the message, but finally quit and summoned Halford. The President, Halford wrote in his diary, "said he never cared for office, felt that he had no taste for public life; felt so when Senator and if he could choose to wake up President or lawyer of Indianapolis he would choose the latter."[16]

Beyond doubt, Harrison was worried about the outcome of the Free Silver Convention in St. Louis. Farmers in the West and Midwest felt a great deal of interest in the action of the convention, and the Farmers' Alliance had already declared itself in favor of free coinage of silver. Michener warned Washington that only wise legislation could prevent disaster to the Republican party. And there was the imminent threat that the Knights of Labor would combine with the Alliance. Unless Harrison and Windom could satisfy these elements without doing material injury to other interests in the country, the future of the Republican Party would

13 *Journal,* November 3, 1889; Richard Simons, "Great Dakota Mystery," in the Indianapolis *Star Magazine,* March 28, 1954. A recent study by Howard Roberts Lamar, *Dakota Territory, 1861–1889: A Study of Frontier Politics,* portrays Harrison's role in statehood for the Dakotas on pp. 247, 256–59, 264, and his denunciation of sectionalism, p. 272.

14 Figures derived from *Biographical Directory of the American Congress, 1774–1949.*

15 Michener to Halford, November 25, 1889, (L.C.), Vol. 91.

16 Halford's Diary, November 22, 1889, in (L.C.).

be blighted. The President was well aware that the farmers, laborers, and miners wanted free coinage of silver, free sugar, and some anti-trust legislation that might result in lower prices under free competition.[17]

On Thanksgiving Eve, Secretary Halford reported Harrison still at work on the message but not as harried. "After dinner I came over and the President read some portions of it and said that he would not try to do any more work on it that night but go and read one of Cooper's novels. We also walked out before dinner."[18] Three days later: "At work on the message. President gave it a final revision at night. Mr. Blaine read it and sent a very flattering letter to the President which greatly pleased him. I called over and saw Mr. Blaine at his house. The President said he felt very much relieved and very grateful to Mr. Blaine for his kind note."[19] Apparently things had worked out. In Blaine's view it was "a splendid message, clean, comprehensive, direct and meaty—I have read it with delight—a large part of it twice."[20]

Visibly encouraged, the President made final corrections on the proof and released it to the Government Printing Office. Unlike his predecessors, however, Harrison banned advance copies to the newspapers and the press associations. Shortly after 4:00 P.M. on Monday, December 2nd, Colonel William H. Crook, confidential White House clerk, with sealed copies in hand, boarded a Pennsylvania Railroad train for Baltimore, Philadelphia, and New York. At Baltimore and Philadelphia, trusted agents signed for the copy and pledged no release until Congress had received the message. These extra precautions against embarrassing leaks, though irksome to some, had been devised by Halford, an old newspaper hand.[21]

17 L. T. Michener to E. W. Halford, (L.C.), November 26, 1889, Vol. 91.

18 Halford's Diary, November 27, 1889, (L.C.).

19 November 30, 1889. Ibid.

20 Blaine to Harrison, November 30, 1889, (L.C.), Vol. 91. Blaine's letter included some suggestions generally slight in character but of some interest. "If by your 'Sunday law' recommendation you refer to the closing of saloons on that day I am heartily with you. But if you mean the interference with what are called 'innocent games' as the German Schutzenfest—I beg you to think well before you do it. It will in my belief prove abortive, if enacted. It will not I think be enacted and will widely and severely affect our party by driving the Germans from us. If you mean saloon I beg you will make that point very clear." Harrison discarded the Sunday Law recommendation.

21 Harrison Papers on Microfilm, Series 2, Reel 68, contains the telegrams received at the White House. On December 2 and 3 Halford had arranged the itinerary of Col. Crook. All out-of-city media received the same consideration. Halford himself delivered the message to the Washington papers about 9:30 A.M. on December 3.

About the time Colonel Crook reached the Associated Press office at 13 Park Row, New York, the White House heard that there was a good deal of nervousness in the financial heart of the nation. Moneylenders were alarmed by the Administration order requiring banks to transfer surplus deposits to the U.S. Treasury. They pleaded tight money; immediately interest rates shot skyward. On December 2nd, Grenville M. Dodge "saw money loaned here [New York] for 90 days at twelve percent which shows the temper of the streets—and this was a good house, too."[22] Harrison was not unaware of the widespread fear of a financial panic, and along with the pension question, the tariff, and the rights of Negroes, the problem only added to the suspense until he could face Congress and the country with his message.

Following the practice begun by Thomas Jefferson, Harrison sent Executive Secretary Pruden to Capitol Hill at noon on December 3rd. After the usual ceremony of accepting and opening the two envelopes, Senate and House clerks read the President's message to Congress.[23]

While in no sense minimizing foreign policy, which he dealt with first, Harrison devoted most of the message to domestic affairs. In treating of the financial problem, including the Treasury surplus, currency, and the silver question, he proclaimed himself a friend of silver, and therefore promised to protect it from the danger and evils that might result from excessive coinage.[24] A special message to Congress on silver would follow. There were strong, outstanding statements on veterans' pensions, civil service reform, the race question, and on the hazardous conditions under which railway men worked and were often killed. In each instance, Harrison made specific recommendations for new laws. The London *Morning Post* thereupon observed: "If President Harrison carries out in practice the peaceful and progressive principles indicated in his message, the whole world will be the gainers

22 Dodge to George C. Tichenor, Assistant Secretary of the Navy, December 2, 1889, Dodge Records, Vol. 12, p. 893. Dodge, who had been a major general of volunteers in the Civil War and then became chief engineer of the Union Pacific Railroad, was also an able financier. See *CDAB*, p. 239.

23 *Journal*, December 4, 1889. The New York *Sun* reported that the reading consumed nearly two hours.

24 Harrison clearly shared Windom's fears that unlimited or excessive coinage of silver at the current ratio would only result in further depreciation and thus cause gold and silver to part company permanently. (Windom to Harrison, November 30, 1889, (L.C.), Vol. 91.)

thereby."[25] But the President also called for a new navy, a new merchant marine, and stronger coastal defenses in line with the ideas of Navy Secretary Tracy and naval strategist Alfred Thayer Mahan.[26]

Press reaction, in general, followed strict party lines. Led by the New York *Sun,* which could not find the "faintest sign of intellectual promise" or "the least indication of a power to rise above the dull deadly line of mediocrity," Democratic papers agreed that the message was "sluggish and uninspiring literature," a "scrapbook of comparatively unimportant facts" which disclosed "a President without ideas and an Administration without a policy."[27] The New York *Times* urged that the message "be accepted as the measure of the man . . . and the policy he complacently announces and approves is to 'let things drift.' "[28]

Republican papers thought otherwise and balanced the partisan criticism with undisguised delight. The Boston *Advertiser* hailed the message as "comprehensive in scope, discreet and conservative in manner and tone" and lauded the "positive recommendations of policy on nearly every prominent question."[29] The Cincinnati *Commercial Gazette* detected "unusual diligence and capacity in the study of public affairs of the highest moment." Nor had there ever been "a stronger presentation than the President makes of the necessity of the protection of the Colored people, or a clearer and more business-like advocacy of tariff reform and reduction of the revenue."[30] Similar tributes came from the New York *Tribune,* the St. Louis *Globe-Democrat,* the Chicago *Inter-Ocean,* and, of course, the Indianapolis *Journal.*

The first senator to send a congratulatory message was George Edmunds, a duck-hunting partner as well as political friend. The

25 December 4, 1889, as cited by the *Journal,* same date.

26 Walter Russell Herrick, Jr., "General Tracy's Navy: A Study of the Development of American Sea Power, 1889–1893" (unpublished Ph.D. dissertation, Univ. of Virginia, 1962), pp. 106–7.

27 New York *Sun,* editorial of December 4, 1889. Among the American papers consulted were the New York *World,* Louisville *Courier-Journal,* and the New York *Times.* Canadian papers following the Democratic line were the Toronto *Empire,* Toronto *Globe,* Toronto *Mail,* and the St. Louis *Republic.* Only the New York *Herald* granted that the message "was a plain business document, well written, and making recommendations strictly in the line of the Republican platform."

28 December 4, 1889. The *Times* did concede that "as a mere reference index, the message may have some value in Congress and newspaper offices."

29 As cited in the *Journal,* December 4, 1889.

30 *Ibid.*

Vermonter expressed his "great satisfaction" and added: "If, now, Congress will really go to work and *do* the things, all will be well with the party and the country. I earnestly hope that summer will meet us with all our great work accomplished, and not as matters merely talked of."[31]

Mounting mail in Halford's basket revealed a wealth of popular support from nearly every state in the Union. That wide interest had been aroused could not be doubted. A letter from a Buffalo citizen interested Harrison:

Your message has made a marked impression upon the people in this vicinity. I find all classes already familiar with your views upon trusts, the railroad cars and changes in the tariff. It has been a continual surprise to discover so many persons, many of them of that class who now read for themselves, so familiar with your *exact phraseology*. Your views have made you *many new friends*."[32]

From Indianapolis, where the friends of ousted Tanner and hordes of unsuccessful office-seekers had been critical of Harrison, came the glowing report that "no state paper published at any time within the past 25 years has been seized upon by the Indianapolis reading public as has that of President Harrison." Lawyers, preachers and business men generally, Harrison learned, had read the document and were talking about it.[33] Young Albert J. Beveridge, now a young lawyer but destined to make and to write American history, called it "a message of unusual strength."[34]

Thus Harrison received early and outspoken support in his program to enfranchise the Negro in the South, to strengthen civil service reform, to obtain new silver legislation, and to enact an anti-trust law. He had made a strong bid to secure the backing of labor as well as business, to satisfy the silverites as well as the eastern bankers, to protect farmers as well as veterans.

The President early let it be known that his policy regarding the election of a Speaker of the House was "hands off."[35] Thomas B.

---

31 George B. Edmunds to Harrison, December 4, 1889, (L.C.), Vol. 92.

32 D. S. Alexander to Harrison, December 8, 1889, (L.C.), Vol. 92.

33 *Journal*, December 5, 1889.

34 *Ibid*. (interview with A. J. Beveridge).

35 The Administration's views were published in the Indianapolis *Journal* of Wednesday, August 21, 1889, as special from Washington, quite probably written by Perry S. Heath, Harrison's friend and the paper's Washington correspondent. It appeared on the day Harrison came home to the cornerstone laying in Indianapolis.

Reed of Maine, an able if not nimble parliamentarian, had been tirelessly campaigning for the post east and west. Harrison had declined Reed's invitation to spend three days at his Portland home in July, despite the promise of "a delightful excursion to the White Mountains . . . and an equally delightful sail in Casco Bay,"[36] although he did arrange to shake the hands of some of the Congressman's constituents en route to Bar Harbor. Of candidate William McKinley, rival candidate Joe Cannon remarked: "McKinley keeps his ear to the ground so close that he gets it full of grasshoppers much of the time."[37] During a day spent with the President at Deer Park, McKinley probably learned only that the selection of a Speaker would be left entirely to the House. It was a personal triumph for Reed in the face of strong competition when he won a party caucus on the second ballot—85 votes to McKinley's 38 and Cannon's 19, with 24 going to others. As Congress opened on December 2nd, Reed received an almost full party vote of 166, or 12 more than Democrat John G. Carlisle whom he replaced. McKinley was named chairman of the important Ways and Means Committee, a useful stepping-stone.

To replace Supreme Court Justice Stanley Matthews of Ohio, who had died in March, Harrison looked for a man of independent judgment, and after long deliberation selected Judge David J. Brewer of Kansas, aged 52 years, a nephew of Associate Justice Stephen J. Field. Brewer, a tall, sturdy man with a reputation for carrying his full share of the work, had the active support of Kansas Senator Preston B. Plumb, who obtained further help from Arkansas and Nebraska to make a trans-Mississippi crusade. Hearing rumors that another would be named, Plumb managed to create a snarl by continuing to argue his case at the White House where, unknown to him, Brewer's appointment already had been signed. It was one of those days when Harrison let his visitors run on without saying much himself; resisting the impulse to tear up the paper with Brewer's name on it, he sent it to the Senate on December 4th. The appointment was confirmed two weeks later by a vote of 53 to 11.[38] A letter written by Attorney General Miller

---

36 Reed to Harrison, July 21, 1889, (L.C.), Vol. 83.

37 William Allen White, *Masks in a Pageant*, p. 156. McKinley had returned to Ohio to campaign for the re-election of Governor Foraker—a vain effort as it turned out.

38 Willard L. King, *Melville Weston Fuller*, p. 155.

to an opponent of the nomination probably summed up Administration views:

From my examination of his decisions and record, I have come to the conclusion that he [Brewer] has not only the courage to decide against wealth and power and corporation, but what is a much more severe test to decide in their favor when the law and justice of a case demand it. To do the latter requires courage of a kind which demagogues lack.[39]

Harrison was discovering that the presidency as well as the candidacy entailed a great deal of train travel. He left Washington quietly on December 6th, bound for Indianapolis and Chicago, where he was to help dedicate a new auditorium. A stir was created when word was brought to the train that Jefferson Davis had died in New Orleans. Secretary of War Proctor sent a telegram asking whether the flag should be displayed at half-mast on War Department buildings as was customary upon the death of a former Secretary. Considering all circumstances, it was wise to inquire.

Harrison, of course, could not sanction it. The Indianapolis *Journal* firmly wrote Davis down as "the President of a greater amount of national disaster, human suffering and organized hell than any man of modern times,"[40] and had the decision been otherwise, the home town paper opined,

Old veterans, bent under years and disease, would have forgotten age and decrepitude to voice their wrath. . . . We all remember the protest which deterred Grover Cleveland from returning the captured flags. That . . . was a summer's effort compared to the cyclone of wrath and indignation which would have swept the country had Secretary Proctor half-masted the flag in honor of Jeff Davis.[41]

From various sources—North and South respectively—would come praise and aggrieved voices. The Atlanta *Constitution* considered the omission a mark of disrespect and "the National Shame," which brought light-hearted rejoinders from the North.[42] Harrison managed to avoid making any public statement meanwhile.

He attended Sunday services at his old church—First Presbyterian—with the McKees whom he was visiting, greeted a host of

---

[39] W. H. H. Miller to A. J. Durand, December 11, 1889, Miller Letterbooks.

[40] December 7, 1889.

[41] *Journal*, December 10, 1889.

[42] "A vast majority of the American people," the *Journal* remarked, "will accept their share of the shame" (December 9, 1889).

callers that afternoon, and then boarded a sleeper for Chicago, where he was to view a recently erected modern Parthenon. Designed by Louis Sullivan, the Auditorium, as it was called, was truly a great building of granite block and brick with a tower 270 feet high.[43] A tremendous pipe organ was heard, the famed Adelina Patti sang, and Harrison's remarks so aptly personified the building that some of his words were later inscribed on a bronze tablet attached to the structure (now Roosevelt University).[44] The President's talk was extemporaneous—the star billing went to Illinois Governor Fifer.

Christmas would be spent at the White House. Two deaths in the family had occurred meanwhile—first, that of Mrs. Harrison's beloved sister, Elizabeth Scott Lord, in Washington;[45] and, a few days later, that of the President's 25-year-old nephew, William Sheets Harrison of Chicago.[46] A favorite nephew, young William had supported a widowed mother and three sisters through his work as assistant general freight agent for the Chicago, Milwaukee & St. Paul. For both the President and Mrs. Harrison it was a sorrowful fortnight preceding the holiday which was, nevertheless, a merry one for the grandchildren.[47]

[43] The building, which fronted more than 710 feet of Congress Street, Michigan and Wabash Avenues, was probably the nation's most famous structure of that time.

[44] Harrison concluded his remarks as follows: "It is my wish, and may it be the wish of all that this great building may continue to be to all your population that which it should be—an edifice opening its doors from night to night, calling your people away from the care of business to those enjoyments and pursuits and entertainments which develop the souls of men, which will have power to inspire those whose lives are heavy with daily toil, and in its magnificent and enchanting presence, lift them for a time out of these dull things into those higher things where men should live." See text clipped to a letter, F. W. Peck to Halford, December 12, 1889, (L.C.), Vol. 92.

[45] Journal, December 11, 1889. Mrs. Harrison had remained in Washington to be with her sister, who had been removed from a New York hospital to the Capital. Some 50 carriages made up the funeral procession to Rock Creek Cemetery.

[46] Journal, December 19, 1889.

[47] New York Sun, December 26, 1889.

CHAPTER XII

Launching the New Year

O N JANUARY 1, 1890, an early morning drizzle had turned into a cold, steady rain by 11:00, the hour set for the usual White House reception. Outside the doors, white-coated coachmen shivered on their unprotected perches. In the vestibule of the Mansion, red-clad musicians of the Marine Band awaited John Philip Sousa's signal to strike up "Hail to the Chief" the moment the President and Mrs. McKee (substituting for her mother, who was still in mourning) should start to descend to the Blue Room. Favored callers were assembled in the East Room, the only one of the four public reception halls bathed in natural light.

Here as elsewhere in the Executive Mansion, spreading palms and tall rubber plants crowded every nook and corner, while hyacinths, azaleas, and ferns banked the mantels. In the Red and Green Rooms were gathered the diplomatic corps, consular officials, and delegates to the International Maritime Conference and the Pan-American Conference. Their combined presence on this day lent brilliance to a White House dreamily described as "a wilderness of lights and flowers, filled with brave men and fair women, gay uniforms and rich toilet."[1]

With Vice-President Levi Morton and Mrs. Morton at his left and right, the President shook hands with the hundreds of visitors for nearly three hours. Secretary of State Blaine presented Baron Fava, the Italian Minister and dean of the diplomatic corps, and then the Russian, British, and German Ministers, "all men of splendid physique."[2] In regular order came the Supreme Court

1 The New York *Tribune* and the Indianapolis *Journal* of January 2, 1890, carried fulsome accounts of the event.

2 New York *Tribune*, January 2, 1890.

Justices and their wives, members of the Cabinet, senators, congressmen and their ladies, followed in turn by Army and Navy officers in full dress. The G.A.R. made a full turnout and at about 12:30 P.M. the reception to the public got under way. The line moved quickly into the East Room. By 2:00 the doors were locked, the President's family sat down to lunch, and the crowd was making the rounds of receptions provided by various members of the Cabinet.

Dinners and receptions on the White House social calendar that season suffered a series of postponements or cancellations in mid-January. On the 15th there occurred the sudden death of Walker Blaine, the promising first son of the Secretary of State.[3] The younger Blaine had been serving as Examiner of Claims in the Department. His unexpected death after only a brief illness greatly shocked the President, who had called to see him less than twenty minutes before he died.[4] On hearing the news, Harrison and his wife returned immediately to console the bereaved family. Private Secretary Halford noted in his diary: "There is great grief over the death of Walker Blaine and fear for the result on Mr. Blaine."[5] With nearly all of official Washington in attendance at the Church of the Covenant, the sad obsequies were only little short of a state funeral.

A double tragedy then struck the household of Navy Secretary Benjamin F. Tracy, who had just taken possession of a splendid home on I Street facing Farragut Square. At about 7:00 on the morning of February 3rd, fire swept the home while the family slept. Trapped on the second story were the Secretary's invalid wife, a married daughter, and a great-granddaughter. Awakened by horrifying black smoke, they sought safety by jumping from a window, but the fall proved fatal to Mrs. Tracy, although the others escaped with minor injuries. Rescuers who entered the building managed to carry out an unconscious Secretary at the point of suffocation. A second daughter, Mary, and a French maid had already perished in the smoke and flames.

Harrison, who soon learned where the fire was, lost no time in

3 William T. Sherman to Whitelaw Reid, January 21, 1890, Reid MSS.; New York *Tribune*, January 6, 1890. The sudden death was described as a "national loss" by the Indianapolis *Journal*, January 16, 1890. Newspaper articles praised Walker Blaine as a lawyer, student of literature, politician, and statesman.

4 Halford's Diary, January 16, 1890, (L.C.). During Walker's illness Harrison had called daily at the Blaine residence.

5 *Ibid.* Mrs. Alice Coppinger, Secretary Blaine's daughter, died only a few days later.

getting there, since Farragut Square was hardly more than two blocks away. Finding Secretary Tracy still unconscious, he took his turn in administering artificial respiration which helped save the man's life. As the victim regained consciousness, he barely recognized the President, who was holding his head, and finally, when normal pulse and breathing returned, the dazed man's questions were directed at Harrison, who had no choice but to break the news of the double tragedy as best he could.[6]

Harrison saw that the bodies were brought to the East Room where the open casket of Delinda Tracy and the closed coffin of daughter Mary were arranged together, and services were held. Deep was the sorrow of that day just as of other recent days.[7]

Harrison referred to these depressing matters in a letter to Ambassador Whitelaw Reid, then in Paris, who had reported that the President's message to Congress had been very well received in Europe. "The sadness in Mr. Blaine's family," Harrison wrote,

. . . and the awful tragedy of the house of Secretary Tracy have not only made me inexpressibly sad but have made heavy demands upon my time and strength. Both have needed to be braced up and happily strong and sympathetic friends have not been wanting. Tracy is with me—is entirely well in body, and shows a brave spirit. He said yesterday that he wanted to resume his work and he will probably do so within a few days. Mr. Blaine also seems to bear up with fine courage —tho at times, when he is not engaged, his face is a very sad sight to look upon. Still he has in a measure already taken up his work and I do not much fear that he will break down.

It has been a winter very full of sickness and death, but our immediate household has been spared. I sometimes wonder that I am alive—but that I should have escaped a single day's sickness is amazing and a source of great thankfulness.[8]

6 *Journal*, February 4, 1890. Tracy, who had a genial personality, was a favorite with Harrison. The New York *Tribune*, February 4, 1889, carried a front page diagram of Gen. Tracy's house, calling it one of the best known of the present Cabinet houses.

7 W. H. H. Miller to Howard Cale, February 3, 1890, Miller Letterbooks. The Attorney General wrote: "We are all in dreadful distress here today from the calamity to Gen'l Tracy this morning. It looked at first as if Gen'l Tracy might go too, but fortunately he has revived and the Dr. assured me a short time ago that he would get along alright." *Journal*, February 5, 1890; New York *Tribune*, February 5, 6, 1890. Mrs. Harrison, upon learning that the Tracy maid was without relatives in this country, arranged for her funeral and interment in Mount Olivet Cemetery.

8 Harrison to Reid, February 7, 1890, Reid MSS. No sooner had the President posted his letter to Reid than he received a heartwarming message of appreciation from United States Attorney S. N. Chambers in Vincennes, Indiana. He praised Harrison's "strength, courage and ability," adding that "the country now fully knows, what we knew all the time, that in you dwelt the tenderest sympathy for your fellow men and that as you valued your own manhood as you have respect and love for mankind" (Chambers to Harrison, February 7, 1890, (L.C.), Vol. 98).

By the end of 1889, the barrenness of the Forty-ninth and Fiftieth Congresses had given way to the hope that a Republican-controlled Congress would keep in stride with those who envisioned a consolidated empire at home and a high rank among the commercial powers of the world. A mood of expectancy had been created. Farmers, debt-ridden and mortgaged, needed more income and ampler foreign markets for their products. Mining states were ready to produce more silver for coinage, and the President had showed himself convinced that agricultural and mining interests deserved and required as much tariff protection as did eastern industrialists. Harrison's message to Congress had called for a tariff to protect all sections.[9] Negroes clamored for the vote, for greater economic opportunities, and for a proportionate share in government and patronage. Harrison pledged himself and Congress to satisfy their demands. Various citizens, including many business men, had testified before a Senate committee that they were embittered and impoverished by corporate trusts and by the economic lawlessness of the railroads, but this was perhaps a problem for another generation to solve.

Congress had no sooner reconvened after the Christmas holiday recess than Harrison was locked in a dispute with Catholic leaders who violently protested his appointments of General Thomas J. Morgan as Indian Commissioner and of Dr. Daniel Dorchester as Commissioner of Indian Education. After a bitter battle in the press and in the Senate, both men survived charges of anti-Catholic bias and were confirmed by a vote of 28 to 16.[10]

Thereafter, national problems developed so rapidly that the President was soon struggling with a bewildering variety of them at the same time. There were thorny questions raised by trouble with the Navajos;[11] unsettling disturbances in the Cherokee strip; the movement by farmers and mining-camp senators for free

[9] New York *Tribune*, January 1, 1890. The Ways and Means Committee began hearings in December 1889, and it heard from all parts of the country during the long session of the 51st Congress.

[10] Details of the appointment have been recounted in Harry J. Sievers, "The Catholic Indian School Issue and the Presidential Election of 1892," *Catholic Historical Review*, XXXVIII, No. 2 (July 1952), 129–55. See also New York *Tribune*, February 12, 1890.

[11] New York *Tribune*, February 11, 1890, editorial entitled "The Trouble with the Navajos," blamed the difficulty on the inadequacy of their reservations in northern Arizona. Some 20,000 Indians were beginning to spill over into white man's territory and incidents ensued.

coinage of silver; the relentless pressure by veterans for a service pension; a party schism over the tariff; official appointments; a federal elections bill; and lengthy, acrimonious debates over Senator Blair's Education Bill. Of all these, the elections bill, the silver problem, and the tariff rates claimed first importance, although the other issues, which had dramatic aspects, would put Harrison's Administration to a severe test.

Highest on his legislative list were a protective tariff, and a bill guaranteeing the southern Negro an actual, countable vote in federal elections. Getting these measures through the House by a strict party vote would be relatively easy. The Senate, however, would require cajoling. Although Republicans did have a bare majority, sixteen or more western senators held the balance of power. Known as the "silver bloc,"[12] they were loud in their demands for the free coinage of silver, and as a start they asked for a liberalization of the Bland-Allison Act, which in 1878 had become law over the veto of President Hayes. Harrison's task was to win western Republican support for his chief Administration measures. To accomplish this, he first had to settle the silver question without going to the extreme of a free-coinage law.

Six years in the Senate had taught Harrison a great deal about the operation of the Bland-Allison Act, which had provided for government purchase of $2,000,000 worth of bullion each month to be coined into silver dollars. Although fears of inflation never materialized, still the desires of free silverites had scarcely been met, for the market price of silver had declined to a ratio of twenty to one in relation to gold.

Harrison soon learned that the leaders in the movement for free silver were the senators from the newly admitted mining states. Under the leadership of Teller and Wolcott of Colorado, these Republicans vigorously urged free coinage, although the President supposed that they might be satisfied with something less. He enjoyed some advantage over Cleveland, who had shown himself a resolute foe of silver, while Harrison had posed as a friend to silver without ever committing himself to free coinage. In order now to implement the party platform on tariffs and civil rights, he needed the support of the silverites as much as they needed the backing of the Administration for financial relief. At the same time, it was

12 Fred Wellborn, "The Influence of the Silver-Republican Senators, 1889–1891," *Mississippi Valley Historical Review*, XIV, No. 4 (1928), 462–80.

essential to stave off a threatened alliance between western senators of his own party with the southern Democrats, who might well adopt filibustering tactics.

Although Harrison would shun free coinage, he did tell Congress in his first annual message on December 3, 1889: "I have always been an advocate of the use of silver in our currency. We are large producers of that metal and should not discredit it."[13] In mid-January, the President and Secretary Windom exchanged views on how best to draft a bill which would authorize the issue of Treasury notes on deposits of silver bullion. Upon reaching agreement, Harrison provided copies for the Cabinet, which unanimously approved the proposed measure.[14]

It was essential for a Republican to espouse the bill which on January 20, 1890 was introduced in the House by Edwin H. Conger of Iowa. After about three months, the Committee on Coinage, Weights and Measures would report it back; meanwhile, violent opposition to the bill was voiced both by sound-currency men who feared inflation and silver advocates who wanted free coinage. Inside and outside the Committee room the debate raged, and Harrison and Windom were attacked on the Senate floor. Excessive speech-making in behalf of free and unlimited coinage led Attorney General Miller to observe that "the trouble is . . . Congress seems to be in a dilly-dally mood."[15] The Windom bill, which came out of committee on March 26th, received no real attention in the House until June. The Senate meanwhile was debating silver legislation of its own. Occasionally the atmosphere grew tense. On April 5th, Leonidas L. Polk, President of the Farmers Alliance and Industrial Union, predicted in a letter to Populist leader James B. Weaver that

The silver states of the West are ready for a revolt, and you may listen for thunderbolts from that quarter to fall upon the Republicans in the Senate during this week. . . . The lines are being drawn

13 *Public Papers and Addresses of Benjamin Harrison*, pp. 45–46. Harrison went on record to say that "any safe legislation . . . must secure the equality of the two coins in their commercial uses." The President suggested that he might communicate further with Congress on the subject of silver.

14 Windom to Harrison, January 14, 1890, (L.C.), Vol. 96. Also Philadelphia *Press* as cited in the Indianapolis *Journal*, January 24, 1890, and the New York *Tribune*, January 20, 23, 1890. Editorials on "The Silver Bullion Bill" praised Harrison and Windom for a joint "endeavor to solve the silver problem on the basis of justice to all."

15 W. H. H. Miller to John E. Sparn, March 13, 1890, Miller Letterbooks.

very tightly through the South and will result in a most signal division of the Democratic party.[16]

With the aid of "Czar" Reed in the House, Harrison was able to hold the party line there. A bill passed on June 7th called for the purchase of $4,500,000 worth of silver per month backed by U.S. Treasury notes. The cautious provision was made that coinage "should only be in such amounts as necessary to provide for redemption."[17] In other words, practically all the nation's silver output would be purchased and free coinage avoided.

Harrison tried to conciliate the various Republican views in order to win in the Senate, but met with temporary failure when Senator Preston B. Plumb of Kansas got a free-coinage amendment adopted. The bill as amended passed the Senate by a vote of 42 to 25, thus necessitating a conference.

Pressure mounted on all sides. The president of the Mercantile Bank of New York advised compromise,[18] while a Colorado lawyer urged that Harrison "sign any silver bill that may be presented to him, leaving the responsibility of the measure to the test of actual experience and to the representatives of the people, whose duty it is to legislate on the subject."[19] A British diplomat in America saw it this way:

The probablity is . . . a compromise between the Administration and House and the Senate. . . . Free coinage itself will not pass unless the feeling alters. Its real meaning is the fearful burden of debt of the South and West—, which is mortgaged to the N E and is naturally anxious for cheap money. The farmers here are in a terribly bad way, worse than in England, because they own their own land and are so heavily mortgaged.[20]

Harrison himself lost no time in arranging a series of White House conferences aimed at persuading the free-silver senators to

16 James Baird Weaver Papers. (The author is indebted to the late Claude R. Cook, amiable archivist at the Iowa State Dept. of History and Archives.)

17 Wellborn, art. cit., p. 466.

18 The bank official was William P. St. John, prominent in Union League and Republican circles, who had been in Washington on June 14 and who urged the compromise ultimately adopted by the Administration.

19 D. V. Burns to Halford, June 19, 1890, Harrison Papers on Microfilm, Series 2, also assured the White House that "General Harrison's administration is giving satisfaction to the great majority of the people of this state, irrespective of party, notwithstanding the attacks that have been made upon him by some of our representative citizens."

20 Stephen Gwynn (ed.), Letters and Friendships of Sir Cecil Spring-Rice I, 102-4.

accept a compromise bill. Reiterating his opposition to free coinage, he threw the weight of his office behind a bill that he hoped
would please the whole country.[21] Actually this was impossible—
gold reserves had shrunk and would shrink further, but at least the
conference committee killed the free-coinage amendment.[22] Now
required was the purchase of 4,500,000 ounces of silver per month
at the market price, through the issuance of Treasury notes re-
deemable in gold or silver coin at the option of the Treasurer. At
an average price of $1.00 per ounce, this meant an increase of 125
percent in silver coinage. Paper money would flow more freely,
putting a strain on Treasury reserves of gold.

The compromise, known as the Sherman Silver Purchase Act,
was adopted by the Senate on July 10th, and by the House two days
later. A victory of a kind, it was celebrated by faithful G.O.P.
senators and congressmen at a White House dinner, followed by a
Sousa band concert. A note to Mrs. Harrison, then at Cape May
Point, New Jersey, reflected the President's sentiments on the eve
of signing:

The passage of the Silver Bill by the House yesterday (July 12) was
very gratifying to all our people. I have been asking for a Republican
bill and this must be one—for no Democrats voted for it in either
House. It is not just what I wanted, but it is not so far away but
that I shall be glad to end a controversy by signing it, when it comes
to me tomorrow.[23]

Yet as Sir Thomas Gresham had seen, lightweight or cheap
money tends to drive out the dearer, and the nation would soon
see the principle realized. Human nature and the love of sound
money being what they are, it becomes impossible to tinker with
an established currency system without causing future difficulty.
While trouble from this source was mounting, Harrison would
have other legislative matters to consider and the current session of
Congress would be protracted.

Of Harrison's four years in the White House, the most difficult
was 1890 when a so-called Federal Elections bill (as well as anti-
trust tariff legislation) coincided with the battle over free silver.

21 *Journal*, June 21, 25, 1890.

22 Wellborn, *art. cit.*, pp. 467–68. The entire story has been since told in full detail by W. A. Robinson, *Thomas B. Reed*, pp. 244–46.

23 The President to Mrs. Harrison, July 13, 1890, Marthena Harrison Williams MSS.
(copies in the possession of the author).

The Democratic minorities in Congress had assembled after New Year's Day, 1890, in a hostile mood. As true party members, they nursed a smoldering resentment over Cleveland's defeat in 1888; moreover, they had been stung by final failure to indict and convict William Wade Dudley, charged with ballot fraud,[24] and they were intensely irritated by several bills aimed at guaranteeing the Negro a vote in federal elections. Now and again they looked for some means to break Speaker Tom Reed's iron rule so as to hamstring the Republican program.

Not unexpectedly, the Senate welcomed any opportunity to embarrass the Chief Executive. It was natural that the first onslaught be aimed at a policy which envisioned federal control of elections so that Negroes might vote freely and have their votes counted. Harrison had asked that legal protection be extended to colored citizens who "did not intrude themselves upon us." No political or civil rights should be withheld and "no question in our country can be at rest except upon the firm base of justice and the law."[25]

In these latter postwar years, Negro mass meetings were held all over the country, including the District of Columbia. From these were issued scores of protests that federal, as well as local, elections in the South saw the suppression of Negro votes by violence or fraud. Too, Harrison was advised that "our wives and daughters, our mothers and sisters, are forced, in consequence of . . . legislation to occupy seats . . . in filthy and inferior cars." The White House was reminded that "in the execution of justice Negroes are cowardly lynched and murdered without a hearing and without even a semblance of a trial."[26] Harrison acknowledged each mes-

24 W. H. H. Miller to Sen. George F. Edmunds, January 7, 1890, Miller Letterbooks, recalled that "a very large number of witnesses were subpoenaed," a full investigation conducted by Democratic district attorneys, "but the grand jury refused to find indictment"; also New York *Tribune*, January 9, 1890. For the full story on W. W. Dudley, see Harry J. Sievers, *Benjamin Harrison: Hoosier Statesman*, pp. 417–21.

25 *Public Papers and Addresses of Benjamin Harrison*, pp. 62–63.

26 Harrison Papers on Microfilm, Series 2, Reel 70, "An Address to the President" issued by Colored Americans meeting in Washington, D.C., on February 3, 1890. Other complaints placed before Harrison read as follows: (1) our children are not afforded the school facilities to which they are justly entitled; (2) the labor system in most of the Southern States is unjust and unfair to Colored Americans; (3) we are compelled to obey laws that we have no voice in making; (4) we petition the federal courts be organized and that juries be drawn that will be favorable to the enforcement of the laws; (5) we petition enactment of the "Blair Educational Bill" and request appropriated monies be apportioned on the basis of illiteracy; (6) we also petition the present Congress to pass such laws as will put federal elections under federal control. It can be noted that Harrison received many similar appeals (Reels 69, 70, *passim*).

sage by a personal reply and meanwhile told Congress that the
Negro "should be protected in all his relations to the Federal
Government, whether as litigant, juror, or witness in our courts,
as an elector for member of Congress, or as a peaceful traveler
upon our interstate railways."[27] Whatever Harrison's emotional
reaction may have been, he had witnessed northern sacrifices during the war and he well knew the cost of Union and liberty. Politics aside, he would exclude no man from these benefits. His was a
responsible administration, and as a western newspaper stated:

Harrison may just as well understand it now as later on, that the
Negro is restless and dissatisfied with his administration and has no
confidence in his pretended promises, but desires facts and facts alone
. . . the Negro is sore and mighty sore.[28]

But Harrison would try to fulfill what, in effect, were past political pledges. In 1885, as a United States Senator, he had shown
concern over "the suppressed Republican vote of the South," and
in a humane speech on the Senate floor in the spring of 1886, he
had declared himself "one of those who feel that the colored race
in the South since the war has been subjected to indignities, cruel-
ties, outrages, and a repression of rights such as find no parallel in
the history of civilization."[29]

Inasmuch as his views were known, ministers, educators, and
politicians alike were confident of a sympathetic hearing in urging
civil and political rights for the Negro. Some were former slaves—
"preachers and teachers [who] presented the subject with great
power and earnestness."[30]

The problem was all the more immediate now, since southern
Negroes who had suffered little mistreatment when Democrats under Cleveland had been securely in power, were killed off or outraged in large numbers after the Republicans returned. Indiana
State Attorney General Michener, who was well informed, saw
that the remedy would lie in legislation backed by rigorous en-

[27] *Public Papers and Addresses of Benjamin Harrison,* "Annual Message of 1889,"
p. 63.

[28] An undated clipping (Detroit *Plain-Dealer,* a weekly; November, 1889?) in
Harrison Papers on Microfilm, Series 2; also H. C. Astwood to Harrison, December 3,
1889, *ibid.*

[29] New Orleans *Weekly Pelican,* December 1, 1888.

[30] L. T. Michener to E. W. Halford, October 1, 1889, (L.C.), Vol. 88.

forcement. "I am earnestly in favor of such legislation," he wrote Harrison. . . .

It may be true that the enforcement of such laws will cause bloodshed in some portions of the South, but better bloodshed than slavery and outrages and murder for political reasons in this civilized nation.[31]

There came a heavy mail from Negro individuals and groups in both the North and the South. They joined northern whites in their endorsement of and support for honest elections and fair play. Harrison received from John M. Langston, the first Negro congressman from Virginia, a letter expressing "grateful, profound thanks for your warmest, brave and opportune words employed in your excellent message."[32] A sixteen-year-old Pennsylvania boy was proud of his President and "pleased with his principles"; and a senior Illinois citizen, a Harrison voter in 1840, strongly endorsed the plea for "free and untrammeled exercise of the right of suffrage." He added:

I hope Congress at this session will pass laws giving the Executive power to place troops at the polls in the election of members of Congress wherever fraud and intimidation are practiced to deprive the Negro of his political rights.[33]

Northern Republicans introduced several election bills in the new Congress. Among the prime movers were Senators George Frisbee Hoar of Massachusetts, John Sherman of Ohio, John C. Spooner of Wisconsin, and William C. Chandler of New Hampshire, and Representatives Henry Cabot Lodge of Massachusetts, Jonathan H. Rawell of Illinois, and Harrison Kelley of Kansas. Speaker Reed cooperated in pushing for the desired legislation. Toward the end of April 1890, House Republicans instructed Lodge to make order out of the several bills. Lodge talked with Senator Hoar, a leader of the movement, and in due course there came to Congress the Lodge Bill, which provided for Federal supervision of elections in the South.

The measure that became known as the Force Bill would pass in the House but fail in the Senate. At no time could Harrison count on the full support of his party. Early opposition came from Sena-

31 *Ibid.*

32 Langston to Harrison, December 3, 1889, Harrison Papers on Microfilm, Series 2.

33 J. P. Bartlett to Harrison, December 6, 1889, *ibid.*

tors J. Donald Cameron and Matthew Quay, both of Pennsylvania, where corporate interests with holdings in the South feared that business might be disturbed.[34] Spooner said of these two and of other Republican recalcitrants:

The Almighty dollar obscures their vision. I mean by that, that the commercial spirit which held back the anti-slavery men, is holding them back against anything that might sacrifice commerce to the right of citizenship.[35]

During the spirited debates, Harrison was privately urged to use the weight and power of office to lead a public crusade for Negro rights in the South. Chief proponent of the idea was the Ohio-born war veteran Albion W. Tourgee, lawyer, former carpetbagger and onetime justice of the North Carolina Superior Court, whose novels, *A Fool's Errand* and *Bricks Without Straw*, had dramatized Negro problems. He wrote Harrison:

The colored man North and South firmly believes . . . that a Republican President, a Republican House and a Republican Senate, are able to *do something* to secure free speech, a free ballot and a fair return of votes at the South.[36]

Tourgee, who had drafted an election bill introduced by a congressman from Kansas, urged that a special message, "terse, pertinent and original, like one of your campaign speeches, would secure the passage of such a law." Tourgee had the idea that such a message "would thrill like an electric flash—especially if it came unheralded, as your personal act."[37] Tourgee wrote quite a number of pleading letters, arguing at one point that a bold, urgent message to Congress "would rouse the country as one of Napoleon's proclamations did his army."

But, unable to consider himself a Paul Revere, let alone a Napoleon, Harrison depended on "Czar" Reed who, by limiting each speaker to forty minutes (but changing this rule when necessary), and brooking no interference or delay, justified his election as a partisan Speaker. Not only did he control members of his own party, but he also blocked all efforts of the opposition to emascu-

---

[34] E. J. Gibson to Halford, January 5, 1890, (L.C.), Vol. 95. Gibson showed conclusively that Cameron tried to discredit the Administration and block legislation in the Senate.

[35] Dorothy Ganfield Fowler, *John Coit Spooner*, p. 138.

[36] Tourgee to Harrison, April 12, 1890, (L.C.), Vol. 103.

[37] *Ibid.*

late the Lodge Bill or delay a vote on it. On July 2nd, the House passed the measure by the narrow margin of 155 votes to 149. A greater struggle, however, would take place in the Senate.

In many ways the date of July 2, 1890 would live long in the memory of Benjamin Harrison. In addition to the satisfaction afforded by the House passage of the Lodge Bill, the President signed into law the major measure so far passed by the Fifty-first Congress—the Sherman Anti-Trust Act, which still remains on the statute books. The next day he would admit Idaho into the Union as the forty-third state.[38] Harrison could look back on the first six months with some satisfaction. A pledge to needy veterans had been redeemed,[39] the door to trade with South America had been swung open,[40] and the House had completed work—long and hard —on a controversial tariff bill. No one could deny that much remained on the agenda but on that evening, as the Marine Band played on the White House lawn, most of the guests—like the President himself—were looking forward to the long Fourth of July weekend away from the depressing humidity of the capital city.

[38] *Journal*, July 4, 1890.

[39] On June 27, 1890, a bill passed granting pensions to soldiers and sailors who served 90 days in the Civil War, now or hereafter disabled, and to widows and minor children and dependent parents. (See Chapter X, pp. 127-28.)

[40] The Pan-American Conference adjourned on April 19, 1890, and the U.S. would soon push for reciprocity agreements. See *Journal*, April 21, 1890, editorial entitled "Work of the All-American Conference."

CHAPTER XIII

A Splendid Cottage and a Lottery

A NATURALLY CORPULENT Benjamin Harrison had grown even more stout as a result of keeping quite close to his desk during the first several months of the Fifty-first Congress. White House confinement was broken by a trip to Cleveland where, on May 30th, he assisted in the dedication of a monument to James A. Garfield marking the late President's tomb. In addition, there had been some weekend hunting and shooting, as well as a sea cruise to Fortress Monroe. No real vacation or long walks were possible, however, until Harrison left the heated city on July 3, 1890, to join his family at Cape May Point. Meanwhile, the White House was to undergo extensive repair, including electrical wiring, over the next four months.

A sizable, newly built furnished cottage, which the President later saw fit to purchase, had originally been presented to Mrs. Harrison by Postmaster General John Wanamaker and some Philadelphia friends. The gift, which was made by private subscription, had been almost settled when Harrison told his Postmaster that, after occupying the cottage, he would advise him as to the conditions of its acceptance.[1] As it turned out, Mrs. Harrison, who had gone there in June, was so delighted with the sea breezes, the broad porches, and the twenty airy rooms, that her husband decided, as he put it, "to become the donor" while acknowledging his debt to those who had supervised the construction and elegant furnishings.[2] His $10,000 check to John Wanamaker was dated July 2nd.

Meanwhile a storm had blown up. The Indianapolis *Journal,* as

1 Harrison recalled this detail in a letter to John Wanamaker dated July 2, 1890, in which the $10,000 check was enclosed (L.C.)., Vol. 108. Wanamaker to Harrison, June 26, 1896, (L.C.), Vol. 165, stipulates re-sale by Harrison to Wanamaker six years later.
2 Harrison to Wanamaker, July 2, 1890, *loc cit.*

usual, was first in reporting family news. On May 29th, a special dispatch to the paper from Washington stated briefly: "The President and his family will summer at Cape May Point, New Jersey, either with the Postmaster General, who has a cottage there, or in a cottage that is being specially constructed for that purpose." And when the deed and keys to the cottage were presented to Mrs. Harrison a few days later, the faithful *Journal* so reported, adding that the President "was greatly surprised."[3] Other papers were quick to pick up the scent. "Who are those generous individuals," the New York *Sun* queried editorially, "that have bestowed upon MRS. BENJAMIN HARRISON a cottage at Cape May Point, clear of encumbance and with floors swept clean for BABY MC KEE to creep over this summer?" It was urged that the subscribers' names be made public and that Harrison return the gift forthwith. "The President who takes a bribe is a lost President," the *Sun* argued sententiously.[4]

The story was too good to let go, and the Philadelphia *Inquirer* (Republican) was able to obtain some remarks from Mrs. Harrison, who said, in effect, that she was really pleased although holding to the idea of only temporary occupancy rather than complete acceptance.[5] Photographs of the house began to appear, and while the editorial attacks on the President spread out in widening circles ("Gift Grabber," "disgraceful proceeding," and the like),[6] the so-called Cape May Improvement Company and other real-estate promoters began to preen themselves on a land-office business that placed a premium on "certain sandy reaches and mammoth patches in Southern Jersey."[7] For a week or more following Mrs. Harrison's arrival there, property near "The President's Home" was being advertised in Philadelphia and Baltimore newspapers, while news columns detailed Mrs. Harrison's movements and speculated about the loan of a carriage and horses. The Philadelphia *Inquirer* ably summed up the matter by stating that "the Cape May proceeding is a vulgar business driven along without regard to the feelings of the President and his family, and Mr. Har-

3 *Journal*, June 7, 1890.

4 New York *Sun*, June 11, 1890. The *Sun* was joined by the Philadelphia *Record* (quoted by the *Sun* on June 16) in launching the attack on Harrison.

5 Philadelphia *Inquirer*, June 13, 1890.

6 Philadelphia *Record*, quoted in the New York *Sun*, June 16, 1890; New York *Sun*, June 18, 1890. Said the *Sun*: "The establishment is, in plain words, an eleemosynary institution."

7 Philadelphia *Inquirer*, June 23, 1890.

rison, who has nerve and common sense, should put an end to it."[8]

Back at the White House, Harrison appeared more concerned over Pension, Post Office, and Naval Appropriation bills which awaited his study and signature; and on July 2nd, after signing into law the Sherman Anti-Trust Act, he wrote John Wanamaker a letter gracious in tone but somewhat businesslike in that the Postmaster was asked to "be good enough to see to the right disposition of the check inclosed."[9] Inasmuch as the letter was private, it could hardly end the criticism, which friendly newspapers tried to lessen by relating that while the cottage was originally built as a gift to the President, just as one at Long Branch had been presented to President Grant, Harrison had declined to accept it as such.[10] The New York *Times* (Democratic) then argued that Harrison had bought it only after he had felt the attacks on him.[11] No attention was paid to the possibility that the President or his wife might have wished to examine this new home before concluding the sale. The sympathetic Washington *Star* argued that:

So far as accepting the cottage as a gift, the moment the matter was brought to the President's attention he thanked the gentlemen for their great kindness but distinctly declined to accept it as a gift, saying that the terms upon which it would be occupied would be left to future determination. The matter had gone so far that he could not well say more or less than this without appearing churlish and rude. So far as the main point is concerned, it is enough that he promptly declined to accept the property as a gift. That left him free to decide on further action, and this was the payment of its full value.[12]

Further plans, in view of prolonged White House alterations and repairs, were to spend September in a mountain cottage at Cresson, Pennsylvania, near Altoona. When the story was circulated that this would be a rent-free gratuity of the Pennsylvania Railroad, a company spokesman stated that the cottage had been leased by a realty company to the President "at a fair price," and there the matter rested.[13]

Harrison continued to occupy the Cape May Point cottage in

8 *Ibid.*

9 Harrison to Wanamaker, July 2, 1890, *loc. cit.*

10 Philadelphia *Press* dispatch, reprinted by the Indianapolis *Journal,* July 15, 1890.

11 As quoted in the *Journal* of July 28, 1890, in an editorial headed "The Malice of the Opposition."

12 Quoted *ibid.*

13 The *Journal* of July 10, 1890 quoted the Pennsylvania Railroad's general passenger agent as saying that there was "absolutely no warrant for the assertion that the cottage was tendered him by anyone."

later years, although following its sale for the very reasonable sum of $10,000, in 1896, he would transfer his allegiance from the Jersey shore to the Adirondack mountains. The $10,000, which was received from John Wanamaker, was the same as the price paid. It was still remembered that President Grover Cleveland had purchased a property of 27 acres, located three miles from the White House for $21,500 in 1886 and had sold it some years later "for far more."[14] Although quite aware that critical eyes scanned every real-estate transaction affecting the presidential purse, Harrison was unlikely to use his high office to gain monetary profit. Perhaps a little tardily, but no less earnestly, he acted so as to avoid any suspicion of it.

Relations with Postmaster General Wanamaker, long one of Philadelphia's religious leaders, were all the closer that summer because of a joint struggle with the well-known Louisiana lottery, which could be briefly described as a spreading morass of corruption. The diversion of household funds by wives, grocery money by servants, and office cash by numerous clerks was encouraged if not abetted by the phantom lure of gold. If household meals were sometimes skimpy, the cook had her reasons; while employers were often hard put to balance the office books. The funds involved were huge, just as the odds were long and the payments lean. Thefts of letters containing cash for lottery tickets were common although complaints were seldom lodged.[15]

Harrison, who in his first message to Congress had asked for a more stringent law relating to the use of mails by lottery promoters, called on the Postmaster General to find out the facts and report directly to him; for the lottery company had altogether too many legal tricks for the Justice Department to handle. Wanamaker did not have to go to Louisana to discover that the lottery ring mailed out about 50,000 letters a month to Washington alone, while the mail it received could be measured by the ton. He estimated that the lottery had increased the postal traffic by five to one.[16]

14 *Journal*, July 15, 1890. John Wanamaker offered to take the property for $10,000, but in order to forestall criticism the title was placed in the name of a third party. (See W. V. McKean [editor of the Philadelphia *Ledger*, and Wanamaker's close friend] to Harrison, May 5 and 29, 1895; and Wanamaker to McKean, June 24, 1895, Harrison Papers on Microfilm, Series 2. Also Harrison to McKean, June 24, 1896, (L.C.), Vol. 165.)

15 John S. Ezell, *Fortune's Merry Wheel: The Lottery in America*, devotes Ch. 13 (pp. 242–70) to the Louisiana Lottery and its political activities including bribery.

16 Wanamaker to Harrison, June 28, 1890, as cited in Ezell, *op. cit.*, p. 262; *Journal*, July 18, 1890.

The overt act, which in the end had drastic effect, had been the lottery company's efforts to obtain a franchise, through bribery, in the infant state of North Dakota. A whopping state debt of $539,807 could easily be paid off, it was stressed. The lottery agents would settle for $100,000 per year plus 150,000 bushels of wheat seed if granted the franchise. The measure carried the state senate without much difficulty (over a two-thirds majority), but strong voices began to make themselves heard.

Governor John Miller, for example, reported to Harrison that the lottery lobby was indeed powerful. He charged that with ample funds at its command, "income from this unholy business will be able to control the politics."[17] North Dakota's Chief Justice Guy Corliss wired: "public sentiment prostituted, pressure of national sentiment our only hope."[18] The club that Harrison then used was the publication of reports to him that the lottery people had reached persons "appointed to office or candidates for appointment." Should it be found that such were promoting the legislation, "it would likely prove fatal to them."[19] Postmaster General Wanamaker and Attorney General Miller joined in. Theirs was "astonishment beyond measure," and reaching for the strongest statement he could find, Miller observed that for North Dakota to sanction lottery "would be like Massachusetts legalizing polygamy."[20] One could hardly go much beyond that.

But there was no lack of pressure on the side of the angels. Pinkerton detectives on the ground could readily threaten public exposure of the corrupted. It was noised about that Harrison would withhold nomination of any further appointments in North Dakota until the lottery scheme was scuttled. The thrusts hit home, despite censorship efforts by certain Northern Pacific Railroad officials who cut the Western Union wires at Bismarck.[21] North Dakota's lower house could not help but indefinitely postpone the lottery measure. An impetus toward a complete probe of the lottery company's methods was what this all amounted to; hence John Wanamaker's examination of the mails and the insistent stand taken by Harrison to obtain an effective law.

17 Telegram from John Miller to Harrison, February 3, 1890, and letter of February 4, 1890, (L.C.), Vol. 97, and Vol. 98. Miller warned that the bill probably would pass the North Dakota senate as matters then stood.
18 Telegram from Corliss to Harrison, February 7, 1890, (L.C.), Vol. 98.
19 Journal, February 8, 1890.
20 Ibid.
21 Minneapolis Tribune, May 31, 1890; Indianapolis Journal, June 1, 1890.

Wanamaker tried to get the Post Office Committee of the House to act, but apparently lacked personal influence in the face of able lobbyists. Harrison then had the committee members call on him at the White House, three times in all, but the President's humorless attitude did not serve him well in personal conferences where a more hearty personality might have asserted itself. Finally, his Presbyterian patience worn thin, Harrison warned the Congress that "unless a bill was voluntarily reported from the Committee" he would produce a special message urging immediate action.[22] It was now late July, and the President had returned to Washington for a few days.

Little time was lost in waiting for the House to act. Dated July 29, 1890, Harrison's special message to Congress requested "severe and effective legislation . . . to purge the mails of all letters, newspapers and circulars" relating to the lottery. It was a matter of record, he pointed out, that the national capital had become a potent center of lottery agents whose "corrupting touch . . . had been felt by the clerks in the postal service and by some of the police officers of the District." In a more casual manner, Harrison declared that it was hardly necessary for him "to attempt to portray the robbery of the poor and the widespread corruption of public and private morals which are the necessary incidents of these lottery schemes."[23]

About the only newspaper critical of the bill was the New Orleans *Times-Democrat*, which was well recompensed for lottery advertising and other paid notices. Harrison and Wanamaker were soundly upbraided as themselves being agents of corruption, as exemplified by the "gift of a cottage-by-the-sea." The situation presented, the writer went on, "is verily next-door neighbor to the spectacle of Satan reproving sin."[24] Other journals, regardless of party politics, took an opposite view.[25] With party lines no barrier,

22 *Journal*, July 26, 1890.

23 *Public Papers and Addresses of Benjamin Harrison*, pp. 165–66.

24 The editorial, headed "Harrison and Wanamaker on Corruption," asked where the President got his information and concluded that "it came from that other twin saint, Wanamaker, peer of even Ben Harrison himself in canting sanctimoniousness" (dated August 1, 1890, a clipping in (L.C.), Vol. 110).

25 The Chicago *Post*, although Democratic, stated: "The anti-lottery message of the President has met with the cordial approval of nearly every daily paper of any reputation in the country, regardless of politics, which shows decidedly the most intelligent sentiment . . . is against the scheme of demoralization" (quoted approvingly by Indianapolis *Journal*, August 1, 1890).

Harrison obtained favorable House action within three weeks after his special message to Congress; for, on August 16th, Congressman John A. Caldwell of Ohio brought in a stringent measure, barring the lottery and its customers from use of the mails, that was passed in a first reading the same day.

In the Senate, Philetus Sawyer of Wisconsin, an outspoken lottery foe, eagerly received the bill on September 2nd. Final passage without debate and without amendment would be achieved only two weeks later, and on September 19th Harrison signed the bill into law.[26] Sundry arrests, indictments and convictions would follow. Although the maximum fine under the bill was only $500, a year in prison could be added to the penalty or decreed alone.

Back at the Cape May cottage, Harrison would next concern himself with the tariff, reciprocity of trade, and the Negro question. Of any issue he was called upon to face, the tariff was probably the most difficult, and, in the long run, it would prove the most troublesome.

26 Ezell, *op. cit.*, p. 263, states that the new law "barred all letters, postal cards, circulars, lists of drawings, tickets and other materials referring to lotteries from the mails. No check, draft bill, money . . . could be transported. . . . Registered letters would be returned unopened."

CHAPTER XIV

A Tariff Won, A Panic Averted

IF A PROTECTIVE tariff was the foremost party pledge to be redeemed by the Fifty-first Congress, it also would become the chief cause of dissension in Republican ranks and ultimately a thorn in the side of the party. As presidential candidate in 1888, Harrison had espoused high tariff doctrine as well as the principle of duty-free imports from those countries that would extend the same privilege to the United States, i.e., reciprocity.[1] Harrison told farmers that the wider market to be gained was part and parcel of the framework of tariff protection. They believed him and voted for him. Long before his inauguration, he had determined to ask Congress for a tariff that would include the reciprocity principle.[2]

He reiterated the same idea during the Pan-American Conference.[3] The national goal, in his mind, was that of larger and better markets at home and abroad, "more constant employment and better wages."[4] Secretary of State James Blaine could easily agree on reciprocity, a favorite program for trade between the United States and Latin America. But when the William McKin-

---

[1] Harrison had staked his campaign and election on the principle of protection. See Sievers, *Benjamin Harrison: Hoosier Statesman*, pp. 375–76; also L. T. Michener to E. W. Halford, August 26, 1890, (L.C.), Vol. 111, wrote: "My notion has been that reciprocity is a part of protection, and especially when it is brought about in a way recently advocated by Mr. Blaine. My recollection is that the President had considerable to say to the same effect in his speeches in the campaign of 1888."

[2] Harrison to Blaine, January 17, 1889, cited in Volwiler, *Correspondence Between Harrison and Blaine*, p. 44, and Michener stated that "the reciprocity doctrine has hosts of adherents among the Indiana Republicans." Michener to E. W. Halford, August 26, 1890, (L.C.), Vol 111.

[3] *Public Papers and Addresses of Benjamin Harrison*, pp. 31–37.

[4] *Ibid.*, pp. 79–80. The quotation is from Harrison's second annual message to Congress, December 1, 1890. This official document mirrors well the thinking of Harrison between January and November of 1890. He took pride in announcing that the value of American exports in 1889 increased $115,000,000 over 1888, and he advised farmers that "about $100,000,000 of this excess was in agricultural products."

ley Bill, sponsored by the Ohio Congressman, who was now chairman of Ways and Means, provided for repeal of the duty on raw sugar, Blaine could not agree; nor, indeed, could all party men.[5]

"The people are patiently waiting for Congress to act on the tariff bill," a one-time Indiana Congressman wrote Secretary Halford in mid-March, 1890. "I fear they will be disappointed, as nearly four months of the session has now elapsed and there still appears to be a disagreement on the sugar schedule."[6] Republicans could agree that tariff *revenues* should be reduced because of a surplus of funds in the U.S. Treasury. Duty-free sugar would help tip the scales just as higher duties on manufactured items would tend to lessen the flow of imports.

Blaine, however, was arguing that too many Latin American products were being admitted free already.[7] "May I hope that you will not consent to the throwing away of a hundred million [dollars worth] of sugar with nothing in return," he wrote Harrison from Bar Harbor on July 19th. "I want *you* first and last to keep yourself and your administration free from mistakes and especially from gigantic blunders. . . . It will be a bad political blow if the Bill passes in its present shape."[8] Blaine had reference to passage in the Senate; the bill had already been railroaded through the House by Speaker Tom Reed by a party vote of 138 to 121.

Since the chief obstacle appeared to be the sugar question, Harrison assured the Secretary that he would have an amendment included to provide for the reimposition of tariffs if reciprocal advantages were withheld by other nations.[9] So it was done, although it seemed clear that a Senate majority favored lower

5 New York *Tribune*, February 20, 1890. Any change save a slight or token reduction was opposed by the Sugar Trust which counted among its supporters Secretary Blaine and Gen. W. J. Sewell. See Sewell to the President, July 14, 1890, (L.C.), Vol. 109. As a former Senate crony and personal hunting companion, Sewell, now a rich railroad magnate, advised the President that the sugar refiners were entitled to consideration, since "they are suffering from the bad repute of a trust." Also the Indianapolis *Journal*, February 15, 1890, noted: "The Sugar Trust does not want free sugar, and their attorneys in Washington are using all possible persuasion. . . ."

6 S. J. Peele to E. W. Halford, March 18, 1890, (L.C.), Vol. 101.

7 Blaine to Harrison, July 22, 1890, *ibid.* "Eighty per cent of the Latin American goods were already admitted free," he pointed out, "while many American exports to Latin America had to pay high duties." Also see H. U. Faulkner, *Politics, Reform and Expansion*, p. 108.

8 Blaine to Harrison, July 19, 21, 1890, (L.C.), Vol. 110.

9 Harrison to Blaine, July 17, 1890, as cited in Volwiler, *op. cit.*, p. 109, noted that "things have gone so far that I do not think we can avoid free sugar, but if my plan will stand criticism, as I believe it will, we can still hold the strings in our hands. I am in negotiations for reciprocity."

sugar duties or none at all. The free list also included molasses, coffee and tea, and hides.

But duties on other farm products, including butter, barley, hams and bacon, would be higher, and refined sugar would continue to be taxed, permitting a bit of leeway for the American Sugar Company. Louisiana cane producers, meanwhile, would receive a protective bounty of two cents a pound. All manufactured goods subject to competition between U.S. and foreign plants would have a higher duty. The ultimate effect on the purchasing power of the wage earner and low salaried individual was given little thought.

An amendment postponing the free entry of raw sugar for six months after passage of the bill also helped mollify Secretary Blaine, who, late in July was invited to visit the President at Cape May Point. Harrison and several friends visited him at the Congress Hall Hotel in Cape May the day after his arrival. Then the party moved on to the cottage at the Point, where Blaine was to remain for several days. Informal talks on the shaded veranda, aboard the steam launch *Juno,* or during carriage rides about the countryside were quite private. Postmaster General Wanamaker and Secretary Halford were also seen at the cottage by visiting reporters who could do little more than file stories that bespoke peace and harmony within the official family.[10]

Returning to Washington while Blaine made his way back to Bar Harbor, Maine, Harrison told newsmen that he was confident that the Senate would pass the McKinley Bill.[11] Which indeed it would, free sugar and all, after some weeks of further debate, although not without some 460 amendments and a bad party split prior to final agreement.

A political message from Maine, which apparently was looking forward to 1892, was forwarded to Cape May. In a statement dated August 2nd, the Republican State Chairman there had declared Maine for Harrison in that future election year, noting too that "Mr. Blaine . . . has no presidential ambitions."[12]

10 *Journal,* July 17, August 2, 3, 5 and 8, 1890. See also Harrison to Blaine (telegram), July 25, 1890, as cited by Volwiler, *op. cit.* p. 114. The *Journal* announced that "The President and Mr. Blaine . . . have worked together on the same line concerning reciprocity."

11 *Journal,* August 9, 1890. Asked by reporters if he thought Congress would pass the McKinley Bill and an election bill, Harrison retorted: "I am surer than ever."

12 J. H. Manley to L. T. Michener, August 2, 1890, Michener Papers, Box 1, (L.C.). A copy of same was clipped to the L. T. Michener to E. W. Halford letter, August 4, 1890, (L.C.), Vol. 110.

Blaine, in fact, would not and could not be an avowed candidate for obvious reasons. An appreciative note from the Secretary, who had returned to Bar Harbor, assured the President that "if anyone needs a rest, and has fairly earned it, I am sure you are the man."[13] Harrison felt rested enough to travel to Boston, leaving the train at Jersey City to be transferred aboard the U.S. cruiser *Baltimore,* to attend the G.A.R. National Encampment. Flying the President's flag, the *Baltimore* was formally greeted by six other Navy ships as she arrived in Boston harbor on August 11th. With cannon mouths ablaze right and left, Harrison disembarked and received a military escort to the Hotel Vendome.[14]

The President's facility of phrase in remarking upon patriotism and love of country won him several ovations in Boston, where he addressed his G.A.R. comrades as "men who upheld the flag of the nation in those days when it was in peril," and reminded a thronged house the following evening of "magnificent evidence of what Massachusetts has done in defence of the Union and of the flag and . . . promise of what she would do again if the exigencies should call upon her to give her blood in a similar cause."[15] A spectacular parade of veterans had consumed more than five and a half hours that afternoon as, among many thousands, Harrison, Congressmen William McKinley and Henry Cabot Lodge, and the great soprano Lillian Nordica looked on.[16] Later that evening, at a joint reception of the Grand Army of the Republic and the Women's Relief Corps, Harrison told of "those silent battalions of the dead" at Arlington Cemetery and hailed "those magnificent battalions of the Sons of the Veterans" in whom could be seen the resurrection.[17]

Because of an apparently serious conflict on the tariff bill, Har-

13 Blaine to Harrison, August 7, 1890, (L.C.), Vol. 111.

14 R. A. Alger to Harrison, July 18, 1890, (L.C.), Vol. 109; C. Hedges (ed.), *Speeches of Benjamin Harrison,* p. 226; *Journal,* August 10, 1890. On the *Baltimore,* the President's flag was unfurled and a salute of twenty-one guns was fired.

15 Hedges *op. cit.,* pp. 228–29.

16 Nordica was the stage name of Lillian Norton born in Farmington, Maine, 1859. She made her debut as a soprano soloist in New York City with Patrick Gilmore's band c. 1876 at age 17. After studies in Milan, Italy, she made her operatic debut in Brescia in *La Traviata,* 1879; first appeared as prima donna as Marguerite in *Faust,* in Paris, 1882. Nordica was outstanding in Wagnerian roles, and by 1890 was celebrated for the richness of her tones, a notable coloratura range, and supreme artistic ability. See *CDAB,* p. 736.

17 Hedges, *op. cit.,* pp. 230–31. Among those greeting "Comrade" Harrison was Clara Barton, President of the Red Cross Association. Born in Oxford, Mass., in 1821, she had nursed during the Civil War and then devoted her life to Red Cross affairs until a few years before her death in 1912. See *CDAB,* pp. 52–53.

rison lost no time in returning to Washington by train. He was
back at his desk by late afternoon, August 13th, and had begun to
consider what might be done at a caucus of Republican Senators
to be held the next evening. Although it is not clear what part
he might have played in the affair, it was essentially a test of
political pragmatism. It had become all too clear that southern
Senators would not support the tariff bill unless the Federal
Elections Bill upholding Negro voting rights was scrapped. Outspoken advocates of Negro suffrage, whom Harrison supported,
were Wisconsin Senator John C. Spooner who took a stern moral
view; white-haired and portly George F. Hoar of Massachusetts,
and the veteran abolitionist William E. Chandler of New Hampshire. On the other hand, the National G.O.P. Committee Chairman, Senator Matthew Quay of Pennsylvania, could visualize
victory on the tariff issue only if the bill so distasteful to the
southern members was dropped. It seemed purely a matter of
give one and take one, vote and go home, but Spooner's indignation reached such heights that others too had to climb to keep
near him.[18]

In the background, Harrison appears to have exerted sufficient
strength to keep Republican ranks from breaking wide open.
Senator James McMillan of Michigan, Chairman of the Committee on Manufactures, invited the warring members to his
home. Pragmatism of a sort did win out.[19] It was agreed that action on the Federal Elections Bill would be postponed until the
second session of the Fifty-first Congress. Senator Hoar seemed satisfied, even if others were not entirely at ease with such pure pragmatism.[20] But at least there had been no surrender of the Negro
suffrage measure as yet.

18 John C. Spooner to Henry C. Payne, August 13, 1890, Spooner Letterbooks, Book
13, wrote that "it looks as if Aldrich and Quay had sold us out on the Federal Election
Bill. Cannot tell for a day or two, however." Likewise Congressman Robert P. Kennedy,
Republican Eighth Ohio District, linked Quay and August 13th with the emergence of
the Judas Iscariot of today. See Public Opinion, IX, 519; Fowler, John Coit Spooner,
p. 133; Indianapolis Journal, July 12, August 17, 1890; Leon Burr Richardson, William
E. Chandler: Republican, pp. 390, 395–97.

19 Richard E. Welch, Jr., "The Federal Elections Bill of 1890; Postscripts and Prelude," The Journal of American History, Vol. LII, No. 3 (December 1965), 511–26,
dramatically contrasts the figures of Quay and Hoar. "In the eyes of certain newspaper
editors in New England, Quay was the leader of the "trade-and-dicker faction" of the
party, ready to jettison the opportunity to advance the cause of the Negro . . . to . . . the
desires of those special interests to whom he was beholden."

20 Fowler, op. cit., p. 138; and Welch, art cit., p. 517. Hoar secured the signatures of
34 out of 35 Republicans in caucus to take up the consideration of the Federal Elections
Bill at the second session and "to keep it before the Senate to the exclusion of other
legislative business, until it is disposed of by vote."

Too, the tariff bill, though not yet passed, was linked with a threatened gold famine. Because higher duties were expected, imports of foreign merchandise had so increased, as laden ships raced to our ports, as to unbalance America's trade position. Gold was flowing abroad not only on this account but because of the greater demand here for silver, which it was replacing in foreign shipments. Certain silver legislation had been passed—another economic variance.[21] And a rise in the Bank of England's discount rate to five percent was luring money abroad.[22]

Bankers who flocked as usual to Bar Harbor in the summer called on Secretary Blaine who took pen in hand. "My dear Mr. President," he wrote, "several gentlemen from New York . . . have spoken to me in urgent tones about the business condition of the country. They are gentlemen of high character, with long experience in financial matters. They are most anxious that the Government should more rapidly supply money for the present demands of the country."[23] Since money was scarce, the cost of doing business had gone up and so had prices now that the McKinley Bill seemed sure of passage.

It appeared fortunate for the President—and for the country—that industrial production was continuing at a high rate with full employment of labor.[24] A long discussion with Treasury people, particularly with General A. B. Nettleton,[25] formerly of Jay Cooke and Company, now an Assistant Secretary, yielded assurance that the economic situation was sound, particularly since an unusually large cotton crop had sold high. Harrison purchased 45 shares of Great Falls Water Power and 600 of Red Mountain Consolidated Mining, both steady dividend payers, and departed

---

21 Editorial entitled "The Stringent Money Market," *Journal*, August 23, 1890.

22 Windom to Harrison, September 14, 1890, Vol. 112, claimed that these fears grew "not so much out of conditions as theories, and my impression is that the tightness of the money market is due in great measure to an anticipation of what may be required as a result of pending tariff legislation. Some . . . are no doubt true but most . . . are greatly exaggerated."

23 Blaine to Harrison, August 22, 1890, (L.C.), Vol. 111.

24 *Journal*, August 23, 1890. Large amounts of money had been put into iron furnaces, rolling mills, mines, and machinery.

25 Alfred Bayard Nettleton also had been editor and proprietor of the Minneapolis *Tribune* and had gained earlier editorial experience in the office of the *Register*, at Sandusky, Ohio. He owed his appointment to Windom with whom he was intimate. Indianapolis *Journal*, July 10, 1890, and *CDAB*, p. 724.

for Cape May.[26] To Secretary Blaine and the gentlemen of high character went the following assurance: "Everything in reason will be done and I hope an easier money market will be the result. . . . I notice . . . an upward tendency in the market in spite of the money stringency."[27]

From Cape May the Harrisons moved on to Cresson, Pennsylvania, a hillside town in the Alleghenies, a few miles southwest of Altoona. The presidential party, including Mrs. McKee, Mrs. Dimmick and little Benjamin McKee, occupied a spacious cottage near the Mountain House, the center of social activity, and the Halfords took residence in a smaller dwelling. One day Harrison drove to nearby Clearfield where bituminous coal was mined, descended a shaft, greeted sooty miners, and at the day's end met their wives and children. On September 8th he visited Loretto and nearby Gallitzin, which had been founded as a Catholic colony in 1799 by Prince Gallitzin, an exiled Russian priest. There he inspected a famed one-hundred-year-old convent and its adjoining chapel.[28]

But while Harrison had been enjoying his scheduled three week stay in Pennsylvania, a Broadway exporting firm failed for $1.5 million and financial fears grew.[29] Other news was good, R. G. Dunn reporting that "legitimate business . . . was never in a more healthy condition."[30] On September 10th, the Senate passed its own version of the tariff bill and Maine went solidly Republican by the largest majority ever.[31]

The stock market, however, was shaky. There was talk of "enormous demands for payment of duties if the new tariff should go into effect October 1"[32] which had to be countered by

26 Howard Cale to General Harrison, July 5, 10, 1890, and Charles Webster, Secretary of the Great Falls Water Power and Town Site Co., to Harrison, July 5, 1890, (L.C.), Vol. 109.

27 Harrison to Blaine, August 29, 1890, ibid.

28 Russell and Mrs. May Harrison joined the family later. Press coverage of the trip and subsequent vacation activity are reported in the Journal, September 6–24, 1890.

29 Journal, September 13, 1890. The stock market dipped sharply and reports had it that the money stringency would in time "prostrate the business of the whole country."

30 Ibid. Failures reflected bad loans made upon "giddy speculative enterprises" and were not charged to legitimate interests.

31 J. H. Manley to Harrison, (L.C.), September 8, 1890, Vol. 112. In addition to Reed, Congressmen Nelson Dingley, Jr., Charles A. Boutelle, and Seth L. Milliken were easily re-elected.

32 Harrison to Windom, September 13, 1890, ibid., a series of telegrams in rough draft, and Journal, September 13, 1890.

an official estimate that less than $9 million would pay the full duties on all goods in warehouses on which tariff rates had been raised. For Harrison and most of the Cabinet to be away at this time was hardly reassuring, however. Treasury Secretary William Windom was at Williamstown, Massachusetts, on his way to visit War Secretary Redfield Proctor in Vermont. The Attorney General, Secretary of the Interior, and Secretary Blaine also were out of town. The carriages of Agriculture Secretary Rusk, Navy Secretary Tracy and Postmaster General Wanamaker were seen waiting outside the Treasury building.

Communication was by telegraph. Harrison wired Windom and two Assistant Treasury Secretaries in Washington that effective action was needed to increase the money supply, and he instructed Windom to go to New York. It was decided to prepay $5 million worth of interest on government bonds, and the rate of four percent was raised. "Mr. Windom will do all the Treasury can do," Harrison assured Secretary Tracy. "I have urged him to act with promptness and to do enough at once."[33] Senate and House managers of the tariff legislation, which was being handled by a joint committee to work out existing differences, were urged to confer with Tracy and Assistant Treasury Secretary Nettleton at the White House.[34]

It was believed that bond men in Wall Street were waiting for Windom. Secretary Tracy had word, Harrison was notified, that they "are expecting to offer bonds at from 128 to 130, and a very strong pressure will be brought upon the Secretary to accept up to the amount of $16,000,000."[35] Harrison was satisfied that Windom would wisely withhold any specific commitment. After the Treasury Secretary had talked in New York with Mr. Parker, Mr. Coe, Mr. Knox, Mr. Perkins and Mr. Vermilye, bankers all,[36] he wired the President: "There appears to be considerable stringency but no reason to apprehend serious consequences. I . . . will take such action as I think the situation requires." He wrote the next day that the large amounts of money to be required for customs duties at a time when it was necessary to lay out increased

33 Harrison to Tracy, September 13, 1890, (L.C.), Vol. 112.

34 Harrison to Windom and Nettleton, ibid.

35 Tracy to Harrison, September 16, 1890, ibid.

36 Windom to Harrison, September 14, 1890, ibid. Windom admitted that only in New York could he "promptly and accurately learn the situation and its necessities." The gentlemen named were all bank presidents.

funds for large crops that year appeared to underlie the financial disturbance.[37] On September 18th he publicly announced that he would purchase four percent bonds in the amount of $16 million "if a reasonable price is asked for them."[38] Harrison warmly approved. Summing up in a letter of September 18th, Windom reported the bond men were found ready to sell at fair prices and that the United States Treasury in the last 33 days had paid out more than $65 million in excess of receipts during that time.[39] The Secretary was now able to resume his trip to Vermont. Harrison had a few days left at Cresson, returning to Washington in time to receive a plea from a New England delegation for a special session to allow the Senate to act on the Election Bill, presumably after the November elections.[40] The President reserved decision.

October 1st marked the final day of the long session. As the hands of the clock moved toward the hour when the first session of the Fifty-first Congress would adjourn, a state of nervous expectancy prevailed. Frustrated lobbyists who had spent months in trying to secure passage of bills were besieging members to make one last effort. Women were imploring Congressmen to get their private pension bills approved. Others, in trying to buttonhole this or that Senator or Representative, succeeded only in blocking the corridors and doorways. And there were the clerks who labored furiously to transcribe enacted bills on parchment for the President's signature.

At 2:00 P.M., Harrison arrived at the Capitol and entered the President's room just off the lobby. His presence emptied both Chambers, and what was intended as a visit merely to sign bills soon turned into a full scale reception. Leaders of both parties came to pay respects to the Chief Executive and to the Cabinet members who flanked him. The first to take Harrison's hand was William McKinley, the leader in the tariff and reciprocity legislation. After McKinley, Joe Cannon and others had received a

---

37 *Ibid.*

38 B. F. Tracy to the President, September 16, 1890, (L.C.), Vol. 112, believed that "126 or 127 at most would bring sufficient to relieve the market, provided the Secretary absolutely refuses to go above that price." Next day Windom wired Harrison that he was well pleased with the result—the fair buying price being 126 to 126¾ flat.

39 William Windom to the President, September 18, 1890, (L.C.), Vol. 113.

40 *Journal*, September 9, 1890. See also William P. Frye to Harrison, September 8, 11, 1890, (L.C.), Vol. 112, George S. Edmunds to J. S. Morrill, September 9, 1890, Morrill MSS., Vol. 40.

cordial handshake, the tariff bill was signed at 3:22 P.M.[41] In raising the level of customs duties to an average of 49.5 percent the G.O.P. had redeemed its pledge to business and industry and the opposition now had a key issue on the eve of the November elections.

The President congratulated the Congress and thanked Vice-President Morton, Kansas Senator John Ingalls (Senate President pro tempore) and Speaker Tom Reed for their dignified, impartial and courteous leadership. Before the 6:00 adjournment, he signed many more bills and vetoed three, striking down the Washington Jockey Club's bid for a monopoly on horse racing and bookmaking in the District. Harrison left the Capitol well satisfied. All in all, during the ten month session only twelve of nearly 4,000 presidential appointments had been rejected by the Senate, which had passed a record number of 1,085 bills during the historic first session.[42]

41 *Journal*, October 2, 1890.
42 *Ibid*. On September 28, 1890 it was noted that during the two sessions of the 50th Congress the Senate had passed 1,110 bills—a record until the 51st Congress.

CHAPTER XV

A Congress Lost

URING THE LONG SUMMER OF 1890, Harrison was preoccupied with the approaching off-year elections. The White House mail and visits from G.O.P. leaders underscored the important fact that in some 40 states the November balloting would decide the makeup of the Fifty-second Congress. Several important governorships also hung in the balance; but unless the G.O.P. could counter the adverse trend common to by-election years, the party's slim majorities in the Senate and House would disappear.

A survey of affairs in Indiana, where the President was anxious to make a good appearance,[1] showed Louis T. Michener with a firm grasp on the party reins, while law partner John B. Elam had drafted the platform for the state convention. A ringing endorsement by the Indiana G.O.P. came in September.[2]

Early signs elsewhere were also good. James S. Clarkson resigned as First Assistant Postmaster General in order to devote full time to the congressional campaign.[3] Every Cabinet member stood ready to hit various campaign trails, and it was no secret that party leaders counted heavily on Blaine, Rusk, Tracy, and Windom for supporting speeches, especially in close districts. At Harrison's suggestion, U.S. Marshal Dan Ransdell was signing up key senators and congressmen for political harangues away from their home districts. No help was needed in either Maine or Vermont, where G.O.P. men had already been elected.

On the other hand, several problems had arisen, none of which could be swept under the rug. Foremost was an undisguised dis-

---

1 Harrison to George W. Steele, September 27, 1890, (L.C.), Vol. 113.
2 L. T. Michener to E. W. Halford, August 20, 29, 1890, (L.C.), Vol. 111.
3 J. S. Clarkson to Harrison, September 3, 1890, (L.C.), Vol. 112.

sension within the Republican ranks. Although Harrison had co-operated in getting the party program through Congress, his unbending ways, mostly in patronage matters, had aroused the ill will of some powerful G.O.P. men. Boss Platt, for instance, irked by the President's idea that he would be "His Own Boss," had been unfriendly from the beginning. Boss Quay of Pennsylvania, who had sabotaged Senate efforts to enact a federal elections bill, muttered his complaints that he had little influence in appointments. Harrison indeed would soon welcome Quay's resignation as chairman of the national committee, inasmuch as some shady financial dealings when he held a state office had been exposed.[4] Senators C. B. Farwell and S. M. Cullom of Illinois felt snubbed because Congressman Joseph G. Cannon, an original Harrison man, controlled state appointments; and occasionally there could be heard the strident voice of Stephen B. Elkins who, his recommendations passed over, complained now and again of shabby treatment by the Chief Executive.[5]

No one could deny that a studied distribution of patronage had swelled the ranks of the disappointed. The President once summed up matters in a letter to a former judge, a Negro who was seeking a place on the Interstate Commerce Commission. Harrison wrote consolingly to Albion W. Tourgee of New York: "The number of applications is large and most of the gentlemen who have been named are men of character and influence," but

... I am glad that you are philosopher enough to understand that in a matter of this sort I can only wait till the applications are all in and then address myself to them, in a judicial way, to decide what appointment on the whole ought to be made. Public considerations, which involve geography and a great many other things, being in control. When you were on the bench you were never compelled to punish a man unless you found him unworthy (guilty) ; but unfortunately I am every day compelled to inflict disappointments upon those whom I highly esteem, and who are worthy of reward and recognition.[6]

In other words, one man got the job while many others were ruled out, and the same was true for every position.

4 Eugene H. Roseboom, A History of Presidential Elections, pp. 286–87. On Harrison's previous silence on the charges against Quay, see R. S. Murphy to the President, May 1, 1890, (L.C.), Vol. 104. Murphy was Quay's private secretary.

5 C. B. Farwell to E. W. Halford, April 19, 1890, (L.C.), Vol. 103, S. B. Elkins to L. T. Michener, June 12, 1890, (L.C.), Vol. 107; Congressman Abner Taylor (R., Ill.) to John B. Arthur, August 2, 1890, Harrison Papers on Microfilm, Series 2.

6 Harrison to Albion W. Tourgee, December 3, 1890, (L.C.), Vol. 115.

Former President Harrison at Long Beach, N.J., with his daughter, Mamie (Mrs. J. Robert McKee), and her children, Benjamin Harrison ("Baby") McKee and Mary Lodge McKee, August, 1894.

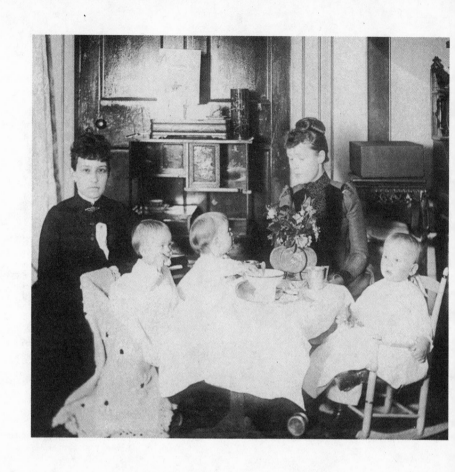

Harrison's daughter and daughter-in-law, (left) Mary ("Mamie") Harrison McKee and (right) May Saunders Harrison, in the White House with their children, (l. to r.) "Baby" McKee, Marthena Harrison, Mary Lodge McKee.

Russell Harrison, the President's son, on the White House lawn with his daughter, Mary, and pet dog, "Dash." In the goat cart drawn by "Whiskers" are his son, Benjamin ("Baby"), and his niece, Marthena Harrison.

Inside the White House, about 1893: (upper left) the Blue Room, (lower left) the President's Office, (upper right) the Cabinet Room, (lower right) the President's Bedroom.

(above) Funeral cortege of Benjamin Harrison, forming at Illinois and Georgia Streets in downtown Indianapolis, March, 1901.

(below) Dignitaries entering the First Presbyterian Church in Indianapolis for the funeral service of Benjamin Harrison.

(above) California triumphal arch erected for Harrison's visit during his transcontinental tour of 1891.

(below) Presidential party in electric car at St. Elmo, at foot of Lookout Mountain Incline, April 8, 1891, during Harrison's visit to Chattanooga. With the President on the platform are Secretary of Agriculture J. M. Rusk (left) and Postmaster General John Wanamaker right).

Caroline ("Carrie") Scott Harrison, First Lady and first president general of the Daughters of the American Revolution, in 1890.

(above) Tombstone of Benjamin Harrison, Crown Hill Cemetery, Indianapolis, with citation reading: "Statesman, yet friend to truth. Of soul sincere. In action faithful and in honour clear."

(below) President Harrison reviews Baltimore parade on the 75th anniversary (September 9, 1889) of the British bombardment of Fort McHenry, birthplace of "The Star-Spangled Banner."

(above) President Harrison and his Cabinet, 1892.

(below) Original Cabinet, March, 1889.

(left) Badge worn at the 1892 Republican Convention by the Alternate Delegate from Williamsport (Pa.).

(top right) Guest's ticket to the 1892 Republican National Convention in Minneapolis.

(bottom right) Six 13¢ U.S. Harrison stamps, given by the President to his grandson, "Baby" McKee.

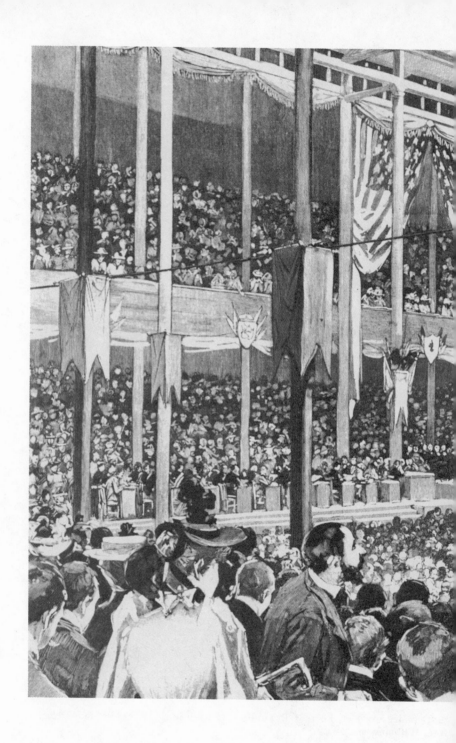

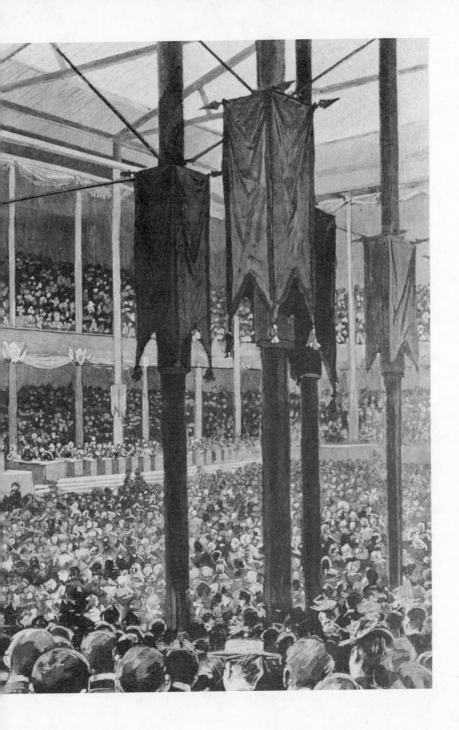

The 1892 Republican National Convention in Minneapolis, as depicted in *Harper's Weekly*, June 11, 1892. According to the report, the auditorium was "built within an industrial exposition building." It was a "vast room with admirable acoustics, well suited to the demands of the hour" but "has little to commend it in aesthetics."

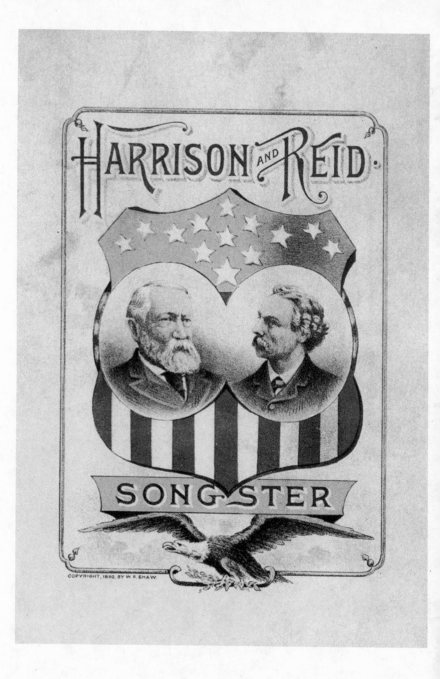

1892 Republican campaign songbook, featuring presidential candidate Harrison and his running mate, Whitelaw Reid.

My dear, dear Boy

Three pictures of the Ships of the North Atlantic Squadron were given to me by the Chief Engineer of the Indiana — and I thought you would like to have them

Your loving Grandpa

Sept 25th 1896.

Benj Harrison

U.S. battleship *Indiana* of the Navy's North Atlantic Squadron. Picture given to Harrison in 1896 by the ship's chief engineer, and sent by the former President to his grandson with the accompanying note.

The Benjamin Harrison Memorial Home, Indianapolis, now a National Historical Landmark.

(above) Library in the home of Benjamin Harrison, Indianapolis.

(below) Back parlor in the Harrison Memorial Home, Indianapolis.

Matthew Brady's official photograph of Benjamin Harrison.

(above) James G. Blaine, the "Plumed Knight."

(below) "Czar" Thomas B. Reed, Speaker of the House.

(above) Senator John Sherman, father of the first anti-trust law.

(below) Mark Hanna, square-shooting G.O.P. boss, McKinley's lieutenant.

(above) Admiral Alfred Thayer Mahan, naval historian, helped revolutionize American Navy.

(below) Andrew Carnegie, industrialist.

(above) Chauncey M. Depew, New York Central's president, a Harrison devotee.

(below) Editor William Allen White, who called Harrison our "greatest Constitutional President."

Albert J. Beveridge, Indiana campaigner for Harrison.

"God Help the Surplus" was the motto of Harrison's Pension Commissioner, "Corporal Tanner," here lampooned by *Puck*.

Harrison, under his "grandfather's hat," broods before the ancestral Raven—a *Puck* cartoon.

(above) Orator Harrison and future Speaker of the House Thomas B. Reed in a group at "Roseland," Woodstock, Connecticut, July 4, 1889.

(below) President and Mrs. Harrison enjoy a visit at the John Wanamakers' country estate near Philadelphia.

(below) The Harrisons welcomed at Bar Harbor by the Blaines and Senator Henry Cabot Lodge.

(above) Harrison, second wife, Mary, and baby, Elizabeth.

(above) The Homestead Strike, 1892: strikers on lookout at the Carnegie Mills.

(below) The Homestead Strike, 1892: Pennsylvania state militia enters Homestead.

The Grand Army of the Republic parades (1892) on Washington's Pennsylvania
Avenue—"Avenue of the Presidents"—with U.S. Capitol in the distance.

(inset) Senator Matthew S. Quay of Pennsylvania.

Senator M. S. Quay in Indian regalia.

(above) Delegates to Inter-American Conference of 1889, pictured in Washington, D.C. (building and individuals unidentified).

(below) Henry Clay Frick.

1889 portrait of Vice-President Levi P. Morton.

Democratic gerrymandering in Ohio, Kentucky, Maryland, and Tennessee brought James Clarkson on the scene[7] while Harrison reacted vigorously to reports that listlessness and apparent indifference had engulfed certain gentlemen who "smoked their cigars in the hotel and did nothing."[8] Inasmuch as some were federal office-holders drawing good salaries, Harrison took pen in hand. "A word now and then from the President," as Secretary Michener observed, had such effect that by late September, Republicans were reported working four times as hard as the opposition.[9] Nor was Harrison's literary talent confined to letter-writing. Clarkson, a veteran reporter with an eye for good style, one day begged the President to receive Lemuel Ely Quigg of the New York *Tribune* who had been commissioned to get out an eight page pamphlet detailing the good things done by the Administration. Although Clarkson found Quigg's work "superior" and "effective," still, he assured Harrison that "if you will give him five minutes, you can imbue . . . [the work] with the spirit of the great things done."[10] The President obliged.

Even before adjournment, Congressmen had mounted platforms back home. Certain features of the new tariff law were being exploited by Democratic campaigners coincident with actual price rises of food or of household wares or notice that they would be raised because of the McKinley Bill. It soon appeared that the new tariff would increase the cost of living. Persons of limited means, who made up the majority, would be the first to complain.[11]

Republicans lost no time in preparing campaign documents to be sent out by the million. One, entitled "Facts from the Treasury," argued that the G.O.P. Administration had "saved the people no less than $51 million on its redemption of bonded debts," while another, entitled "Better Days for Farmers" told how the McKinley tariff would benefit agriculture without raising prices or increasing the cost of living[12]—a neat trick.

---

[7] J. S. Clarkson to Harrison, September 13, 1890, (L.C.), Vol. 113, and November 20, 1890, (L.C.), Vol. 114, in which the effects of gerrymandering are discussed.

[8] L. T. Michener to E. W. Halford, September 15, 1890, (L.C.), Vol. 112.

[9] Michener to Halford, September 15, 1890, (L.C.), Vol. 112, also September 22, 1890, (L.C.), Vol. 113. Michener advised Halford that "in the last four days . . . the Democratic State Committee received 94 letters, whereas this Committee received more than 94 letters on each of those days."

[10] J. S. Clarkson to Harrison, September 28, 1890, (L.C.), Vol. 113.

[11] Harry Thurston Peck, *Twenty Years of the Republic 1885–1905*, p. 212.

[12] *Journal*, October 4, 1890.

More than pamphlets was needed. In Ohio, which had been gerrymandered, McKinley's own district had been invaded by Democrats who had engaged some hucksters to rig up old wagons, stock them with tinware, and then visit every Amish farm in Holmes County to offer ordinary 5¢ tin cups for $1.00. (It was explained that ordinary dishpans could be afforded only by millionaire capitalists.) When the startled Amish farmer objected, he was told that under the circumstances, $1.00 per cup was a low price; buy now before further inflation![13] Once the Amish people got the idea, G.O.P. campaign documents would prove useless. In Indiana as in Ohio, Democrats encouraged price manipulation or actively worked on it.[14]

Further westward, the G.O.P. was in serious trouble. Illinois, Iowa, and Missouri, all of which reported labor problems and partial crop failures, loomed as doubtful states in November. Kansas, a bellwether of farmer discontent, appeared to be in open revolt against the idea of a beneficent McKinley tariff.

Reading the signs, Harrison reconsidered his refusal of an invitation to attend a reunion of his old command at Galesburg, Illinois, in the heart of the Midwest. Perhaps too, he had erred in canceling an appearance with General William Sherman, at an Army of the Cumberland reunion at Toledo in mid-September. Now a hastily arranged itinerary over a 3,000-mile political course was charted on the very day the McKinley Bill was signed into law.[15]

Popular men and good speakers were wanted. Harrison was therefore accompanied by General Tracy, Secretary of the Navy, whose efficient handling of the fleet was very popular with the people;[16] also by Ohio Congressman Charles H. Grosvenor, "renowned as a bitter partisan debater,"[17] and by General Thomas J.

---

13 *Journal*, November 9, 1890.

14 Harrison himself believed that such activity had not really hurt the G.O.P. in Ohio. See E. F. Tibbott's Diary, November 8, 1890, (L.C.), Vol. 114.

15 Benjamin Harrison to J. S. Harrison, October 2, 1890, (L.C.), Vol. 113, told his brother that "my trip west is unsettled, except as to three points. I am to be in Galesburg the 8th and Ottumwa the 9th, and Topeka the 10th. The route to Galesburg and the return from Topeka remain unsettled." A copy of the itinerary was released by the Passenger Department of the Chesapeake and Ohio Railway Company on October 4, 1890 (see Harrison Papers on Microfilm, Series 2).

16 J. S. Clarkson to B. F. Tracy, September 17, 1890, B. F. Tracy MSS.

17 C. H. Grosvenor to E. W. Halford, October 4, 1890, Harrison Papers on Microfilm, Series 2. For a sketch of Grosvenor, see *CDAB*, p. 377.

Morgan, the Indian Commissioner, well known in Illinois. Less well known, although good politicians, were U.S. Marshal Dan Ransdell and Captain William M. Meredith, a veteran of the Seventieth Indiana; Secretary Halford and White House stenographer E. F. Tibbott. A. P. Jones of the Associated Press and G. G. Bain of the United Press completed the party. On October 6th, the Pullman car "Haslemere" was boarded for Galesburg and intermediate stops along the route of the Chesapeake and Ohio.[18]

For a President to journey to meet old comrades in an election year meant forty speeches along the way.[19] A prime objective of the second day was Terre Haute, home of R. W. Thompson, onetime Navy Secretary, where "every bell and steam whistle . . . added its tribute" to the cheers of more than 10,000.

At Danville, Illinois, Joe Cannon ground, Harrison had praise for the congressman, and he told some 10,000 farmers that they "were the repository of all power, the originator of all policy."[20] Among other stops in a busy day was one at Peoria, where Harrison accepted a bouquet of roses from a child actress of "Little Lord Fauntleroy" fame.[21] During the final run to Galesburg next day, he rode in the engine cab with Frank Hilton, who had served in the 102nd Illinois of Harrison's command during the Atlanta campaign. The cab was a little crowded. At all crossings and stations Harrison pulled on the whistle cord while Secretary Tracy handled the bell rope with equal force and frequency.[22]

Of the more than 25,000 attracted to Galesburg, many came forward to take the President's hand. Harrison spoke five times, twice on the campus of Knox College, where a cornerstone was laid and where he sat at dinner with his old fraternity. Appearing before the veterans and their families, the President took his stand on the side of individual liberty and self-government:

It is the great thought of our country that man shall be governed as little as possible, but full liberty shall be given to individual effort,

18 *Journal*, October 7, 1890. J. S. Runnells to E. W. Halford, October 3, 1890, Harrison Papers on Microfilm, Series 2 (telegram), reveals that George W. Pullman furnished the car for the trip.

19 *Speeches of Benjamin Harrison*, Charles Hedges (comp.), pp. 234–86, contains a majority of the addresses made during the western tour of 1890.

20 *Journal*, October 8, 1890.

21 Elsie Leslie Lynde, the actress, had made the presentation on behalf of several G.A.R. posts (*Journal*, October 9, 1890).

22 *Ibid.*

and that restraints of law shall be reserved for the turbulent and disorderly. What is it that makes our communities peaceful? What makes these farm houses safe? It is not the policemen. It is not the soldiers. It is this great and all pervading American sentiment that exalts the law, that stands with threatening warning to the law-breaker, and above all, the pervading thought that gives to every man what is his and claims only what is his own.[23]

A band concert, a review of the ex-soldiers, two banquets and more speeches completed the reunion festivities that day, October 8, 1890. Near midnight, the President was heard to remark: "This day in Galesburg I shall long remember."

On to Iowa. Ottumwa held a double attraction. Harrison's sister Sallie Devin served breakfast and his brother John Scott Harrison from Kansas City was there. At the city's celebrated "Coal Palace," the President was welcomed by Democratic Governor Horace Boies and Republican Senator William B. Allison. Reporters noted the absence of General James B. Weaver, a popular vote-getter with the farmers, who, two years later, would return to do battle as the People's Party candidate.

In troubled Kansas, perhaps the hardest hit financially of the midwestern States,[24] Harrison saw only the familiar cheering children, waving flags, and bouquets of roses at the several whistle-stops. Topeka seemed in a festive mood. Avowed intentions in the state to raise "less corn and more hell"[25] brought from the President an admonition:

A single year of disappointment in agricultural returns should not make you despair of the future or tempt you to unsafe expedients. Life is made up of averages, and I think you will show a good average. . . . Kansas and her people have an assured and happy future.[26]

Others had spread the word that Kansas suffered from a great robber, the Santa Fe Railroad, as well as from the loan companies;[27] but without attempting to meet this awkward issue, Harri-

[23] Hedges, op. cit., pp. 243–52. According to Harrison, the Civil War was fought only "that law might not lose its sanction and its sanctity. Every man shall keep the law."

[24] Russell B. Nye, *Midwestern Progressive Politics*, pp. 60–68, demonstrates that between 75 and 90 percent of all Kansas farmers were mortgaged at an average interest rate of 9 percent. In prosperous Lyon County, whose total valuation was $6,500,000, there was a mortgaged indebtedness of $5,500,000. Between 1880 and 1890 an estimated one-third of all farm mortgages in the state were foreclosed.

[25] *Ibid.*

[26] Hedges, op. cit., p. 263.

[27] Nye, op. cit., p. 61. The Union Pacific and the Southern Pacific railroads shared the reputation of the Santa Fe.

son left Topeka for Kansas City, where he was pictured as exhausted and nursing a limp right hand.[28] He spoke only briefly at the Board of Trade, then was escorted to St. Louis where an autumn festival and annual folk fair were in progress.[29] Greeted by some 200,000 festive folk, the President reviewed a parade and toured the Fair grounds. In two unscheduled speeches he promised federal aid to improve the Mississippi River channel and forecast substantial railroad growth in the South and Southwest.[30] At about ˙10 P.M. he returned to the "Haslemere" carrying with him a copy of the St. Louis *Post-Dispatch* account of the reception. Printed on a silk handkerchief, it was the first known instance of a web press used to impress silk.[31]

The return trip took Harrison back through Indiana and Ohio, where crowds gathered at every scheduled stop. At Massillon, Ohio, where industry was growing, he observed:

Our strength, our promise for the future, our security for social happiness are in the contentment of the great masses who toil. It is in kindly intercourse and relationship between capital and labor, each having its appropriate increase, that we shall find the highest good, the capitalist and employer everywhere extending to those who work for human rights a kindly consideration with compensatory wages.[32]

Just how could this be brought about? The nearest that Harrison could get to it was an appeal at Canton, Ohio, McKinley's home town,[33] for closer labor-capital relations. Employers, he said, should be "more thoughtful of those who work for them."[34] In a final public speech at Alliance, he thanked Republicans and Democrats alike for their warm reception, and charged them to elect good men to Congress. From what he had seen of the country,

28 *Journal*, October 11, 1890.

29 R. C. Kearns to R. B. Harrison, October 15, 1890, Russell Harrison MSS.

30 Farmer organizations (and secret societies) demanded such improvements of the Mississippi River as would fully develop its carrying capacities and make it the natural competitor of the railroad companies in the transportation of farm products. See L. T. Michener to E. W. Halford, November 8, 1890, (L.C.), Vol. 114.

31 Hedges, *op. cit.*, pp. 269–70; *Journal*, October 13, 1890.

32 *Journal*, October 14, 1890.

33 From Kalamazoo, McKinley wired: "Allow me to congratulate you on the hearty reception everywhere received by you. I regret that I was not in my district to welcome you. Many thanks for the kind words you said for me" (William McKinley, Jr., to Harrison, October 14, 1890, (L.C.), Vol. 113).

34 Hedges, *op. cit.*, pp. 283–84.

he said, he believed it to be entering "upon an upgrade . . . of business."[35]

The press of both parties hailed the tour as one "continuous ovation";[36] and journalist George Alfred Townsend noted in the Cincinnati *Inquirer*:

President Arthur or President Hayes could not have made Harrison's speeches. Garfield fell into the oratorical method too promptly, and was somewhat too scholastic to get down to the pithy generalizations of Harrison. We perhaps live at the time of which Henry Clay spoke, when, profoundly disappointed with John Tyler, he said: "Whigs, pick up your flints and try again." The grandson of that old Harrison speaks as if he were picking his flint. In the meantime the hour is one of the quietest in the history of the land.[37]

Harrison was content to leave to others the campaigning of the final two weeks. Reports received scarcely forecast hope for G.O.P. success. Michener felt that the "High Price Scare" would lose the party 2,000 to 3,000 votes in closely divided Indiana. Similar warnings poured in from other states.[38] An empty money chest restricted party efforts, particularly in Ohio and Pennsylvania.[39] Too, fears mounted that the partial crop failure as well as voters' apathy would result in a large stay-at-home protest. "I think we will carry the state," Michener wrote Harrison but without much conviction.[40] Harrison replied that although he did not relish the idea of another trip west, still he would cast his vote in Indianapolis "for friends who have done so much for me and for what I believe to be the cause of good government."

Secretary Blaine took a rather relaxed attitude, declaring in

35 *Ibid.*, pp. 284–86; *Journal*, October 14, 1890.

36 Denver *Republican* and Philadelphia *North American*, as cited by the Indianapolis *Journal*, October 14, 18, 1890. Similar sentiments were voiced by the Cleveland *Leader* and the county newspapers of Indiana.

37 Published also in a number of other newspapers including the *Journal*, October 25, 1890. Townsend's book, *Washington Outside and Inside*, had a wide circulation.

38 L. T. Michener to E. W. Halford, October 21, 1890, (L.C.), Vol. 114, spoke of the high price scare as well as Democratic designs to "practice fraud, intimidation and bribery." Also Michener to Halford, October 25, 1890, (L.C.), Vol. 114.

39 In Ohio, Sherman learned that "it has been almost impossible to raise means even for printing campaign documents—we have from office-holders and clerks—all told $70.00" (Marshall Cushing to John Sherman, October 14, 1890, John Sherman MSS., Vol. 529). In Pennsylvania, Quay and Cameron contrived to cut off G.O.P. congressional candidates without funds (J. S. Clarkson to Harrison, October 30, 1890, (L.C.), Vol. 114).

40 October 29, 1890, (L.C.), Vol. 114, is a masterful six-page election eve analysis; also Harrison to Michener, October 31, 1890, Michener MSS.

Philadelphia that the loss of the House would merely be "one of the natural reactions that comes between two presidential terms . . . so frequent that it creates no disturbance on the one side and no elation on the other."[41] The next day Clarkson told Harrison: "I fear Mr. Blaine's statement . . . will be taken as the cue of permission by Republicans who were already half-willing to trade off Congress for State and local offices." Clarkson's final forecast was "practically a tie." In any event, he added, "we have had a campaign on a high plane, honorable, fair and clean. No surrender will follow it."[42] Civil Service Commissioner Theodore Roosevelt expressed a common feeling in that he hoped for victory, rather than expected it.[43]

The results, in fact, were far worse than even the most pessimistic of Republican predictions. The majority in the House was wiped out: 235 Democrats and 10 Populists and Independents had been elected to only 86 Republicans. The Senate, however, remained Republican by a majority of 8.[44] The tidal wave had engulfed and retired a host of G.O.P. notables, including McKinley and Cannon of the House, and Kansan John Ingalls of the Senate.

The tariff was blamed by some and absolved by others. Some ascribed the defeat to the silver legislation. Some thought that too many voters had stayed at home: a party failure.[45] When all the returns were in, Harrison asked his old friend Frank Tibbott, now a White House stenographer, to accompany him on his daily stroll. With possibly an eye to history, Tibbott entered some enlightening remarks in his diary on November 8th:

The President . . . talked very freely as to the result of the elections. It would be hard for me to sum up his explanation. In fact he hardly attempted to explain it. He spoke of the result in Indiana and thought that the "sore toe," although possibly pretty well covered up, was still *sore*. He did not think that many Republicans voted against us but that they lacked interest and simply stayed away. He remarked he would like to have the vote analyzed to see if it were possible whether the Republicans had voted against us.

41 *Journal*, November 2, 1890.

42 J. S. Clarkson to Harrison, November 2, 1890, (L.C.), Vol. 114.

43 Theodore Roosevelt to Henry Cabot Lodge, October 31, 1890, Lodge MSS.

44 Harold U. Faulkner, *Politics, Reform and Expansion*, pp. 116–17. Roseboom, *op. cit.*, p. 286, agrees with the Faulkner figure of 235 Democrats, but lists 88 Republicans and 9 Farmers' Alliance men.

45 J. S. Clarkson, November 20, 1890, (L.C.), Vol. 114.

He said that the preponderance was against us in the fight. In the first place the very fact that [the] "off-yrs." rule was that we lost, had a tendency to hurt us, and produced an apathy that could not be coaxed into life—the claim being that it was no use. Then the gerrymander necessarily worked against us. To the suggestion that the tariff had hurt us he said that was contradicted by Ohio and California going strongly for us, while Montana which should be helped by the tariff had really not entered very largely into the question. In Wisconsin the Dems. claimed the tariff as the cause when the school law was probably largely responsible. In Massachusetts there was a man running for Gov. who had barely pulled through two years ago. The people there should have taken warning and not re-nominated a weak man. In Minn. while the result was still uncertain, if we lost it was because another weak man was nominated. In Illinois it was a fight against Farwell and his bossism. In Penna. it was a personal quarrel— a fight against Quay. . . . Said of course Quay would step down and out. Said in looking at the result of vote for Gov. and for other state offices—so widely different could not see why Mr. Quay did not recognize it as a personal defeat. . . .[46]

To another, Harrison asserted that he did not believe that the opposition had actually acquired any more of the nation's confidence "nor been augmented by any permanent accessions."[47] In other words, he was not depressed.

[46] Tibbott's Diary, entry for November 8, 1890, (L.C.), Vol. 114.
[47] Harrison to R. S. Taylor, November 29, 1890, (L.C.), Vol. 115.

CHAPTER XVI

The Cost of Bloodshed

GRAVE DIPLOMATIC PROBLEMS arising from capital crimes occupied the President and the State Department for many months. Two ugly episodes were largely concurrent, and for a time war was threatened on both sides of the globe. Harrison was to learn much, however painfully, about the two nations concerned—Italy and Chile.

Immigrants to New Orleans after the Civil War included many Italian subjects from Sicily, some with a criminal background, many of them linked with the Mafia Black Hand Society.[1] Bloody vendettas, chiefly among Sicilians at first, resulted in many unsolved crimes in and about the city. Disquiet naturally arose and antagonism between Italians and native Americans deepened. Crime and the Mafia became synonymous in New Orleans.

One brave man tried to ferret out the evildoers. This was the city's superintendent of police, the 32-year-old David C. Hennessey, a likable Irishman. Chief Hennessey was well known to the Mafia. He had refused its bribes and thus incurred its emnity. An expected witness before a grand jury scheduled to sit on October 22, 1890, Hennessey never lived to testify. On the 15th, a rainy, dark night, he was waylaid, fired upon, and mortally hurt. The volley brought Detective William J. O'Connor running. "Who did this, Dave?" O'Connor asked. "The Dagoes," Hennessey said.[2]

The murder became known as the Mafia Incident. Hennessey's death on October 16, 1890, was the first in a series of happenings

---

1 Ed Reid, *Mafia*, is a satisfactory introduction to a mysterious subject. Chapter 14 entitled "The New Orleans Incident," pp. 135–60, is based on written as well as oral testimony. On the activities of the Mafia in Italy during the last two decades, see Camillo Anbert, "The Mafia: Crime Inc. (Italy), *Réalités*, November 1954, pp. 4–10.

2 For the most detailed account see John E. Coxe, "The New Orleans Mafia Incident," *Louisiana Historical Quarterly*, XX, No. 4 (October 1937), 1067–1110.

that eventually resulted in large international problems. The fact that the victim had named Italians as his assassins sufficed to establish in the minds of the police and the public the nature of the crime. A volatile press reflected rising resentment in the city. Mass meetings were called "to assist the officers of the law in driving the murderous Mafia from our midst." On the day of the Hennessey funeral, Mayor Joseph A. Shakespeare called the city council in special session to tell them why police evidence proved beyond any doubt that the dead man "was the victim of the Sicilian vengeance." Declared the Mayor: "No community can exist with murder societies in its midst." Several prominent citizens were named to a White Citizens Committee charged with the duty of "total annihilation of such hell-born associations."[3]

The arrests of many Italians followed. Some, unjustly detained in the parish prison, suffered physical beatings and other indignities. Protests by Pasquale Corte, the Italian consul at New Orleans, were brushed aside by the Mayor, whereupon Corte wired Baron Francesco Fava, Italian Minister at Washington, and cabled the Foreign Office in Rome. The United States government was asked to look into the activities of the White Citizens' Committees and to stop the arrests.

Advised that New Orleans was threatened by a bloody riot, Harrison directed Secretary Blaine to wire Louisiana's Governor Francis T. Nichols for a full report. Blaine's wire cited the Italian Minister as "confident that the great body of Italians in New Orleans repudiate with horror the act of a few criminals" and desire only "to see the law take its course and punish the murderers of the chief of police."

Governor Nichols replied that the initial excitement had subsided and that he did not anticipate any trouble. With reference to charges of prison brutality, he advised Blaine that a grand jury had indicted two guards for various acts of brutality. Actually, he said, "the nationality of the prisoners had not been the cause of maltreatment." The Italian Government appeared satisfied with these assurances and Harrison breathed a bit more easily.[4] With good conscience he told the Congress in his annual message of

3 Coxe, art. cit., pp. 1073–78.

4 Foreign Relations of the U.S. (1891) under "Italy," pp. 658–728, carries all "correspondence in relation to the killing of prisoners in New Orleans, March 14, 1891."

December 1, 1890 that "no community will find lawlessness profitable," adding:

No community can afford to have it known that the officers who are charged with the preservation of the public peace and the restraint of criminal classes are themselves the product of fraud or violence. The magistrate is then without respect, the law without sanction.[5]

For the next three months diplomatic relations with Italy remained normal, although in New Orleans the wheels of justice were turning.

A grand jury which convened on November 9th finally indicted nineteen Italians on two counts—murder, and "shooting while lying in wait with the intent to murder." But at the arraignment on the 30th, a motion to quash the indictments on the grounds of illegal procedure was entered and ultimately sustained. Fresh resentment among New Orleans citizens arose.

A new grand jury assembled and four days later reindicted the nineteen for the same crimes while motions to dismiss were denied. All the prisoners pleaded not guilty. When the case finally came to trial on February 16, 1891, public feeling ran high. Each day as the prisoners rode to court in a mule-drawn Black Maria, children filled the air with taunts of "Who killa da Chief?"[6]

The trial proved to be one of the most bizarre in Louisiana's history. At the outset it took eleven days to select a jury from among some 1,375 examined. Next the state obtained an order to excuse ten of the prisoners so as to base its case on the supposed guilt of nine. After some 67 witnesses had testified for the state and 84 for the defense, the jury got the case on March 12th. The next day, Friday the 13th, it found six not guilty, and could not agree on the remaining three, for whom the judge declared it a mistrial.[7]

Tension in New Orleans, which had smoldered for several weeks, now burst forth in full fury. Almost immediately handbills hit the streets, calling on "all good citizens" to attend a March 14th meeting that would seek steps to remedy the failure of justice. Eight thousand citizens answered the summons, and the prison

---

5 *Public Papers and Addresses of Benjamin Harrison*, pp. 89–90.

6 Coxe, *art. cit.*, pp. 1080–81.

7 Reid, *op. cit.*, p. 140, calls the trial "the most botched up . . . in the history of Louisiana jurisprudence."

was stormed and searched. Some of the nineteen Italians were shot down and others hanged, until the bloody toll stood at eleven. Satisfied that justice had been done, a leader dispersed the mob with a "God bless you." That same afternoon the New Orleans *States* rejoiced in the lynching but counseled calm:

Citizens of New Orleans you have in one righteous upheaval, in one fateful gust of mighty wrath, vindicated your laws, heretofore desecrated and trampled underfoot by oath-bound aliens who had thought to substitute murder for justice, and the suborner's gold for the freeman's honest verdict. Your vengeance is consecrated in the forfeited blood of the assassins. Stop there. Return to your homes and resume the peaceful pursuit of avocations.

The Louisiana press as a whole voiced approval, as did most Southern newspapers. In the North and overseas a sense of shock was felt. Many agreed with the London comment that "Italy's indignation is shared by the whole civilized world."[8]

A terrified Italian consul wired Baron Fava in Washington: "Fear further murders. I also am in great danger." Secretary Blaine, who read of "the dreadful mob at New Orleans" in the Washington papers, sent word that evening to the White House: "The Italian Minister is half-crazed over the tragedy & wants you to make some inquiry of the Governor of Louisiana."

In the morning, a Sunday, a deeply disturbed President took pen in hand. "As to the New Orleans lynching," he wrote Secretary Blaine,

. . . it is very appalling, but under our federal system, while the United States is responsible to other nations for injuries done to their citizens, it is without jurisdiction to interfere for their protection, except by suggestion, or appeal, to the State authorities. If any representations have been made by the Italian Minister we must consider whether this important intimation should not be used. If it serves no other use it will prove our good will and regard for the law. How well this tragic incident illustrates the fact that social order cannot exist when the rights of a class and a whole body of laws are persistently and by consent of the community annulled. If any man's rights under the law may be violently denied him, then every man's may be.[9]

[8] Coxe, *art. cit.*, pp. 1085–92. For a more complete account of press reaction, see J. Alexander Karlin, "Some Repercussions of the New Orleans Mafia Incident of 1891," *Research Studies of the State College of Washington*, XI, No. 4 (December 1943), 267–82.

[9] A. T. Volwiler (ed.), *Correspondence Between Harrison and Blaine*, pp. 141–43.

Harrison later went to the ailing Blaine's bedside and dictated a telegram to Governor Nichols. He referred to the "deplorable massacre," and requested state cooperation in protecting the treaty rights of Italians in New Orleans, in preventing further bloodshed, and in bringing to justice those responsible for the lynching. The wire, signed by Blaine, noted specifically that "the President deeply regrets that the citizens of New Orleans should have so disparaged the purity and adequacy of their own judicial tribunals as to transfer to the passionate judgment of a mob a question that should have been judged dispassionately by the settled rules of law."

Copies of the dispatch were handed to Baron Fava and cabled to American Minister Albert G. Porter in Rome with instructions to get it to the foreign office promptly. The desire and intention of the President to do justice seemed clear.[10]

Harrison's good will and prompt action satisfied neither Italy nor Italian-Americans. In Chicago, Italians shouted that "if justice be not rendered, full and prompt, our native land will speak even with the voice of her guns."[11] Similar threats reached the White House and the State Department.[12] Even Baron Fava, alarmed by the intensity of the Italo-American emotions, wired all Italian consuls in the United States "to use their influence and authority to urge" former nationals to show themselves "by dignified, calm and strictly legal behavior . . . worthy of their civilized country." This advice went unheeded. Italian colonials preferred to follow the lead of the mother country, which instructed Baron Fava to press for immediate and direct federal action. "Our right . . . to demand and obtain the punishment of the murderers, and an indemnity for the victims is unquestionable."[13] King Humberto and Foreign Minister Rudini stood adamant.

Harrison directed Secretary Blaine in Washington and Minis-

10 *Foreign Relations of the U.S. (1891)*, pp. 666–70.

11 Karlin, *art. cit.*, p. 272.

12 March 20, 1891, Newark resolutions deplored and denounced "the occurrence as wanton, cruel and an indefensible crime against American law and justice as well as against humanity and civilization" (L.C.), Vol. 120. Copies were also sent to the authorities of the U.S. and Italy, and to the Governor of Louisiana. Dr. Botello to Harrison, March 23, 1891, (L.C.), Vol. 121, wired from New Haven that "Eight hundred Italians protest against New Orleans massacre and demand that justice should be done."

13 *Foreign Relations of the U.S. (1891)*, p. 673.

ter Porter in Rome to explain "the embarrassing gap in federalism—that in such cases the state alone has jurisdiction." Italians, who found this somewhat of an anomaly, kept insisting on formal, written guarantees from the national government. To Fava's continued and heated importunities Blaine used some nondiplomatic language:

I do not recognize the right of any government to tell the United States what it should do. We have never received orders from any foreign power and we will not begin now. . . . It is a matter of total indifference to me what persons in Italy may think of our institutions. I cannot change them, still less violate them.[14]

This vigorous assertion of American rights, so stated the Chicago *Tribune*, would knock the "breath from the monkey and the hand-organ man" so that the Italians and the Italo-Americans would at once change their tune.

Just the opposite happened. In Italy the populace vented its wrath in impromptu meetings and heaped indignities on touring Americans. The shaky Italian ministry found it necessary to make some face-saving gesture; and finding Blaine powerless to do anything, abruptly withdrew Baron Fava from Washington on March 31, 1891. Harrison instructed Minister Porter in Rome to come home on leave of absence. To avoid a complete diplomatic break, however, each nation left its legation in the hands of subordinates.

War talk heated the press on both sides of the ocean. After it was pointed out that in armored ships Italy outnumbered the United States nineteen to one, rumor had it that an Italian squadron might soon appear off eastern coastal cities or near the mouth of the Mississippi to menace New Orleans. An English naval officer in New York at the time made a joking comment. "You people," said he, "want more ships for your navy. Just let those Italian fellows send over a fleet. Then you take the fleet, and there you are."[15]

14 Thomas A. Bailey, *A Diplomatic History of the American People*, p. 450. This was a reporter's version which Fava transmitted to Italy, which published it in a "Green Book," together with other relevant documents. Blaine's written account to Marquis Imperiali, April 1, 1891, is milder. "The Government of the United States is utterly unable to give the assurance which the Marquis Rudini has demanded. Even if the National Government had entire jurisdiction over the alleged murderers, it could not give assurance to any foreign power that they should be punished. The President is unable to see how any government could justly give an assurance of this character in advance of investigation or trial" (*Foreign Relations of the U.S. (1891)*, pp. 676–77).

15 Harry T. Peck, *Twenty Years of the Republic*, pp. 226–27. The Atlanta *Journal* jokingly hoped that Italy was sending a warship to New Orleans, as rumored. "We

Harrison sought more news from New Orleans. John W. Luck, special agent of the Treasury Department, observed that "it is so easy, you see, to pass from the killing of Negroes to the killing of Dagos."[16] U.S. Attorney William Grant wrote the Attorney General in Washington: "I am unable to obtain any direct evidence connecting these persons [those indicted for the murder of Hennessey and acquitted] with the Mafia, or any other association of a similar character in the city."[17]

Soon the war scare evaporated and for nearly six months a diplomatic silence reigned. Italy took the first step in breaking the impasse when Minister of Foreign Affairs Rudini called on the American diplomatic officer in Rome. Harrison then wrote Secretary Blaine:

It is quite evident that the Italian Government is very anxious to let go and not well advised as to how it can be done gracefully. It seems to me that . . . the correspondence upon the subject could not be opened by us; certainly not in the absence of a duly accredited Minister of the Italian Government from Washington. They withdrew Baron Fava and should re-equip the Legation here as the first step towards any further friendly discussion. If this intimation is given I think we should carefully avoid any implication that our action could be favorable upon the renewed suggestion of indemnity.[18]

Italian Chargé d'affaires Marquis Imperiali called on the Secretary at his Augusta, Maine retreat and Blaine reported the visit to Harrison. He "fairly teased me to a talk in full, [but] I told him I could do nothing until I could return to Washington and get your directions and instructions in the premises. . . . I hope to be in Washington within a fortnight and I should like to treat the Italian matter. . . . I think if we strongly adhere to the ground you intimate, we shall gain everything."[19]

Ten days later it was learned that Italian restrictions against

---

are," it said, "too much in need of a navy to let a thing like that escape." See *Public Opinion*, X, 588 (March 28, 1891) for the contemptuous treatment afforded Italy as "absolutely powerless" and "financially . . . almost bankrupt."

16 John W. Luck to E. W. Halford, March 22, 1891, Harrison Papers on Microfilm, Series 2.

17 *Foreign Relations of the U.S. (1891)*, pp. 687–89. Grant concluded that "I do not draw the inference myself from the facts disclosed by this statement [made by the chief of police of New Orleans] that these crimes were all the work of the Mafia, but they are attributed to that Society generally by the public."

18 Harrison to Blaine, September 23, 1891, as cited by Volwiler, *op. cit.*, pp. 192–93.

19 Blaine to Harrison, October 12, 1891 (*ibid.*, p. 205).

the importation of U.S. hog products had been lifted. Perhaps it was possible, Harrison agreed, to satisfy Italy and have her send a minister here."[20] The view taken in his message to Congress of December 9, 1891, was conciliatory. The New Orleans tragedy was frankly termed "the lynching," and reference was made to "the fury of the mob" and "this offense against law and humanity." An indemnity had been demanded rather than requested, but diplomatic correspondence had been held up by the absence of Italy's minister to Washington. Still, "it is not doubted that a friendly conclusion is attainable."[21]

Some three months from the date of the message, Harrison, nudged by Blaine, offered an indemnity of 100,000 francs ($20,-000). Rome now asked 150,000 (Rudini had been criticized in Italy for not being sufficiently aggressive in asserting the rights of Italians abroad), and to get it over with Blaine proposed 125,000 francs ($25,000).

Blaine seemed a bit angry and dashed off a blunt note to the President. "No minister is here yet. We have waited eleven months during which period our Minister has been passing his time in Indianapolis drawing $12,000 a year from the Treasury."[22] Harrison at once yielded the point and advised the Secretary to take such action as he thought best.

The joint production of Harrison and Blaine—a cordial note from Washington to Rome plus payment of 125,000 francs ($25,-000) helped soothe outraged feelings. The incident was considered closed as King Humberto of Italy ordered the resumption of full relations between the two nations. Harrison's words at least had been remembered, the King expressing pleasure "with the language used by the President in his message of December last."[23]

The pleasure was not entirely mutual on this side of the water. New Orleans again flared up and the U.S. Congress was displeased. In facilitating payment to Italy, Harrison and Blaine had recourse to the State Department emergency fund, bypassing Capitol Hill.[24]

20 Blaine to Harrison, March 26, 1892 (*ibid.*, pp. 247–48).

21 *Public Papers and Addresses of Benjamin Harrison*, pp. 93–94.

22 Correspondence in Volwiler, *op. cit.*, pp. 246–51. Also (L.C.), Vol. 138, contains copies of letters exchanged. (March 23–29, 1892.)

23 Marquis Imperiali to Blaine, April 12, 1892, as cited in *Foreign Relations of the U.S. (1891)*, p. 728.

24 Coxe, *art. cit.*, pp. 1098–1101, discusses the row in Congress. See also the New Orleans *Times-Democrat* of May 5, 1892.

The impact of the Mafia Incident had nearly caused postponement of a scheduled tour through the South and to the Pacific Coast and back, a round trip of 9,232 miles. Senator William B. Allison of Iowa was one who urged Harrison to go, saying: "It will do you and the country good."[25] The President and Mrs. Harrison, Postmaster General John Wanamaker and party of fifteen, which was occasionally enlarged, left Washington on April 14, 1891, to return about five weeks later. Word of another apparent emergency arising from an impending revolution in Chile was received on May 6th, when Harrison reached Seattle. Reassured by wire that he need not cut his trip short, he made the 33 more stops on the return circuit as scheduled.[26]

The affair, which proved serious, got its start on the West Coast where Chilean revolutionaries had been hard at work acquiring arms and munitions. Their vessel, the *Itata*, stole out of San Diego harbor in order to take on this cargo from an American schooner waiting at San Clemente Island about 50 miles off shore. The initial question had been one of search and seizure in view of possible violation of neutrality laws,[27] but since the *Itata*, now vanished, had already been searched, the U.S.S. *Charleston* was sent in pursuit.[28] Secretary Blaine was in New York, where he became quite ill, almost on the verge of physical collapse; and Navy Secretary Tracy stepped into the breach. Ultimately, the closely-pressed *Itata* surrendered her munitions of war to the U.S. Navy off the rebel-held Chilean port of Iquique. The appearance of other United States ships in those waters doubtless helped in the decision arrived at.

As the Presidential tour continued through the Northwest, the Prairie States, and the Midwest, no doubt could exist that it had

25 Allison to Harrison, April 4, 1891, (L.C.), Vol. 121.

26 Charles Hedges (comp.). *Speeches of Benjamin Harrison*, pp. 416–90.

27 W. H. H. Miller to the President, May 6, 1891, (L.C.), Vol. 122, (telegram). Miller also reported that the Chilean Minister had demanded enforcement of American neutrality laws and that Secretary of State Blaine had called on the Attorney General "to take the necessary action to that end."

28 Harrison to Miller, May 6, 1891, (L.C.), Vol. 122, (telegram), approved the pursuit. Frederick B. Pike, *Chile and the United States 1880–1962*, p. 330, n. 119, states: "The Chilean interpretation of the troublesome incident was that the United States Government had resorted to an unduly narrow and unjustified interpretation of neutrality laws to prevent delivery to the congressional forces at Iquique of arms purchased in the United States—and very possibly loaded onto the 'Itata' outside of United States territorial waters."

been a success, a great improvement over the last. A nonpolitical journal, commenting on the President's "refinement and breadth of vision," found the variety and skill of his speeches "very striking."[29] Andrew Carnegie, who was about to sail for Europe, left word that he knew of "but one voice and that of praise and gratitude for what you have done."[30] It was, in truth, something of a feat to have delivered 140 impromptu addresses in about thirty days and at the same time to have greeted hundreds of admirers.

The Chilean difficulty, which persisted on top of the Italian matter, proved aggravating. A U.S. court eventually decided that the *Itata* mission had not violated American neutrality after all.[31] But an American naval officer did violate neutrality when he revealed to loyalist shore batteries the location of a rebel invasion force on the Chilean coast.[32] Emotion blazed white-hot south of the equator.[33] To make matters worse for official Washington, it was the rebel forces that ultimately prevailed.

Recognition was, of course, delayed. With Chilean President Balmaceda deposed, a number of prominent Chileans, fleeing Congressional vengeance, received asylum within the American legation at Santiago "as a humane expedient" rather than as a "recognized privilege under international law."[34] Harrison and Blaine were thus improvising. The President was unable to warm to the rebels who "do not know how to use victory and moderation."

So it would prove. All things considered, it was perhaps unwise of Captain Winfield Scott Schley of the U.S.S. *Baltimore* to grant shore liberty to 117 seamen, some of whom were in Valparaiso's True Blue Saloon when one of the party was spat upon. In the ensuing brawl, two bluejackets were stabbed to death, seventeen others knifed, shot, or beaten. Chilean rioters, perhaps aided by

29 *Congregationalist*, May 7, 1891.

30 Carnegie to Harrison, May 14, 1891, (L.C.), Vol. 122, (telegram).

31 Walter La Feber, *The New Empire*, p. 132; Alice Felt Tyler, *Foreign Policy of James G. Blaine*, pp. 135–41. As Pike, *op. cit.*, p. 330, n. 119, concludes: "Chileans were confirmed in their viewpoint when in 1891 the United States Court for the southern district of California, located in San Diego and presided over by Judge E. M. Ross, decided that the law had not been violated in the arms transaction and dismissed all charges."

32 R. D. Evans, *A Sailor's Log: Recollections of Forty Years of Naval Life*, pp. 266–67, as cited by La Feber, *op. cit.*, pp. 132–34.

33 Pike, *op. cit.*, pp. 68–73.

34 Harrison to Blaine, September 26, 1891, in Volwiler, *op. cit.*, pp. 195–97, and Blaine's reply, September 28, 1891, *ibid.*, pp. 197–98. Originals are in (L.C.), Vol. 130.

local police, chased other U.S. sailors here and there about the city. October 16, 1891, proved a bad day for the hated U.S. Navy.[35]

The reaction by the U.S. press can be readily imagined, with a war of vengeance the consensus. In the White House a lonely President (in the absence of Mr. Blaine and the illness of Mr. Halford) found himself "almost to the point of distraction and exhaustion," as he told his clerical friend, Dr. George H. Corey.[36] A cable from Andrew Carnegie, a peace-lover by nature, a shrinker from brawls, carried the warning: "Chile very weak and sorely tried. Her giant sister should be patient and forbearing."[37] Yet from Chile came no apology, no expression of regret.

Harrison directed Joseph Wharton, Acting Secretary of State, to send a sharp note complaining of the delay. The new regime waited still longer before replying, and then made an apology unsatisfactory to the United States. The Chilean Foreign Minister merely excused himself on the score that in Chile the law was "slow in its processes" but "exact in its conclusions."[38] The trials were at that time being held in criminal court in Valparaiso.

The slowness of the process was one thing, but the Chilean method so outraged Harrison's sense of justice that he asked for an explanation through diplomatic channels. In his annual message to Congress on December 9, 1891, he hoped that the investigation would bring full satisfaction to the United States, adding the warning that "if these just expectations should be disappointed or further needless delay intervene, I will by special message bring the matter again to the attention of Congress for such action as may be necessary." The President called the attack "savage, brutal, unprovoked."[39] It had been a flagrantly unjust attack on the American uniform. Apology and indemnity must come.

35 Captain Schley's own report along with that of the American Consul at Valparaiso and other witnesses are in *Foreign Relations* . . . (*1891*), pp. 204 ff. The crew was extended "the usual courtesy and hospitality of the city . . . by the captain of the port."

36 Harrison to Corey, October 16, 1891, (L.C.), Vol. 131. Harrison, though admitting that "every additional pull on me now brings the blood," attended a meeting of the Ecumenical Conference and gave the membership a conference.

37 Carnegie to Harrison, October 26, 1891, Carnegie MSS., Vol. 13, Carnegie added: "Why Americans are unpopular in any sister republic needs inquiry."

38 Bailey, *op. cit.*, p. 453. For a recent evaluation favorable to Chile and the Chilean judicial process see Pike, *op. cit.*, pp. 71–76.

39 Annual Message, December 9, 1891, in *Foreign Relations* . . . (*1891*), pp.ix–x. Harrison promised to submit "the entire correspondence with the Government of Chile at any early day." The Valparaiso affair was termed "so serious and tragic in its circumstances and results as to very justly excite the indignation of our people and to call for prompt and decided action on the part of this government."

In Chile an angry foreign minister publicly attacked and maligned the U.S. President, Navy Secretary Tracy, and American Minister Patrick Egan.[40] Viewing this as "an atrocious insult to the American government," Harrison ordered the Navy to prepare for action. Unprepared at the time of the Mafia affair some nine months earlier, Tracy, who had a battle plan ready, alerted the fleet. His naval yards were working overtime. Only Blaine, somewhat ill at ease in the garb of a pacifist, sought to defend the Chileans. Heated Cabinet discussions followed, and at one meeting the President leaned forward and with an emphatic gesture declared: "Mr. Secretary, that insult was to the uniform of the United States sailors."[41]

War feeling ran dangerously high. Civil Service Commissioner Theodore Roosevelt thirsted to lead a cavalry charge against the Chileans.[42] Other offers of military service were entertained. To a nephew in Kansas, Colonel James F. Harrison, the President wrote: "Certainly I ought not to be unwilling to sacrifice my relations, as Mark Twain would say, if there is a war with Chile. . . . I . . . have always been hopeful that a sense of justice would lead the Government of Chile to do that which would avoid a collision."[43] A Kentucky congressman declared that over a million men would respond to a call to arms. When the body of one of the murdered seamen lay for a time in state in Independence Hall, Philadelphia—an honor previously accorded only to Abraham Lin-

---

[40] Chile's Minister of Foreign Relations, M. A. Matta, had been a leader among Radical and Liberty party politicians who viewed the U.S. with extreme distrust and dislike. Infuriated by Harrison's message, Matta wired Pedro Montt, then Chile's envoy in Washington, that Harrison had been guilty of deliberate inaccuracies. See Pike, *op. cit.*, pp. 72–77. La Feber, *op. cit.*, p. 134, calls the remarks of Matta "an inexcusable public note which maligned both Egan and Harrison."

[41] Harrison's statement is cited by Robert H. Ferrell, *American Diplomacy*, p. 186. For details on Tracy's battle plans for the Caribbean area, see Walter R. Herrick, Jr., "General Tracy's Navy: A Study of the Development of American Sea Power, 1889–1893," (Ph.D. dissertation, Univ. of Va., 1962), pp. 217–18. There is substantial evidence that "Mahan, Soley, Folger, and Tracy formed an informal strategy board . . . for naval operations in Chilean waters."

[42] H. F. Pringle, *Theodore Roosevelt*, p. 167. In article entitled "The Foreign Policy of Benjamin Harrison," in the *Independent* (N.Y.), August 11, 1892, No. 1, pp. 2–3, Roosevelt characteristically stated: "The United States was absolutely in the right and Chile absolutely in the wrong." He judged Harrison's foreign policy as one of "dignified firmness and wise liberality."

[43] Benjamin Harrison to Col. J. F. Harrison, January 26, 1892, Harrison Papers on Microfilm, Series 2. For commentary on this exchange, see A. T. Volwiler, "Harrison, Blaine, and American Foreign Policy, 1889–1893," *Proceedings of the American Philosophical Society*, LXXIX, No. 4 (November 1938), 644.

coln and Henry Clay—the American feeling became more emotional.

Chileans seemed no less warlike. Encouraged by the successful revolution, they boasted of what their navy would do if war came. Still, as matters then stood, the U.S. had 63 million people within its bounds to Chile's three million.

During the first three weeks of January 1892, Blaine alone prevented Harrison from sending an ultimatum, though Secretary Halford recorded in his diary: "The President stated that all members of the Cabinet are for war."[44] Then, on January 20th, Chile demanded Minister Egan's recall. This so stirred Harrison's militancy that Blaine sent on an ultimatum written by the President himself. It read:

I am now . . . directed by the President to say that if the offensive parts of despatch of the 11th of December are not at once withdrawn, and a suitable apology offered, with the same publicity that was given to the offensive expressions, he will have no other course open to him except to terminate diplomatic relations with the Government of Chile.[45]

This ultimatum of January 21, 1892 probably surprised Chile more than it did European nations which had cultivated that country's trade. The British Foreign Office already had a report that "unless Chile apologized promptly the United States would declare war and seize nitrate territories as an indemnity."[46] Paris and Berlin, informed that war between the United States and Chile seemed imminent, joined London in declaring that not one European nation would come to Chile's aid if United States forces invaded.[47] Sir Cecil Spring-Rice, Secretary of the British Legation in Washington, already had noted "the verge of war here . . . the President and the Navy are bent on it."[48]

44 As cited in La Feber, op. cit., p. 134.

45 House Ex. Doc. [52nd Cong., 1st sess.], I, 308. For the background of Harrison's insistence on writing the note himself, see the exchange of published letters with Blaine in Volwiler, op. cit., pp. 235–39.

46 Pike, op. cit., p. 78.

47 Ibid.; also John A. S. Grenville and George B. Young, Politics, Strategy, and American Diplomacy, p. 98, described the Chilean revolution as an "interested movement of political parties for obtaining power . . . and the question of principle found little place in that struggle."

48 Stephen Gwynn (ed.), Letters and Friendships of Sir Cecil Spring-Rice, p. 118. Spring-Rice attributed the war scare to "inconceivable stupidity" on the American side and "trickery" on the part of Chile. He also noted Blaine's influence for peace and styled him as "anti-Jingo."

Four days passed without answer from Chile. Harrison meanwhile was working on a special message to Congress that reviewed the assault upon the *Baltimore's* crew and the insulting Chilean message of December 12th. On January 25th, Congress was told that protection must be afforded all U.S. citizens in foreign lands who suffered brutality and injury inflicted out of a spirit of animosity. Harrison asked Congress, which then had the sole power to declare war, to take "such action as may be deemed appropriate."[49]

Public response was favorable. Harrison informed the editor of the New York *Mail Express* that "it has been very gratifying to know that my communication yesterday to Congress has been so well supported, and so kindly received."[50] American unity had its effect, as did the influence of the European powers. Within 24 hours Chile backed down, a capitulation which Blaine had expected hourly.

An entry in the Henry Cabot Lodge diary indicates that the Chilean dispatch, which Blaine regarded as "so complete an apology," did not completely satisfy the President,[51] who could and did haggle over words. Blaine submitted to Harrison a reply to Chile, and added: "It may seem to you too cordial, but I believe it to be in the highest sense expedient. I have relied on Chile's good sense for reparation, and I believe we will get it more easily that way than by arbitration."[52] Harrison reworked Blaine's draft, convinced, as he told his Secretary of State, that "what I have said . . . has rather enlarged than diminished the expressions of cordiality." "My dear Mr. President," wrote an obviously relieved Blaine, "I liked your despatch better than mine. I have had it put in cipher and it is just about to be telegraphed to Santiago where I have no doubt it will give great satisfaction and relief."[53] Harrison not only lauded Chile's "spirit of justice," but offered congratulations for

49 *Public Papers and Addresses of Benjamin Harrison*, pp. 174–86.

50 Harrison to Colonel Elliott F. Shepherd, January 26, 1892, Harrison Papers on Microfilm, Series 2.

51 Lodge MSS., January 27, 1892, copy furnished by the late Howard K. Beale. See also John A. Garraty, *Henry Cabot Lodge*, p. 149.

52 Blaine to Harrison, January 29, 1892, as cited in Volwiler, *op. cit.*, p. 238. Blaine said: "We can afford to be very generous in our language and thus make a friend of Chile–if that is possible. At all events we can afford to venture $5,000 on it, and that is all we will get for the two sailors."

53 *Ibid.*, pp. 238–39. The President submitted his revision to Blaine and offered to discuss it with him.

the "cordial, frank and ample withdrawal of Señor Matta's tele-graphic instructions."[54]

As Theodore Roosevelt viewed the climax to the matter, Harrison's "timely display of firmness . . . produced a change of heart in our opponents."[55] Chile gave an indemnity of $75,000, which was generous, and the funds were distributed among the injured sailors and the families of the slain. Attorney General Miller drew a moral, writing a volunteer for military service that day:

It is quite certain . . . that the only way to make it sure that we shall have no need for wars with foreign powers is to be prompt, vigorous and peremptory in demanding that our flag and uniform shall always and everywhere be respected. With comparatively few exceptions, this seems to be the sentiment of the whole people, and the fact that the sentiment was so unanimous no doubt contributed to the desired results.[56]

Concerning the charge that Harrison's conduct during the Chilean revolution poisoned relations between the two countries for many years, one may reflect that even today there seems no easy solution to the problem of how to foster a friendly Pan-American spirit "without seeming to side with the ruling party in each country, thereby earning the hatred of the opposition, the rulers of tomorrow."[57]

54 *Foreign Relations . . . 1891*, pp. 312–13, give the text as written by Harrison and dispatched by Blaine.

55 Howard K. Beale, *Theodore Roosevelt and the Rise of America to World Power*, p. 43.

56 W. H. H. Miller to R. C. Bell, January 30, 1892, Miller Letterbooks.

57 Grenville and Young, *op. cit.*, p. 96.

CHAPTER XVII

The Political Winds

POLITICAL EFFORT to regain the ground lost in the 1890 election would not necessarily be expended in the President's behalf. The negative element of party patronage—the disappointed office-seeker—could be important, as workers who had not shared in jobs became idle hands, or at best lukewarm in the support of their chief. Ambassador Whitelaw Reid in Paris could well agree with a concerned correspondent who wrote that "no man could possibly change the entire patronage of the nation from one party to another and not engender many hostilities; an angel from the skies could not avoid such a result."[1] Grover Cleveland, the first Democrat to rule after six G.O.P. administrations, well knew this, and Harrison would experience the same trials, as party bosses sought to ally themselves with the man of the moment wherever found.

It seemed, then, that his chief opponent in 1892 would be Secretary Blaine rather than the Democratic candidate of whatever stripe. An untimely rivalry engendered by some personal hostility and much talk led United States Attorney E. G. Hay, who had been Senator Harrison's secretary, to complain of "too many fool friends" on both sides of the fence. Hay further opined that "the apparent effort on the part of somebody to compel Mr. Blaine to say whether he is a candidate . . . will hurt President Harrison very much."[2] Minnesota Senator W. D. Washburn, who may have been shown this letter, argued succinctly: "There are two serious objections to Harrison's renomination; first, no one cares anything for him personally, secondly, no one, as far as I know, thinks he could be elected if nominated."[3]

These and other pinpricks were felt by members of the inner

1 R. G. Horr to Reid, September 13, 1891, Reid MSS.
2 Hay to L. T. Michener, April 29, 1891, E. G. Hay MSS., Letterbook A-5.
3 Washburn to E. G. Hay, May 20, 1891, *ibid.*, Vol. 9.

circle of the President's official family; and if Harrison made a move, someone was likely to pounce or sulk. What could be done, for example, when former G.O.P. National Chairman W. W. Dudley, the present party treasurer, bought up three acres of filled-in land in the District for about 50 cents a square foot, then offered them to the U.S. Government for three times that amount as a site for a new Printing Office? Treasury Secretary Windom routinely signed the land condemnation measure to give the Government clear title, but Attorney General Miller advised that unless the White House intervened "you will have . . . a scandal."[4] Harrison, aided by Massachusetts Senator Hoar and Kansas Senator Plumb, forcefully opposed any further move. Yet the project failed in the Senate by only seventeen votes, and no further political support from Dudley would be forthcoming.[5] The faithful Michener, who had taken up law practice in Dudley's office, would be writing Secretary Halford some months later: "I know of many men who were sincere Harrison men . . . who are now veering about in the other direction."[6] Men at listening posts throughout the nation crowded the mails with opinions and surmises.

The economic tide, meanwhile, did not favor the course of the ship. Late in the old year another near panic, caused chiefly by tight money, hit Wall Street, and this time bankers called early at the White House. Soon Drexel, Morgan and Co. of Philadelphia and New York worked out a solution with Secretary Windom, although, inasmuch as gold was still being drained away by monthly purchases of silver as required by the Silver Purchase Act and, quite as bad, greenbacks could be redeemed in gold without being retired, there would still be the piper to pay some day.[7] Harrison took pleasure in proclaiming Chicago as the site of the Columbian Exposition of 1892, a 400th anniversary date, and in promoting Judge Henry B. Brown, an authority on admiralty law rather than a political creditor to be satisfied, to the Supreme Court, replacing

4 W. H. H. Miller to Harrison, December 8, 1890, (L.C.), Vol. 115. Congressional watchdog J. B. Cheadle (R., Ind.) first got wind of the scheme, known as "Dudley's baseball park ring," and alerted Miller (J. B. Cheadle to W. H. H. Miller, December 6, 1890, (L.C.), Vol. 115).

5 With 39 Senators absent the vote against the appropriation was 32 to 16. For the full Senate debate in which Dudley's proposal was called "a little fishy" and covered with "certain badges of fraud," see *Congressional Record* [51st Cong., 2nd sess.], Vol. 22, Part I (1891), pp. 3294 (February 26, 1891), 3315–21 (February 27, 1891).

6 L. T. Michener to E. W. Halford, August 10, 1891, (L.C.), Vol. 127.

7 William Windom to Harrison, December 12, 1890, (L.C.), Vol. 115; Wanamaker to Harrison, December 13, *ibid.*

the late Justice Samuel Miller. Even the Democratic press applauded that.[8]

The seasonal round of dinners at the White House and the
homes of Cabinet members came to an untimely end on January
29, 1891, at the home of John Wanamaker, a famed host. With the
exception of Secretary Windom, who had gone to New York to
address a Board of Trade dinner, and of Secretary Tracy and Attorney General Miller, who accompanied him, everybody was there,
including Windom's own family. Harrison left the party rather
early and was about to retire when a servant handed him a telegram from Tracy telling of Windom's sudden collapse and death
in New York at the close of his speech. Able, dignified, and genial,
Windom had been closer to the President than any other Cabinet
member.

Harrison called for his carriage and rushed to the Wanamaker
home. Blaine was informed, then War Secretary Redfield Proctor,
and finally Wanamaker, who had been busy with departing guests.
The host saw the Windoms to their carriage and, with Harrison
and Proctor, followed them home. The news then had to be broken
and Harrison could not help but feel the strain as he consoled the
bereaved. He returned next morning to escort Mrs. Windom to the
cemetery where he selected the burial lot, then went to the railroad
station where Cabinet men and other officials stood in silence as
the coffin was borne from the train. Flags flew at half-staff and all
social activity was canceled until after the Lenten season.[9]

Flags again were half-masted upon the death, a few days later, of
Admiral David D. Porter in Washington and that of General William T. Sherman on February 14th in New York. Harrison jour-
neyed to that city to pay last respects to his old commander in the
Georgia campaign, and, on the day of the funeral, business was
suspended both in Washington and in St. Louis, the place of
burial. A letter to Harrison's brother Carter in Tennessee reveals
the President's personal feelings at this time:

I have been, as you can well imagine, overwhelmed with care and
anxiety and work . . . The rush connected with the last days of Congress, and the anxiety connected with the three deaths in the official
circle, have quite overwhelmed me; though I hope to hold out without
any break now until rest comes.[10]

8 New York *Herald* (Dem.) as cited by Indianapolis *Journal,* December 26, 29, 31,
1890.

9 In addition to routine press coverage, intimate details of the tragedy are entered
in the Mary Lord Dimmick Diary, January 29, 30, 31, 1891 (Walker MSS.).

10 Benjamin Harrison to Carter Harrison, February 16, 1891, (L.C.), Vol. 119.

Who would succeed Windom? Well aware of the risk involved in any choice, since he could hardly please at the same time Boss Platt of New York, Matt Quay of Pennsylvania, Elkins of West Virginia and certain Westerners with claims, Harrison nominated Charles Foster, an Ohio merchant, financial conservative and long-time friend. Foster was promptly confirmed by the Senate and was well received by the press.[11]

As the 51st Congress came to a close, Harrison signed an historic measure creating a Circuit Court of Appeals, thus freeing U.S. Supreme Court Justices from the arduous duty of service wherever called.[12] Harrison also helped speed a million-dollar improvement of the Mississippi River channel, thus redeeming a personal and party pledge to midwestern farming and shipping interests.

On the debit side was the failure of the Federal Elections Bill to reach a vote in the Senate, and the passage of the Silver Purchase Act, largely through cloakroom deals by silver-state Senators and anti-Harrison forces led by Senators Cameron and Quay of Pennsylvania, the National Republican Chairman.[13] "We have fallen upon bad times for the party," Wisconsin's Senator Spooner summed up. "The Confederacy and the western mining camps are in the legislative supremacy."[14] Put in another way, in the words of U.S. Attorney Hay: "We have had too much . . . of what may be

11 Charles Foster to Harrison, February 23, 1891, (L.C.), Vol. 120, gives evidence that the new Secretary shared Harrison's views and promised that "the welfare of the country and the success of your administration will be the guiding star of my conduct."

12 Sr. Maria Margaret Quinn, "William Henry Harrison Miller" (unpublished Ph.D. dissertation, Catholic Univ. of America, 1965), pp. 111–16, calls the action the first structural modification of the federal judicial system in more than one hundred years. Harrison had called for the reform to avoid delays which "amounted practically to a denial of justice in a large number of cases." Salaries of U.S. judges were also increased by the 51st Congress. While in the Senate Harrison more than once succeeded in getting such a bill passed and he continued to advocate it. See W. H. H. Miller to Judge A. N. Thayer, February 28, 1891, Miller Letterbooks.

13 Richard E. Welch, Jr., "The Federal Elections Bill of 1890: Postscripts and Prelude," Journal of American History, LII, No. 3 (December 1965), 511–26. Welch correctly observes that "the maneuver of the silver bloc delivered a most damaging blow to the elections bill but it did not secure the enactment of additional silver legislation. Stewart's bill passed the Senate on January 14 but was buried in the House" (p. 520).

14 J. C. Spooner to Major J. M. Bundy, and to Alex Meggert, January 27, 1891, Spooner Letterbooks, Box 15. The Wisconsin Senator charged Nevada's two Senators with betraying "the Republican party and the rights of citizenship for silver." In Spooner's eyes the failure of the elections bill was a punishment to the G.O.P. "for making too easy the admission of western boroughs into the Union."

called 'strictly business' politics and . . . the abandonment of healthy sentiment."[15] To that extent the President shared in the disappointment.

A man whose name was not associated with national legislation, or with political failures to obtain appointments, was Secretary of State James G. Blaine, who had been eulogized, while Harrison was ignored, by former Governor J. B. Foraker of Ohio. The Foraker incident, so called, occurred at the 1891 convention of Republican League Clubs in Cincinnati where it was said that Blaine "has given us an admirable administration."[16] Whether or not Foraker meant to say Harrison instead of Blaine cannot be known, nor did this influential midwesterner ever say—at least not publicly. But he did set tongues wagging at the time, and gave an impetus to the Blaine bandwagon. William McKinley spoke for Harrison, but when General James S. Clarkson of Iowa, a silent Blaine supporter, was named Republican League president, most delegates began to look for a seat on the Blaine wagon. It was significant, too, that Clarkson succeeded Matt Quay as National Chairman when the latter somewhat belatedly resigned on July 29th. "I have no personal choice for President . . . time will indicate the man," said Clarkson, who considered Harrison lacking in "personal popularity" and thus unavailable for the national ticket. Insofar as other qualities were to be considered, Clarkson conceded in a press interview that Harrison was second to none in intellectual ability, including "his phenomenal Secretary of State."[17] It was at about this time that U.S. Attorney Hay complained of "too many fool friends."

It was not that Clarkson discouraged Harrison; it was more of a case of let the better man win. "I have always found you ready and anxious to promote the party interest in every possible line," he wrote Harrison meaningfully.[18] Party unity was the key to success.

If Harrison was second to none in intellectual ability, he also was a man of great patience and strong endurance. So certain mem-

15 E. G. Hay to W. D. Washburn, January 27, 1891, E. G. Hay MSS., Letterbrook A-5, pp. 179–82.

16 Hay to Washburn, April 28, 1891, ibid., pp. 238–44.

17 During the Cincinnati convention Clarkson was in Boston where his press interview was given wide circulation. Harrison saw a copy on the West Coast. See H. Casson to J. M. Rusk, April 24, 1891, Rusk MSS.

18 J. S. Clarkson to Harrison, May 5, 1891, (L.C.), Volume 122. Clarkson's great political power and influence in inner circles was described by L. T. Michener in a letter to Halford, September 3, 1891, (L.C.), Vol. 129.

bers of his official staff thought as they witnessed his long labors during the diplomatic differences with Italy, Chile, and Great Britain, and the negotiating of reciprocity agreements with Spain, France, and Germany in 1891. Harrison had to be foremost because of Blaine's illness (a nervous disorder) from May until October of that year. Meanwhile, Interior Secretary Noble, who was ailing, had to have an extended leave of absence, while War Secretary Proctor resigned his portfolio to enter the United States Senate from Vermont. The additional work caused by the absence of these three gave rise to Harrison's remark: "The President is a good deal like the old camp horse that Dickens described; he is strapped up so he can't fall down."[19]

Blaine's condition made news on dull days when newspapers had to be sold in a competitive market. Lacking other topflight material, James Gordon Bennett's New York *Herald* flared with these headlines on May 22 and 23, 1891, and who could resist them? "Is Blaine's Mind Giving Way? Flashes of Intense Brain Activity Followed by Periods of Extreme Mental Depression . . . Diplomatic Business Suffers . . . Blaine Breaking Down, Though Friends Deny It . . . Continued Work Would Render Him Liable to Falling in the Harness," and so on.

Inevitably, there followed a report that Blaine was dying, which the Secretary read with interest; he then sent word to an inquiring reporter that he would not contradict the story. Later he went out driving, and on some days twice. Friendly letters from Harriet Blaine to Carrie Harrison gave assurance that the Secretary was on the mend. Harrison was moved to write him: "The over-readiness of the newspapers to kill off public men is one of the curious and discreditable phases of modern journalism."[20]

A dying public man is always news but now that Blaine was on the mend, stories were heard of a personal feud with the Harrisons that would end the Secretary's hopes of becoming a presidential candidate in 1892. Lawyer Michener, still on the inside of affairs, assured E. G. Hay that a sincere friendship existed between the two men and that Blaine was not only greatly annoyed but would not wish to be a candidate "under any circumstances."[21] Blaine well knew that Harrison had been doing and would con-

19 Harrison to William McKinley, February 4, 1892, (L.C.), Vol. 135.
20 July 18, 1891, (L.C.), Vol. 126. Mrs. Blaine's letters to Mrs. Harrison, May 27, July 4, 1891, have been preserved by the President's granddaughter (Marthena Harrison Williams Collection).
21 May 2, 1891, E. G. Hay MSS.

tinue to do most of his work, at least until his return which apparently was still several months away. For a while Harrison was busy with the claims of Canada and England concerning the right to hunt seals in the Bering Sea. Several new reciprocity agreements were concluded and signed, including long-deferred consent by France to admit U.S. pork into her ports. An international Monetary Conference to regulate the use of silver was organized while gold still continued its outward flow. Remarking upon a business trip to Europe by railroad magnate Chauncey M. Depew and Commodore Vanderbilt, Harrison observed wryly: "I cannot help feeling a little malice toward the American citizens, members of my own family included, who are carrying our good money across the sea."[22] Vacation days at Cape May Point were spent in ocean fishing, carriage rides, and beachside saunters with Baby McKee, although Harrison still found his work consuming an average of four hours daily.

Uncertainty over the candidacy of James G. Blaine would occupy the minds and the talk of leading men until the nomination could be arrived at in June 1892. The uncertainty was sometimes veiled, even by the loyal Michener, who assured E. G. Hay that a majority opinion had Blaine well out of it. Yet the situation did present a base for political maneuvering and bargaining, and energetic men of varying political hues could hardly be inactive.

General Clarkson, who offered to resign from G.O.P. leadership "to relieve you of any possible embarrassment," so he wrote the President, may have wished for more of a free hand, with influence perhaps undiminished.[23] There was no question but that he leaned more to Blaine in his fence-straddle. Harrison dutifully reminded him that G.O.P. leaders "shall be men . . . who have the zeal, enthusiasm to combat the work [of the campaign] in such a way as to unite the party."[24] So Clarkson must stay on, even after he said to his fellow workers that "Blaine . . . would not be a candi-

22 Harrison to Depew, July 1, 1891, (L.C.), Vol. 125.
23 J. S. Clarkson to Harrison, July 22, 1891, (L.C.), Vol. 126. Clarkson expressed the view that "all the men in controlling places ought to be those who possess your confidence and can be fully trusted by you." The Iowan desired "union and harmony as the first prerequisite for success in '92" and offered the suggestion that "there need not be any demoralizing contest over the next ticket."
24 Harrison to Clarkson, July 27, 1891, ibid. The President repeated his desire for harmony and union, reminding Clarkson that "there has been no time, I think, in my limited public career when my name has been a shibboleth to those who would introduce distractions, and no time when my personal ambitions were not in all respects subordinate to the public good and to party success which is only another expression of the same thing."

date but would accept if the Convention saw fit to tender the nomination in such a way as to make it complimentary."[25] A complimentary nomination for Blaine! While this sounded rather tentative, a responsive New York *Herald* found it not difficult to discover a general feeling "in every quarter of the United States . . . that if health is restored to him, James G. Blaine and no other, must head the ticket in 1892."[26]

Michener, who had been Harrison's manager in 1888, scented blackmail although there was no question but that true Blaine feeling abounded. Chauncey Depew, an influential New York supporter of Harrison, called the movement "more than a sentiment . . . a craze," after the man from Maine was "cheered to the echo" by a Republican League gathering at Syracuse.[27] All this would inevitably lead to some polite suggestions for Harrison to consider, with bargaining plainly inferred.

It was Michener who carried the word to Harrison after Clarkson met at Bar Harbor with Matt Quay, Tom Platt, Samuel Fessenden of Connecticut and other influential members of the National Committee, a meeting assembled for the purpose of discussing how to influence the President according to the rules of the game. The word went out that Harrison should consult with them on future appointments and give them some actual influence in policy. Was Blaine the wedge? The boom and the cheers would then subside as a consequence. It was significant, however, that no direct move was made to undermine the President's chances for the nomination—he was still the frontrunner as the race now went.[28]

Harrison summoned Michener to Cape May for talks that lasted for days. The President's position at this time was the same as

25 Michener to Halford, July 30, 1891, *ibid.*

26 As cited by George H. Knoles, *The Presidential Campaign and Election of 1892*, p. 37.

27 Depew to Whitelaw Reid, August 30, 1891, Reid MSS. Yet D. S. Alexander to Harrison, August 12, 1891, (L.C.), Vol. 127, having attended the Syracuse convention concluded that all predicted Harrison's renomination, since both the country and the G.O.P. felt *"absolutely safe"* in Harrison's hands.

28 L. T. Michener to E. W. Halford, September 3, 1891, (L.C.), Vol. 129. The results of the Bar Harbor conference were given by Clarkson in a personal interview with Michener on September 2, 1891 in Washington. Harrison's manager of '88 learned that Blaine felt kindly enough but his family felt bitter towards the President. The significant factor was that Blaine-for-President supporters "are not at heart for Blaine but really wish to crush the President and nominate a man of their own selection."

that of every public man who would really prefer to be out than in, but who did not wish to be pushed out or even pushed. Nor would he make any move that would cause intraparty squabbles over pieces of power once his own hold had been relaxed. Harrison now told Michener that he did not wish to run again (being naturally influenced by an ailing Mrs. Harrison, who was of the same mind although the White House had ceased to have charms many months before);[29] but at the same time he made it clear that he could hardly place a blanket mortgage on his official conduct. A little boldly, perhaps, Harrison advised Michener to tell Clarkson that he wished neither a bargain nor a renomination. Thereupon Clarkson decided to keep the Blaine boom moving despite the threat to party harmony, although he would continue to be personally friendly to Harrison, even conspicuously so.[30]

Mrs. Harrison remained at Cape May when her husband returned to Washington to inspect a refurbished White House and to resume his work there. The mansion "looks very clean and much improved," Harrison reported, although some scaffolding was still up. "The greatest beauty of all is the work in the bathroom—with the white tile and marble and porcelain-lined tub. They would tempt a duck to wash himself every day. The state dining room will be very handsome when the hangings are up and the whole table is covered and decked out. Your room and the Green room are very tasteful."[31] By the end of September, after having dinner guests every evening, including General Clarkson, Harrison felt weary but composed in mind. "You can rest assured that . . . the average good sense and fairness of our people is asserting itself," he wrote Carrie. "Senator Pettigrew has come out in the *Inter Ocean* with a most friendly interview, giving me credit for 'having the directing hand even in diplomatic matters.' " The September heat would be worth "millions to the cornfields" and incidentally to the Republican party, personal comfort aside.[32]

29 Mrs. Harrison's health had deteriorated during the summer of 1891. Unknown at the time, her persistent cough was a sign of incipient tuberculosis which left her listless and physically weak during the winter of 1892.

30 Undated memorandum by L. T. Michener entitled "A Proposal to End Hostilities," pp. 1–3, Michener MSS. The phrase "blanket mortgage" was Harrison's and he expressed the desire only "to be allowed to complete his term honorably."

31 Benjamin Harrison to Mrs. Benjamin Harrison, September 16, 1891, a holograph in Marthena Harrison Williams MSS. The basement and laundry had also been refurbished, but upstairs had yet to be carpeted and curtained.

32 Harrison to Mrs. Harrison, September 19, 1891, *ibid.*

Harrison concealed from his wife the fact that the White House was infested with mosquitoes, of which he advised Secretary Blaine, then added comfortingly: "You are fortunate in being away from here just now."[33]

Blaine had been freed of the trouble and perplexity of the Chilean and Italian episodes, and upon his return toward the end of October he thanked Harrison for doing his work but hedged on the issue of a second term for Harrison. Harrison took Blaine's words as meaning that he should say nothing about a second term, that he remain noncommittal.[34] This aspect of Harrison's position seemed to annoy his friends who hardly wished to surrender his prestige and advantage of position. William McKinley, backed by Mark Hanna, Ohio's leading Republican who had McKinley's presidential possibilities in mind, won the race for governor in that state during the fall although Democrat Russell Flower won in New York. Whitelaw Reid, writing from Paris, saw no loss of prestige: "In New York we fought on local issues and gained only a partial success. In Ohio we fought on the principles and splendid record of your administration, and gained a victory that inspires our friends everywhere."[35]

Harrison's largest problem, since it involved a delicate choice, lay in appointing a successor to War Secretary Redfield Proctor, and again there were those who would be offended, on one side or the other, whichever way the decision went. Backing former governor Cheney of New Hampshire, a member of the G.O.P. National Committee, were the New Englanders Proctor and Chandler; Cheney was also favored by Michener, who had first-hand knowledge of his value as a political worker.[36]

Of superior claim was Stephen B. Elkins, a native Ohioan. Elkins had made money in New Mexico minerals, later acquiring other interests in land, timber, mines, and the West Virginia Central Railroad, which had been founded by his business partner

[33] Harrison to Blaine, September 23, 26, 1891, as cited in Volwiler, *Correspondence Between Harrison and Blaine*, pp. 192–97.

[34] Volwiler, *op. cit.*, pp. 294–303.

[35] November 13, 1891, (L.C.), Vol. 132.

[36] P. C. Cheney to Michener, December 14, 1891, Michener MSS., Box 1. Person Colby Cheney, five years older than Harrison, had achieved success as a paper manufacturer. He served as Republican governor of New Hampshire, 1875–77, and remained active in national G.O.P. politics.

and father-in-law, the wealthy Henry G. Davis.[37] Campaign manager for Blaine in 1888, Elkins had been living in New York but
now made his home in the newly established town of Elkins, West
Virginia, where on occasion he entertained members of the Harrison family; and Harrison had been his guest at Deer Park in western Maryland. The President's own finances were largely in the
safe custody of Elkins and Davis, who served him as personal advisers, and it was known that Elkins had the confidence of Secretary Blaine. Harrison's son Russell, writing from New York, got
right to the point: "Elkins could have joined Clarkson . . . in
the [Blaine] movement [but] he got a number of influential people to change front and go to work in your interest. . . . Mr. Elkins
informs me that he is going over Saturday to see Blaine again and
push to get a letter of the right character and tone. . . . The rallying to Blaine is not because of his popularity but is because of a
very strong feeling all over the country that you are adverse to
recognizing the leaders and workers of the party. . . . I am praying
that you will counteract this feeling and honor a warm personal
friend and wise leader by appointing Elkins to your Cabinet as
Secretary of War."[38]

The letter to be solicited from Blaine would comprise a statement along the lines of "I do not choose to run," but it could
hardly be immediately forthcoming. Indeed, if the appointment
of Elkins smacked of a deal, Harrison could not afford to overlook
a well-known and able public man who for months had openly
supported and predicted his renomination and re-election. Furthermore, Elkins could command a measure of bipartisan support
inasmuch as his partner and father-in-law Henry G. Davis was
an influential Democrat.[39] Little trouble, certainly, would be faced

37 Elkins, who had just turned fifty, had been raised in Westport, Missouri, and
graduated from the University of Missouri. In addition to an active law practice and
far-flung investments, he founded and became first president of the Santa Fe National
Bank. Oscar D. Lambert, *Stephen Benton Elkins: American Foursquare*, is a well-
researched biography, published in 1955.

38 Russell Harrison to Benjamin Harrison, undated holograph (November 1891[?]),
in Russell Harrison MSS. Russell, in addition to being a close friend, had borrowed
money from Elkins. The President's son inaugurated the campaign to secure the
Cabinet portfolio for Elkins as soon as word came that War Secretary Proctor would
enter the United States Senate. See Lambert, *op. cit.*, pp. 135–40.

39 G.O.P. leaders supporting Elkins included John M. Mason, of Grafton, West
Virginia, whom Harrison made U.S. Commissioner of Internal Revenue; N. B. Scott,
later United States Senator; George W. Atkinson, a Wheeling lawyer who became
governor of West Virginia; B. F. Jones, President of the Jones & Laughlin Steel Works,
Pittsburgh; and, of course, James G. Blaine. Also G. A. Hobart to Elkins, November
14, 1891, Elkins MSS., confirms Senate support for the post of Secretary of War.

with the appointment of Elkins, which Harrison made hard on the heels of his annual message to Congress. On December 20, 1891, four days after receiving the nomination, the Senate confirmed it without opposition. Public response was favorable on the whole, although one G.A.R. man wired from Wisconsin that Elkins did not possess the courage to be on either side in the late war (he had in fact enlisted in the Union army from Missouri although both his father and a brother were Confederates.) [40]

For Christmas came some gifts of English pheasants and Scotch whisky from abroad, and some fine cigars from Vice-President Morton, who Harrison hoped would run with him again provided he himself ran. It seemed hardly likely that there would be any clean way out of it; he would be attacked in any event and he could hardly decline to run while under fire. Secretary Blaine was proving unexpectedly difficult. Harrison, on December 29th, jotted on an "Excuse me!" note from the Secretary: "This was the third appointment I had . . . the other two he forgot—this one was made at his suggestion and after waiting an hour this is rec'd." [41] Subsequent notes from the White House to State had a rather sharp tone, and not until after the Chilean crisis had been finally settled did the President and the Secretary resume their onetime cordial relations.

Harrison privately acknowledged Indiana's pledge of a solid delegation to him at the forthcoming convention: "A renomination for the Presidency is a thing I could very well forego [but] it would have been disappointing if the Indiana Republicans had shown indifference in view of the organized attack that has been attempted." [42] If only his political foes and lukewarm friends had left him alone, Harrison might have gracefully withdrawn, always provided that a strong enough G.O.P. candidate presented himself; but after a conference with Boss Platt and others in New York,

---

[40] Lambert, *op. cit.*, pp. 10–22, summarizes the military record. The disaffected Wisconsin soldier was Francis Downs, who wrote to Harrison a letter of complaint on December 17, 1891, (L.C.), Vol. 133. One correspondent advised Judge Gresham that as War Secretary Elkins would be just the man to aid Blaine and Harrison in plunging the country into war with Chile in an election year in order to continue the present administration (J. H. Woodward to Gresham, December 20, 1891, Gresham MSS., Vol. 38).

[41] Letters and annotations in Volwiler, *op. cit.*, pp. 215–16 and n. 51.

[42] Harrison to Louis Hartman, December 26, 1891, (L.C.), Vol. 134.

Chairman Clarkson sought to obtain the word from Blaine that
he would run. Certainly the nation's businessmen looked to him
for continued prosperity based on reciprocity, Clarkson ran on,
and it was felt too that he alone could draw a sufficient number
of voters from the Farmers' Alliance to keep the Republicans in
power in the Northwest.[43]

While Blaine mulled over a reply, possibly in conference with
Elkins, pressure was brought to bear on Harrison to speak out.
Lawyer Michener, who was permitted several patient hearings,
argued at length that it was "his duty to allow his friends to see
that delegates friendly to him were chosen . . . also that the coming campaign would have to be made on the record of his administration and that he alone was the one who should win or lose on
that record."[44] Yet the talk always ended with Harrison saying that
he did not wish to be re-elected and that in good time he would
decline to run. So if Harrison would decline to run, then Blaine
should also, one might reasonably expect. Dated February 6, 1892,
Blaine's statement to Clarkson that "I am not a candidate for the
Presidency" failed to mention Harrison. The letter in fact contained this rather curious verbiage: "To those who have tendered
me their support I owe sincere thanks and am most grateful for
their confidence. They will, I am sure, make earnest effort in the
approaching contest, which is rendered specially important by reason of the industrial and financial policies of the government being
at stake."[45]

Awaiting the opening of a Cabinet meeting at the White House,
Treasury Secretary Foster felt impelled to scribble a note to the
President in the way of unburdening himself and giving Harrison
the word: "The Blaine letter is not all that could reasonably have
been expected [but] do not fail to be cordial and gracious about
it to Blaine. The election is now the matter to be carefully
watched."[46] With Blaine seated at his right, the President quietly
composed himself.

43 Knoles, *op. cit.*, pp. 38–40, described the anti-Harrison caucus at "Amen Corner"
in New York's Fifth Avenue Hotel on January 15, 1892.

44 Undated memorandum by Michener, "Harrison Prior to the National Convention of 1892," pp. 1–4, Michener MSS.

45 *Journal*, February 8, 1892. Blaine's declination was widely published on an
otherwise dull Monday morning.

46 February 8, 1892, (L.C.), Vol. 135.

CHAPTER XVIII

Action for and by Blaine

A s THE WINTER WANED, both major parties turned their attention to the coming national conventions. The Republicans would meet first at Minneapolis on June 7th, the first time a presidential nomination would be made west of the Mississippi River. Two weeks later, on June 21st, the Democrats would convene in Chicago.

As the party out of power, the Democrats were frankly divided and somewhat apprehensive. Not a few thought that Harrison might repeat his electoral triumph of 1888, while of their own leader they were not sure. As preconvention matters stood, the onetime winner and onetime loser Grover Cleveland of New York —still the party's idol—faced strong opposition within his own state and from Tammany Hall.

The chief contender was U.S. Senator David B. Hill, who had won the New York governorship in 1888 while Harrison carried the state for the presidency. And Maryland Senator Arthur Pue Gorman, the successful foe of the federal elections bill, was not to be dismissed lightly. However, the party had no big issue other than the McKinley tariff over which to fight. Already the southern question of equal suffrage seemed settled by neglect; the country was relatively prosperous except for some distress among the farmers and unrest in the ranks of labor; the questions of free coinage of silver and currency were too dangerous politically to touch.

The Republicans seemed equally divided although more confident of victory in the end. Harrison was by no means a great favorite. Several party leaders viewed the President as unmanageable, stubborn, plainspoken, and aloof. Those estranged, who boasted that they controlled nominating conventions, still looked hopefully to Blaine, or if not to him, to McKinley, ex-Speaker

Tom Reed, John Sherman, or to some pliable dark-horse candidate. Still, rank-and-file Republicans felt that they could win again with Harrison. Party men and independents alike would say that he had been a good President. It seemed no small matter that John Thompson, co-founder of the Chase National Bank, gladly admitted that "it would give me great pleasure to go . . . to Minneapolis if I could be of service to Harrison, for I believe him to be most thoroughly honest, truthful and a lover of his country. He is the best and truest American that has been in the White House for years and deserves the nomination by acclamation."[1] It would be the judgment of historian Henry Adams: "Mr. Harrison was an excellent President, a man of ability and force; perhaps the best President the Republican party had put forward since Lincoln's death. . . ."[2] Notable too was the radical reversal of the strongly independent Benjamin Bristow, who, as Grant's Treasury Secretary, had uncovered the Whiskey Ring. In January this New York lawyer had longed for the passing of the current Administration.[3] Yet some months later he assured Harrison by letter that "your fearless expression of sound opinions upon vital financial questions, your steadfast opposition to the fatal heresies of 'Jeffersonian Democracy' and your intelligent, conscientious, and painstaking performance of public duties entitle you to the confidence and support of all who put the desire for good government and national prosperity ahead of every other consideration in the selection of a Chief Executive."[4] This was practically the G.O.P. Bible.

Democrats would attack Harrison on the score of inconsistency —for vetoing small public-works bills, while signing a rivers and harbors bill full of jobbery. Efforts would be made to prove him indifferent to the plight of the farmers. It would be said that he never really understood or tried to acquaint himself with the views and problems of the Alliance people and the Silverites. Yet it seemed that if the G.O.P. walked and talked carefully, and avoided offending important sectional interests, its victory of 1888 would be repeated. Harrison's policies of protection, pensions, reciprocity, trade expansion, and Pan Americanism needed only to be continued.

1 Thompson to A. E. Bateman, June 1, 1892, Harrison Papers on Microfilm, Series 2.
2 Henry Adams, *The Education of Henry Adams*, p. 321.
3 Bristow to W. Q. Gresham, January 7, 1892, Gresham MSS., Vol. 38.
4 Bristow to Harrison, June 20, 1892, Bristow Letterbooks.

The battle lines, however, were only beginning to form. Secretary Blaine's letter stating that his name would not go before the Minneapolis Convention apparently meant what it said despite its failure to mention Harrison. The President and his circle, as well as those personally devoted to the Secretary of State, had no reason to question the sincerity of the statement. Those opposed to Harrison's renomination chose to believe that either the statement had been forced by Elkins, or, if spontaneous, that it would have only temporary effect.[5] In April, both the Chicago *Post* and the New York *Sun* carried Washington dispatches stating that Blaine wanted to make the race that he had foregone in 1888, and that he was showing an "anxiety to get the nomination." The story was given to the press by William H. Grace, a Brooklyn politician and office-holder and for many years a friend to Blaine.[6] Grace, a guest at the Blaine mansion, nevertheless quoted Blaine as saying that he would be unavailable. There simply would not be, he said, enough votes.[7]

A politician believes what he wants to believe but such stories naturally annoyed Harrison's friends as much as they intrigued Blaine's followers. The relations between the President and his Secretary continued to be cordial and Harrison accepted Blaine's choice in naming a Collector of Customs at Portland, Maine. Speaker Reed had his man, the Secretary another. Harrison would have liked to oblige Reed, but finally yielded to Blaine, a choice that bitterly angered the Speaker. Later, when invited to "board the Harrison band wagon," Reed made the reply: "I never ride in an ice-cart."[8] Again the exercise of patronage had created an enemy.[9]

As the preconvention campaign advanced, anti-Harrison assaults

5 A delegate to the Minneapolis Convention was quoted as saying: "I have positive knowledge that Blaine wrote his letter, not because he wanted to, but because Harrison and Elkins harassed him into writing it" (New York *Sun*, April 3, 1892). This was categorically denied by Blaine's closest friends. See P. E. Studebaker to Russell Harrison, June 20, 25, 1892 (Russell Harrison MSS.).

6 William H. Grace to B. F. Tracy, June 1, 1892, Tracy MSS., Box 22, admitted: "I would like to see Mr. Blaine President," and in March he thought only Blaine could carry New York. At the April state convention Grace supported Harrison.

7 Chicago *Post* as cited by New York *Sun*, April 3, 1892.

8 D. S. Alexander, *Four Famous New Yorkers*, p. 183; Springfield *Republican*, May 20, 1892; Harrison to Blaine, September 22, 1890, Blaine MSS., Vol. 3.

9 L. E. Quigg to Whitelaw Reid, May 21, 1892, Reid MSS.; and the Springfield *Republican*, May 20, 1892, which reported Reed's stinging retort. The betting was $5,000 even that Harrison will not be nominated, and $10,000 against $5,000 that he cannot be elected.

became more strident. The silver-producing states found Harrison a disbeliever in the free and unlimited coinage of silver, and other elements objected to his enforcement of the Silver Act of 1890. California thought him favorably disposed to Chinese immigration. Mrs. Blaine, so the Capital grapevine had it, had been trying to get her husband to rescind the letter that apparently took him out of the race, and to declare himself a candidate. In mid-April she sought an interview with the President, to ask him to promote her son-in-law, John J. Coppinger, a newly created colonel, to the rank of brigadier general. It occurred to Harrison that the Colonel stood near the bottom of the list of 70 then in line for higher rank.[10] Halford's diary quoted Harrison as saying that after "fierce words . . . Mrs. Blaine went out of the room with a harsh look on her face. . . . 'You had a chance to please us once,' she said, referring to the failure to appoint Walker Blaine as First Assistant Secretary of State."[11] The Coppinger decision, which actually had Secretary Blaine's blessing, became grist in the mill of the anti-Harrison forces, and accounts of Mrs. Blaine's wrath were legion. Newspaper stories dealt with a "stormy interview" which Mrs. Blaine broke off by saying that the President's "decision would cost him a renomination and that she would now force Mr. Blaine to take the field against him."[12]

Matters worsened when the New York *World* (Democratic) on May 7th quoted Russell Harrison, the President's son, as telling at least a half dozen people in the Fifth Avenue Hotel that "Mr. Blaine's condition is such that all talk of his nomination, even if he should be a candidate, is out of the question. He is completely broken down both mentally and physically. He cannot remember the simplest things, and all the work has been on my father's shoulders for over two years. It is simply absurd to talk of nominating Mr. Blaine. He can scarcely more than sign his name to documents . . . and rarely, if ever, reads any of them. He is almost as helpless as a child and it is downright cruelty to be continually

[10] Coppinger had been promoted by Harrison to a colonelcy on January 15, 1891 and ranked 56 out of 70 in seniority for further promotion.

[11] Halford's Diary, April 16, 1892, as cited by A. T. Volwiler, *Correspondence Between Harrison and Blaine*, p. 245, n. 9.

[12] Mary A. Dodge to Harrison, February 20, 1893, cited in *ibid.*, pp. 291–92. Miss Dodge was a cousin of Mrs. Blaine, and had much ability and influence. Under the pseudonym "Gail Hamilton" she wrote numerous magazine articles and several books. Her biography of James G. Blaine appeared in 1895.

bringing his name to the front as a presidential candidate."[13] The fury this article created in the Blaine household can only be imagined. With a cold "My dear Sir" letter the Secretary sent the clipping to the White House and sharply observed: "I have seen no withdrawal of these statements or denial of their authenticity. . . . I have at different times . . . heard of similar rumours purporting to have emanated from the White House, but have not deemed them worthy of notice. They could derive importance only from the accompanying publication."[14]

Private Secretary Halford and War Secretary Elkins hurriedly took counsel lest Blaine should suddenly resign. A wire to Russell Harrison was answered by word of denial already given to the newspapers and by letter to Blaine who was told: "The story is wholly and unqualifiedly false and I so stated to reporters of other papers who called on me during the afternoon. I hardly think it necessary for me to give you this assurance as you have much experience with newspapers and disreputable reporters but I thought I would drop you a line to convey my assurances of respect and express regret that such a story had any publicity whatever."

Blaine replied that everything would be satisfactory "provided it [the denial] be published in the columns of the *World* where the report complained of appeared. I think it will occur to you that that is the proper manner of proceeding." Young Russell had already tried to gain access to the *World,* which refused outright to publish a denial.[15] A worried President also sought to mollify Blaine.

As to the paragraph from the New York *World* which you inclose, imputing certain statements respecting yourself to my son Russell— not as an interview but as second or third hand—I would have supposed that your experience as a public man would have led you to discredit the story. The motive was very apparent. An explicit denial has, as I am advised, now been made by Russell. As to the "rumors purporting to emanate from the White House," you rightly judged them to be unworthy of your notice and will not fail to see that any notice of them by me is impossible. Will you permit me to add that I am always accessible to you for an open and frank talk upon any matter of a personal nature.

13 The clipping is reproduced in *ibid.,* p. 274.

14 This exchange of correspondence between the Harrisons and Blaine is in (L.C.), Vol. 140, and in Volwiler, *op. cit.,* pp. 273–78.

15 Neither the *World* nor the *Herald* saw fit to publish Russell's denials (Russell Harrison to Blaine, May 11, 1892, *loc. cit.*).

Blaine however still desired to have the *World* print the denial, and he complained (erroneously) that Russell had allowed three days to elapse without any action. And there would be no "open and frank talk." Blaine closed the door by replying: "Will you permit me to suggest that talk on so unpleasant a subject would be painful if not impossible. Writing is better."[16]

Harrison could see for himself that Blaine had failed physically. A few days after the New York *World* incident, Senator James S. Barbour of Virginia died, and at his funeral ceremonies in the Senate Chamber on May 16th everyone had a good look at Mr. Blaine. Democratic Congressman Frank Coburn of Wisconsin, who sat nearby, wrote privately to a constituent back home: "I saw him standing, sitting and walking. His countenance is that of a man standing in the shadow of death, the face . . . flabby and wrinkled, is the face of a broken down old man. His walk is not strong and his form is bent as he walks. To talk of nominating him is nonsense, to nominate him would be an act of selfish cruelty on the part of the party. He would die because of the worry and work of the campaign, a worry and work that he nor any other man as a candidate could not escape, and he and his friends know it unless they are blind. But if nominated he is a weak candidate. He is the candidate of those dissatisfied with Harrison, the disappointed politicians of the party, and it does not take as many people to get up a furor of enthusiasm and make a great noise as it does voters to elect the candidate."[17] Whatever the true state of Blaine's health—and he had not a year to live—his home had become headquarters for those "who desired the President's destruction."[18]

Harrison, meanwhile, had to deal with his wife's failing health. A condition diagnosed in April as nervous prostration kept her bedridden until early May when the President managed to get her outdoors for a carriage ride. Soon she was able to make a health excursion with her husband and a doctor to Fortress Monroe

---

[16] Harrison to Blaine, May 10, and Blaine to Harrison, May 11, as cited in Volwiler, pp. 276–78. Russell wrote the Secretary a second letter on May 11, saying that "the 'World' no doubt had a purpose in printing what it said and the publication of my denial would have defeated that purpose."

[17] Frank Coburn to Ellis B. Usher, May 17, 1892, Usher MSS. The Congressman concluded with George W. Curtis' comment that "the same reasons why Mr. Blaine should not be elected in 1884 exist in 1892."

[18] D. S. Alexander, *op. cit.*, p. 184.

where a penciled note by Harrison to his daughter Mame McKee revealed that she was not much better:

She has not shown the improvement we had hoped. There seems to be no reason why she doesn't come right up except her nerves. . . . It is hard to get her to brace up and take an interest in anything.[19]

It was hoped to get her to try a little fishing but when the doctor considered the air too damp the trip was curtailed immediately. Back at the White House the President spent several hours each day in his wife's sickroom, freely admitting that her illness had withdrawn him from business and politics.[20] He left her side only to lay the cornerstone for Grant's Tomb on Riverside Drive in New York, and to dedicate a soldiers' monument at Rochester, New York, on Memorial Day. He answered one letter critical of Blaine for "appropriating honors to himself" by stating: "I have not given myself a moment's concern about the matter. . . . My position, as you know, from the beginning has been that if a re-nomination had to be schemed for by me it was, first, pretty clear evidence that it ought not come to me; and, secondly, rather a discouraging prospect of success. If we have a degree of unanimity and enthusiasm, I think prospects are hopeful; if we fall into distractions, they may be hopeless."[21]

No friends had remained more loyal than Michener, E. G. Hay and D. S. Alexander, the two last having once served as personal secretaries. None, however, believed that Harrison should wait for the voice of the people to be heard at Minneapolis. Already the politically strong state of New York was preparing to send Platt men to the convention. Alexander complained to Halford: "I don't like this 'let-alone' policy."[22] Michener, who had often voiced disappointment that Harrison had forbidden the launching of an organization similar to the one created in 1888, informed Harrison one April night that "hostile delegates were being chosen in regions where the great majority of Republicans wished him to be

19 Harrison to Mrs. J. R. McKee, May 16, 1892, Harrison Home MSS. Mrs. Harrison's indisposition became serious in early April (Harrison to Mrs. Mary S. Dimmick, April 8, 1892, Walker MSS. [telegram]).

20 Harrison to P. C. Cheney, May 10, 1892, (L.C.), Vol. 140; to Gil Pierce, May 21, *ibid.;* and Harrison Papers on Microfilm, Series 2, *passim.*

21 Harrison to P. C. Cheney, May 10, (L.C.), Vol. 140.

22 D. S. Alexander to Halford, March 15, 1892, (L.C.), Vol. 137. Alexander warned that Platt and Hiscock "are letting things drift so that at Minneapolis they can construe the delegates for someone else if there is a chance."

the nominee." He asked the President to lift the embargo on his true friends before it was too late. Harrison's gentle but firm refusal to change his position found Michener loyal to the end: "Mr. President, you are my Commander-in-Chief. I now put my hands over my head and there they will remain until you take them down."[23] But quite aware of shrewd maneuvers to defeat Harrison, Michener told Hay that the President had vetoed "any organized movement in his behalf." So, he complained, "I am told that it is a 'go as you please' movement . . . without cohesion or direction. I am considerably vexed. . . . When things 'go as they will,' they go to the dogs."[24]

Although the Springfield *Republican* (an organ critical of Harrison) pronounced the opposition as "feeble,"[25] stories appearing daily in the Washington *Post* predicted what would be done to defeat the renomination of the President. Unanimity of opinion pointed to Blaine, either as a volunteer or as a draft candidate, althought William McKinley was favored in Ohio and by "malcontents."[26] War Secretary Elkins, the most astute politician in the Cabinet, now asked Whitelaw Reid, chief owner of the New York *Tribune,* to publish "a few strong articles . . . to clear the atmosphere." Reid, who had retired as Minister to France and was quietly fishing for second place on the ticket, was cautioned: "The time is short and the opportunity passing."[27] The publisher would have to avoid displeasing Boss Platt and the New York delegation but still he obliged. A leading Republican organ could hardly do less unless it wished to divide and rule, or to lend a hand in that direction.[28] "The *Tribune,*" Reid confided to Elkins, "is certainly going as far, for the President, as the condition of things . . . would warrant." Indeed both the editorial and news columns of the paper supported Harrison with "great discretion, in the friend-

---

[23] L. T. Michener prepared a statement of his 1892 activities for the late A. T. Volwiler, then engaged in the preparation of Harrison's biography. Copies may be found in both the Michener and Harrison Papers. The author has verified details and finds Michener's version substantially accurate but somewhat incomplete.

[24] L. T. Michener to E. G. Hay, April 29, 1892, Hay MSS., Vol. 10.

[25] May 18, 1892. The paper claimed the anti-Harrison men continually turned back to Blaine "after trying to convince themselves that they can nominate some other candidate at Minneapolis."

[26] The "malcontents" were Platt, Quay and Clarkson.

[27] Elkins to Reid, May 19, 1892, Reid MSS. Elkins postscripted a prediction that Harrison already had over 600 delegates.

[28] L. E. Quigg to Reid, May 21, 23, 24, 30, 1892, *ibid.*

liest spirit and as vigorously" as the strained situation would bear.[29]

With the G.O.P. convention scheduled to open June 7th, late May was a time for action. Led by National Chairman Clarkson, and Platt's henchman J. S. Fassett, one Blaine faction gathered at General Russell Alger's home in Detroit to promote a united front for the onetime Plumed Knight.[30] Others, party men, not wholly in love with Blaine but still opposed to Harrison, met at the Shoreham Hotel in Washington. There Tom Reed spoke of the White House as an icebox and its occupant as an iceberg.[31] Secretary Blaine made no comment during the continual fire directed at Harrison, and as D. S. Alexander put it:

It seemed almost tragic that he [Blaine] did not censure such attacks, if sincere in his February letter or in his expressed regard for the President, especially as his name furnished the only rally-point for the Harrison opponents. One sentence must have cleared the atmosphere. Yet assaults multiplied while the apparent beneficiary remained silent."[32]

Harrison now decided to do something else other than yield the field by default. He sent a carriage for Michener and for nearly an hour reviewed the attacks known to have been made by Clarkson, Platt, and Matt Quay. Michener glowed inwardly as he heard the President say: "No Harrison has ever retreated in the presence of a foe without giving battle, and so I have determined to stand and fight." It would be Michener's task to take charge of the Harrison campaign at the convention. "Do whatever can be done honorably for me."[33] With Michener in charge, Harrison could sleep nights leaving it to his lieutenant to work until 3:00 or 4:00 A.M.

An angry man was James S. Clarkson, who had hoped to head

[29] Reid to Elkins, May 26, 1892, *ibid.* Reid indicated that he had not yet resumed the editor's chair but saw that "the gentlemen in charge did the right thing by Harrison and the administration."

[30] Springfield *Republican*, May 20, 1892. Carter B. Harrison to the President, May 25, enclosing a clipping from the Nashville *American* (May 22), detailed the conference at Alger's home where "Blaine's friends give every assurance that the Plumed Knight would accept the nomination—in no event will Harrison be the nominee" (Harrison Papers on Microfilm, Series 2).

[31] L. E. Quigg to Whitelaw Reid, May 21, 23, 24, 1892, Reid MSS.; and Springfield *Republican*, May 20, 1892.

[32] D. S. Alexander, *op. cit.*, p. 184.

[33] Undated memorandum, "Harrison Prior to the National Convention of 1892," Michener MSS. He recalled the date as Monday, May 23, 1892, but his own correspondence file fixes the true date as May 21.

Harrison off. Racing to the Shoreham Hotel, he was heard to declare that Harrison "was figuring now entirely on the support of Providence and sincerely believed that the Lord of Hosts would smite Platt as Samson had smitten the impious Ishmaelites." He brushed aside suggestions that he call at the White House but consented finally to dine with Elkins, only to laugh at his host's claim that Harrison had nearly 600 delegates solidly pledged. When Elkins predicted Harrison on the "first ballot" and dismissed talk "of a stampede to Blaine," Clarkson retorted that Elkins "was crazy . . . talking moonshine; that Blaine could lift his finger and leave Harrison without delegates enough to serve as pallbearers." It was not altogether a happy meeting. Clarkson made the sarcastic thrust that there was no occasion to call at the White House since "everything was going so beautifully."[34]

Harrison had already moved to set Clarkson aside and make U.S. Land Commissioner Thomas H. Carter Chairman of the G.O.P. National Committee. A strong partisan of Western interests, Carter could do much to offset the influence of Clarkson, owner of the Iowa *State Register* of Des Moines.[35]

Closest to Harrison in battle, Private Secretary Halford was quoted as saying that the President would accept any result at Minneapolis, *except Blaine*. It was understood that the opposition planned to nominate Blaine "with a whoop and a hurrah"; then the Secretary of State could either accept or telegraph his refusal. But in the latter event, Harrison would forbid the use of his own name, "having no desire," as Halford put it, "to be served with warmed over victuals."[36]

Blaine had gone to New York where, with Mrs. Blaine, he stayed at the Fifth Avenue Hotel, site of the "Amen Corner" of Boss Platt. Some 400 news-hungry reporters called, only to be told that he came to visit a little granddaughter and to consult a noted oculist. He repeatedly denied any "public side to my visit." But he could hardly avoid twice meeting Boss Platt, and delayed his

---

[34] An eyewitness account of Clarkson's antics is given in L. E. Quigg to Whitelaw Reid, May 21, 23, 24, 1892, Reid MSS. Accounts in the New York *Sun* and *Tribune* for May 22–June 4 substantially corroborate Quigg's report.

[35] Quigg to Reid, May 24, 1892, Reid MSS.

[36] Quigg to Reid, May 21, *ibid*. Tom Reed admitted that he had heard of the Platt-Quay scheme but said he was convinced that "Blaine will not take nomination" and believed he would never consent to be used in that way. Also Michener to Halford, September 3, 1891, (L.C.), Vol. 129.

return to Washington until J. S. Clarkson arrived on the scene. The New York *Tribune*'s well-informed editor, Whitelaw Reid, doubtless knew better than to say that "nothing political" transpired, but others could see that Platt wore a confident smile. Assured that he would be solidly backed by Pennsylvania and warmly supported by New York, Blaine, said Platt, would accept although with some misgivings.

Right in the midst of the talk . . . Blaine looked up and said, "But if I am elected, I shall have to stay . . . in Washington during the summer months of the long term of each Congress, and that will kill me."[37]

On May 28th, Blaine concluded his New York sojourn by receiving Clarkson and several members of the National Committee, and on the day appointed the news was heralded by headline:

Blaine Now A Candidate—Made So By The Attacks
of Harrison and The Cabinet.[38]

Widely published articles pictured the President as the true architect of reciprocity, the "firm friend of silver," and the consistent bimetallist. White House interviews described Harrison as quiet and self-reliant, stressing also "his great physical strength." A heavy mail tokened good strength nationally. A shirt-sleeved Michener was busy collecting funds.[39] But it would be a battle, certainly; as state delegations crowded the rails to Minnesota, the magic name of James G. Blaine was much in evidence. The Chicago *Tribune* carried a page-wide view of trains steaming over the prairies to Minneapolis to the support of the Plumed Knight, with banners, eagles, plumes, and Blaine portraits. As the delegates passed through Chicago, there were added two dining cars, each "stacked with one hundred cases of champagne and everything else the boys want" to enable them to "kindle a blaze of enthusiasm that will fire the Republican convention."[40]

Favorite sons abounded, and Ohio had McKinley and John Sherman. Mark Hanna, the influential coal, ore, and shipping

37 New York *Tribune*, May 22–June 4, 1892 and Quigg to Reid, May 21, 23, 24, 1892, Reid MSS.
38 New York *Sun*, June 1, 1892.
39 Michener to Hay, May 28, 1892, Hay MSS., Vol. 10. Michener spent $717.71 in Washington and $6,613.69 at Minneapolis. During the campaign he collected $9,172.29 and turned over to the National Committee the sum of $2,150.00 (Michener to Harrison, April 14, 1893, (L.C.), Vol. 157).
40 Springfield *Republican*, May 28, 1892.

magnate, supplied thousands of McKinley buttons and flags, and General Nelson Miles, for one, was active behind Sherman. Senator William B. Allison of Iowa, Reed of Maine and others were cited as dark-horse candidates, once the Harrison and Blaine forces had exhausted themselves.[41] There was anxiety at the White House, but mainly because of Mrs. Harrison's continued poor health. "Mrs. Harrison had a restless night last, getting very little sleep," the President wrote son-in-law J. R. McKee. "I was up with her until 2:00 and am a good deal worn out myself, what with anxiety and nursing and the rush that is upon me just now."[42]

First reports from Minneapolis were consoling. Boasting that "we are first on the ground," Michener claimed pro-Harrison sentiment stronger than expected.[43] Harrison declared himself "carrying no anxiety," on that account but rather was satisfied "that the people who talk against my renomination are not able to point to any official delinquency or inadequacy."[44]

On Friday morning, June 4th, at a brief Cabinet meeting which Blaine attended, it seemed as if the Secretary had finally decided to remain in the Harrison camp. This attitude made his backers uneasy. The necessity of Blaine's severing his Cabinet tie with the President became apparent, especially since reports from Minneapolis showed him to be gaining ground. In fact, it became known that day that a Blaine and Alger boom, planned in secret, would be launched "with much noise" next morning (June 5th).[45] Too, the Secretary's son, Emmons Blaine, was known to be conferring with the anti-Harrison clique.

It was left to Emmons to advise his father to resign, a step which all the rest of the Blaine family approved. Dated June 4th, and presumably written after the Cabinet meeting, the official tidings reached the White House at 12:45 P.M. Noting Blaine's request that his resignation . . . "be accepted immediately,"[46] Harrison re-

41 General Nelson Miles to John Sherman, June 1, 1892, John Sherman MSS., Vol. 582. Miles forsook his own presidential aspirations to back Sherman, stating that "the hostility between the President's forces and those of Mr. Blaine may become so strong that neither may be nominated and there is certainly a very strong undercurrent and public opinion in your favor. . . ."

42 June 2, 1892, (L.C.), Vol. 141.

43 Michener to Halford, June 1, 1892, (L.C.), Vol. 141, (telegram).

44 Harrison to William A. Russell, June 2, 1892, ibid.

45 D. M. Dozer, "Benjamin Harrison and the Presidential Campaign of 1892," American Historical Review, LIV, No. 1 (October 1948), 61; Alexander, op. cit., pp. 184–85.

46 Dozer art. cit.; also a copy in Harrison MSS.

marked to Halford: "Well, the crisis has come." Only 45 minutes later, Halford delivered the President's prompt acceptance. Word went out to Michener at Convention headquarters to observe caution and not attack Blaine.

At least the Secretary was no longer acting as a loyal Cabinet member. The resignation the President would charitably ascribe to Blaine's poor health and ill-starred advisers.[47] Although Blaine's sudden action was unexpected at the moment, Harrison seemed relieved. The June 5th entry in the diary of presidential stenographer E. F. Tibbott accurately reflected his feelings at that hour:

Blaine's resignation yesterday seemed to make the President more comfortable. He remarked to me . . . "Well there is one thing, I am sure to be comfortable for the next 8 or 9 months at any rate." His telegram (dictated by him but signed by Halford) to Michener is characteristic. "The President is indignant that anybody should suspect him of weakening when a fight is on. If the lines stand till he retreats there will be no retreat." After this he went calmly off to church.[48]

47 Volwiler, *op. cit.*, p. 288, n. 32. Endless speculation has been made on the possible reasons for the sudden resignation, since Blaine offered none himself. See Dozer, *art. cit.*, pp. 62–63. Blaine's most recent biographer (D. S. Muzzey) cites strained relations with Harrison, waning health, and the zeal of political friends, but concluded that "it is doubtful whether the Secretary himself really knew what his own mind was on the matter." Harrison's own friends "laid the use of Blaine's name at the door of Mrs. Blaine" and "with her assistance" Platt, Quay and Clarkson drove "the sick man into resignation."

48 Tibbott Diary, as cited by Dozer, *art. cit.*, pp. 63–64.

CHAPTER XIX

Harrison's Name Is Offered

O N THE WEST BANK of the Mississippi stood the Minneapolis Industrial Exposition Building, site of the 1892 G.O.P. National Convention. Conveniently close was the West House, the city's largest hotel, which quite outranked Convention Hall as an arena of political intrigue. It housed headquarters for Harrison, Blaine, and McKinley, and through the hot nights of the preconvention maneuvering its walls would vibrate with the rumbling tones of the political managers. Among those looking after the President's interests were many Indianapolis friends and neighbors, plus a clan of some forty Harrison kinsmen.[1] Advisers to Michener included Chauncey M. Depew and Senator Frank Hiscock of New York, Thomas Carter of Montana, John C. New of Indianapolis, and William E. Mason and A. M. (Long) Jones of Illinois—Administration men all. Prominent also were the Mc-Kinley and Sherman followers who looked to Mark Hanna for strategy and support. The Blaine faction naturally gravitated to Clarkson, Platt, and Quay.

Arriving Saturday morning, June 4th, Mark Hanna found the Blaine faction "very active and . . . doing most of the talking."[2] On Sunday, in fact, he noted a large number of Blaine delegates about, and on Monday there occurred a demonstration perhaps designed to look like a Blaine stampede. Enthused delegates and marching clubs roamed the streets, all chanting "Blaine, Blaine, James G. Blaine."[3]

1 The number included Harrison's two sisters, two brothers, and their families (Harrison Papers on Microfilm, Series 2).
2 Mark Hanna to John Sherman, June 14, 1892, John Sherman MSS., Vol. 583 (copy in (L.C.), Vol. 142).
3 "Blaine, Blaine, James G. Blaine, The Continental liar from the State of Maine," was used by the Democrats in the campaign of 1884.

Michener and conferees had quite approved Blaine's resignation and its prompt acceptance. "He is now out in the open," remarked Chauncey Depew, "is a proper subject for attack, and we should act accordingly."[4] Since Blaine now appeared as a leading rival, not a phantom, it was determined to give him a smashing defeat. As Michener recalled it: "The actual battle began at that moment." A polling committee was set up to locate every delegate to the convention and to keep a finger on every pulse. "[Blaine's] resignation has strengthened the lines here; our forces are united and determined . . . they rallied far more promptly than in 1888," Michener reported to Harrison late on June 5th.[5]

Harrison supporters on the lookout could see the Blaine boom begin to fade, and on June 6th the White House was told: "There was a time when the nomination of Mr. Blaine would electrify the party—*now* it would electrocute it."[6] Blaine's action had aroused criticism even by old friends—political maneuvering seemed to lie back of it.[7]

Up very late that night, Michener sent off two wires for Harrison to read at breakfast. One stamped 2:50 A.M., June 7th, read: "We believe that the Blaine men are about to abandon him—at any rate they are now making desperate attempts to find new candidates. . . ." A second dispatch told of 511 delegates safe for Harrison. "All looks well."[8]

As the convention opened, with the Blaine crowd very restless and uneasy, prior activity by Mark Hanna began to have effect. Badges were ready, McKinley's name printed on tally sheets,[9] and now came Clarkson, Quay and Platt with advice and support.

---

4 Undated memorandum, "Harrison Prior to the National Convention of 1892," Michener MSS., p. 10. Hanna, however, told John Sherman that Depew and Sen. Sawyer of Wisconsin both leaned to a third man (Hanna to Sherman, June 14, 1892, *loc. cit.*).

5 Michener, "Harrison Prior to . . . Convention of 1892," p. 11; Mason to Halford, telegrams, June 7, 8, 1892, and Michener to Halford, telegrams, June 4, 5, Harrison Papers on Microfilm, Series 2. The Michener memorandum recalled that A. M. Jones "is with us heart and soul."

6 Charles S. T. Collis to Halford, June 6, 1892, (L.C.), Vol. 141.

7 General H. V. Boynton to Harrison, June 5, 1892, Harrison Papers on Microfilm, Series 2; Felix Agnus to Harrison, June 6, 1892, (L.C.), Vol. 141. W. J. Arkell to Halford, *ibid.*, advised that "Blaine men are getting ready for dark horse. Harrison figures nominate him on first ballot and look reliable. This is the situation this morning. If convention is protracted a dark horse will win. Watch McKinley. Confidential."

8 (L.C.), Vol. 141.

9 Margaret Leech, *In the Days of McKinley*, p. 56, corrects the impression that Hanna "for several reasons did not press the claims of McKinley on the Convention," as stated by C. S. Olcott, *The Life of William McKinley*, I, 285-86.

If McKinley could inherit the loose Blaine strength, his name and influence might serve as the rallying point for all anti-Harrison men, it was agreed. Since he needed delegates already pledged to the President, his managers sought to obtain them. Minneapolis hummed with activity once the keynoter's speech was over. Secretary Halford at the White House was told all:

. . .They do not have any hope of nominating Blaine, but are laboring to get our delegates to agree to vote for some other man than Harrison on the first ballot. I never saw a hotter fight.·. . . The Blaine people want to nominate McKinley, but he is standing firm to us this hour. National Committee in violation of law, precedent, justice. . . ."[10]

Michener was indignant because the National Committee in fact was running the anti-Harrison campaign. To prevent the McKinley bandwagon from getting up steam it became imperative to insure Harrison's nomination on the first roll call. The Harrison forces would gladly give McKinley his hour of glory by making him Permanent Chairman. Once he began playing the role of presiding officer, "making rulings and doing things that would cause discontent—always the lot of the presiding officer"[11] he would be no hero. So McKinley was marched to the chair. It was also necessary to prevent the National Committee from wooing Harrison delegates prior to the first roll call scheduled for June 10th. Michener was confident that the President would win on the first ballot, if the pledged delegates came through; but it had to be the first ballot. Such was the situation late on June 7th when the White House was notified: "every device of avarice, malice and revenge is being used against us."[12] Telegrams went out, from friends in Washington as well as from Minneapolis, and mighty was the response. From all across the land, wires from businessmen, bankers, shippers, and political clubs poured into Minneapolis: "Stand by Harrison."[13]

10 Michener to Charles Foster and to Halford, June 7, 1892, (L.C.), Vol. 141.

11 Michener memorandum, *loc. cit.*, pp. 9–10. Leech, *op. cit.*, p. 56, says that McKinley appeared to ignore activities on his behalf, and repeatedly affirmed his strong allegiance to Harrison. This Michener denies.

12 John C. New to Halford, June 7, 1892, (L.C.), Vol. 141.

13 Michener memorandum, pp. 13–14. There was ample evidence that the opposition tried to break Harrison's hold on southern delegates (Michener to Halford, June 7, 1892, (L.C.), Vol. 141). Former Secretary Proctor and current War Secretary Elkins also expressed alarm at the methods and motives of the anti-Harrison forces (Proctor to W. B. Allison, June 8, 1892, Allison MSS., Vol. 288; Elkins to Reid, June 9, Reid MSS.). Only Navy Secretary Tracy remained confident: "Was in N.Y. yesterday. Went around to gather the feeling. Was amazed at the strength of the feeling for Harrison" (B. F. Tracy to Hiscock, June 8, 1892, Tracy MSS., Letterbook No. 3).

If the opposition could stop a nomination on the first roll call, McKinley's prospects would brighten. When Platt and Quay assured Hanna that a solid Ohio delegation for McKinley would tip the scales against the President, Hanna worked all night toward this end. Pennsylvania and New York delegates, under such urging, could also drift away.[14] It was thus necessary to insure Harrison's choice on the first ballot. The sole job of "Long" Jones was to hold Harrison votes in line, to see that the pledged delegates stayed pledged. His Committee of 40, as now known, agreed to collar every Harrison delegate at a secret meeting. An invitation was framed both to entice and to serve as a blind: "Come with me and you will see something that has never before been seen, and that you will love to think of all your life." Who could resist it? At 1:00 P.M. on June 9th, just after convention adjournment for the day, 468 curious delegates crowded into nearby Market Hall. It soon became apparent that they were there for business, not pleasure. Chauncey Depew was made chairman and the roll of states was called even before Hanna, Platt, Quay, or Clarkson knew that the meeting was in progress.[15] Michener flew to the telegraph office to inform the President: "Low-water estimate asked for and 520 votes was the result. Depew stated on announcing the vote that there were present a majority of the Nat'l Republican Convention. . . ."[16]

The word went out in Minneapolis: "Tell everybody." Matt Quay swore that "the fight would go on just the same"—[17] an empty threat that bothered no one. At the White House, Harrison read some wires that "seemed surely to presage victory." Someone with him thought him "as cool and self-possessed as if it was a democratic convention."[18]

On Friday afternoon, June 10th, Senator Wolcott of Colorado arose and presented the name of Blaine in an effective speech:

14 Mark Hanna to John Sherman, June 14, 1892, loc. cit.

15 New York Tribune, June 10, 1892, completely confirms Michener's memo on the Market Hall meeting, the paper claiming it as "a stroke which paralyzed the opposition."

16 Michener to Halford, June 9, 1892, (L.C.), Vol. 141.

17 Michener memorandum, p. 16. New York Tribune, June 10, reported Quay "as amused at the accounts given of the Administration caucus." Others who dismissed the report as untrue were Clarkson, Conger, Fessenden, and other members of the National Committee.

18 Entry in Tibbott Diary, June 9 at 8:15 P.M., (L.C.), Vol. 141.

"Blaine deserves now to be called upon to lead the party he has done so much to shape."[19] And so Blaine was cheered, while Chairman McKinley had great difficulty in restoring order. The roll call advanced to Indiana whose delegates escorted to the platform the venerable R. W. Thompson, Navy Secretary under President Hayes, and "the warrior statesman, Benjamin Harrison," was placed in nomination.[20] A New York *Tribune* reporter reported the cheers "deafening in discord and volume" as fans and umbrellas were waved aloft.[21]

A demonstration of nearly 30 minutes followed speeches seconding Blaine's nomination, then Chauncey Depew arose "to recount the services of President Harrison and to enforce his claim to the nomination." Blaine banners became liberally mixed with flags for Harrison in a prolonged demonstration, and after speeches by Wisconsin delegates for the President the excitement was quieted as the delegates turned to voting.[22] Few surprises marked the balloting. Indiana voted a solid 30 for Harrison, and Maine's twelve went to Blaine. When Ohio was reached, the hand of Mark Hanna became apparent in a vote of 44 for McKinley and two for Harrison. Chairman McKinley challenged Ohio's votes on his own part and insisted that he personally be recorded for Harrison,[23] who seemed to be safely ahead. There he remained, and when Texas voted 22 for Harrison, renomination was won. As "the convention went wild," Boss Platt left the hall with sad face and a deep sigh.[24] Harrison had received 535 votes, Blaine 182, McKinley 182, Thomas B. Reed 4, and Robert T. Lincoln 1, of the 904 cast. The vote was now made unanimous.

Looking cool and composed, the President accepted congratulations from the Cabinet, from his daughter and two nieces, and

19 *Proceedings of the Tenth Republican National Convention,* pp. 117–19, as cited by Knoles, *The Presidential Campaign and Election of 1892,* p. 66.

20 New York *Tribune,* June 11, 1892.

21 *Ibid.*

22 Knoles, *op. cit.,* p. 67; New York *Tribune,* June 11, 1892.

23 Leech, *op. cit.,* p. 57; Michener claimed that "this was a farcical attempt to save McKinley from the charges of breaking his promises to support the President for renomination. It deceived no one. It was unworthy of those who staged the performance" (Michener memorandum, pp. 18–19).

24 A. E. Bateman to Harrison, (L.C.), Vol. 143 (dated June 1892). Bateman wrote: "I just returned tonight from Minneapolis . . . have been to four conventions and never before have I seen so many mean tricks against a candidate and against you."

some 30 newspapermen assembled before his desk at the White House:

I have a sincere love for all our people he said. . . . I have asked of all public officers a faithful performance of their duty. I have felt great regret that I was unable to find a suitable place for every deserving friend. . . . As I have had light and strength I have tried to discharge my duties for the public good.[25]

Harrison had expected that the convention would renominate Vice-President Levi P. Morton of New York as his running mate, and had so informed Michener. He retired early that Friday evening and while he slept, the Platt forces had partial revenge. Their choice was Whitelaw Reid whose name was presented by New York State Senator Edmund O'Connor and was seconded by General Horace Porter and Governor Morgan Bulkeley of Connecticut.[26] Former Speaker Reed's name also came before the convention, but when the Maine delegation withdrew it, the New Yorker won second place on the ticket by acclamation. Harrison was disappointed that Morton had been bypassed, remarking to Michener that Reid's bitter battles with the typographical union as publisher of the New York *Tribune* would more than likely antagonize organized labor.[27] Many others, particularly in the U.S. Senate, were displeased, and the key state of New York was left doubtful politically.[28]

25 New York *Tribune,* June 11, 1892.

26 Michener memorandum, pp. 19–20. Morton and Reid exchanged cordial notes in which Reid claimed that he was not a candidate for the vice-presidency and had expected Morton's renomination "if you had not been quoted as saying you didn't want it" (Levi P. Morton to Reid, June 24, 1892, and Reid to Morton, July 2, Reid MSS.). In his *Autobiography,* p. 247 (published 1910) Platt wrote Reid off as a "persistent assailant of the N.Y. organization," but on June 15, 1892, he claimed that the credit for nominating Whitelaw Reid belonged to the New York delegation which he controlled. He told L. E. Quigg: "I don't care who takes the credit for Harrison but if anybody robs Milholland of the credit of securing Reid's nomination, I shall be furious" (L. E. Quigg to Reid, June 15, 1892, Reid MSS.).

27 The labor dispute had been settled before the convention, as was pointed out on the floor at Minneapolis. A typical editorial reaction came on the pages of the Lafayette (Indiana) *Journal,* June 24, 1892, which approvingly cited the Chicago *Herald's* advice: "The bargain effected a few days before the Minneapolis Convention, by which a powerful candidate for Vice-President made his peace with a labor union, is not going to bear its expected, perhaps promised fruit. Mr. Reid hopes that by yielding . . . to a demand that he has rejected for years—the right of the typographical union to rule his printing office—he would not only disarm hostility that was mischievous to his party eight years ago but would bring himself a support among organized trades. In this he is to be grievously disappointed."

28 The Levi P. Morton MSS. contain many expressions of the esteem in which senatorial colleagues held the Vice-President. Though disappointed, he remained loyal and supported the national ticket.

The final chapter of the Minneapolis episode was written in the White House on Monday, June 20th, when a committee headed by Governor McKinley notified Harrison that he had been duly chosen to make the race. Michener felt that Harrison seemed stern and McKinley embarrassed, although newspaper stories reflected a spirit of harmony.[29] "Your Administration has more than justified your nomination four years ago and the confidence of the people implied by your election," said McKinley, to which Harrison responded that "no charge of inadequacy or delinquency to principle has been lodged against the administration."[30] It had been a matter of high devotion to duty, even if, it may be admitted, it had been rather humdrum and dull.

Two days later, the Democratic National Convention, meeting in Chicago, renominated Grover Cleveland on the first ballot by 617 votes to 114 for Senator David B. Hill of New York and 103 for Horace Boies of Iowa. Thus Cleveland would run for the third time.

---

29 Michener memorandum, p. 21, "The Notification": "The occasion was most embarrassing to the Governor . . . he did not receive the cordial greeting that is usual on such occasions; on the contrary the bearing of the President was cold and stern." This is balanced by the McKinley-Harrison exchange in (L.C.), Vol. 141, and by Perry Heath's accounts in the *Journal*, June 21, 1892.

30 *Journal*, June 21, 1892.

CHAPTER XX

Down to the Wire

LONG AFTER MIDNIGHT on June 22nd, the Democratic National
Convention in Chicago prepared for its first ballot. The
forces of Grover Cleveland were confident that they could
turn back a last minute drive by Tammany Hall and other supporters of New York's David B. Hill. At that late hour even the
brilliant oratory of Tammany chieftain Bourke Cochran would
fail to stem the Cleveland tide. Finally, at 3:00 A.M. the roll call of
states began, with 607 votes necessary for a choice. Outside the
convention hall, thunder, lightning and storm heightened the tension within.

At that same hour, in far-away Gray Gables on Cape Cod,
Grover Cleveland relaxed with a few friends in his gun room,
awaiting the returns by special wire. The Democratic candidate
had been through this experience twice before. "If the nomination passes me by," he remarked, "I shall be anything but disappointed or afflicted."[1] The suspense during the roll call was rather
easily endured in view of the 617 votes he got, with 114 for Hill
and 103 for Horace Boies of Iowa. The nominee then issued the
usual statement asking the support of every party member and
predicting victory in November. On July 4th, the Populist party,
standing for free silver and free trade, nominated General James
B. Weaver,[2] founder of the agrarian reform movement known as

---

[1] Allan Nevins (ed.), *Letters of Grover Cleveland*, p. 287.

[2] Born in Dayton, Ohio, in 1833 (the same year as Harrison) Weaver became a
lawyer, Union soldier, and a Republican who denounced predatory corporations.
By 1878 he espoused the Greenback cause and served as their presidential candidate in
1880. He ran successfully for Congress in both 1884 and 1886, and had a strong political
following by 1892.

the Farmers' Alliance, and prepared to fight "for human liberty and for the rights of man."[3]

The more or less radical Democratic wing was trying to do something along this line by means of a plank in the party platform denouncing tariff protection as robbery and fraud, and the McKinley bill as the "culminating atrocity of class legislation."[4] Harrison countered at once with a letter to Colonel E. A. McAlpin, president of New York's Republican League, criticizing the statement as heedless of effect "upon the wages of American workingmen and without thought of its destructive effect upon American industries."[5] The message was cheered by a convention of Republican League clubs at Rochester on June 28th, while Diplomat John Hay predicted that the restrictive plank would swing thousands of votes into the Harrison column.

Grover Cleveland, a reasonable man, threatened to repudiate it but was persuaded to avoid arbitrary action. The prevailing bimetallism and moderation in tariff reform was therefore favored. Business, in fact, could feel safe in either party camp, particularly after Cleveland personally named William C. Whitney, a man of great energy and ability as well as Standard Oil wealth, as National Democratic Chairman. The nation's press predicted a hard battle. Governor Hill's sulking supporters were a source of concern in Cleveland's home state of New York; while Harrison had to face the fact that certain important G.O.P. leaders not only in New York and Pennsylvania but in the Midwest had declined a seat on his bandwagon.[6]

With the passage of weeks, in fact, little interest in the result was shown. Some emotion, mostly on the Democratic side, was stirred by Cleveland's choice of Chairman Whitney; but neither Harrison nor running mate Whitelaw Reid seemed able to arouse lasting fervor. Most voters seemed to agree that either candidate would fill the presidential chair with credit, as indeed each already had done. It was, in fact, the nation's only presidential election in which each major candidate had been a White House resident.[7]

3 Hamlin Garland to Weaver, July 23, 1892, Weaver Papers.

4 Allan Nevins, *Grover Cleveland*, p. 491.

5 Harrison to McAlpin, June 24, 1892, (L.C.), Vol. 143.

6 D. S. Alexander, *Four Famous New Yorkers*, pp. 188–89; Nevins, *Cleveland*, p. 189. The New York *Times, Harper's Weekly,* and the New York *Sun* regarded New York as a toss-up.

7 In 1912, Theodore Roosevelt would run on the Progressive ticket.

Harrison left it to the National Committee to elect a slate of new officers, which was done. Hailed by Whitelaw Reid's New York *Tribune* as "energetic and intelligent,"[8] these individuals as a group were still relatively unknown and innocuous, as the President was pointedly reminded. "We are not organizing a Sunday school convention or a prohibition meeting but are preparing ourselves for an attack on the devil," Secretary Halford was told by the two-fisted Michener, who seemed to be rowing against the current. "In warfare of this kind, a good long club is more effective than a sprinkle of Eau-de-Cologne."[9] Following protracted talks and a few false starts, since it was admittedly difficult to find "a capable man whose business interests would permit him to accept," Harrison replaced Chairman W. J. Campbell of Illinois with 38-year-old Thomas H. Carter of Montana, "bright, judicious, level-headed,"[10] raising him from the post of Secretary. Carter, who headed the General Land Office, took charge on July 16th while the Democratic press observed, perhaps self-consciously, that "Mr. Harrison intends to superintend his own campaign through personal agents."[11] Carter retained the services of James S. Clarkson on the Executive Committee, with offices in New York's Fifth Avenue Hotel. National Treasurer C. N. Bliss of New York appeared to satisfy everyone.

The Empire State remained a battleground, with Boss Platt dead set against giving Harrison the slightest nod; while Cleveland, in a complaining mood, appeared to feel that he was in the same fix, in view of noncooperation from Hill. "It's a funny thing," he once remarked, "for a man to be running for the presidency with all the politicians against him."[12] For each candidate, for a while, it was an uncertain tide. Tragedy at the Homestead Works of the Carnegie Steel Company, where twenty men were killed in a battle between locked-out workers and armed Pinkerton emissaries, resulted in a strong military guard for the nonunion

8 New York *Tribune*, June 28, 1892.

9 Michener to Halford, July 1, 1892, (L.C.), Vol. 144. Agriculture Secretary Rusk was also advised that "Providence is on the side of the heaviest battalions," E. W. Keyes to Rusk, July 6, 1892, Rusk MSS.

10 Harrison to Whitelaw Reid, July 19, 1892, (L.C.), Vol. 144.

11 G. H. Knoles, *The Presidential Campaign and Election of 1892*, pp. 124–25 and n. 19.

12 Nevins, *Letters of Grover Cleveland*, pp. 294–303.

labor that was brought in.[13] It then could be argued that the protective tariff served to protect wage-cutting—it certainly did not protect jobs.

Neither Cleveland nor Harrison would come to grips with the issue. While summering at the Adirondack village of Loon Lake, New York, the President addressed the annual conference of the National Educational Association in Saratoga and came out for law and order. "Obedience to law; deference to public authority; a self-sacrificing purpose to stand by established and orderly administration of government,"[14] he said, must be respected in all disputes. Arbitrary and punitive action on the part of either labor or management was not opposed. "If the injustice of his employer tempts the workman to strike back," Harrison stated on another occasion, "he should be very sure that his blow does not fall upon his own head or upon his wife and children."[15] In riots in July at a rich silver mine in Idaho where wages had repeatedly been cut until the miners rebelled, 30 fell dead in a fight with new nonunion help. At the request of the governor, Harrison instructed the Secretary of War to send troops, and the trouble was quelled. The Chicago Tribune praised the President for crushing out every vestige of "anarchical tyranny" with no fear that his party might lose some votes by antagonizing union strikers;[16] but again the action taken had been without reference to the workers' side of the case.

To his credit, Harrison did entertain the proposition advanced by Hugh O'Donnell, who led the unionized iron and steel workers, that the Carnegie Steel Company should recognize the Amalgamated Association by reopening conferences "for the sake of the men, women and little children that make up our present distressed community" of some 12,000 souls at Homestead.[17] White-

---

13 Richard Wilmer Rowan, The Pinkertons: A Detective Dynasty, pp. 299–312; and accounts in the Chicago Tribune, Indianapolis Journal, and New York Tribune, July 7, 1892.

14 Journal, July 14, 1892.

15 Public Papers and Addresses of Benjamin Harrison, pp. 17–18. Harrison's labor record is discussed in Sievers, Benjamin Harrison: Hoosier Statesman, pp. 154, 284, 375–76, and 395–97. A year before the Homestead trouble, Harrison told the factory workers at Troy, N. Y., that Americans had a "stronger claim on my sympathy and help" than workmen in other lands.

16 Editorial, July 15, 1892.

17 Hugh O'Donnell to Whitelaw Reid, July 16, 1892, Reid MSS. Given the close relationships of Harrison and Reid with Andrew Carnegie, prospects for a peaceful settlement seemed bright.

law Reid accepted the assignment, but even he was unable to make himself heard by any company official, including Andrew Carnegie's partner Henry Clay Frick. By means of a State Department cipher, finally, Carnegie, who had fled to Scotland some weeks before, was reached.[18] A lover of peace, particularly when beyond the reach and influence of the bellicose Frick, Carnegie had responded on the side of mercy when a Polish-Russian immigrant entered Frick's office to shoot and stab the hard-shelled tycoon, who somehow survived.[19]

It would have been far better for the strikers if Harrison's "obedience to law" had been observed. Unyielding before, Frick at last was so stonily unmovable that it was just as well for small Andrew, who hated and feared violence, to prolong his stay in Scotland, speaking unguardedly only to the liberal Gladstone.[20]

Two more crises served to widen anti-Republican sentiment: first in eastern Tennessee, where miners battled convict labor which had been brought in to work certain struck mines; then in New York State, where a switchmen's strike resulted in arson, train-wrecking and casual murder. Among lessons learned, the fact stood out that thousands of workers would vote the Populist ticket in the forthcoming election, while other thousands would shift from the Republican to the Democratic side. The steel labor leader, Hugh O'Donnell, for one, would carry his people with him.

Honest party men were disturbed. Hawkins Taylor, a midwestern Republican visiting Washington, complained to Senator William B. Allison that "what was once a grand honest people's party" had now become "the slave of the money power." How could anyone expect to ask the laboring man to vote the Republican ticket in the fall?

Carnegie . . . lets assistants reduce the scale of pay of the working men and thereby promote a strike, and then like the New York Central

18 Vice-presidential candidate Reid employed John Milholland as emissary of the Administration to both Carnegie and Frick. See memorandum of the visit to H. C. Frick, Pittsburgh, Pa., July 30, 1892, Reid MSS.
19 Details of the attempted assassination of Frick are dramatically presented by Stewart H. Holbrook, *The Age of the Moguls*, p. 83–88; and in the pages of the Indianapolis *Journal*, the Chicago *Tribune*, and the New York *Tribune*, July 24, 25, 26, 1892.
20 Carnegie to W. E. Gladstone, September 24, 1892, Carnegie MSS., Vol. 17, called Homestead "the trial of my life" and confessed that "it is expecting too much to expect poor men to stand by and see their work taken by others—*their daily bread.*" In July, however, Carnegie simply reported that "my lips are sealed." See Carnegie to William T. Stead, August 6, 1892, Carnegie MSS., Vol. 17.

brings the Pinkerton murderers to murder the workmen, and . . . they commence the bloody wars. . . . It is enough to make a man ashamed of being an American when he finds that sixty-five millions boast that they are the greatest nation on the earth and *surrender to the money gamblers of this and the old wealth and allow cut-throat Pinkerton protectors to swarm over the country at will and murder workmen.* And now I grieve the Republicans in Congress will be on the side of Carnegie and the Pinkerton murderers. How can you all proudly ask the laboring man . . . [etc.]?[21]

So much was true; but when the labor picture seemed blackest, the Republican cause experienced a sudden change of fortune. Late in August, New York State Labor Commissioner Charles F. Peck made himself famous by revealing in his annual report how the McKinley tariff, far from being "the culminating atrocity of class legislation" as charged, had resulted "not only in increased production of goods but also increased wages for workmen."[22]

This unwelcome news naturally shocked advocates of free trade, especially since Peck was a Democrat appointed in 1883 by Grover Cleveland, then governor, and his integrity was considered beyond question. Republicans manifested an undisguised joy over "the best witness that has yet appeared in behalf of the McKinley tariff."[23] Cleveland supporters denounced it as a campaign trick engineered by Peck in collusion with Senator Hill, who had yet to ally himself with the Democratic candidate. Both Hill and Peck made public denials, the latter declaring: "It is all nonsense to call it a political document."[24]

The report quickly took on further significance. When the New York *Times* and other party journals failed to publish even a brief abstract, the G.O.P. press gave it national circulation, while Republican speakers cited it as the best official document on the tariff yet produced by anybody except McKinley. Harrison was quite favorably impressed; National Chairman Carter crowed that the favorable trend grew clearer every hour; and New York *Sun* editor Charles A. Dana confided to free trader John Bigelow that he did not see how Cleveland could be elected.[25]

21 September 6, 1892, Allison MSS., Vol. 289.
22 Knoles, *op. cit.*, p. 158.
23 *Journal*, August 30, 1892.
24 *Journal*, August 31, 1892, citing the New York *Herald* in an editorial.
25 Bigelow Diary, August 28, 1892. John Bigelow was the former editor of the New York *Post*.

Amid shifting trends and uncertain tides throughout the sum·
mer, both Democratic and G.O.P. national chairmen, as might
be expected, predicted victory in November. They agreed only
that the final vote would be close. As the hot season wore on, Harrison declared himself so removed from the canvass that he scarcely
realized that he was a candidate for re-election. While it was true
that the campaign needed new life, with every doubtful state
clamoring for the President to make at least one speech to help
the G.O.P. cause, the beleaguered candidate, who considered himself "a leader in prison,"[26] could not comply. Vice-President Morton joined with Henry Cabot Lodge in urging Harrison to schedule personal appearances;[27] but it became clear that the man in
the White House faced the dilemma of choosing between political
and public duty on the one hand, and a personal and family obligation on the other. When G.O.P. managers recalled his success
as a front-porch campaigner in 1888, they sought his appearance
on the stump at any cost. But Harrison felt constrained to sacrifice political opportunity to be at the side of his wife, whose struggle for life would keep him close by during the summer and early
fall.

Weakened by coughing spasms and a lung hemorrhage, Mrs.
Harrison had been confined to her bed since May. It was early
determined that she was suffering from tuberculosis—a diagnosis
her husband chose to keep to himself.[28] It was advised that she be
taken to Loon Lake, a quiet Adirondack village in northern New
York. At first she responded so well that daily carriage rides were
enjoyed, as well as an occasional row on the lake; so that Harrison
felt it safe to leave her in good hands and to return to Washington where a dilatory Congress was still in session.

In many ways the separation proved difficult. Congressional fili-
busters, coupled with a siege of heat and humidity, gave Harrison
some uncomfortable days and sleepless nights. "Politics and business," he wrote his daughter who was in Boston with the grandchildren, "have been crowding me day and night, and with the

26 Harrison to William O. Bradley, November 16, 1892, (L.C.), Vol. 152.

27 Morton to Harrison, Lodge to Harrison, July 28, and Harrison to Lodge, July 30,
Harrison Papers on Microfilm, Series 2.

28 The complete medical report became public on October 25, 1892 (New York
Tribune).

anxiety about your mother, makes life just now a burden and ambition a delusion."[29]

Early in August, Congress finally quit, and the President returned to Loon Lake. Though the brisk mountain air revived him physically, it had failed to restore health to his wife. She seemed more depressed than ever; husband, children, nor grandchildren could raise her spirits. Doctors could do little but counsel patience. In September, Carrie Harrison contracted pleurisy. Hope grew dim and the presidential cottage "lived in hourly anxiety."[30]

On September 14th, the public learned that the First Lady had been stricken with pulmonary tuberculosis. Expressions of concern and sympathy flooded the rural telegraph office, and the family drew consolation from a mounting national crusade of prayers for Mrs. Harrison's recovery. Subsequent medical bulletins were pessimistic. One that described the illness as fatal was changed by the family to read "the issue is uncertain"—all in an effort to soften the blow. Personal and family friends who read between the lines could see no hope.

Unaware of her true condition, Mrs. Harrison often remarked that "if they would only take her back to Washington," she would get better. The President arranged for a special car equipped with a hospital bed for the 500-mile rail journey. At 9:00 A.M. on September 21st, an Army ambulance met the train in Washington and a newspaper reporter caught a glimpse of the President climbing in. By nightfall the country could read that he was "much afflicted, and his eyes, red from weeping, and with dark rings under them, told the tale of his deep distress and sleepless nights at the bedside of his wife."[31] At the White House the family vigils continued for another long month.

Mrs. Harrison's last moments were peaceful, as the end came early in the morning of October 25th. An avalanche of telegrams, letters of condolence, and tokens of sympathy came to the White House before and after the funeral, which took place in the East Room on Thursday morning, October 27th. In a circle around the chrysanthemum-covered casket crowded nearly all of official Washington directly behind the family and retinue of

29 Harrison to Mary McKee, July 30, 1892, Harrison Home MSS. He complained that the mercury ranged from 92 to 103 in the shade.
30 Mame Dimmick to Howard Cale, September 23, 1892, Cale MSS.
31 *Journal*, September 22, 1892.

the White House staff. Flanked by son Russell and daughter Mary, the President stood next to his wife's father, Dr. John W. Scott, who hid his 92 years within an unusually "symmetrical and strong frame."[32]

Spectators by the thousands lined Pennsylvania Avenue as the funeral party made its way to the depot for the last journey to Indianapolis, where services were held in the First Presbyterian Church. From there, a cortege of more than a hundred carriages moved slowly in a five-mile procession to the Harrison plot in Crown Hill cemetery, where it was observed that the President was indeed shaken. Late that same afternoon he departed for Washington to try to forget his sorrows, and later he wrote a warm letter of public thanks. "My dear Old Friends and Neighbors," it began,

I cannot leave you without saying that the tender and gracious sympathy which you have today shown for me and for my children, and much more the touching evidence that you have given of your love for the dear wife and mother, have deeply moved our hearts. We yearn to tarry with you and to rest near the hallowed spots where your loving hands have laid our dead; but the little grandchildren watch in wondering silence for our return and need our care, and some public business will not longer wait upon my sorrow. May a gracious God keep and bless you all!

Most gratefully yours,
Benjamin Harrison.

Harrison's letter of acceptance of the G.O.P. nomination had been released in early September. In the past, such letters had been brief formal notes of acknowledgment, but had grown in length and importance—equaling or exceeding party platforms as campaign documents.

The Harrison letter[33] appealed to business to continue the G.O.P. in power, warning that the Democratic party was the party of demolition. Republicans, Harrison maintained, had inaugurated a policy of "safe progression and development" which would continue to offer a program of national expansion based on "new factories, new markets and new ships." He lashed out against the Democratic offer of state bank issues, and criticized that party's pledge to abandon the protective system. Cleveland's tariff views

32 New York *Tribune* and Indianapolis *Journal*, October 29, 1892.

33 *Public Papers and Addresses of Benjamin Harrison*, pp. 8–25, contains the full text of the acceptance letter.

were branded as "destructive and un-American," and free trade
was characterized as nothing less than a "mad crusade against
American shops and . . . manufacturers." No thoughtful business-
man, Harrison argued, could afford to vote approval of the Democratic tariff plank which "would at once plunge the country into
a business convulsion such as it has never seen." More than half
of the letter was devoted to a defense of reciprocity and the Mc-
Kinley tariff as a triple blessing for every citizen.

Despite mixed feelings within the G.O.P. on the issue of free
elections in the South, the President refused to abandon the Administration's familiar battle cry of a "free ballot and a fair count"
for the enfranchised Negro, even if this should require a commission to police national elections in the Democratic South.[34]

In the area of foreign policy, Harrison defended Administration
actions, since in Europe as well as in both hemispheres of the
Americas, never had the honor and influence of the United States
been held in higher esteem. "The strength of our cause and not
the strength of our adversary" had given tone to our diplomatic
correspondence.[35]

Unable to take the stump, the President had written a document
of 6,000 words, which not only tripled his effort of 1888 but also
proved three times as long as Cleveland's current acceptance.
When contender Grover Cleveland labeled it "a long and dreary
deliverance,"[36] Blaine broke a long silence to observe that none of
Harrison's predecessors had spoken more clearly or more ex-
haustively on national issues.[37] All in all, Harrison had made an
able presentation of the Republican cause, and party leaders were
confident that the letter had enhanced the national platform. Since
circumstances had prevented a speaking tour, the document became the President's chief contribution to the campaign.

Nor would Grover Cleveland campaign, once he became aware
of Mrs. Harrison's serious condition.[38] He issued a brief letter,

34 *Ibid.*, pp. 19–21. Also J. A. Sleicher to Harrison, August 5, Harrison Papers on
Microfilm, Series 2, and Harrison's undated reply.

35 *Ibid.*, p. 23.

36 Cleveland to Edward M. Shepard, September 14, 1892, cited in Nevins, *Letters of
Grover Cleveland*, p. 308.

37 James G. Blaine, "The Presidential Campaign and Election of 1892," *North
American Review*, CLV (1892), 514, as cited by G. H. Knoles, *op. cit.*, p. 172.

38 Cleveland spent the summer at Gray Gables, and made but one major address
to some 20,000 in Madison Square Garden.

half of which he devoted to the tariff as a "question of morals as well as a question of markets."[39] The McKinley tariff was attacked, but Cleveland denied the charge that Democrats intended to wage war against business.

Political omens scarcely encouraged the G.O.P., inasmuch as September victories in Maine and Vermont showed a 40 percent slump in the total vote cast compared with 1888 campaign figures.[40] Joseph H. Manley, Maine state chairman, advised Harrison that it was the "most difficult campaign I have ever been connected with," partly because Czar Reed had refused to take the stump. Redfield Proctor attributed Vermont's poor turnout to the use of the Australian ballot, but had no explanation for Harrison's twenty percent loss in the popular vote.[41] The only encouraging sign was the Republican recovery from the debacle of 1890. Still, a general lack of enthusiasm and a pathetic leadership were manifest.

State elections in the South demonstrated that Cleveland could count on the traditionally Democratic strongholds. G.O.P. plans to effect a fusion to break the solid South broke down because white voters preferred the *status quo,* while intimidated Negroes either stayed away from the polls or, if they showed up, saw their votes challenged and disallowed. Republicans lost badly in Alabama, Arkansas, Florida, and Georgia, while Cleveland widened his favorable vote of 1888.[42]

Seldom would a national contest be so confused by third party activity. In the western states of Colorado, Idaho, Kansas, North Dakota, and Wyoming, where Democrats could scarcely expect to win, they nominated no electors so that they might throw their strength to Populist candidate Weaver as the best means of defeating the G.O.P. Even Harrison managers admitted that such a fusion would give John B. Weaver four electors in Colorado and

39 Knoles, *op. cit.,* p. 174. Cleveland contended that tariff protection promoted special interests and thus invited corruption of the ballot. The letter of acceptance was published in the New York *Herald,* September 28, 1892.

40 W. Dean Burnham, *Presidential Ballots,* p. 247. In Maine the total vote fell from 128,000 to 116,000 and the G.O.P. majority slipped from 23,000 to 12,000. Vermont cast 8,000 less votes and the Republican majority dropped from 30,000 to 20,000.

41 Proctor to Harrison, September 7, 1892, (L.C.), Vol. 147.

42 Burnham, *op. cit.,* pp. 253–55.

ten in Kansas. An effort was made to persuade General Weaver to withdraw and throw his support to Harrison.[43] The effort failed, although Mrs. Mary Lease of Kansas, who had campaigned extensively with Weaver in the South and in the West, later advised the people to vote for Harrison.[44]

Down to the last day an optimistic Harrison regarded the contest as extremely close. In early October he noted that "there is a substantial *drift* to us of old soldiers and of protection Democrats, and if these can be *added* to a *full* Republican vote, we shall win."[45] William Henry Smith, the general manager of the combined New York Associated Press and Western Associated Press, shared Harrison's feeling: "The situation is changing, and if there is no backset, I should think that the Republicans will win." He predicted a G.O.P. sweep of New York, Illinois, and of all western and northwestern states, and claimed that "the money question in the West and . . . the money and tariff question in New York,"[46] would insure a Republican victory. Former Attorney General Benjamin H. Bristow returned from Europe to join the chorus of optimists who felt certain that Harrison would get a second term.[47]

Late in October, G.O.P. figures gave Harrison 210 votes and Cleveland 131, with more than 100 votes still in doubt. National committeeman William Hahn gave the following explanation to the White House:

I think it is safe to put North Carolina, Tennessee and Alabama in the columns of safe Democratic states as the Democrats do the counting there. Even if we were to carry them, I am afraid that the electoral vote would not be ours. You will notice in the list of doubtful states we have New York, Connecticut, Indiana, Nevada, West Virginia and Delaware. If we carry Indiana in addition to the sure Republican states, that will settle it, or if we lost Indiana and carry New York, that

43 G. M. Dodge to Weaver, October 14, 1892, Dodge Records, Vol. 13, p. 885; and Judge Albion Tourgee to Weaver, October 19, 1892, Weaver Papers.

44 J. S. Clarkson to Dodge, October 15, 1892, Dodge Records, Vol. 13, p. 887. Weaver issued a public denial.

45 Harrison to Russell Alger, October 3, 1892, as cited in Alger to Clarkson, October 6, Clarkson MSS., Box 4, (L.C.).

46 W. H. Smith to W. W. Phelps, October 7, 1892, Smith MSS. Smith had purchased joint ownership of the Indianapolis *News* which had declared for Harrison in early October.

47 B. H. Bristow to the editor of the New York *World*, October 25, 1892, Bristow Letterbooks.

will settle it; or if we lose both those states and carry Connecticut and West Virginia and then give the Democrats but four of the electoral votes in Michigan, that would just elect our ticket.[48]

But as the parties rounded the final turn in November, the front-running Republicans encountered two serious difficulties: Federal Judge Walter Q. Gresham bolted the party to endorse Grover Cleveland, and the National Committee found itself on the brink of collapse due to illnesses suffered by General Clarkson and Treasurer Bliss.

Gresham's defection created great rejoicing in the Democratic camp and sparked Cleveland's final drive with undisguised enthusiasm.[49] Another serious G.O.P. loss occurred when campaign difficulties in Missouri and in West Virginia forced Executive Committeeman Richard C. Kerens to absent himself from the New York headquarters when he was needed most.[50] At this point Louis T. Michener charged Thomas Carter and the National Committee with sheer incompetence particularly in Indiana where rumor had it that Democrats would carry the state by a majority of nearly 20,000.[51]

Since Harrison had just returned from his wife's funeral, Carter turned to Private Secretary Halford to justify himself. "I cannot at this moment," wrote Carter, "be either charitable or just to General Michener. He manifests zeal without knowledge, and malice without provocation."[52] He denied Michener's charge by detailing specifically what the Committee had done for Indiana, and promised that the state would stand by Harrison.

Yet Michener's blast had inflicted a serious wound. From Indianapolis on election eve Halford warned the President: "The net result of all I have seen and heard is to leave one only anxious and doubtful."[53]

48 W. H. Hahn to Halford, October 28, 1892, (L.C.), Vol. 149.

49 Nevins, Grover Cleveland, p. 505; Matilda Gresham, Life of Walter Q. Gresham, II, 669–72. Personal hostility towards Harrison and disbelief in the protective tariff helped Gresham make up his mind.

50 W. O. Bradley to Halford, October 22, 1892, (L.C.), Vol 149; Carter to Halford, November 1, 1892, (L.C.), Vol. 150.

51 Indiana National Committee member W. T. Durbin had complained to Michener that Chairman Carter had neglected Harrison's own state (Carter to Halford, November 1, 1892, (L.C.), Vol. 150; and Michener to Halford, October 11, 1892, (L.C.), Vol. 148).

52 Carter to Halford, November 1, 2, 1892, (L.C.), Vol. 150.

53 November 6, 1892, (L.C.), Vol. 151. Halford reported that "The National Committee moved pretty late."

Confidence pervaded the Cleveland camp where managers predicted a close victory, claiming both Indiana and New York for the Democrats. Betting odds, which at first favored the G.O.P., changed suddenly when William Whitney walked into the Fifth Avenue Hotel and dumped a half-million Cleveland dollars into the pool.[54]

On election evening President Harrison awaited the returns in the Cabinet room. With him were Mrs. McKee and two nieces, Mrs. Dimmick and Mrs. Parker. At the telegraph instrument across the hall were son Russell, Lieutenant Charles F. Parker, U.S.N. (a nephew), and Cabinet members Tracy, Charles Foster, and Miller. At three in the morning Harrison retired knowing that he had been defeated.[55] At about the same hour in the Cleveland home on West 51st Street in New York the winner sagely remarked: "It is a solemn thing to be President."[56]

Cleveland had secured a majority of slightly under 375,000 and in the electoral college had won 277 to 145 votes for Harrison, and 22 for James Weaver. Twelve million citizens had voted and Weaver had polled 1,029,846.[57] The result, the most decisive since Lincoln's re-election in 1864, showed that the doubtful states of New York, New Jersey, Connecticut, and Indiana had slipped easily into the Cleveland column. The Democrats swept Illinois and Wisconsin, although California went to Cleveland by less than 150 votes. Even in Michigan, which Harrison carried by 20,000, the Democrats chalked up five electoral votes, and in rock-ribbed Republican Ohio the new President obtained one elector.

Many and various reasons for the outcome found expression. William Whitney and David Hill agreed that it represented a popular uprising against the McKinley tariff and a protest against the Force Bill. Editor Henry Watterson attributed it "to the Homestead riots which transferred the labour vote bodily from the Republicans to the Democrats."[58] Leading Republicans shared this view, and New York Union League President Charles St.

54 Alexander, op. cit., p. 191, n. 12.

55 Knoles, op. cit., p. 228.

56 Nevins, Grover Cleveland, p. 508.

57 This marked the first time in American history that a third party had polled over a million popular votes.

58 Alexander, op. cit., p. 191.

Collis informed Harrison that "our overwhelming defeat is attributable to the 'employee' class who secretly and deceitfully voted against their employers from 'pure cussedness.' "[59]

Judicial opinion on "the causes of the recent disaster," found Supreme Court Justice John M. Harlan outspoken. "It is difficult for anyone to tell what was the chief cause of the defeat," he wrote William Howard Taft, but "it is a mistake to lay it all, or for that matter, any of it, to the doctrine of protection. My own judgment is that the Homestead affair had more to do with the result than any other single cause." He censured Henry Clay Frick as "that eminent Republican" who betrayed his party

to add to his reputation as a man who had nerve and genius enough to tame any combination of workmen. So while Mr. Carnegie was in Europe amusing himself in various ways, his man Friday entered upon the work of disuniting the labor element of the country from the party of protection . . . [so] that the great mass of laborers . . . felt that Frick's success was the triumph of Pinkertonism and the destruction of the rights of labor.[60]

Post-election explanations multiplied rapidly and ranged from allegations of Democratic fraud in Indiana and New York, coupled with the anti-Republicanism of Catholics and the "foreign element"[61] on the one hand, to widespread charges of mismanagement by the National Committee on the other.[62] Harrison read his heavy mail and gradually dictated replies. He had kind words for the work of the National Committee and faulted no one.[63]

The magnitude of Cleveland's victory caused Harrison to tell

[59] November 18, 1892, (L.C.), Vol. 152.

[60] Harlan to Taft, November 13, 1892, Taft Papers (General Correspondence, Box 60). Taft, himself headed for the White House and the Chief Justiceship, agreed with this and with Harlan's further analysis that injustice to the farmer had a significant role in the Republican rout. "A great mass of men in the West whose lands were under mortgage to 'bloated bondholders' at large rates of interest, and who thought that the free coinage of silver would give every man his 'sheer' of this world's goods and thereby enable him to get even again," had quietly ditched the Republican party on the principle that a change could make their lot no worse.

[61] Harrison's mail abounded with charges that the Jesuits in particular and Roman Catholics in general had caused the G.O.P. defeat.

[62] George W. Steele to Halford, November 11, 1892, (L.C.), Vol. 151.

[63] Harrison to Clem Studebaker, November 16, 1892, (L.C.), Vol. 152. The President avoided discussion of the causes of the G.O.P. defeat but chose to express relief that the people voted to end his responsibility. "It seems to me, as I look back, that I have already been here ten years. There has been no pleasant break in all that time. It has been one continuous strain, pull and worry . . . owing to my constitutional habits . . . of carrying everything heavily."

C. N. Bliss that "the result is more surprising to the victor than to me. For me there is no sting in it. Indeed after the heavy blow the death of my wife dealt me, I do not think I could have stood the strain a re-election would have brought."[64]

Political defeat, as Harrison put it, "carries no personal disappointments or griefs." Yet he confessed chagrin that

perhaps we were mistaken in our belief that we had marked out lines of progress, and even of glory, for our country; but my heart was full of that thought; and I shall greatly regret to see the tariff, reciprocity and shipping legislation destroyed. The people are entitled to their will, and if the democratic theories of this campaign are as wrong and destructive as we believe them to be they will find it out and, as Mr. Lincoln said, "wobble right." The "protection" campaign has been for some years a difficult one, owing to the fact that it involved the cooperation of the workman and his employer; and these classes have been growing apart—a sad thing to contemplate.[65]

Harrison accepted the people's verdict more calmly than Whitelaw Reid, who concluded that "a success won by such incongruous allies cannot be maintained." He predicted that the "Republicans must come in again," and advised Harrison that the role of ex-President would lend "immense importance [to] your every movement. You will be the first American private citizen; and will have a degree of esteem among the people of all parties such as no man, similarly placed, has enjoyed in our time."[66]

The President replied serenely and somewhat humorously:

You take a just and philosophical view of the election result . . . faults of management . . . cannot account for the result, which had more general causes. The workingman declined to walk under the protective umbrella because it sheltered his employer also. He has smashed it for the fun of seeing the silk stockings take the rain. If he finds that the employer has a waterproof coat, while he is undefended, he may help rig up the umbrella.[67]

64 November 16, 1892, (L.C.), Vol. 152.

65 Harrison to Gilbert A. Pierce, ibid.

66 Reid had no regrets and no complaints about the work of the campaign. His letter to Harrison, dated November 28, has been reproduced in Cortissoz, The Life of Whitelaw Reid, II, 187.

67 Ibid., p. 188.

CHAPTER XXI

The Later Years

HARRISON'S FINAL WEEKS as President began quietly, with no apparent indications that a series of crises was imminent. On New Year's Day of 1893, "the quietest within living memory"[1] of the Capital, the traditional reception was not held, as mourning for Mrs. Harrison continued in official circles. When scarlet fever struck Marthena Harrison, the President's little granddaughter, the White House was isolated by a quarantine.[2]

During January the deaths of former President Rutherford B. Hayes and James G. Blaine occurred. Physicians reported that Blaine died from endema of the lungs, among other causes, although it was the opinion of General Alger that he simply lacked the courage to live.[3] Harrison paid his respects to the bereaved family, then announced his former Secretary's death by executive proclamation. Blaine's death brought to twenty the number of fatalities connected with Harrison's Administration—"a record . . . unprecedented."[4]

Routine correspondence, which Harrison handled personally, reveals the generalized depression of the Chief Executive. In Vienna, General Grant's son learned from the President that "I

[1] *Journal*, January 3, 1893.

[2] Harrison to Capt. T. M. Little, January 12, 1893, (L.C.), Vol. 155; Harrison to Carter Harrison, January 26, *ibid*.

[3] *Journal* January 28, 1893, reported that gout, Bright's disease of the kidneys and heart failure also contributed to Blaine's death. R. A. Alger to J. S. Clarkson, January 23, J. S. Clarkson MSS., Box 4.

[4] *Journal*, November 14, 1892. The executive staff of the White House had been reduced to almost half by death, and the figure reached fourteen before Thanksgiving with the death of Captain Dinsmore, chief doorkeeper at the Executive Mansion. Dr. John W. Scott followed Mrs. Harrison to the grave within a month, and the list of notables included Secretary of the Treasury Windom, Mrs. Harrison, Mrs. Halford and two Senators.

would hasten, if I could, the time when I can surrender all public cares,"[5] while another friend was informed: "My period in the Executive Mansion has been full of care and labor, and I am now very much worn out and full of longing for rest."[6] With some feeling Harrison told Whitelaw Reid that "I shall feel a great sense of relief when public affairs have for me only an interest and no responsibility."[7] The President's only misgiving, as his family realized, was the distressing prospect of resuming family life in Indianapolis.

Meanwhile, an international monetary conference on silver in Brussels ended in failure. Wall Street demanded a bond issue both to prevent a panic and to protect the gold supply. Harrison resolutely argued against the bond issue as being merely a scheme, and won the point without unsettling the stock market.[8] A minor crisis arose with the death of Supreme Court Justice Lucius Q. C. Lamar. Democrats felt that propriety should prevent the lameduck Harrison from appointing a successor to the Mississippi Democrat. Some Republicans suggested that Harrison resign so that he might be nominated to the Court by Levi P. Morton. The President had no patience with either suggestion, promptly sending to the Senate the name of Federal Judge Howell E. Jackson, a Tennessee Democrat. Criticized by his own party, Harrison rejoined that he had never believed in a partisan judiciary. The nominee, he added, had shown himself to be "of the highest integrity and [with] the finest sense of what the judicial office implies."[9]

In the Hawaiian Islands, long of interest to Harrison and his Cabinet, a revolution unseated native Queen Lydia Liliuokalani, whose policy of "Hawaii for the Hawaiians" had failed. U.S. Minister John L. Stevens sent 150 marines to protect American lives and property, and proclaimed Hawaii a U.S. protectorate. Stevens and Provisional President Sanford B. Dole collaborated in drawing up a treaty of annexation that was entrusted to a Commission ordered to the White House.[10]

5 Harrison to Colonel Fred Grant, January 10, 1893, (L.C.), Vol. 155.

6 Harrison to Captain Thomas M. Little, January 12, ibid.

7 Harrison to Whitelaw Reid, December 5, 1892, as cited in Cortissoz, Whitelaw Reid, II, p. 188.

8 Charles H. T. Collis to Harrison, February 15, 1893, (L.C.), Vol. 156; Harrison to Collis, February 20, ibid.

9 Harrison to George L. Pullman, February 3, 1893, (L.C.), Vol. 155.

10 Walter La Feber, The New Empire: An Interpretation of American Expansion, pp. 142–43. George W. Baker, "Benjamin Harrison and Hawaiian Annexation: A Re-

In the absence of cable communication, news of the revolt was brought to San Francisco by the Commissioners on January 28th. The next morning Harrison had Stevens' report that "the Hawaiian pear is now fully ripe, and this is the golden hour for the United States to pluck it."[11] Harrison let it be known that the Administration would cordially welcome the Commissioners, who were received by Secretary of State John W. Foster and Navy Secretary Tracy.[12]

Privately, Harrison left no doubt that he viewed annexation as a fitting climax to his expansive foreign policy. He regretted that the Hawaiian question did not arise six months sooner or sixty days later, as time for completion of the pact was lacking. Nonetheless, Harrison managed to get a treaty before the Senate on February 16th, asking for "annexation full and complete." He denied that the United States had sought the Queen's overthrow. On the other hand, he believed that annexation "would best serve the interests of the Hawaiian people and of the Americans domiciled in the islands," and he called for prompt action.[13]

---

interpretation," *Pacific Historical Review*, XLV, No. 3 (September, 1964), 295–309, is a cogent review which unfortunately overlooks the findings of La Feber; J. A. S. Grenville and George B. Young, *Politics, Strategy and American Diplomacy*, cc. 3 and 4, "The Challenge of Latin America and An Administration in Search of a Policy: Hawaii and Latin America," pp. 74–124, are provocative and well balanced; see also R. H. Ferrell, *American Diplomacy*, p. 185. The troops were landed for the presumed purpose of protecting American life and property, but as T. A. Bailey, in *A Diplomatic History of the American People*, p. 470, observes, "It is remarkable . . . that most of these troops were not stationed near the American property, but where their presence would intimidate the Queen." See Julius W. Pratt, *The Expansionists of 1898*, pp. 74–109; William A. Russ, Jr., *The Hawaiian Revolution*; and Queen Liliuokalani, *Hawaii's Story*, pp. 243–50.

11 Charles C. Tansill, *Diplomatic Relations Between the United States and Hawaii*, p. 467, quotes Secretary of State Thomas F. Bayard (Cleveland's first term), dated February 15, 1889, saying that "Hawaiian annexation to the United States was merely a matter of a comparatively short time."

12 Walter R. Herrick, Jr., *The American Naval Revolution*, pp. 103–7; Indianapolis *Journal*, January 30, 31. The editorial of February 1, 1893, alleged that "Uncle Sam was not asleep." Headlines screamed: He Knew That A Revolution Was Pending and Prepared for It—Minister Stevens and Captain Wiltsie of The Cruiser Boston, Had Instructions to Land Blue-Jackets at The First Sign of Trouble. Indianapolis *Journal*, January 30, cites the English press as setting up a howl over possible annexation. For example, the London *Daily News*, January 29, said: "The overthrow of the Queen appears to be an American coup." Similar editorials in other London papers, The *Daily Telegraph*, *Daily Chronicle*, *Standard*, and *Times*, give evidence that is at variance with the interpretation of Walter La Feber, *op. cit.*, pp. 142–47.

13 *Public Papers of Benjamin Harrison*, pp. 214–15, contains the full text of the special message. Harrison observed that it was essential that no other foreign power should secure Hawaii, for "such a possession would not consist with our safety and with the peace of the world." Harrison to C. C. Hines, February 3, 1893, (L.C.), Vol. 155.

Harrison had the support of the big navy advocates, territorial expansionists, and most Republicans in both houses of Congress. The New York *Tribune* observed that "the popular verdict is clear, unequivocal and practically unanimous."[14] Led by E. L. Godkin, editor of the *Nation,* and by vocal Democrats, those opposed deplored Harrison's course as a strange mixture of "rash imperialism and colonialism."[15]

As matters turned out, a badly divided Senate refused to act before the expiration of Harrison's term. When Grover Cleveland resumed the presidency, his Secretary of State, W. Q. Gresham, condemned the treaty as a "hasty and botched piece of work,"[16] and the new President withdrew it as peremptorily as Harrison had submitted it. During the remainder of 1893, despite efforts to the contrary, the Hawaiian question remained unsolved. Not until the Spanish-American War, and then by a joint resolution of Congress, was the annexation of Hawaii completed.

Harrison described his final day in Washington as "fearfully bad . . . in that it was colder than my Inauguration day. For rain they had snow."[17] Returning from the ceremony at the Capitol, he and Cleveland discussed a forthcoming presidential trip to Chicago to open the Columbian Exposition. Harrison, who would have been delighted to go, felt distressed that Cleveland seemed bored by the idea. Following routine farewells, Harrison was escorted to the railroad station by the out-going Cabinet. When he arrived at Indianapolis, he was almost overwhelmed by a cheering throng, as hundreds sought to shake his hand. Harrison later commented to his son: "I made no mistake in coming home at once—there are no friends like the old ones."[18]

Settling into a domestic routine proved difficult. "My house," he complained, "needed the labor of almost every known trade to

14 On February 21, Reid's paper strongly supported annexation. An editorial said, in part: "The views of the American people have grown with their growing empire . . . the necessity for new markets is upon us. . . . As a prime condition of extending this influence, the duty of controlling the Isthmian routes is clear to every intelligent mind. . . . To render that control sufficient, the sovereignty of Caribbean territory and of Hawaii is absolutely necessary." See also Bailey, *op. cit.,* p. 471.

15 Baker, *art. cit.,* p. 307; W. M. Armstrong, *E. L. Godkin and American Foreign Policy,* 1865–1900, p. 177.

16 Harrison to E. W. Halford, March 12, 1893, (L.C.), Vol. 156.

17 Harrison to E. W. Halford, March 12, 1893, (L.C.), Vol. 156; Harrison to Gen. W. J. Sewell, May 1, 1893, (L.C.), Vol. 157.

18 Harrison to Russell B. Harrison, March 8, 1893, (R. B. Harrison MSS.).

restore the waste of the campaign of 1888 and also of the tenants who have occupied it in my absence."[19] A new stable, the addition of a new front porch, the interior renovation and painting could be put out for contract, but the major task of unpacking papers, books and china had to be tackled alone or sometimes with the help of Secretary Frank Tibbott, who had come from Washington. Harrison confessed to John Wanamaker that "I find myself exceedingly lazy, unable yet to do much of any work."[20]

Harrison derived his greatest pleasure from his two grandchildren, Mary and Benjamin, who had come with their mother, Mame McKee. A goat which once had graced the White House lawn became a neighborhood attraction, and in late May it was joined by a burro, a Wanamaker gift.[21]

He looked for limited professional employment, letting it be known that he would accept no retainer of less than $500 and then only in the capacity of associate counsel. Personal appearances in court, he advised clients, would be restricted to very important cases. Even during the panic of 1893, he adhered to these rules.

Returning for the summer to Cape May, Harrison devoted a part of each day to the preparation of six law lectures to be delivered at Stanford University. The $25,000 stipend was attractive, but the research and writing proved to be long and tedious.[22]

Harrison presided at an annual G.A.R. encampment held in Indianapolis during the first week of September 1893, and spoke in Philadelphia in December at the request of Wanamaker. By February 1894, he had completed the six lectures, which were given at Stanford during the spring. (Revised for publication, they later appeared in *Views of an Ex-President.*) Accompanied by his daughter and his grandchildren, Harrison took pleasure in sightseeing and in visiting with West Coast friends before returning home. He resolutely declined several invitations to lecture at other colleges.

19 Harrison to Thomas H. Carter, April 15, 1893, (L.C.), Vol. 157.

20 Harrison to John Wanamaker, May 25, *ibid.*, and Harrison to J. R. McKee, May 9, 1893, Harrison Home MSS. Harrison opened and unpacked five barrels of china by himself one day and went to bed very lame.

21 Harrison to John Wanamaker, May 28, 1893, (L.C.), Vol. 157.

22 Harrison to Hon. Leland Stanford, March 2, 1893, (L.C.), Vol. 156, and Harrison to President David S. Jordan, May 22, 1893, (L.C.), Vol. 157. He confided that "I would like to cultivate not only a love of our institutions but an understanding of them among the young men and women you have gathered about you."

Law cases were tried in Indianapolis, Chicago and before the U.S. Supreme Court, but Harrison was glad to admit that for the first time in his life, he was "not to be under the spur."[23] It was quite possibly for this reason that he refused an offer to become president of a bank. The offer of a professor's chair, handsomely endowed, at the University of Chicago did not appeal to him. Inasmuch as he realized nearly $50,000 in 1894–95 from his law practice in state and federal courts, with other income derived from investments and from magazine articles and lectures, he could feel extremely well off. The *Ladies' Home Journal* paid $5,000 for nine articles of only 3,000 words each, and from this beginning sprang a book, *This Country of Ours*, which had a large sale in the U.S., as well as in South America and abroad when translated into five foreign languages. Harrison was satisfied that his writings had "promoted an interest in our public institutions," particularly in view of the wide circulation.[24]

His charitable work continued to expand, and it included a sizable annual contribution for the education of Negroes in the South. This donation was given through the Presbyterian Church in which he held a national office. The Indianapolis Orphan Asylum claimed him for its advisory board, and his purse was also open to other local causes. Family gifts or loans were continued.

Now 62 years old, Harrison considered it time to remarry, choosing as his second wife a member of the family through his first marriage. This was the widow Mary Lord Dimmick, daughter of the first Mrs. Harrison's sister, who had attended her aunt at the Adirondack retreat and later in the White House during those last months. It is likely that some jealousy existed between Mrs. Dimmick and her cousins, Mary and Russell, for when Harrison broke the news to his two children he was a bit shaken by their cool disapproval.[25]

23 Harrison to Gen. Henry B. Carrington, June 25, 1894 (Tibbott transcript).

24 Harrison to J. D. Gustus, November 11, 1896, Harrison Papers on Microfilm, Series 2. Scribner's paid Harrison a 20 percent royalty on each copy and it should be noted that this was the highest royalty that firm had ever offered to an author. (See Bok to Harrison, August 6, 1896, (L.C.), Vol. 166.)

25 Benjamin Harrison to Russell B. Harrison, December 3, 1895, William Henry Harrison MSS. "It is natural," he told his son, "that a man's former children should not be pleased ordinarily, with a second marriage. It would not have been possible for me to marry one I did not very highly respect and very warmly love. But my life now, and much more as I grow older, is and will be a very lonely one and I cannot go on as now. A home is life's essential to me and it must be the old home. Neither ·of my children live here—nor are they likely to do so, and I am sure they will not wish me to live the years that remain to me in solitude."

The announcement was made during the Christmas season of 1895, and it was decided to hold the wedding the following April at St. Thomas's Episcopal Church in New York City, rather far removed from family scenes. Former Vice-President Levi P. Morton and most ex-members of Harrison's Cabinet attended, with former Navy Secretary Benjamin F. Tracy serving as best man. Attendance was limited to 40 guests. Returning immediately to Indianapolis with his bride, Harrison soon found himself much more active socially, being called upon to attend dinner parties, flower shows and even concerts. "I am not devoted to music but Mrs. Harrison is," he explained, "and I am devoted to her."[26] A daughter named Elizabeth, who was born on February 21, 1897, was one of the few children to be born to an ex-President.

Before and after his second marriage, Harrison discouraged speculation that he would be a presidential candidate in 1896, and yet talk of it would not die. Other G.O.P. hopefuls, including William McKinley and potential kingmaker Mark Hanna,[27] felt overshadowed by the ex-President's good press, as reporters stressed the greater geniality of manner"[28] manifested by the facile lecturer, the competent author, and the successful lawyer of Indianapolis. Freedom from the grind and worry of work was Harrison's secret. "Few of the newspaper writers," he joked, "seem to get on to the fact that a poor ass, that is carrying three loads, cannot expect to be [as] frisky as a led colt."[29]

Whenever Harrison appeared professionally or socially in New York, Chicago or Washington, the press reported that he was on a "political errand." This he called "ridiculous," and, when broached on the subject, he vehemently disclaimed any desire for a renomination or for public service of any sort. Repeatedly he advised party leaders: "I do not see anything but labor and worry and distress in another campaign or in another term in the White House."[30]

After a summer at Monmouth Beach, New Jersey, in 1894, Harrison returned home and remained determined to avoid politics. Even when John Philip Sousa wrote from the St. Louis Exposition that the name of Harrison was "nearer the hearts of the

26 Harrison to Edward W. Bok, May 18, 1896, (L.C.), Vol. 158 (Tibbott transcript).
27 Stanley L. Jones, The Presidential Election of 1896, p. 116.
28 Murat Halstead to Harrison, May 11, 1894, (L.C.), Vol. 160.
29 Harrison to Halstead, May 17, 1894, ibid. (Tibbott transcript).
30 Harrison to Frank Hiscock, May 17, 1894, (L.C.), Vol. 160 (Tibbott transcript).

people than ever before,"[31] he still refused to flirt with political ambition. Under mounting pressure from state party leaders, however, he consented to make two token speeches in Indiana—one in the northern and the other in the southern sector. This, he soon discovered, was a mistake. The two major addresses mushroomed into twenty speeches on each trip—"ten . . . getting there and ten . . . getting home again."[32]

1894 was Harrison's fortieth year on the political stump and he refused all invitations to leave the state—except one. Former Vice-President Levi P. Morton had accepted the G.O.P. gubernatorial nomination in New York and requested just one speech.[33] Harrison obliged with a ringing speech at the end of October in the Carnegie Music Hall. There in the balcony, where he was to sketch the Hoosier, sat the Canadian artist, John Colin Forbes, famous for his full-length, life-size portrait of Gladstone. He caught some good poses of the orator in action, and Harrison found himself back in the national news, both verbally and pictorially.[34] As Patrick Ford, editor of the Irish World, told him: "The ovation last night was worthy of you. . . . You are one of the few speakers whose utterances retain their force and vividness even when transferred to type." He praised the ex-President's "lucidity of statement, keen analysis, and broad and elevated views," and concluded that "last night's speech is truly a masterpiece."[35]

Even this limited exposure, however, failed to lure Harrison into thinking that he might go before the people in 1896. Yet when the election results showed a Republican landslide in Indiana and in New York, he described it "the most extraordinary political revolution the country has ever witnessed,"[36] and White

31 Sousa to Harrison, September 6, 1894, (L.C.), Vol. 160.

32 Harrison to Halford, September 24, 1894, ibid.

33 In reply to Harrison's telegram of congratulations Morton wrote: "If I had not been left off the ticket with you in 1892, I do not think I could have been prevailed upon to allow the use of my name as a candidate." (L. P. Morton to Harrison, September 25, 1894, ibid.).

34 Harrison to Mrs. McKee, October 30, 1894, Harrison Home MSS.

35 Patrick Ford to Harrison, November 1, 1894, (L.C.), Vol. 161. Harrison had prepared notes but chose to discard them in favor of an extemporaneous speech.

36 This phrase appeared in a handwritten statement prepared by Harrison for a press interview on November 7, 1894. The full text can be found in (L.C.), Vol. 161. In a personal letter to the victorious Levi P. Morton, Harrison stated that language failed to express his thoughts about the election results. He felt that "cyclone," "landslide," "earthquake," and "waterloo" were too tame. (Harrison to Morton, November 7, 1894, (L.C.), Vol. 161.)

House talk began anew in the press and among friends. P. C. Cheney called for the renomination of the old ticket of 1888, and former Navy Secretary Tracy predicted that the team of Harrison and Morton would waltz into the White House in 1896.[37]

Harrison would have none of it. "The repugnance to further public service," he assured Wanamaker, "deepens with me every day."[38] Michener, chief victim of the new political fever, heard directly from Harrison. "I am not insensible to approval or applause, but I am not very anxious just now to make myself more popular." As Harrison saw it, he said, "I am sometimes strongly tempted to do something very unpopular for safety."[39]

During 1895 things went more to Harrison's liking. Except for a serious bout with "la grippe" in March, he continued in good health through an important will litigation at Richmond, Indiana, which lasted from January to May. Despite innumerable obstacles within and without the courtroom, Harrison gained a victory for his clients and a fee of $25,000. Only when he returned to the Eastman Johnson Studios in New York to sit for his official White House portrait, or when he vacationed with Wanamaker outside Philadelphia, did stories circulate that he was angling for another term. Such talk annoyed Harrison, who found it difficult to counter the idea that he was manipulating a presidential nomination.[40]

Only with the advent of a summer vacation in the Adirondacks could he claim immunity from the press and its reporters. His first camp was a "rude primitive board shanty house," where somehow he managed to write articles, to hunt, and to fish. As he told Senator Elkins, he devoted the summer "to the entertainment of my grandchildren and some other friends."[41] Harrison so enjoyed

37 P. C. Cheney to Michener, November 8, 1894, Michener MSS., B. F. Tracy to Harrison, May 1, 1896, (L.C.), Vol. 164.

38 Harrison to Wanamaker, November 12, 1894, (L.C.), Vol. 161 (Tibbott transcript).

39 Harrison to Michener, November 12, 1894, Michener MSS.

40 Harrison to D. S. Alexander, June 14, 1895, (L.C.), Vol. 162 (Tibbott transcript). Harrison added: "I have never been very eager in the pursuit of fame for its own sake and I do not see that my fame is likely to be increased by going again to Washington. Have not said this to the newspapers recently though I did a year ago, simply because there seems to be no use in it. I was strongly tempted to give the *Journal* an interview to that effect when I arrived at home, but their reporter did not call."

41 Harrison to S. B. Elkins, August 1, 1895, (L.C.), Vol. 163 (Tibbott transcript). Harrison described his location at Old Forge, N.Y., as a "beautiful and delightful region" and volunteered the information that "we have not had a hot day or night since we have been here."

the outdoor life that he decided to build his own camp the following summer, and to name it "Berkeley Lodge" after the Virginia plantation of Governor Benjamin Harrison V, the great-grandfather who signed the Declaration of Independence.[42]

The winter of 1895 and the spring of 1896—despite the G.O.P. national convention scheduled for St. Louis—found Harrison withdrawing more and more from public life. On February 3, 1896, in a public letter to the chairman of the Indiana Republican Committee, he declined to be a candidate before the national convention.[43] Some preferred not to believe him, yet to all Harrison stated that "another term at Washington would [be] . . . full of cares and trouble for me, and that only. I have thought that a fresh pilot might steer the ship more satisfactorily than I."[44] McKinley and Hanna rejoiced, and Senator William B. Allison (whom Harrison personally favored)[45] took new hope.[46]

With the June convention only six weeks away, letters from friends, so reads Halford's diary for April 30, 1896, "kept coming in . . . insisting that General Harrison allow his name to be used for the nomination of the presidency. To all the General returns a final answer that he cannot change his determination."[47] Even Tracy's importunity that only Harrison could beat McKinley failed to budge him. Although Harrison believed that Allison

42 Asa E. Martin, *After the White House*, p. 349. The summer home was located on the Fulton Chain of Lakes in Herkimer County, N.Y. Ultimately Harrison deeded this property to his second wife because, as he stated, "She has helped me to create this little place and we have spent many happy days there."

43 Harrison to J. K. Gowdy, second draft of letter, February 3, 1896, (L.C.), Vol. 163; also entry from Halford's diary, February 3, 1896, *ibid.*, testifying that Harrison refused "his consent to the use of his name in the St. Louis Convention." As to his motives Harrison explained: "I do not like to appear to be in the attitude of the little boy that followed the apple-cart up the hill, hoping the tail-board might fall out! It is not a dignified position." (Harrison to Elkins, February 3, 1896, a copy (L.C.), Vol. 164.)

44 Harrison to Colonel R. S. Robertson, February 15, 1896, Harrison Papers on Microfilm, Series 2.

45 Harrison to John H. Gear, May 8, 1896, (L.C.), Vol. 165 (Tibbott transcript). He complained that "Mr. Allison's managers have been too cautious." It should be noted that after Harrison's letter of February 3, 1896, Hanna and McKinley controlled the Indiana delegates to the national convention.

46 Harrison to S. B. Elkins, April 23, 1896, Elkins MSS. As between Allison and others in the field, or as Harrison put it, "as between the field and myself, I am for anybody to beat Harrison."

47 Entry from Halford's diary, April 30, 1896, (L.C.), Vol. 163. Harrison's former White House secretary noted that "Gowdy insists on instructions by state convention for McKinley. He is evidently in Mark Hanna's hands. Letters which fall into certain hands show him unfriendly toward Harrison."

would give the country a "safe and conservative administration," he gave no public endorsement lest he himself become involved in a convention squabble. To the end he spiked every attempt to launch a "unite on Harrison" movement.[48]

As a result, Hanna dominated the convention, McKinley got the nod, and Harrison wired congratulations and predicted a November victory. Then he told friends: "I am altogether pleased to be out of the political struggle which is now waxing warm. It is a great comfort to have the newspapers turn their attention to somebody else, to say nothing of office-seekers."[49]

In July he fled to the Adirondacks where he found grading, tree trimming and floating logs to the mill more enjoyable than a political canvass.[50] But the candidacy of William Jennings Bryan followed him even to the recesses of the Adirondacks. Mark Hanna, evidently worried, approached Harrison for help. He wanted him to speak in New York and across the nation, so that the "issue may not be switched off to silver."[51] Personally and by letter, Hanna begged Harrison to come to New York and sound the keynote for McKinley.[52]

Harrison demurred but finally agreed to make the speech in late August. Party men who either wrote or visited him, insisted that neither Bourke Cochran nor Chauncey Depew could launch the New York campaign as well as he.[53] In agreeing, Harrison advised Hanna that the money question could not and should not be subordinated. "We cannot make the issues—they make themselves"; and declared that "silver is the leading issue that most agitates and interests the people." He urged that free silver arguments be

48 L. T. Michener to E. F. Tibbott, May 8, 1898, (L.C.), Vol. 165.

49 Harrison to W. V. McKean, June 24, 1896, (L.C.), Vol. 165 (Tibbott transcript).

50 Harrison to W. H. H. Miller, August 6, 1896, (L.C.), Vol. 166. When outdoor work resulted in lameness, Harrison quipped: "I can sit on a stump and give orders as well as anybody."

51 M. A. Hanna to Harrison, July 8, 1896, (L.C.), Vol. 165.

52 Harrison to C. W. Hackett, August 4, 1896, (L.C.), Vol. 166, detailed that when last in New York (July 28–30) "Mr. Hanna pressed upon me with great urgency a request that I should make a speech in New York City in August."

53 Powell Clayton to Harrison, August 7, 1896, (L.C.), Vol. 166. As chairman of the Speakers' Bureau Clayton told General Harrison that "the consensus of opinion, not only of the National Committee, but of all prominent Republicans we have consulted, is that the 'keynote' of the campaign should be sounded at a meeting in New York City." He continued: "You, of all the Republicans in America, are the one man upon whom all agree the responsibility of this great service should be placed and who is best able to perform it." See also C. W. Hackett to Harrison, August 7, 1896, ibid.

refuted, and further advised that the party make an aggressive fight for the protective tariff.[54] Hanna agreed with Harrison's suggestions and the date was set for August 27th.

Harrison's prior complaints about the poor acoustics in Madison Square Garden resulted in the rental of Carnegie Hall where, before a packed house, and with his wife in the audience, he spoke without a manuscript but with what John Hay called "splendor of diction" and "mastery of method."[55] The G.O.P. press ranked it next in imp' '.nce to Major McKinley's letter of acceptance. Magazine editor Edward Bok claimed: "No speech has gone through the country like yours—every paper . . . Maine to California . . . has been filled with it."[56]

Harrison brushed aside further demands to enter into a general campaign, saying that "I can't be expected to do the work I used to do."[57] When he closed down the Adirondack camp, he believed that Bryan was politically dead, adding: "I think we shall win easily."[58] From New York City Harrison returned to Indianapolis by the Chesapeake and Ohio route in order to speak at Richmond, Virginia, and at Charleston, West Virginia. And finally, in response to a personal plea from McKinley, he also spoke at Cincinnati, but did refuse Mark Hanna's request for a speech to 20,000 Poles in Chicago.[59] At home he made 40 speeches. White House telegrapher B. F. Montgomery styled Harrison as

54 Harrison to M. A. Hanna, July 10, 1896, (L.C.), Vol. 165. This holograph letter by Harrison best summarizes his views on the issues of the campaign and the way in which leading speakers should handle them.

55 John Hay to Harrison, August 29, 1896, (L.C.), Vol. 166. The general reaction to Harrison's speech was a full chorus of praise. John Hay, who was scarcely a personal friend, concluded that: "It is difficult to imagine any treatment of the subject which should be clearer, more exhaustive, more dignified, more saturated with that commanding authority, which finishes discussion—which requires and admits no answer."

56 Edward W. Bok to Harrison, September 10, 1896, (L.C.), Vol. 166; also W. C. Gray to Harrison, September 8, 1896, ibid.

57 Harrison to W. T. Durbin, September 16, 1896, (L.C.), Vol. 166 (Tibbott transcript). On the same day Harrison assured former Secretary of the Treasury Charles Foster that the "speech I made in New York has had so wide a circulation that no one can doubt either my interest in the campaign or the views I take of the questions before the people. If I should speak one hundred times it would be only a reiteration." (Harrison to Charles Foster, September 16, ibid.)

58 Harrison to W. J. Steele, September 18, 1896, (L.C.), Vol. 166 (Tibbott transcript).

59 M. A. Hanna to Harrison, October 21, 1896, (L.C.), Vol. 167. Harrison to M. A. Hanna, October 22, 1896, testifies to the fact: "I will have made over forty speeches in the state when the trip is completed and I have, as you know, spoken for other states. I think this ought to be accepted as my contribution to the campaign."

one of the best speakers of the day. He "can think on his feet and never slop over when he says it."[60] McKinley won the battle, but Harrison retired gracefully from further political association with the new President, whom he had helped to put in the White House. Law, not politics, would engage him for the four remaining years of his life.

The last years, extending from 1897 until 1901 and paralleling McKinley's presidency, proved to be the busiest, happiest, and most rewarding of Harrison's career. They saw him reach full stature as elder statesman, while achieving lasting fame as an international lawyer.

In February 1897, the birth of his daughter Elizabeth, named after his own mother,[61] brought new joy to a once broken household. The General appeared to enjoy the new domestic cares and duties, even to the point of complaining when professional engagements called and kept him from Indianapolis.[62] Much sought after by the nation's educators as a lecturer or as a trustee, in 1895 he consented only to serve on the board of Purdue University,[63] an appointment he accepted in 1895, and where President J. B. Smart lauded his interest and contributions to the school's rapid growth in both numbers and excellence.

Clearly Mrs. Harrison and baby Elizabeth claimed first place, as he regretfully declined invitations to address annual conventions of the American Bar Association and the National Educa-

60 B. F. Montgomery to E. F. Tibbott, October 31, 1896, (L.C.), Vol. 167. In Montgomery's judgment Harrison "is the best and biggest single force on either side in this canvass."

61 Harrison to Miss Catherine Pearl Engle, March 2, 1897, Harrison Papers on Microfilm, Series 2. In part, the letter read: ". . . We have called our little girl Elizabeth after her mother's mother and my mother, which I am sure you will think to be appropriate."

62 Harrison to Charles R. Skinner, April 17, 1897, Harrison Papers on Microfilm, Series 2. ". . . I do not want to be ridden with a spur, and in spite of all my efforts to limit my work I find myself this spring with more upon my hands than I can do with comfort."

63 Indiana Governor Claude Mathews offered Harrison the appointment as trustee of Purdue University on June 10, 1895. In accepting the commission Harrison wrote: "I have felt a real interest in the school, growing out of a visit to one of their recent commencements and out of my acquaintance and esteem for President Smart. This morning I had a conversation with him and as a result of it beg to say to you that I will accept such an appointment and will endeavor to make such contribution as I can to the success of the university." (Harrison to Claude Mathews, June 14, 1895, (L.C.), Vol. 162 (Tibbott transcript).) An examination of the Minutes of the Purdue Board of Trustees between 1895 and 1900 show Harrison with a good record for attendance and for good and constructive advice. He was often in demand at university functions and spoke frequently to student groups.

tion Association. Likewise, when his family could not accompany him, he declined generous offers of all-expense paid trips to Europe and Japan.[64] Moreover, he let it be known that he had cut all his connections with national politics. Legal retainers, however, continued to be plentiful. One domestic action, the Illinois Inheritance Tax Cases, brought him to the Supreme Court early in 1898. Here he won a clear-cut victory on behalf of plaintiffs in error and appellant in support of the contention that the Illinois Inheritance tax law was unconstitutional because it was in conflict with the provisions of the 14th amendment.[65] Lesser cases, which he handled between vacations at the Jersey shore or in the Adirondacks, involved libel, patent and railroad litigations in state and federal courts.

Following his success before the U.S. Supreme Court, Venezuela unexpectedly retained Harrison as chief counsel in a boundary dispute with British Guiana.[66] The case was to be tried before a five-man arbitral court during the summer of 1899.

Harrison faced the immense task of sifting through documentary evidence covering four centuries and dating back to the period of European discovery and colonization of South America. At the outset, the non-Spanish speaking Harrison knew but little of the entire history. Within two years he would come close to qualifying as an expert.[67]

When Venezuela achieved independence in 1821, the boundary

[64] Wanamaker had offered him a 66-day sail and tour of Europe and another business friend tried to entice him to Japan. Still others felt that Harrison would enjoy a trip to South America where he could see the results of the Pan-American Conference. (Harrison Papers on Microfilm, Series 2, Reels 92, 93 hold scores of refusals.)

[65] Benjamin Harrison, *Views of An Ex-President*, comp. Mary Lord Harrison, pp. 298–330, has the full text of the argument before the Supreme Court of the United States. In this case Harrison was associate counsel with Seward, Guthrie and Steele, a New York firm. Harrison received a fee of $5,000.00. See W. D. Guthrie to Harrison, January 12, 1898, Harrison Papers on Microfilm, Series 2.

[66] Grover Cleveland declined the position of chief counsel for Venezuela, and the ex-President's suggestion that Joseph Choate, Frederick Coudert, or George Edmunds might be approached as counsel, apparently did not meet favor with the Venezuelan government. See Nevins, *Letters of Grover Cleveland*, pp. 477–78. During December of 1897 and January 1898, Jose Maria Andrade, the Minister of Venezuela at Washington, and the Marquis de Rojas, Agent for the Venezuelan government before the Arbitral Tribunal, approached Harrison and following two months of negotiation, the General accepted a retainer on his own grounds. Jose Andrade to Harrison, January 4, 1898, (L.C.), Vol. 170. Correspondence covering subsequent negotiations is to be found in Vols. 170–71.

[67] Indianapolis *News*, May 6, 1899. A lengthy article detailing Harrison's "employment and task" claimed that Harrison at the time (1898) knew little more of the case than many other readers of newspapers and periodicals.. Actually the case was

between herself and British Guiana (now known as independent Guyana) was somewhere between the Essequibo river in Guiana and the Orinoco river in the new republic. Spain had claimed the territory up to the Essequibo, although the region was at times sparsely and sporadically occupied by the British. Between 1835 and 1844, a British agent, Robert Hermann Schomburgk,[68] crossed the region and mapped it, laying down a boundary line which gave to British Guiana the larger part of the disputed territory. Venezuela promptly protested and in 1844 England declared the Schomburgk line unofficial and merely preliminary to further negotiation.[69]

All attempts of Venezuela, however, to secure arbitration failed. In 1886 England occupied the mouth of the Orinoco and fortified her position there.[70] Immediately, Venezuela broke off all diplomatic relations with England and sent to the United States an agent who successfully aroused American interest in the dispute.[71] In 1895, after Congress passed a resolution recommending arbitration, Richard Olney, Secretary of State, sent a strong note to England which asked for arbitration, thereby further extending the Monroe Doctrine.[72] The British government replied that it had nothing to arbitrate. Cleveland sent a special message on the

---

only a minor incident in Harrison's own administration and was mentioned by him in his annual messages to Congress. The paper further noted that "General Harrison enagaged in a case for a Spanish-speaking country, and one in which documents translated from foreign languages are numerous, is familiar only with the English language."

68 For the best description of the activity and findings of Robert H. Schomburgk, and of his brother and part-time assistant, Richard Schomburgk, a trained botanist, see Marcus Baker, "The Anglo-Venezuelan Boundary Dispute," The National Geographic Magazine, XI No. 4 (April 1900), 134.

69 George Lincoln Burr, "The Search for the Venezuela-Guiana Boundary," American Historical Review, IV, No. 3 (April 1899), 470-77, summarizes the major difficulties encountered both in ascertaining and in interpreting the historical facts in this protracted boundary dispute.

70 Henry Cabot Lodge, "England, Venezuela, and the Monroe Doctrine," North American Review, CLX, No. 463, (June 1895), 651-58 is a violent indictment of British imperialism and a forthright charge that the object of British policy was the control of the mouth of the Orinoco. Further details can be found in Elting Morison (ed.), The Letters of Theodore Roosevelt, I, 460, n. 3.

71 In charge of their propaganda efforts was William L. Scruggs, who had recently served as the American Minister at Caracas under Benjamin Harrison. For the best background material see T. D. Jervey, "William Lindsay Scruggs, a Forgotten Diplomat," South Atlantic Quarterly, XXVII, No. 3 (July 1928), 292-309.

72 For an authoritative treatment of the Olney corollary see George B. Young, "Intervention Under the Monroe Doctrine; The Olney Corollary," Political Science Quarterly, LVII, No. 2 (June 1942) 247-48. Young was the first scholar to use the papers of William Lindsay Scruggs, whose heirs have made the former Minister's diary and other papers available to this biographer.

issue to Congress and they appropriated $100,000 for a commission to investigate the true divisional line between Venezuela and British Guiana.[73] The five-man unilateral American Boundary Commission pursued its work vigorously, but in November of 1896 Great Britain yielded to the demands of the United States for arbitration.[74] Three months later, in February of 1897, an agreement was reached and a treaty of arbitration signed between England and Venezuela. Under pressure from the United States, Venezuela signed the arbitration treaty, thus setting the stage for General Harrison's appearance in the arena of international law.[75]

Harrison drove a hard bargain with the agents of the Venezuelan government, stipulating a retainer of $20,000, and requesting quarterly payments of $10,000 until the international tribunal in Paris had rendered a decision. Convinced that he would need competent assistants, Harrison persuaded the Caracas government to employ the services of former Navy Secretary B. F. Tracy, for whom Harrison asked and obtained a fee of $50,000. Later, as the workload increased, James R. Soley, Tracy's law partner, was also retained for an undisclosed sum. To complete the legal battery, the brilliant international lawyer Severo Mallet-Prevost, former Secretary to the American Boundary Commission, entered the case. Together counsel conferred and agreed on a timetable of March 15, 1898 for the printed case, December 15, 1898 for the

[73] Excellent background material is supplied by Joseph J. Mathews, "Informal Diplomacy in the Venezuelan Crisis of 1896," *Mississippi Valley Historical Review*, L, No. 2. (September 1963), 195–212. This author maintains (p. 196) that "jingo feeling proved to be stronger in the United States than had been anticipated by Cleveland or by Richard Olney, Secretary of State and chief architect of the American diplomatic offensive."

[74] The American Boundary Commission, headed by Supreme Court Justice David J. Brewer, issued an official report published in four volumes in 1897 (Washington: Government Printing Office). S. N. MacVane critically reviewed this report for the *American Historical Review*, II, No. 3 (April 1897), 34–36. It should be noted that the private correspondence of the Commission president, David J. Brewer (Yale University Library) and the Commission secretary, Severo Mallet-Prevost (privately held), coupled with the papers of former Cornell president, Andrew J. White (Cornell University Library) and former Johns Hopkins University president, Daniel Coit Gilman (Johns Hopkins University Library) have enabled the biographer to go behind the scenes of the official Commission report.

[75] Charles C. Tansill, *The Foreign Policy of Thomas F. Bayard, 1885–1897*, p. 661, clearly illustrates that Venezuela had long sought the friendly help of the United States in settling her difficulty with Great Britain. It should be noted that the heads of the treaty had been proposed by the United States and the British had assurance from Olney that he would urge Venezuela to sign the treaty. See T. H. Sanderson to Mead, October 13, 1896 (Joseph Chamberlain Papers in Birmingham University Library, Birmingham, England). The archives of the Foreign Minister of Venezuela (Caracas, Venezuela) clearly indicate Venezuelan unwillingness to sign the arbitration treaty until coerced by Secretary of State Olney.

counter-case, and won stipulation that the oral arguments before the arbitral tribunal be held during the summer of 1899.[76]

As chief counsel Harrison divided the work as fairly as possible among his associates, but made it clear that he himself would assume full responsibility for mastering the entire case both as to the involved historical facts and the legal principles in dispute. For fifteen months he refused all other legal employment and devoted his energy and time to the cause of Venezuela. At Indianapolis, for example, he turned his home into a law office in order to avoid the distractions of working downtown; in the Adirondack woods and along the Jersey shore (while his tiny daughter and wife vacationed), he had his private work room; and even atop New York's Fifth Avenue Hotel, the usual place for legal conferences with his colleagues, the General had his own hideaway.[77]

Toward the end of September 1898, from the Adirondacks, Harrison advised Tracy: "I have been working every day this summer except Sundays."[78] Pressure increased as the November deadline approached, and the General found himself "almost to the breaking point."[79] Colleagues Tracy and Mallet-Prevost felt the whip of duty which Harrison so often used on himself. In mid-November 1898, he warned them both "to put everything else aside. If you do not do it, we shall wind up in a sputter and a hurry that will show itself in the work."[80] As it turned out, coun-

76 Harrison realized $80,000 of the $100,000 for which he contracted. See Harrison to Severo Mallet-Prevost, March 12, 17, 1898, (L.C.), Vol. 171. On the question of fees and other expenses connected with the litigation, (L.C.), Vols. 171–74, contain all correspondence from Harrison to Señor Andrade, Señor Rojas, B. F. Tracy, Severo Mallet-Prevost, and Richard Olney. The interested scholar can locate these letters easily; hence they will not be cited unless for some more specific purpose.

77 Harrison to W. H. H. Miller, October 7, 1898, (L.C.), Vol. 173, notes, "I am settled here at the hotel (Fifth Avenue) with a little office room at the top of the house, where I meet with my associate counsel once in a while and review the work that we are each doing on our brief in the Venezuela case."

78 Harrison to B. F. Tracy, September 2, 1898, (L.C.), Vol. 173; Harrison to W. H. H. Miller, September 22, ibid.

79 Harrison to J. M. Andrade, November 12, ibid.

80 Harrison to S. Mallet-Prevost, November 18, and Harrison to B. F. Tracy, November 18, ibid. In writing to Mallet-Prevost Harrison used a sharper tone in expressing disappointment that Mallet-Prevost and Gen. Tracy had not completed their allotment of the work. He wrote: "I know it is hard for a man who is about his office to keep away from other work; but I do most earnestly ask you from now until the brief is completed to put everything else aside." In the Tracy letter Harrison simply wrote: "I have not heard from you since we parted in New York and have not written, because I assumed that you were doing pretty much as I have been— giving all your time and strength to the Venezuela case. I have not lost a day and have fairly worked myself out upon the case. My manuscript is nearly all now in the hands of Mr. Mallet-Prevost."

sel for Venezuela met all deadlines. On March 15, 1898, they had printed one volume stating the position of the South American republic, and added two volumes of appendices and one atlas. Nine months later they had achieved the same objective and printed a counter-case with an equal number of volumes, thus making Venezuela's printed case two volumes, or about 800 pages of primary argumentation. To legal experts this compared favorably "with only one volume of about 65 pages" prepared by Great Britain.[81] Harrison's first reaction was to "evaporate, eviscerate and disperse" the slim British contentions by oral argument before the tribunal.[82]

Family and close associates realized that the harder he worked, the more anxious and nervous the ex-President became. He scarcely took time to note Dewey's victory at Manila Bay and he hardly had time to bid farewell to his son Russell, now Major Harrison, en route to Cuba. Although he had some misgivings about the country's new policy of radical expansion, and would say later that the United States had "no commission from God to police the world,"[83] he had neither the time nor the inclination to make a public comment. Finally, on February 27, 1899 when both

---

81 Indianapolis *News*, May 6, 1899.

82 Harrison to B. F. Tracy, January 12, 1899, (L.C.), Vol. 173, states: "I received yesterday afternoon the British argument. . . . It is to me a great surprise and disappointment. It seems to me that the treaty fairly calls for an argument that would state the legal propositions relied upon and the authorities in support of them. The British argument is less like an argument than their case, for they did announce some legal principles and cited some of the textbooks. The argument is simply a repetition of those broad claims as to Dutch and British occupations which were put forward in the case and counter-case and which Mr. Soley so mercilessly exposed."

83 On May 3, 1898, in an address to the Indiana National Guard, Harrison declared that the Spanish-American War was "a war for humanity. . . . for the oppressed of another race. We could not escape this conflict. Spanish rule has become effete. We dare not say that we have God's commission to deliver the oppressed the world around. To the distant Armenians we could send only the succor of a faith that overcomes death, and the alleviations which the nurse and the commissary give. But the oppressed Cubans and their starving women and children are knocking at our doors; their cries penetrate our slumbers." On July 4, 1899, in speaking to the American Chamber of Commerce in Paris, France, he said that the United States "had let it be known that she reprobated cruelty and persecution, but she has not felt that she had a commission to police the world." And this theme runs through Harrison's public speeches and writings. See *Views of An Ex-President*, pp. 483, 493. The pressure of preparing the Venezuelan case prevented Harrison from making any speeches during the 1898 fall campaign and he excused himself to his old friend Judge R. S. Taylor on this score. He added, however, "I am not right sure that I find myself in sympathy with the extreme expansion views that are being advocated, and I would not want to introduce a discordant note. It has seemed to me that the Administration was drifting, and not steering a marked course."

England and Venezuela had exchanged printed cases, counter-cases, atlases and appendices, totaling 23 volumes, Harrison penned the following note to Venezuelan Minister Jose Andrade in Washington:

I have given myself so absolutely and so constantly to the case of Venezuela since my employment that I have felt recently as if I was on the verge of a breakdown. For one year now I have taken no rest and have not even had the diversion that would have come from other professional engagements. I hope Venezuela is satisfied with the work we have done. My confidence in the case grows with the increasing study of it. Certainly Great Britain has wholly failed, thus far, to bring forward anything in argument that can give us any alarm.[84]

Nearly three months remained before the commencement of the oral argument in Paris. Meanwhile, Harrison and his associates had copies of a cable from the Venezuelan agent, Señor Rojas, sent from London. "Congratulate the counsel. Argument decisive. Masterpiece."[85]

Early in 1899 Harrison booked passage for Europe on the American liner St. Paul, sailing from New York on May 17, 1899. His party would consist of wife, daughter and three servants, including the tireless Frank Tibbott, his personal secretary. Prior to sailing, he devoted much time to conferences with his legal associates in the case, and they carefully planned courtroom strategy and reviewed the significance of the approaching arbitration. In a hand-written memorandum Harrison spoke for his associates and for their South American client:

Venezuela with great respect but with great confidence submits to this high tribunal the very serious issues involved. She does this in the happy belief that in the short but brilliant history of Arbitration Tribunals this one will find a conspicuous place and will recommend to other nations the use of this great agency of peace. Venezuela has no direct representative upon this tribunal and by this fact it is more nearly assimilated to the great courts of justice from which the idea of representation is wholly absent. No other international tribunal has presented this feature—they have been too much the conference of representatives, rather than the consultation of judges, to whom the parties are quite different. The one tends to unsatisfactory compromises, the other to decrees that establish rights.[86]

84 Harrison to Andrade, February 27, 1899, (L.C.), Vol. 174.

85 Severo Mallet-Prevost to Harrison, January 5, 1899, (L.C.), Vol. 173; the postscript contains the cable from Rojas in London.

86 December 6, 1898, (L.C.), Vol. 173.

Before sailing, Harrison took a short rest at Hot Springs, Virginia, where, somewhat pessimistically, he pondered an unexpected development in the composition of the court before which he would appear in Paris. On March 1st, Lord Herschell died in the British Embassy in Washington. Harrison, who had known him personally, deeply regretted that the Paris Tribunal would be deprived of his wisdom and impartiality. Three weeks later England announced that Lord Charles Russell of Killowen would replace Herschell on the court, and this upset Harrison. He advised Mallet-Prevost that "Russell is likely to be aggressively partisan. He has only recently gone up on the Bench and I doubt whether he has acquired the judicial habit." Junior counsel Mallet-Prevost agreed completely: "I had an opportunity of conversing extensively with him, and he struck me as decidedly partisan, and I am afraid we are going to have his influence against us."[87] Developments within the next six months would serve to confirm rather than to allay this fear.

The ocean voyage proved Harrison to be an early riser and a good sailor, as he strolled the decks of the St. Paul with two-year-old Elizabeth, usually dressed in a red coat and hood. During the smooth passage he learned something of the mystery of diplomacy from two table companions: one was Brigadier General S. S. Sumner, the hero of Santiago, who was en route to London as a military attaché; the other was Señor Don José Andrade, Venezuelan Minister to Washington (and brother of the President of Venezuela), who would serve his country as agent in the boundary arbitration.

On June 15th, 1899, in the rooms of the Foreign Office in Paris, where both the Bering Sea Tribunal and the Spanish-American Peace Commissioners had met, the judicial process began. If the diplomatic world focused on the tribunal, Harrison had his eyes fixed on the five arbiters appointed under the Anglo-Venezuelan treaty of 1897. He knew the two American judges personally. White-haired U.S. Supreme Court Chief Justice Melville W. Fuller had sworn him in as President in 1889.[88] The second American, standing in for Venezuela, was the bespectacled younger As-

87 Harrison to Mallet-Prevost, March 20, 1899, and Mallet-Prevost to Harrison, March 22, (L.C.), Vol. 174.

88 Willard M. King, Melville Weston Fuller, pp. 138–39, comments on the Chief Justice's "remarkable capacity for mediation which Oliver Wendel Holmes described as an ability to "tinker a compromise."

sociate Justice David J. Brewer, appointed to the court by Harrison.

Representing England were Lord Russell and Lord Justice Henn-Collins, thin and sharp-featured. President of the Tribunal was Baron Frederic F. de Martens, a Russian jurist and professor in international law.

The British legal battery was headed by Attorney General Sir Richard Webster and former Attorney General Sir Robert Reid. Webster opened for the British and spoke for 52 hours. The case dragged on—and was almost interminable in its tediousness—and Harrison sensed that something other than a judicial trial was taking place. During a recess for the 4th of July, Harrison addressed the American Chamber of Commerce on the Spanish-American War, and defended American foreign policy as humanitarian rather than colonial. He deplored the use of arms in settling international questions, but pointedly observed that "arbitration has halted because of the difficulty there has been in finding a purely judicial tribunal.[89]

Harrison, who was described by Fuller's secretary as "the ablest lawyer to be President,"[90] grew weary and impatient awaiting his turn to speak, which finally came at the end of September. He spoke for a little more than five days—"twenty five hours of talk," and later unburdened himself to former U.S. Attorney General William H. H. Miller:

At last the agony is over. My last word, and the last word from counsel, was spoken at 3:00 P.M. yesterday. . . .

I made a very strong effort to put the hearing purely upon an impartial, judicial basis, but there are two Britons in the panel—men who sitting as judges in an ordinary case would be absolutely impartial and just. But the idea of representation has prevailed in these tribunals and I fear will do so in this. . . .

Great Britain has taken all the territory in dispute, erected police and military stations, made land and mining grants—and it will be a terrible humiliation to have to withdraw. . . . I fancy they (the Tribunal) will have a good deal of debate—and that some compromise line will be adopted instead of the line of right.[91]

89 Harrison to W. H. H. Miller, June 23, 1899, (L.C.), Vol. 175, and N. Y. *Herald* (Paris edition), July 5, 1899. A judicial tribunal, in Harrison's view, should consider international questions with the same indifference to the parties as in any ordinary court of law. He regarded Russell as partisan and Webster as chauvinistic.

90 King, *op. cit.*, p. 258, n. 1.

91 Harrison to Miller, September 28, 1899, (L.C.), Vol. 175.

Five days later, October 3, 1899, Martens read the decision which, except for some territory on the mouth of the Orinoco, confirmed Britain's possession of nine-tenths of the land in dispute. The unanimous decision gave no reasons, and evoked from Mrs. Harrison the pointed remark that "when England will give up anything she has, the world will end," adding in a note to her sister: "We are all furious . . . I never did believe in arbitration, and if such a thing is to be, there should be more than one arbitrator who belongs to another country not concerned in the dispute."[92]

Both sides seemed disappointed, although Harrison admitted that "it might be worse." Webster said "Of course, we wanted more, but we bow respectfully to the decision." The New York *World* and the Chicago *Tribune* cited a prominent official in London as saying: "We got the kernel and Venezuela the shell. All the most valuable gold-bearing region falls within our boundary . . . that was the real source of the trouble and we have gained all we want."[93]

Venezuela, once again in the throes of a revolution, felt cheated and overwhelmed by British power and double-dealing—a sentiment shared by Harrison. "Judged from the standpoint of British claims before the U.S. intervened," he confided to W.H.H. Miller, "it is a very good result—but judged from the standpoint of strict right, it is far from good. . . . the British judges were as always aggressive advocates—rather than judges. Law is nothing to a British judge it seems when it is a matter of extending British domination."[94] Both the European and the American press supported the American counsel's charge that justice had miscarried. The fact was, as a Vatican spokesman pointed out, that the Tribunal had "paid no heed to the arguments of the two parties," and "did not judge according to the rights of the case . . . but arbitrarily drew up, according to its own good pleasure, a would-be conciliatory compromise," conceding "the lion's share to the strongest."[95]

Harrison and his family left Paris as quickly as possible, stopping over two nights at Cologne to see the cathedral, and arriving

[92] Mrs. Benjamin Harrison to Elizabeth Parker, October 3, 1899, James Blaine Walker MSS.

[93] New York *Tribune*, October 4, 5, and Chicago *Tribune*, October 5, 1899.

[94] October 7, 1899, (L.C.), Vol. 176.

[95] Quoted in London *Times*, October 30, 1899.

at Berlin on October 6th. A brief tour of Belgium and England completed his only trip to Europe. He returned to Indianapolis convinced that he had failed to further the cause of international justice. His distinguished colleague, Severo Mallet-Prevost, who returned directly to New York, spoke and wrote freely on the happening at Paris, alleging that a political deal between Great Britain and Russia had vitiated the arbitration. As he told American historian George Lincoln Burr on October 26, 1899: "The decision was forced upon our arbitrators, and, in strict confidence, I have no hesitation in saying to you, that the British arbitrators were not swayed by any consideration of right or justice and that the Russian arbitrator was probably induced to take the stand which he took by considerations entirely foreign to the question."[96]

Mallet-Prevost, who outlived Harrison by some forty-seven years, never deviated from his contention that the decision at Paris clearly reflected "a deal . . . between Russia and Great Britain to decide the case along the lines suggested by Martens and that pressure to that end had been exerted" to secure Fuller's and Brewer's consent to an unanimous decision. The American judges had but two alternatives. In return for a unanimous decision Venezuela would receive Point Barima and a modicum of strategic land to safeguard that country's great inland waterway. If, on the other hand, the Americans objected and filed dissenting opinions, it was threatened that Venezuela would lose all.

If Harrison were alive today, he would scarcely be surprised that Mallet-Prevost had revealed the inside story of the boundary award which appeared in the *American Journal of International Law,* July 1949.[97] It described the Hoosier's indignation and his first reaction to ask Fuller and Brewer to file dissenting opinions. When he cooled down and considered the matter from a practical standpoint, Harrison agreed to accept the alternative. He wrote:

Mallet-Prevost, if it should ever be known that we had it in our power to save for Venezuela the mouth of the Orinoco and failed to do so, we

[96] George L. Burr MSS.

[97] Dr. Otto Schoenrich, "The Venezuela-British Guiana Boundary Dispute," *The American Journal of International Law,* XLIII, No. 3 (July 1949), 523–30. Judge Schoenrich, who recently retired (1966) from the law firm of Curtis, Mallet-Prevost, Colt and Mosle, was associated for many years with Severo Mallet-Prevost. Schoenrich suggested that the memorandum on the boundary dispute be written by Mallet-Prevost. He complied with the understanding that publication of it would be withheld until after his death which came in New York on December 10, 1948.

should never be forgiven. What Martens proposes is iniquitous but I see nothing for Fuller and Brewer to do but to agree.[98]

Harrison took this secret to the grave with him in 1901. Yet, one can scarcely doubt that some sixty years later he would have enjoyed participating in debate before the United Nations which reopened the entire boundary dispute.[99] If he could have sat in on the subsequent discussions before Great Britain and Venezuela at the foreign minister level in London during November of 1963, it is not likely that newly discovered evidence of Russian-British intrigue in 1899 would have startled him.[100] The record shows that by July (mid-way through the Paris proceedings) the boundary line had been so fixed in London that one English spokesman referred to the affair at Paris as a "farce,"[101] and Lord Russell's law clerk confidently told his diary the day before the Tribunal announced its decision: "October 2, 1899: Venezuela—Martens' deal giving us the victory."[102]

Despite the Paris verdict Harrison's associates and clients at home continued to regard him highly. He soon found himself arguing some important cases in the Indiana Supreme Court and in the highest tribunal at Washington. No longer, however, would he become a slave to his profession. In the spring of 1900 he took a long trip through Yellowstone Park and the Northwest rather than attend the G.O.P. convention which renominated McKinley. He did accept a presidential appointment to the International

98 *Ibid.*

99 The case for Venezuela was re-opened on October 1, 1962 by Dr. Marcos Falcon Briceno who addressed the General Assembly in the capacity of his country's Minister of Foreign Affairs. The matter was then referred to a Special Political Committee which on November 12–13, 1962 heard statements by the Foreign Minister of Venezuela and by the representative of the United Kingdom in which they set out the positions of their governments on the entire boundary question and the Arbitral Award made in Paris in 1899. This Special Political Committee adjourned further consideration of the matter when Venezuela, British Guiana and Great Britain agreed to review newly discovered evidence through diplomatic channels.

100 Tripartite discussions between the United Kingdom, British Guiana and Venezuela began in London in November, 1962.

101 The spokesman was Colonial Office agent Charles Alexander Harris who admitted that the decision rendered by the Paris Tribunal was a "farce." See memorandum of Hermann Gonzalez Orapesa (London, December 6, 1963) entitled "Derechos de Venezuela al Territorio Guayanes," p. 22, which is solidly based on the Minutes of C. A. Harris, Colonial Office 111/516, available in Xerox and on microfilm in the archives of the Ministry of Foreign Affairs, Caracas, Venezuela (Direccion Especial de Guayana).

102 Block's Diary, October 2, 1899, a photostat in archives of the Ministry of Foreign Affairs, Caracas, Venezuela (Direccion Especial de Guayana).

Court as it was not likely that the work would be arduous.[103] June through September found him in the Adirondacks, far from politics. He planned an active role in legal and literary circles in the coming year of 1901. Early in March, however, he contracted a severe cold which quickly developed into pneumonia. Great concern arose when he failed to improve, and immediately telegrams of inquiry poured in from family and friends across the land. On March 9th private secretary Frank Tibbott attempted to allay all fears, and most of his letters resembled the hopeful report he penned to L. T. Michener:

The General's attack was quite sudden and unexpected. He was at breakfast . . . and was getting ready to go down town when a chill came on. He had some fever during the day and night—102½ being the highest temperature. A very severe intercostal neuralgia developed and had to be relieved yesterday by hypodermics.[104]

Two days later his condition worsened,[105] and finally when the battery of attending physicians could offer no hope, Mrs. Harrison kept up her watch and took him in her arms as she saw him sinking. On March 13th at 4:45 P.M., Benjamin Harrison died quietly, and any last words have been forgotten.

President McKinley and former President Cleveland headed the list of mourners who wired their condolences and McKinley prepared to start for Indianapolis at once. With appropriate ceremony the body was laid in the State House where on Saturday, March 16th, public demonstration by thousands of Indiana soldiers, led by the survivors of Harrison's old regiment, was followed next day by funeral services at the First Presbyterian Church. Tributes from all over the world poured into Indianapolis, but the man who best measured the worth of the dead statesman was Harrison's neighbor, the Hoosier poet James Whitcomb Riley who spoke briefly at the church services. From my earliest childhood, said Riley,

General Harrison had been a conspicuous figure on the horizon of my world. My father was an earnest admirer of the man as a statesman,

---

103 Harrison to Miller, August 29, 1900, (L.C.), Vol. 178. He regarded it as a distinction rather than as a task.

104 L. T. Michener Papers, Box 2. Tibbott thought that the attack had steadily succumbed to treatment but warned that his condition remained alarming in its possibilities.

105 Harrison to Justice M. Harlan, February 8, 1901, (L.C.), Vol. 180 (Tibbott transcript), called "Washington . . . an infected center in more senses than one just now. The "grip" is there and perhaps some other things more fatal! The "grip" is also here and has been knocking at my door a little." Consequently he did not judge it worthwhile "to go to Washington at the sacrifice and risk that would be involved."

soldier, humanitarian, lawyer and as an element of force for the better-
ment of the world. For the opinions of my father I have the greatest
respect. . . . One of the characteristics of General Harrison always
commanded my profound respect—his fearless independence and stand
for what he believed to be right and just. . . . A fearless man inwardly
commands respect, and above everything else Harrison was fearless
and just.[106]

One might reflect, as did many of the deceased ex-President's
friends, that Benjamin Harrison had died at the time of his
greatest usefulness. They argued that he had shown great wisdom
in guiding public thought in the uncertain days after the Spanish-
American War, "when the tendency [had] been to swing away
from ancient and substantial moorings." To Eugene Hay he
seemed to be "serving a greater purpose than when an active
participant in shaping the Nation's affairs." And yet this was not to
detract from the ability he showed in the White House. Former
Senator Ingalls had once remarked that "Harrison was the only
man who had ever been president who was capable of discharging
with signal ability the duty of every one of his cabinet ministers;
that he was the best equipped man that had ever been in public
life."[107] Michener regarded this opinion as well-founded, recalling
that every member of the Cabinet told me repeatedly that "Harrison knew more about the workings of the various departments
than did their various heads, and they said they never went to him
to discuss departmental matters with him without coming away
filled with amazement, because of his wonderful knowledge, as
well as the unerring accuracy of his mental operations."[108]

Even party members who broke with Harrison in 1892 came to
share this opinion in retrospect. In 1909, a year after Indianapolis
had erected a monument to the only Hoosier to be president,
James S. Clarkson was taking lunch with 79-year-old former Navy
Secretary Tracy in New York and asked "if in any historical way"
the work of the Harrison administration "had been suitably placed
on record for the future." Tracy was unable to answer the query
but suggested that Clarkson put himself in touch with one of many

106 Chicago Inter-Ocean, undated clipping in Russell B. Harrison Scrapbooks, Vol. 3.

107 E. G. Hay to L. T. Michener, March 16, 1901, E. G. Hay MSS., Vol. 19. He concluded his reminiscence with the query: "When shall we see his like again?"

108 L. T. Michener to Hay, March 23, 1901, ibid.

of the ex-President's biographers. So it was that James Clarkson sought out John L. Griffiths:

You know that perhaps the greatest of the several great achievements of Harrison and his administration was the inauguration of the new and modern navy. Cleveland and Secy Whitney had made some start toward it, but had progressed to nothing beyond the building of cruisers or ships of 5,000 tons and under. It was Pres. H. and Secy Tracy who made the departure demanded by this nation's future interests in beginning the building of big warships, and the ships that were built during Harrison's time were the largest warships then in the world; so it is historically true that Pres. Harrison . . . had the wisdom to discern the developments which have since come about in the affairs of the world and the necessity to make our nation a world power.[109]

Neither Griffiths nor other potential biographers lived long enough to write this achievement into the record. Another quarter of a century passed, and Thomas Francis Moran, in his 1933 volume entitled *American Presidents,* conjectured that "the lapse of time will, in all probability, cause us to revise our estimates of the acts and capabilities of our recent Presidents, and I have a feeling that when Benjamin Harrison is viewed in his true historical perspective he will appear larger and more important than he now does."[110]

The Centennial President of the United States, when judged in comparison with Andrew Jackson, Abraham Lincoln, Theodore and Franklin Roosevelt, not to mention more recent leaders in the White House, seems to emerge greater as a man than as a president. His theory of the functions of the presidency differed widely from that of the Jackson and Roosevelt schools where personal appeal and leadership dominated the scene. For his era, however, Benjamin Harrison compiled a strong record of constitutional government which enabled the country to approach the threshold of world power with prudence and caution.

109 James S. Clarkson to John L. Griffiths, May 27, 1909, J. S. Clarkson MSS., Box 1.
110 Thomas Francis Moran, *American Presidents,* p. 217.

Bibliography

Bibliography

Manuscript Sources

The primary sources for the White House years (1889–1893) and for the post-presidential years (1893–1901) in the career of Benjamin Harrison include:

1. The extensive Benjamin Harrison collection housed in the Division of Manuscripts, Library of Congress. Closed to the public and research historians alike until 1948, this is the richest font of information. The collection is described by the Division of Manuscripts card as "Papers of Benjamin Harrison (1833–1901), lawyer, soldier, U.S. Senator, 23rd President of the U.S. Family letters and other papers covering the Civil War period, a large body of papers representing the period of his service as a U.S. Senator, legal and official papers covering his post-presidential career in law, letter-books, scrap-books, etc., dated 1858–1931."

A serviceable breakdown of these materials is as follows:

183 volumes (bound) of approximately 40,000 pieces which, in the judgment of the curator of the Manuscripts Division, deal primarily with Harrison's public life and activities.

55 manuscript boxes (red) judged by library authorities as not pertaining to the public and/or political aspects of Harrison's life. They contain, however, much material essential to the biographer.

58 volumes (bound) of newspaper clippings, now known as the Benjamin Harrison Scrapbook Series. Invaluable material on every phase of Harrison's private as well as his public life.

18 manuscript boxes of Tibbott transcripts. Everard F. Tibbott, once an Associated Press reporter, became Senator Harrison's secretary and remained with him through the presidential and post-presidential years.

8 manuscript boxes: "The Tibbott short hand books." Long after Harrison's death, Tibbott transcribed these thousands of letters from his own stenographic notebooks. These are the contents of the abovementioned eighteen manuscript boxes of Tibbott manuscripts.

7 manuscript boxes of "Legal material from 1851–1900."

3 manuscript boxes of Harrison and Wallace Law Firm correspondence.

80 manuscript boxes of miscellaneous materials: personal bills, checks, notes, lectures, photographs, galley proofs, invitations, guest lists, pamphlets, telegrams, memorials, etc.

The microfilm of the Harrison Papers became available in 1964 as a direct result of the wish of Congress and the President, as expressed in Public Law 85–147 approved August 16, 1957, and amended by Public Law 87–263, approved September 21, 1961, to arrange, index, and microfilm all the Presidential papers held in the Library of Congress. Thus, also in 1964, appeared the *Index to the Benjamin Harrison Papers* (The Library of Congress, Presidents' Papers Index Series, 333 pages). The reproduction of these papers, which number 69,612, cover every aspect of Harrison's life and career. A total of 151 reels represents all the Harrison holdings in the Library of Congress as described in (1) above. Benjamin Harrison letters in other manuscript collections in the Library of Congress or elsewhere are not on microfilm nor are they included in the "Index Volume" so expertly and so thoroughly prepared by the Presidential Papers Section of the Library of Congress. Readers and researchers are referred to the "Introduction" of the *Index,* which features a serviceable "Provenance" and practical guidelines for the use of the microfilm.

2. The next largest collection of Benjamin Harrison Papers is in the private possession of James Blaine Walker and family, New York City. President Harrison's son-in-law, James Blaine Walker, and his two children, Benjamin Harrison Walker and Dr. Jane Harrison Walker, have been most courteous in placing these papers at the author's disposal.

Rich biographical material, including diaries, letters, and Harrisoniana, has helped in drawing an accurate portrait of Benjamin Harrison. Items in this collection extend from 1781 to 1935.

3. The Messinger Collection. These letters from Benjamin Harrison to "Cos. Mag," Mrs. Margaret Peltz of St. Louis, cover the period 1877–1901. They were in the possession of the late Mrs. Clarence W. Messinger, of Houghton, Michigan, a granddaughter of Mrs. Peltz. Since the owner's death the papers have been made available to the Library of Congress but the author thanks the Messinger family for making copies of the letters available to him.

4. Some private and family papers are on file at the President Benjamin Harrison Memorial Home, 1230 North Delaware Street, Indianapolis, Indiana. Personal diaries and financial accounts have provided rich biographical information.

5. A select collection of Benjamin Harrison Papers is also housed in the Indiana Division of the Indiana State Library (Indianapolis).

Sundry items are scattered in the approximately fifty collections, catalogued and indexed, covering the years 1855–1901.

6. Russell B. Harrison Collection. Stored for half a century in the basement of the Terre Haute (Indiana) Savings Bank, these papers were rescued by the Vigo County Historical Society with headquarters in that city. Here, by kind permission of former Congressman William Henry Harrison, son of Colonel Russell Harrison and grandson of President Benjamin Harrison, the author researched the entire collection. These papers are now in the custody of the Indiana University Library, Bloomington, Indiana.

7. The papers of William Henry Harrison Miller, Benjamin Harrison's law partner for a quarter of a century and his Attorney General (1889–1893), were loaned to the author. Particularly valuable were the letterbooks.

8. Other manuscript collections contain material pertinent to Harrison's character and place in history. They have been examined by the author with a view to forming an overall assessment of Benjamin Harrison. In the Division of Manuscripts, Library of Congress, the most helpful were the papers of:

Nelson W. Aldrich, J. C. Bancroft Davis, Wharton Barker, Thomas F. Bayard, Albert J. Beveridge, Jeremiah S. Black, James G. Blaine, the Blair family, the Breckenridge family, Benjamin H. Bristow, Howard Cale, Andrew Carnegie, William E. Chandler, James S. Clarkson, Grover Cleveland, Chauncey M. Depew, William Evarts, John W. Foster, William Dudley Foulke, Walter Q. Gresham, Eugene Hale, Joseph R. Hawley, Eugene Gano Hay, John Hay, William McKinley, Louis T. Michener, Justin S. Morrill, Harry S. New, Richard Olney, Matthew S. Quay, Theodore Roosevelt, Carl Schurz, John Sherman, William T. Sherman, John C. Spooner, William Howard Taft, R. W. Thompson, Benjamin F. Tracy, Henry Watterson, William C. Whitney, John Russell Young.

9. Other archival collections that yielded material were:
The papers of W. H. H. Miller, R. S. Taylor, R. W. Thompson in the Indiana State Library, Indianapolis.
The papers of George S. Bixby in the Manuscripts Division, New York State Library, Albany, New York. Letters, diaries, and scrapbooks pertaining to David B. Hill and New York politics are abundant.
The papers of Silas W. Burt and the William T. Sherman Scrapbooks, New York Historical Society, New York City.
The papers of John Bigelow and Levi P. Morton in the Manuscripts Division, New York Public Library, New York City.
The papers of William Boyd Allison, James S. Clarkson, Grenville Mellen Dodge, and John A. Kasson in the Historical Memorial and Art Department of Iowa, Des Moines, Iowa.
The papers of Nils P. Haugen, Henry Demarest Lloyd, Jeremiah Rusk, Ellis Usher, and William F. Vilas in the State Historical Society of Wisconsin, Madison, Wisconsin.

The papers of David J. Brewer and Chauncey M. Depew, Yale University Library, New Haven, Connecticut.

The papers of George Frisbee Hoar and Henry Cabot Lodge, Massachusetts Historical Society, Boston, Massachusetts.

The papers of S. B. Elkins, University of West Virginia Archives, Morgantown, West Virginia.

The papers of Joseph R. Hawley, State Library, Hartford, Connecticut.

The papers of William T. Sherman in the private possession of the late Miss Eleanor Sherman Fitch, New York City.

The papers of William Henry Smith, Ohio State Archaeological and Historical Society Archives, Columbus, Ohio.

The papers of John Wanamaker, Wanamaker's Department Store, Philadelphia, Pennsylvania.

The diary and papers of Bishop Francis Silas Chatard in the Cathedral Archives, Indianapolis.

The papers of James Cardinal Gibbons in the archives of the Archdiocese of Baltimore, Baltimore, Maryland.

The papers of Terence V. Powderly in the Mullen Library of The Catholic University of America, Washington, D. C.

The papers of Whitelaw Reid in the possession of the Reid Estate and stored in the Tribune Tower Building, New York City. The Division of Manuscripts, Library of Congress, recently acquired this collection.

The Harrison-Hayes Correspondence, photostated at the Rutherford B. Hayes Memorial Library, Fremont, Ohio.

Harrison items in the André deCoppet Collection housed at the Princeton University Library; likewise photostats obtained from the Pennsylvania Historical Society and the Presbyterian Historical Society, both located in Philadelphia.

Marthena Harrison Williams and William Henry Harrison Collections (privately held) yielded diary material, letters, and photographs.

The diary of Caroline Scott Harrison and family letters in the possession of Katherine Scott Brooks, Washington, D.C.

The papers of Richard W. Thompson. Photostats furnished by the Lincoln National Life Foundation, Fort Wayne, Indiana.

On the complex role played by Harrison as Senior Counsel for Venezuela in the arbitration of the boundary dispute between British Guiana and Venezuela, which came before an international tribunal of arbitration at Paris in the summer of 1899, the following archival and personal sources furnished fresh and illuminating evidence:

Personal and legal files of Severo Mallet-Prevost (privately held).

Papers of Andrew D. White and George Lincoln Burr in the Cornell University Archives, Ithaca, New York.

Papers of Melville Weston Fuller in the Chicago Historical Society, Chicago, Illinois.

Papers pertaining to the American Boundary Commission (1896–1897) in the National Archives.

Papers of Daniel Coit Gilman in the archives of The Johns Hopkins University, Baltimore, Maryland.

Papers of José María Andrade in the archives of the Minister of Foreign Relations for the Republic of Venezuela, Caracas, Venezuela.

Papers of Lord Salisbury, Joseph Chamberlain, and Sir Julian Pauncefote from copies available in the archives of the Ministry of Foreign Affairs for the Republic of Venezuela, Caracas, Venezuela.

Papers of William Lindsay Scruggs (privately held) in Atlanta, Georgia, and in Nashville, Tennessee.

Papers of James J. Storrow, pertinent copies in official archives at Caracas.

Papers of William Cullen Dennis, in the private possession of the Dennis Family, Richmond, Indiana.

Papers of John M. Harlan, Law Library, University of Louisville, Louisville, Kentucky.

10. Pertinent newspaper material was culled from the following files in the possession originally of the Harrison Memorial Home, Indianapolis, Indiana: Indianapolis *Journal* (1889–1893), New York *Sun* (1889–1893), New York *Tribune* (1889–1893), and Chicago *Tribune* (1889–1893). These papers were received regularly at the White House and were stored by Harrison in Indianapolis upon his return to private life.

Other newspapers consulted were the Atlanta *Constitution*, Baltimore *American and Commercial Advertiser*, Boston *Traveller*, Chicago *Inter-Ocean*, Chicago *Post*, Denver *Republican*, Frankfort (Indiana) *Evening News*, Huntsville (Alabama) *Gazette*, Indianapolis *Daily Sentinel*, Indianapolis *Evening News*, Indianapolis *Star*, Lafayette (Indiana) *Journal*, Louisville *Courier-Journal*, Minneapolis *Tribune*, Nashville *American*, New Orleans *Times-Democrat*, New Orleans *Weekly Pelican*, New York *Evening Post*, New York *Herald*, New York *Independent*, New York *Times*, New York *World*, Philadelphia *Inquirer*, Philadelphia *North American*, Philadelphia *Times*, Springfield (Massachusetts) *Republican*, St. Louis *Post-Dispatch*, St. Paul *Daily News*, Toronto *Empire*, Toronto *Globe*, Toronto *Mail*, Washington (D.C.) *Post*, Washington (D.C.) *Star*, Worcester (Massachusetts) *Times*, Yonkers (New York) *Statesman*.

In addition to a plenitude of identified newspaper clippings, which form the bulk of the 58-volume Scrapbook Series in the Harrison Papers (Library of Congress), attention is called to a valuable three-volume Scrapbook Series in the Indiana State Library, the gift of Russell B. Harrison, the President's son. Its chief merit lies in the universal newspaper coverage given to the death and funeral of Benjamin Harrison in 1901. Russell Harrison had subscribed to several clipping services, and carefully preserved the unfavorable as well as favorable news and editorial comment.

Published Sources

Adams, Henry. *The Education of Henry Adams.* New York, Modern Library, 1931.

Alexander, De Alva S. *Four Famous New Yorkers.* New York, Holt, 1923.

Anbert, Camillo. "The Mafia: Crime Inc. (Italy)," *Réalités,* XLVIII (November 1954), 4–10.

Andrews, E. Benjamin. *The History of the Last Quarter Century of the United States: 1870–1895.* 2 vols. New York, Charles Scribner's Sons, 1896.

Appleton's Annual Cyclopedia (for the years 1889 through 1893). New York, Appleton, 1889–1893.

Armstrong, W. M. *E. L. Godkin and American Foreign Policy, 1865–1900.* New York, Bookman Associates, 1957.

Bailey, Thomas A. *A Diplomatic History of the American People* (third edition). New York, F. S. Crofts & Co., 1946.

Baker, George W. "Benjamin Harrison and Hawaiian Annexation: A Reinterpretation," *Pacific Historical Review,* XLV, No. 3 (September 1964), 295–309.

Baker, Marcus. "The Anglo-Venezuelan Boundary Dispute," *The National Geographic Magazine,* XI, No. 4 (April 1900), 134.

Beale, Howard K. *Theodore Roosevelt and the Rise of America to World Power.* Baltimore, The Johns Hopkins Press, 1956.

Benjamin Harrison Memorial Commission, Report of. (77th Congress, 1st Session, House Document No. 154.) Washington, D. C., Government Printing Office, 1941.

Biographical Directory of the American Congress, 1774–1949, comp. James L. Harrison. Washington, D.C., Government Printing Office, 1950.

Blaine, James G. "The Presidential Campaign and Election of 1892," *North American Review,* CLV (1892), 512–25.

Borden, Morton (editor). *America's Ten Greatest Presidents.* Chicago, Rand McNally, 1961.

Bowen, C. W. (editor). *The History of the Centennial Celebration of the Inauguration of George Washington as First President of the United States.* New York, Appleton, 1892.

Buchanan, A. Russell. *David S. Terry, Dueling Judge.* San Marino (Calif.), Huntington Library, 1956.

Burnham, W. Dean. *Presidential Ballots 1836–1892.* Baltimore, The Johns Hopkins Press, 1955.

Burr, George Lincoln, "The Search for the Venezuela-Guiana Boundary," *American Historical Review,* IV, No. 3 (April 1899), 470–77.

Carpenter, Frank G. *Carp's Washington.* New York, McGraw-Hill, 1960.

Carson, Hampton. *Supreme Court of the United States: Its History and Its Centennial Celebration.* Philadelphia, John Huber Company, 1891.

Cavanagh, Frances. *They Lived in the White House.* Philadelphia, Macrae Smith Company, 1951.

Cleveland, Grover. *Letters of Grover Cleveland,* ed. Allan Nevins. Boston, Houghton Mifflin, 1933.

Colman, Edna M. *White House Gossip: From Andrew Johnson to Calvin Coolidge.* New York, Doubleday, Page and Company, 1927.

Commager, Henry Steele, *The American Mind.* New Haven, Yale University Press, 1950.

Congressional Record, 1889–1893. Washington, D.C., Government Printing Office, 20–25 (1889–1893).

Cortissoz, Royal. *The Life of Whitelaw Reid.* 2 vols. New York, Charles Scribner's Sons, 1921.

Coxe, John E. "The New Orleans Mafia Incident," *The Louisiana Historical Quarterly,* XX, No. 4 (October 1937), 1067–1110.

Dearing, Mary R., *Veterans in Politics.* Baton Rouge, Louisiana State University Press, 1952.

De Santis, Vincent P. *Republicans Face the Southern Question.* Baltimore, The Johns Hopkins Press, 1959.

Dozer, D. M. "Benjamin Harrison and the Presidential Campaign of 1892," *The American Historical Review,* LIV, No. 1 (October 1948), 61–63.

Durant, John and Alice. *Pictorial History of American Presidents.* New York, A. S. Barnes and Company, 1955.

Ellis, John Tracy. *Life of James Cardinal Gibbons, Archbishop of Baltimore.* 2 vols. Milwaukee, Bruce, 1952.

Evans, R. D. *A Sailor's Log.* New York, D. Appleton and Company, 1901.

Ezell, John S. *Fortune's Merry Wheel: The Lottery in America.* Cambridge, Harvard University Press, 1960.

Fairman, Charles. *Mr. Justice Miller and the Supreme Court, 1882–1890.* Cambridge, Harvard University Press, 1939.

Faulkner, Harold U. *Politics, Reform and Expansion: 1890–1900.* New York, Harper and Brothers, 1959.

Ferrell, Robert H. *American Diplomacy.* New York, W. W. Norton and Company, 1959.

Foulke, William Dudley. *Lucius B. Swift: American Citizen.* New York and Indianapolis, The Bobbs-Merrill Company, 1930.

Fowler, Dorothy Ganfield. *John Coit Spooner: Defender of Presidents.* New York, University Publishers, 1961.

Furman, Bess. *White House Profiles.* Indianapolis and New York, The Bobbs-Merrill Company, 1951.

Gantenbein, James W. (editor). *The Evolution of Our Latin-American Policy.* New York, Columbia University Press, 1950.

Garraty, John A. *Henry Cabot Lodge.* New York, Knopf, 1953.

Gibbons, H. A. *John Wanamaker.* 2 vols. New York and London, Harper & Brothers, 1926.

Glasson, William Henry. *Federal Military Pensions in the United States.* New York, Oxford University Press, 1918.

_____. *History of Military Pension Legislation in the United States.* New York, Columbia University Press, 1900.

Goebel, Dorothy Burne, and Julius Goebel, Jr. *Generals in the White House.* Garden City (N.Y.), Doubleday, Doran and Company, 1945.

Goff, John S. "A Letter from Mrs. David S. Terry to the President's Wife," *Historical Society of Southern California Quarterly,* XXXIX, No. 3 (September 1957), 211–16.

Gorham, George C. *Attempted Assassination of Justice Field.* (In: Field, S. J. *Personal Reminiscences of Early Days in California.*) N. P. [c. 1893], 237–406.

Grenville, J. A. S. and George B. Young. *Politics, Strategy, and American Diplomacy.* New Haven and London, Yale University Press, 1966.

Gresham, Matilda. *Life of Walter Q. Gresham.* 2 vols. Chicago, Rand, McNally and Company, 1919.

Gwynn, Stephen (editor). *The Letters and Friendships of Sir Cecil Spring Rice: A Record.* London, Constable and Company, 1929.

Halford, A. J. "Mrs. Harrison in the White House," *Ladies' Home Journal,* VII, No. 4 (March 1890), 1–2.

Halford, E. W. "General Harrison's Attitude Toward the Presidency," *Century Magazine* (June 1912), 306–10.

Hamilton, Gail. *Biography of James G. Blaine.* Norwich, Henry Bell Publishing Company, 1895.

Hare, Maud Cuney. *Norris Wright Cuney, A Tribune of the Black People.* New York, Crisis Publishing Company, 1913.

Harrison, Benjamin. *Public Papers and Addresses of.* Washington, D.C., Government Printing Office, 1893.

_____. "The Social Life of the President," *Ladies' Home Journal,* XIV, No. 5 (April 1897), 3–4.

_____. *This Country of Ours.* New York, Charles Scribner's Sons, 1922.

_____. *Speeches of Benjamin Harrison,* comp. Charles Hedges. New York, Lovell, Coryell and Company, 1892.

_____. *Views of An Ex-President,* comp. Mary Lord Harrison. Indianapolis, Bowen-Merrill, 1901.

Harvey, George. *Henry Clay Frick the Man.* New York, Charles Scribner's Sons, 1928.

Hays, Samuel P. *The Response to Industrialism: 1885–1914.* Chicago, University of Chicago Press, 1957.

Herrick, Walter Russell, Jr. *The American Naval Revolution.* Baton Rouge, Louisiana State University Press, 1966.

Hirshson, Stanley P. *Farewell to the Bloody Shirt.* Bloomington, Indiana University Press, 1962.

Holbrook, Stewart H. *The Age of the Moguls.* Garden City (N.Y.), Doubleday and Company, 1953.

James, Henry. *Richard Olney and His Public Service.* Boston, Houghton Mifflin Company, 1923.

James, Marquis. *Andrew Jackson.* Indianapolis and New York, Bobbs-Merrill Company, 1938.

Jensen, Amy La Follette. *The White House and Its Thirty-Two Families.* New York, McGraw-Hill Book Company, 1958.

Jervey, T. D. "William Lindsay Scruggs, A Foreign Diplomat." *South Atlantic Quarterly,* XXVII, No. 3 (July 1928), 292–309.

Jones, Stanley L. *The Presidential Election of 1896.* Madison, The University of Wisconsin Press, 1964.

Josephson, Matthew. *The Politicos, 1865–1919.* New York, Harcourt, Brace, 1938.

Karlin, J. Alexander. "Some Repercussions of the New Orleans Mafia Incident of 1891," *Research Studies of the State College of Washington,* XI, No. 4 (December 1943), 267–82.

King, Willard L. *Melville Weston Fuller.* New York, Macmillan Company, 1950.

Knoles, George H., *The Presidential Campaign and Election of 1892.* Palo Alto, California, Stanford University Press, 1942.

La Feber, Walter. *The New Empire: An Interpretation of American Expansion, 1860–1898.* Ithaca, Cornell University Press, 1963.

Lamar, Howard Roberts. *Dakota Territory, 1861–1889: A Study of Frontier Politics.* New Haven, Yale University Press, 1956.

Lambert, Oscar Doane. *Stephen Benton Elkins: American Foursquare.* Pittsburgh, University of Pittsburgh Press, 1955.

Leech, Margaret. *In the Days of McKinley.* New York, Harper and Brothers, 1959.

Liliuokalani, Queen of Hawaii. *Hawaii's Story by Hawaii's Queen, Liliuokalani.* Boston, Lee and Shephard, 1898.

Lloyd, Caro. *Henry Demarest Lloyd: A Biography in Two Volumes.* New York, G. P. Putnam's Sons, 1912.

Lodge, Henry Cabot. "England, Venezuela, and the Monroe Doctrine," *North American Review,* CLX, No. 463 (June 1895), 651–58.

————. *Selections from the Correspondence of Theodore Roosevelt and Henry Cabot Lodge, 1884–1918.* New York, Charles Scribner's Sons, 1925.

MacVane, S. N. "The Report of the Special Commission Appointed by the President January 4, 1896," *American Historical Review,* II, No. 3 (April 1897), 34–36.

McKee, Irving. *"Ben Hur" Wallace.* Berkeley and Los Angeles, University of California Press, 1947.

McMurry, Donald L. "Political Significance of the Pension Question, 1885–1897," *Mississippi Valley Historical Review,* IX, No. 1 (1922), 19–36.

————. "The Bureau of Pensions During the Administration of President Harrison,"*Mississippi Valley Historical Review,* XIII, No. 3 (1926), 343–64.

Martin, Asa E. *After the White House.* State College, Pa., Penns Valley Publishers, Inc., 1951.

Mathews, Joseph J. "Informal Diplomacy in the Venezuela Crisis of 1896," *Mississippi Valley Historical Review,* L, No. 2 (September 1963), 195–212.

May, Ernest R. *Imperial Democracy.* New York, Harcourt, Brace and World, 1961.

Merrill, H. S. *Bourbon Leader: Grover Cleveland and the Democratic Party.* Boston, Little, Brown and Company, 1957.

Moon, Henry Lee. *Balance of Power: The Negro Vote.* New York, Doubleday and Company, 1948.

Moos, Malcolm. *The Republicans: A History of Their Party.* New York, Random House, 1956.

Morgan, H. Wayne. *America's Road to Empire.* New York, John Wiley and Sons, 1965.

Morris, Richard B. (editor). *Encylopedia of American History.* New York, Harper and Brothers, 1953.

Mott, Frank Luther. *American Journalism: A History of Newspapers in the United States Through 250 Years, 1690–1940.* New York, Macmillan Company, 1941.

Muzzey, David Saville. *James G. Blaine, A Political Idol of Other Days.* New York, Dodd, Mead and Company, 1934.

Nevins, Allan. *Grover Cleveland: A Study in Courage.* New York, Dodd, Mead and Company, 1932.

Nye, Russell B. *Midwestern Progressive Politics.* East Lansing, Michigan State College Press, 1951.

Olcott, C. S. *The Life of William McKinley.* 2 vols. Boston, Houghton Mifflin Company, 1916.

Peck, Harry Thurston. *Twenty Years of the Republic, 1885–1905.* New York, Dodd, Mead and Company, 1907.

Pepper, Charles M. *The Life and Times of Henry Gassaway Davis (1823–1916).* New York, The Century Company, 1920.

Perling, J. J., *Presidents' Sons.* New York, The Odyssey Press, 1947.

Pike, Frederick B. *Chile and the United States, 1880–1962.* South Bend (Ind.), University of Notre Dame Press, 1963.

Platt, T. C. *The Autobiography of Thomas Collier Platt,* ed. Louis J. Lang. New York, B. W. Dodge and Company, 1910.

Pollard, James E. *The Presidents and the Press.* New York, Macmillan Company, 1947.

Potter, H. C. "National Bigness or Greatness—Which?" *North American Review,* CLXVIII, No. 509 (April 1899), 433–44.

Pratt, Julius W. *The Expansionists of 1898.* Baltimore, The Johns Hopkins Press, 1936.

Pringle, H. F. *Theodore Roosevelt, A Biography.* New York, Harcourt, Brace and Company, 1931.

Proceedings of the Tenth Republican National Convention, 1892. Printed by order of the Republican National Committee. Minneapolis, Charles W. Johnson, 1892.

Public Opinion. A comprehensive summary of the Press throughout the world. Washington, The Public Opinion Company, 1886–1906.

Reid, Ed. *Mafia.* New York, Random House, 1952.

Richardson, Leon Burr. *William E. Chandler: Republican.* New York, Dodd, Mead and Company, 1940.

Robinson, William Alexander. *Thomas B. Reed: Parliamentarian.* New York, Dodd, Mead and Company, 1930.

Romero, M. "The Pan American Conference," *North American Review,* CLI, No. 406 (September 1890), 356, 365.

Roosevelt, Theodore. *The Letters of Theodore Roosevelt,* ed. Elting E. Morison. 8 vols. Cambridge, Harvard University Press, 1951.

Roseboom, Eugene H. *History of Presidential Elections.* New York, Macmillan Company, 1957.

Rowan, Richard Wilmer. *The Pinkertons: A Detective Dynasty.* Boston, Little, Brown and Company, 1931.

Russ, William A., Jr. *The Hawaiian Revolution, 1893–1894.* Selinsgrove, Pa. Susquehanna University Press, 1959.

Ryden, George H. *The Foreign Policy of the United States in Relation to Samoa.* New Haven, Yale University Press, 1933.

Sage, Leland L. *William Boyd Allison: A Study in Practical Politics.* Iowa City, State Historical Society of Iowa, 1956.

Schoenrich, Otto. "The Venezuela-British Guiana Boundary Dispute," *The American Journal of International Law,* XLIII, No. 3 (July 1949), 523–30.

Sherman, John. *Recollections of Forty Years in the House, Senate and Cabinet.* Chicago and New York, The Werner Company, 1896.

Shuck, Oscar T. *History of the Bench and Bar in California.* Los Angeles, Commercial Printing House, 1901.

Sievers, Harry J. *Benjamin Harrison: Hoosier Statesman (1865–1888).* New York, University Publishers, 1959.

———. *Benjamin Harrison: Hoosier Warrior (1833–1865).* New York, University Publishers, 1952.

———. "The Catholic Indian School Issue and the Presidential Election of 1892," *Catholic Historical Review,* XXXVIII, No. 2 (July 1952), 129–55.

———. *President Benjamin Harrison and Our Country's Flag.* Fort Wayne, Indiana, 1953. (Reprinted from the *D.A.R. Magazine,* November 1952).

Simons, Richard. "Great Dakota Mystery," *Indianapolis Star Magazine,* March 28, 1954, p. 8.

Stanwood, Edward. *James Gillespie Blaine.* Boston, Houghton Mifflin and Company, 1908.

Stoddard, Henry L. *As I Knew Them: Presidents and Politics from Grant to Coolidge.* New York, Harper, 1927.

Stoddard, Lothrop. *Master of Manhattan: The Life of Richard Croker.* New York, Longmans, Green and Company, 1931.

Summers, Festus P. *William L. Wilson and Tariff Reform.* New Brunswick, N. J., Rutgers University Press, 1953.

Swisher, Carl B. *Stephen J. Field: Craftsman of the Law.* Washington, The Brookings Institution, 1930.

Tansill, Charles C. *Diplomatic Relations Between the United States and Hawaii, 1885–1889.* New York, Fordham University Press, 1940.

_____. *The Foreign Policy of Thomas F. Bayard, 1885–1897.* New York, Fordham University Press, 1940.

Tarbell, Ida. *The Tariff in Our Times.* New York, Macmillan Company, 1911.

Townsend, George Alfred. *Washington Outside and Inside.* Hartford and Chicago, J. Betts and Company, 1873.

Tyler, Alice Felt. *Foreign Policy of James G. Blaine.* Minneapolis, University of Minnesota Press, 1927.

U.S. Department of Interior. *Secretary of the Interior, Annual Report of (1889).* Washington, Government Printing Office, 1890.

U.S. Department of State. *Papers Relating to the Foreign Relations of the United States.* Washington, Government Printing Office, 1889–1893.

Volwiler, A. T. "Harrison, Blaine, and American Foreign Policy, 1889–1893," *Proceedings of American Philosophical Society,* LXXIX, No. 4 (November 1938), 644.

_____ (editor). *The Correspondence Between Benjamin Harrison and James G. Blaine, 1882–1893.* Philadelphia, The American Philosophical Society, 1940.

Wagstaff, A. E. *Life of David S. Terry.* San Francisco, Continental Publishing Company, 1892.

Warren, Charles, *Supreme Court in United States History.* 2 vols. Boston, Little, Brown and Company, 1947.

Welch, Richard E., Jr. "The Federal Elections Bill of 1890: Postscripts and Prelude," *The Journal of American History,* LII, No. 3 (December 1965), 511–26.

Wellborn, Fred. "The Influence of the Silver-Republican Senators, 1889–1891," *Mississippi Valley Historical Review,* XIV, No. 4 (1928), 462–80.

White, J. T. (editor). *National Cyclopedia of American Biography,* 6 vols. New York, 1888–93.

White, Leonard D. *The Republican Era, 1869–1901.* New York, Macmillan Company, 1958.

White, William Allen. *Masks in a Pageant.* New York, Macmillan Company, 1928.

Wilgus, A. Curtis. "James G. Blaine and the Pan-American Movement," *The Hispanic American Historical Review*, V (1922), 662–708.

Young, George B. "Intervention Under the Monroe Doctrine: The Olney Corollary," *Political Science Quarterly*, LVII, No. 2 (June 1942), 247–48.

Zeis, Paul M. *American Shipping Policy*. Princeton, Princeton University Press, 1938.

Unpublished Material

Bastert, Russell Henry. "James G. Blaine and the Origins of the First International Conference of American States." Unpublished doctoral dissertation, Yale University, 1952.

Herrick, Walter Russell, Jr. "General Tracy's Navy: A Study of the Development of American Sea Power, 1889–1893." Unpublished doctoral dissertation, Charlottesville, University of Virginia, 1962.

O'Marra, Sr. Mary Lucille. "Quay and Harrison from 1888–1892." Unpublished master's dissertation, Washington, D.C., Catholic University, 1956.

Quinn, Sister Maria Margaret, C.S.J. "William Henry Harrison Miller." Unpublished doctoral dissertation. Washington, D.C., Catholic University, 1965.

Spetler, Allan B. "Harrison and Blaine: Foreign Policy, 1889–1893." Unpublished doctoral dissertation. New Brunswick, N. J., Rutgers University, 1967.

U.S. Department of Justice. *Incoming Correspondence File 8165–88*. Washington, National Archives.

Index

Index

Wanamaker, John (*cont.*)
cific Coast tour, 191; gives burro to
Harrison grandchildren in 1893, 255;
finds Harrison against further public
service, 259; offers ex-President trip to
Europe, 264*n*
Warner, George, refuses post of Commissioner of Pensions, 126
Washburn, William Drew, 14, 15, 199
Washington admitted as state, 131, 132
Washington, George: Centennial commemorating first Inauguration, 61–71;
Harrison sits in his pew at Centennial
service in St. Paul's Chapel, 66; Harrison sits in his chair at Sub-Treasury
Centennial exercises, 68; his Inaugural
Bible at Sub-Treasury Centennial ceremonies, 68
Washington Jockey Club, Harrison vetoes
bill giving monopoly on horse racing
and bookmaking in D.C., 172
Watterson, Henry: on Senate's rejection
of Murat Halstead's nomination, 47, 48;
attributes Republican defeat in 1892 to
defection of labor vote after Homestead
riots, 248
Weaver, James B., 146, 178; as candidate
of Populist party in 1892, 235, 245–246;
total votes for, in 1892 election, 248
Webster, Sir Richard, and Venezuela-
British Guiana boundary dispute, 271;
regarded by Harrison as chauvinistic,
271*n*; on decision by Paris Tribunal,
272
Wellman, Walter, on attitude of Washington and Senate toward Harrison, 43
Wetmore, George P., offers Newport mansion to Harrisons for summer vacation,
83
Wharton, Joseph, 193
White Citizens Committee in New Orleans, 184
White House: post-inaugural open house,
38–39; reorganization of clerical and
domestic staffs, 39; members of Harrison family in, 52; Mrs. Harrison's suggestions for improving living situation
in, 53; Mrs. Harrison's general cleaning
up and repairing of old mansion, 53;
clearing out of goods left by former
tenants, 53; and problems of cuisine,
53–54; methodical running of Harrison
household, 55; charm of official entertaining by Harrisons, 55; Mrs. Harrison
begins White House collection of china
of past Presidents, 55; Harrison grandchildren in, 55–56, 57; dancing made
part of formal receptions, 57; Harri-

White House (*cont.*)
son's lack of feeling of it as a home, 130;
called "my jail" by Harrison, 131; Harrison's routine in fall of 1889, 130–131;
and Christmas 1889 for the Harrisons,
139; New Year's 1890 reception, 141–
142; extensive repairs on, 155, 157, 207;
social activity cancelled in early 1891
because of death of Secretary Windom,
201; infested with mosquitoes, 208;
funeral of Mrs. Harrison in East Room,
242–243
White, William Allen: on Harrison, 4; on
Harrison's campaign fund, 6*n*; on
Blaine, 8*n*
Whitney, William C.: as National Democratic Chairman, 236, 248; gives opinion on reasons for Republican defeat
in 1892 election, 248
Whittier, John Greenleaf, writes "The
Vow of Washington" for Centennial
celebration, 68
Whyte, William Pinckney, 107
Wilkinson, John C., 17*n*
Williams, George B., 35
Wilson, Woodrow, 26
Windom bill on silver purchase, 146–147
Windom, William: as Cabinet possibility,
14–15; Wall Street connections questioned, 15; appointed Secretary of
Treasury, 15, 18; Harrison consults on
Inaugural speech, 33; at Davis's dinner
in Deer Park, 85; accompanies Harrison on trip to Maine, 87; Harrison consults on first message to Congress, 132;
party leaders look to, for aid in 1890
off-year elections, 173; and near-panic
in late 1890, 200; and Dudley land deal,
200; sudden collapse and death of, 201
Wisconsin, and recognition in Harrison's
Cabinet appointments, 20
Wolcott, Senator of Colorado, 145, 230
Woodruff, Franklin, 21*n*
Woodruff, Timothy L., 21*n*
Woodstock, Conn., Harrison celebrates
1889 Fourth of July at, 83–84
World (New York): on Blaine's appointment as Secretary of State, 11; clamors
for Tanner's removal as Commissioner
of Pensions, 119; quotes Russell Harrison on Blaine's health and mental condition, 216–218; quotes London on
Paris Tribunal decision in Venezuela-
British Guiana boundary dispute, 272

Zieman, Hugo, as steward at White
House, 53, 54